GOODBYE TO ALL THAT?

GOODBYE TO ALL THAT?

THE STORY OF EUROPE
SINCE 1945

DAN STONE

OXFORD
UNIVERSITY PRESS

OXFORD
UNIVERSITY PRESS

Great Clarendon Street, Oxford, OX2 6DP,
United Kingdom

Oxford University Press is a department of the University of Oxford.
It furthers the University's objective of excellence in research, scholarship,
and education by publishing worldwide. Oxford is a registered trade mark of
Oxford University Press in the UK and in certain other countries

First Edition published in 2014

Impression: 1

Published in the United States of America by Oxford University Press
198 Madison Avenue, New York, NY 10016, United States of America

British Library Cataloguing in Publication Data

Data available

Library of Congress Control Number: 2013938192

ISBN 978–0–19–969771–7

Printed by
Clays Ltd, St Ives plc

for Libby, Greta, and Clem
and their mum

Preface

In 1946, one of the finest achievements of the newly recreated German film industry, DEFA, was released. *The Murderers Are Among Us (Die Mörder sind unter uns)*, directed by Wolfgang Staudte, was not only a powerful work of film noir, establishing, despite its being in the Soviet zone, DEFA's cinematographic debt to Hollywood, but, for its day, was a remarkably frank assessment of the fact that many of those in successful positions in the postwar western zones of Germany (that later joined together to form the Federal Republic) had already enjoyed successful careers under Nazism, embodied in this instance by a factory owner who had been responsible for murdering civilians. In one particularly powerful scene, when the two protagonists, Susanne Wallner (Hildegard Knef) and Dr Hans Mertens (Ernst Wilhelm Borchert), are together for Christmas, their moment of calm is shattered when, almost unthinkingly, Wallner says, 'Peace, Christmas, how I longed for the day. But now I'm not sure anymore. It all seems so unreal somehow.' Mertens responds with the equally instinctive comment: 'Maybe because in our hearts there is no peace.'

The argument of this book is that there was no peace in the hearts of Europeans in the immediate aftermath of the war because so much of what had happened was being suppressed, as, for example, the wartime careers of many Germans who were able to evade the denazification process. That is hardly novel. What I stress, however, is that this absence of inner peace—in contrast with the absence of war, which was displaced to other parts of the globe, European colonies and Cold War proxy wars—lasted throughout the Cold War. It came increasingly under scrutiny from the 1960s onwards, but only with the end of the Cold War could Europe's wartime record really be examined unblinkingly. Since then, what we see is that this lack of peace in people's hearts not only still animates the way Europeans think, but does so even more than it did in the first few years after 1945. In contemporary Europe, competing memories of the war still lie at the heart of political debates.

Although this is a work of history, it is a resolutely presentist book. For the generation now coming of age born after the end of the Cold War, the 1940s and 1950s might seem as much like ancient history as the Norman Conquest or the Wars of the Roses. In fact, the Second World War and its immediate after-effects shape the world in which we live in many ways. Even more noteworthy is the fact that, for all the many, often extraordinary changes that have taken place in Europe since 1945—socially, economically, technologically, and in every other respect, such that a person who fell asleep in 1950 and woke again in 2000 would hardly recognize the world around them—it is the contention of this book that, paradoxically, the further from the war we get, the more its impact is being felt and the more its meanings are being fought over. In fact, as I will show, although 'postwar' is primarily to be understood chronologically, so that one can agree with commentators who claim that the end of the Cold War marked the end of the postwar period, in another, quasi-philosophical sense, the years since 1989 should be understood as the real postwar years. What I mean by that is that the absence of peace in Europeans' hearts, as articulated by Susanne Wallner in the film, could only be explained in certain officially approved and politically acceptable ways during the Cold War: the ideology of antifascism in communist Eastern Europe and the devotion to reconstruction combined with silence over the widespread collaboration with Nazism—or the failure to prevent its rise—in Western Europe meant that a full and frank discussion of what transpired during the Second World War has only been possible since the end of the Cold War brought about the definitive conclusion of a process that was already in train: the demise of the postwar consensus.

This concept of the 'postwar consensus' should be understood in two senses: first, socio-economically as the creation of welfare-capitalist states and a more or less successful turn to corporate industrial relations in Western Europe, and the building of communism with its concomitant suppression of alternatives in the east (the Iberian peninsula is an exception here, as we will later see, for there was no 'consensus', just continuity in Francoist or Salazarist authoritarianism, connived in by the west, and their gradual unravelling). Second, and no less significant, the consensus meant the triumph of antifascism, officially endorsed and ever more instrumentalized as a tool of legitimacy in Eastern Europe, and providing an intellectual basis in Western Europe for political and social stability, anti-communism, and the turn to consumerism and economic growth.

The major contention of this book, then, is that the postwar consensus went hand in hand with a particular memory of the Second World War, and that the death of that consensus should not be understood only economically (the turn from primary and secondary to tertiary industries, the gradual 'modernization' [=dismantling] of the welfare state, or the abandonment of social democratic values, for example), but also politically, and especially in terms of memory politics. The collapse of the political project of social democracy in the west and communism in the east went hand in hand with the death of antifascism, hence the reappearance of ideas and values which had long been assumed to be dead, or at best marginal and lunatic. If we want to understand the roots of today's right-wing populism, which is taking hold in even normally boringly predictable countries such as Denmark, the Netherlands, and Belgium, then we should look not only to very recent debates about 'radical Islam', the 'war on terror', immigration, or financial crisis, but to the revival of memories—primarily related to Europeans' experiences and commitments during the Second World War—that reveal a deep-seated resentment at the normative values of the years 1945–89, when many, so it now seems, had to hold their tongues.

This analysis should not be interpreted as nostalgia for the brutal stability of the Cold War, which would be a deeply unsavoury position. 'Antifascism', originally a source of inspiration, ended as the cynically deployed basis for the old guard to hang on to power in the communist countries and, in its western variant, it enjoined Western Europeans not to delve too deeply into the murkier aspects of their countries' records during the war. But the argument of this book follows the simple logic of 'don't throw the baby out with the bathwater', as follows: the death of antifascism in both Eastern and Western Europe went hand in hand with a sustained attack on social democracy, which had already been coming under intense pressure since the oil crises and the recessions of the 1970s and 1980s (and, as we will see, social democracy is itself a somewhat awkward term to apply in a Western Europe that was dominated by centre-right Christian Democrats). Memory politics and socio-economic change have been inextricably linked in a way that historians have thus far insufficiently recognized. Tony Judt has hinted at the connection, writing of a 'widely-shared understanding of Europe's recent past [which] blended the memory of Depression, the struggle between Democracy and Fascism, the moral legitimacy of the welfare state and—for many on both sides of the Iron Curtain—the expectation of social progress',

but even in his masterpiece, *Postwar* (2005), this link is not explicitly investigated in detail.[1] In this book, I show that in order to understand the postwar years one needs to know not just what happened ('event history') but
what people at each point in time thought about what had happened in the
past, especially during the war ('history of memory').

Whilst it is liberating and exciting that we are now exposed to the competition of the marketplace of ideas in a way that was not possible during
the Cold War, it is also frightening to see ideas being revived that threaten
the basis of European stability. Certainly it is best to be able to speak freely
about the past, to dispel old myths about, say, resistance or neutrality. But
that also means allowing those nostalgic for fascism to re-emerge and make
their case. Certainly too the challenge of maintaining welfare states in an
age of long life expectancy and a diminished workforce should not be
underestimated. The architects of the welfare states should not be blamed
for not having foreseen the results of their own system's successes. But the
political and economic changes that have occurred since 1989 have been
accompanied by an increasingly shrill and vehement attack on anything
that smacks of the narrative of the 'good war' against fascism, and sometimes it seems that today's Europeans have forgotten what the background
to their unprecedented stability and wealth actually was. Criticisms of the
European Union, for example, are in many instances justified—its secrecy,
clubbable atmosphere, and complex bureaucratic structures, for example,
not to mention the fiasco of the euro taking place as I write—but even so
it bears repeating that the integration of Europe has served its primary
purpose of preventing war. Will we abandon reform of the EU in favour of
a return to protectionism and petty nationalisms? If so, we can be sure that
the cultural accompaniments will include some rather nasty elements rising to the fore in European life.

Some commentators have long maintained that Nazism was never really
buried or tackled head on, but simply smothered, 'like a mad dog', and that
the fascination with it that continually comes to the surface, in rants by
drunken clothes designers, French car advertisements, art installations, or
even beer bottle labels, reminds us that a rejection of social democratic values is not merely a political matter. As I will show in this book, the rise of
social democracy in Western Europe and communism in the east meant the
suppression of Europe's fascist heritage; the demise of social democracy

[1] Tony Judt, *Postwar: A History of Europe since 1945* (London: William Heinemann, 2005), 559.

means not only growing socio-economic divisions, a rise of poverty, unemployment, and crime, and an impoverished cultural life centred mainly around 'celebrities', but also, and as a necessary corollary, the breath of new life for European fascism, however pleasantly and seductively it is packaged in the shape of the *Front National*, the Vlaams Belang, or the various 'Freedom Parties' that have mushroomed in the last decade—not to mention the increasing self-separation from and lack of accountability to society at large of what has been aptly called the 'feral elite' (of politicians, bankers, and the press), for whom the populist right-wingers act as patsies, allowing them to appear 'reasonable'.

Memory of the Second World War is the key to understanding European affairs since 1945, whether one discusses the institutional development of the EEC/EU, the Cold War in Europe, decolonization, the 1968 uprisings, or the demise of the communist regimes. And most striking, when one examines the 'memory wars' of the 1990s and 2000s, one sees a remarkable reassessment of the war being put to work to justify all sorts of positions. The Second World War, then, is not ancient history. All history, as the saying goes, is contemporary history, in the sense that our understanding of the past is always filtered through the norms, mores, and concerns of the present. Perhaps this is especially so when one is indeed writing about how the contemporary came to be.

Acknowledgements

At OUP, my first debt is to Christopher Wheeler, who encouraged me to write this book and set it on its way. Luciana O'Flaherty too helped make the book a reality. But my main thanks go to Matthew Cotton, who has been an absolute pleasure to work with throughout the whole process.

For discussing ideas with me, sharing their forthcoming work with me, or reading parts of the text, my thanks go to: Scott Ashley, Daniel Beer, Paul Betts, Luiza Bialasiewicz, Robert Bideleux, Cathie Carmichael, Geoff Eley, Simone Gigliotti, Helen Graham, Vojtech Mastny, Jens Meierhenrich, Dirk Moses, Rudolf Muhs, Simon Sparks, Emmett Sullivan, Nikolaus Wachsmann, and Anton Weiss-Wendt. Special thanks are due to Mark Donnelly, Michelle Gordon, and Becky Jinks for reading through the whole manuscript and making many helpful suggestions.

Parts of the text have been previously published in the introduction and my two chapters in the *Oxford Handbook of Postwar European History* (2012). My thanks to OUP for permission to reproduce these sections.

A book such as this cannot tackle any subject in great depth and relies heavily on the research of many fine scholars. I hope it does not traduce their work or exploit it unreasonably. I have greatly enjoyed reading in the specialist literature on the history of postwar Europe, in all its aspects, and I have learnt a great deal in the process. I have especially enjoyed the work of some brilliant scholars of international history, including Vojtech Mastny, Vladimir Tismaneanu, Mark Kramer, Vladislav Zubok, Jacques Lévesque, and Odd Arne Westad. That short list is of course not exhaustive and does not mean I have not benefited from many other scholars' work, in many different fields. The endnotes to the book show where my many debts lie, and I hope that this book, albeit only a survey, represents their research fairly.

Contents

List of Figures and Maps

Figures

Maps

Abbreviations

BR	*Brigate Rosse*; Red Brigades (Italy)
CAP	Common Agricultural Policy
CCF	Congress for Cultural Freedom
CDU	*Christdemokratische Union*; Christian Democratic Union (FRG)
CIA	Central Intelligence Agency (US)
CIS	Commonwealth of Independent States
CMEA/ Comecon	Council for Mutual Economic Assistance
CND	Campaign for Nuclear Disarmament (UK)
Cominform	Communist Information Bureau
CPCz	Communist Party of Czechoslovakia
CPSU	Communist Party of the Soviet Union
CSCE	Conference on Security and Cooperation in Europe
DC	*Democrazia Cristiana*; Christian Democrats (Italy)
DP	Displaced Person
EC	European Community
ECA	European Cooperation Administration
ECSC	European Coal and Steel Community
EDC	European Defence Community (Pleven Plan)
EEC	European Economic Community
EFTA	European Free Trade Area
EMS	European Monetary System
EMU	Economic and Monetary Union
EPC	European Political Cooperation
EPU	European Payments Union
ERM	Exchange Rate Mechanism
ERP	European Recovery Program (Marshall Plan)
EU	European Union

FLN   *Front pour la Libération Nationale*; National
                Liberation Front (Algeria)
FN   *Front National*; National Front (France)
FPÖ   *Freiheitspartei Österreichs*; Austrian Freedom Party
FRG   Federal Republic of Germany
FRY   Former Republic of Yugoslavia
GATT   General Agreement on Tariffs and Trade
GDP   Gross Domestic Product
GDR   German Democratic Republic
IBRD   International Bank for Reconstruction and Development
ICBM   Intercontinental Ballistic Missile
ICTY   International Criminal Tribunal for the Former Yugoslavia
IMF   International Monetary Fund
IMT   International Military Tribunal (Nuremberg)
INF   Intermediate Range Nuclear Forces Treaty
IRO   International Refugee Organization
ITO   International Trade Organization
JNA   *Jugoslovenska Narodna Armija*; Yugoslav National Army
KAW   *Komitee der Antifaschistischen Widerstandskämpfer*; Antifascist
                Resistance Fighters' Committee (GDR)
KLA   Kosovo Liberation Army
KPD   *Kommunistische Partei Deutschlands*; German Communist Party
MAD   Mutual Assured Destruction
MFA   *Movimento das Forças Armadas*; Movement
                of the Armed Forces (Portugal)
MKP   *Magyar Kommunista Párt*; Hungarian Communist Party
MRP   *Mouvement Républicain Populaire* (Gaullists)
MSI   *Movimento Sociale Italiano*; Italian Social Movement
NATO   North Atlantic Treaty Organization
NMT   Nuremberg Military Tribunals (successor trials)
OAS   *Organisation de l'Armée Secrète*; Secret Army Organization (France)
OdF   *Hauptausschuß für die Opfer des Faschismus*; Central Authority
                for the Victims of Fascism (GDR)
OECD   Organization for Economic Cooperation and Development
OEEC   Organization for European Economic Cooperation
OPEC   Organization of Petroleum Exporting Countries
OSCE   Organization for Security and Cooperation in Europe
ÖVP   *Österreichische Volkspartei*; Austrian People's Party

PASOK	*Panelinio sosjalistiko cinima*; Panhellenic Socialist Movement (Greece)
PCE	*Partido Comunista Español*; Spanish Communist Party
PCF	*Partie Communiste Française*; French Communist Party
PCI	*Partito Comunista Italiana*; Italian Communist Party
POW	Prisoner of War
PSOE	*Partido Socialista Obrero Español*; Spanish Socialist Party
PZPR	*Polska Zjednoczona Partia Robotnicza*; Polish United Workers' Party
RAF	Red Army Faction (Baader–Meinhof Gang)
RCP	Romanian Communist Party
SALT	Strategic Arms Limitation Talks (or Treaty)
SDI	Strategic Defense Initiative (Star Wars)
SDS	*Sozialistischer Deutscher Studentenbund*; Socialist German Students' Union
SEA	Single European Act (1986)
SED	*Sozialistische Einheitspartei Deutschlands*; Socialist Unity Party (GDR)
SFIO	*Section Française de l'Internationale Ouvrière* (French Socialist Party)
SPD	*Sozialdemokratische Partei Deutschlands*; Social Democratic Party of Germany
SPÖ	*Sozialdemokratische Partei Österreichs*; Austrian Social Democratic Party
SVP	*Schweizerischen Volkspartei*; Swiss People's Party
UN	United Nations
UNESCO	United Nations Educational, Scientific, and Cultural Organization
UNHCR	United Nations High Commission for Refugees
UNRRA	United Nations Relief and Rehabilitation Agency
USSR	Union of Soviet Socialist Republics
VVN	*Vereinigung des Verfolgten des Naziregimes*; Association of Those Persecuted by the Nazi Regime (GDR)
WEU	Western European Union (Brussels Pact)
WP	Warsaw Pact
WTO	World Trade Organization

Chronology of Political Events

1944   D-Day (6 June); Bretton Woods Conference creates World Bank and IMF (July); 'Percentages' Agreement (9 October)

1945   Yalta conference (4–11 February); German surrender (8 May); United Nations Charter (26 June); Potsdam conference opens (17 July); Labour Party victory in UK elections (July); Japanese surrender (15 August); Nuremberg Trials open (20 November)

1946   Kennan's 'long telegram' (22 February); Churchill's Fulton ('Iron Curtain') speech (5 March); French Fourth Republic established; de Gaulle resigns (October); Indochinese War begins (December)

1947   Anglo-American Bizone (1 January); announcement to US of end of British aid to Greece (21 February); Truman Doctrine speech (12 March); communists excluded from government (March); Marshall's Harvard speech (5 June); European Recovery Program conference in Paris (opens 27 June); partition and independence of India and Pakistan (August); foundation of Cominform (5 October); GATT ratified

1948   Start of Marshall Aid; Bevin's 'Western Union' speech (22 January); Benelux Customs Union (January); communists take power in Czechoslovakia (25 February); Brussels Treaty (17 March); OEEC (Organization for European Economic Cooperation) set up to regulate Marshall Plan (16 April); Congress of Europe (7–11 May); Soviet blockade of Berlin and Allied airlift (24 June); expulsion of Yugoslavia from Cominform (28 June) following Tito's split with Stalin; National Health Service starts functioning in Britain (5 July); Anglo-American-French Trizone (18 October); UN Convention on the Prevention and Punishment of Genocide (9 December); UN Declaration on Human Rights (10 December)

1949   Comecon founded (25 January); North Atlantic Treaty (4 April) establishes NATO; Council of Europe created (5 May); end of Berlin blockade (12 May); creation of Federal Republic of Germany (23 May) with Adenauer as Chancellor; creation of German Democratic Republic (7 October) under Ulbricht; Indonesian independence from Dutch rule (December)

1950   Schuman Plan for European Coal & Steel Community (9 May); North Korea invades South (25 June); EPU established (1 July); Pleven Plan for European Defence Committee (24 October)

1951 Treaty of Paris (18 April) establishes European Steel and Coal Community (ECSC); Libyan independence from Italy (December)

1952 Stalin note proposing German unification and neutralization (10 March); Treaty of Paris launches European Defence Community (EDC, 27 May); end of Marshall Aid (30 June); Mau Mau rebellion in Kenya; Treaty of Luxembourg on West German reparations (10 September)

1953 Death of Stalin (5 March); Malenkov calls for 'peaceful coexistence' (15 March); anti-communist uprising in GDR (17 June); arrest and execution of Beria (July/December); Cambodian independence from France (December)

1954 French surrender at Dien Bien Phu (7 May); France's National Assembly rejects EDC (30 August); start of Algerian War (1 November)

1955 Bandung Conference (18–24 April); FRG admitted to NATO (9 May); Warsaw Pact (14 May); end of occupation of Austria (15 May); Geneva Summit (18–23 July)

1956 Khrushchev's 'secret speech' (24 February); workers' uprisings in Poland (October); Hungarian revolution (October–November); Suez War (October–November)

1957 Treaties of Rome establish EEC and Euratom (25 March); independence of Ghana from Britain (6 March); space race begins (October)

1958 Execution of Imre Nagy (16 June); de Gaulle returns to power, Fifth Republic proclaimed (4 October)

1960 EFTA launched (3 May); independence of most African colonies from European rule; OECD Convention (14 December)

1961 Angolan war for independence begins (January); Berlin Wall erected (August); OECD starts functioning (30 September); Algerian protestors killed at Paris rally (17 October); Albania breaks with USSR (October)

1962 Launch of Common Agricultural Policy (CAP); Cuban Missile Crisis (August–November)

1963 Franco-German Treaty of Cooperation (22 January); Kenyan independence from Britain (12 December)

1964 Khrushchev ousted (15 October)

1965 Ceauşescu comes to power in Romania (March)

1966 French withdrawal from NATO command structure (March)

1967 'Merger Treaty' creates EC by merging EEC, ECSC, and Euratom (8 April); military coup in Greece (21 April)

1968 Prague Spring (March) leads to Soviet invasion of Czechoslovakia (20 August); student protests in France, West Germany, Italy, Poland, Spain, and elsewhere; completion of the EC Customs Union

1969 De Gaulle resigns (28 April); Brandt becomes Chancellor of FRG (21 October)

1970 Death of Salazar (27 July); Launch of European Political Cooperation (EPC) for foreign policy coordination (27 October); Brandt's *Ostpolitik* leads to treaties with GDR and USSR

1971 Honecker comes to power in GDR (3 May)

1972 'Snake in the tunnel' coordinates EC exchange rates (March); SALT I treaty (26 May); Basic Treaty between FRG and GDR signed (21 December)

1973 First enlargement of EC: Britain, Denmark, Ireland; oil crisis (October)

1974 Military coup in Portugal ends dictatorship (25 April); Schmidt becomes Chancellor in FRG (16 May); Giscard d'Estaing becomes French President (27 May); end of colonels' rule in Greece (23 July)

1975 Launch of the European Council (10–11 March); Mozambique and Angola independent from Portugal (June/November); Helsinki Final Act signed (30 July–1 August); death of Franco (20 November)

1976 Rise to prominence of Eurocommunism in France, Italy, and Spain

1977 Charter 77 signed in Czechoslovakia (6 January); Amnesty Law in Spain

1978 Murder of Aldo Moro (9 May); accession of Pope John Paul II (16 October)

1979 Second oil crisis (January); launch of EMS (March); Thatcher becomes Prime Minister in Britain (4 May); Pope visits Poland (2 June); SALT II agreement (18 June); start of Euromissile crisis (12 December); Soviet invasion of Afghanistan (24 December)

1980 Zimbabwean independence (18 April); legalization of Solidarity trade union movement in Poland (31 August)

1981 Second enlargement of EC: Greece (January); failure of military coup in Spain (23 February); Mitterrand becomes French President (21 May); Andreas Papandreou becomes Prime Minister in Greece (21 October); Jaruzelski imposes martial law in Poland (13 December)

1982 Falklands War (April–June); Spain joins NATO (May); death of Brezhnev (10 November)

1984 Miners' strike in Britain starts (March)

1985 Gorbachev comes to power in USSR (11 March); death of Hoxha in Albania (11 April)

1986 Third enlargement of EC: Spain, Portugal (January); Single European Act (SEA) launches single market plan (17 February); assassination of Olof Palme (28 February); Chernobyl nuclear meltdown (26 April); Waldheim becomes Austrian President (8 July)

1987 János Kádár ejected from power in Hungary (27 May); Gustáv Husák replaced by Miloš Jakeš as General Secretary of Czechoslovak Communist Party (December)

1988 Soviet withdrawal from Afghanistan begins (15 May)

1989 Delors Report on monetary union (17 April); Solidarity wins Polish elections (4 June); reburial of Imre Nagy (16 June); fall of Berlin Wall (9 November); Kohl's Ten-Point Plan (28 November); loss of communist power in GDR, Hungary, Czechoslovakia, and Bulgaria; revolution in Romania (December)

1990 Lithuania declares independence (11 March); free elections in GDR and Hungary (18/24 March); Gulf War begins (2 August); 2 + 4 Treaty in Germany (12 September); German unification (3 October); Kohl wins all-German election (2 December); Lech Wałesa becomes President of Poland (9 December)

1991 Warsaw Pact dissolved (25 February); Comecon dissolved (28 June); Slovenia and Croatia declare independence, beginning of Yugoslav Wars (June); coup attempt against Gorbachev (19–21 August); independence of Lithuania, Latvia, and Estonia (6 September); rise to power of Yeltsin as Russian President; USSR dissolved through Belovezha Accord (8 December)

1992 Maastricht Treaty on European Union (TEU) sets EU on road to Economic and Monetary Union (7 February); Bosnia and Herzegovina declare independence (3 March); start of Bosnian War (March)

1993 Break-up of Czechoslovakia; Havel becomes Czech President (2 February)

1994 'Second Republic' founded in Italy, Berlusconi becomes Prime Minister (10 May); Norway votes against joining EU (28 November)

1995 Fourth enlargement of EU: Austria, Sweden, Finland (January); Chirac elected President of France (17 May); Srebrenica massacre (12–16 July); Dayton Peace agreement (14 December)

1997 Blair becomes Prime Minister in Britain (2 May); Swiss banks agree payment to Holocaust victims (September); Treaty of Amsterdam dealing with justice, home affairs, immigration, Schengen (2 October)

1998 Establishment of European Central Bank (1 June); Schröder becomes Chancellor in Germany (27 October)

1999 Launch of common monetary policy and single currency (euro) (January); Poland, Hungary, and Czech Republic join NATO (13 March); Rambouillet Accord (18 March); NATO begins bombing Serbia (24 March); resignation of Yeltsin (31 December)

2000 Haider joins Austrian government (4 February); Putin becomes President of Russia (7 May); Milošević overthrown in Serbia (5 October), Vojislav Kostunica becomes President (7 October); EU Intergovernmental Conference at Nice discusses eastern enlargement, re-weighting of commission, European Rapid Reaction Force (7–10 December)

2001 Treaty of Nice on European enlargement (26 February); US-led invasion of Afghanistan (7 October)

2002   Euro enters circulation in 12 EU countries (January); trial of Milošević begins at The Hague (12 February); foundation of International Criminal Court (1 July)

2003   Iraq War begins (19 March); resignation of Shevardnadze as Georgian President (23 November)

2004   Enlargement of EU: 10 new countries join (1 January); Madrid bombings (11 March)

2005   Blair wins third term as Prime Minister (5 May); Merkel becomes Chancellor of Germany (10 October)

2007   Romania and Bulgaria join EU (January); Sarkozy becomes French President (6 May); Brown becomes Prime Minister in UK (27 June); Law of Historical Memory in Spain (31 October); Lisbon Treaty amending basis of EU (13 December)

2008   Financial crisis; Kosovo declares independence from Serbia; (17 February); Medvedev elected President of Russia (2 March); Radovan Karadžić arrested and sent to stand trial in The Hague (21 July); Russia–Georgia War (8–12 August)

2010   'New Start' treaty on nuclear arms control (8 April); Coalition government formed in UK (11 May)

2011   Arrest of Ratko Mladić (26 May); eurozone bailout package (26 October); resignation of Berlusconi (12 November)

2012   Putin elected President in Russia (4 March); Hollande elected President of France (6 May); coalition government formed in Greece (20 June); Russia joins WTO (22 August)

Introduction

The Postwar Aberration

Who would dare to impute to those masses who have risen in Europe against Nazi rule that they are fighting for the revival of a past whose profound weaknesses and irrevocable collapse they have experienced? Their goal is a new world!

Le Franc-tireur, 1 March 1944

We live on the cusp of two worlds. If we find an ethic that will have as its goal the welfare of man and not economic profit or the selfish interests of some race, nation, or social class, then, perhaps, we will be able to clear the rubble from our continent and provide education and comfort to people who crave housing, work, and books more than uniforms, guns, and tanks.

Anatol Girs

The shooting war is over, but the humanitarian democratic ideology has not obtained a clear-cut triumph. We observe that old power conflicts reappear intensified by ideological and social differences, that not a brighter world full of optimism, but a world full of conflicts, fears, and insecurity— even panic—is in the making.

Waldemar Gurian

You are likely to lose faith in yourself and in mankind when you see the survivors of the cataclysm trying to build up a new world by building into it all the same structures that led to the decomposition of the old.

Gregor von Rezzori[1]

Primo Levi is famous as the author of one of the great testimonies of Europe's catastrophe. Indeed, the rise to prominence of the genre of testimony in the late twentieth century is unthinkable without him. But Levi was also the author of numerous short stories, which he published in

Italian journals in the 1960s and 1970s. Where *If This Is a Man* and *The Truce* eventually came to define the Holocaust and to establish Auschwitz as postwar Europe's epitome of evil, 'Gladiators', first published in *L'Automobile* in 1976, seems to sum up many of the postwar period's characteristics: technology, wealth, leisure, sport, and changing gender relations; but also mass consumption, alienation, 'massification', and violence. All are exemplified in Levi's story, in which the eponymous fighters—mostly convicts—are thrown into an arena where, armed only with a hammer, they must face being mown down by cars.[2] The spectators applaud when a gladiator performs an acrobatic manoeuvre that facilitates his escape, but the wildest applause is reserved for the gladiator who smashes in the head of a driver with his hammer. The violence in this story is shocking, all the more so for being juxtaposed with leisure, relaxation, and that epitome of postwar mass culture, the automobile. But coming from the pen of Levi, with the ominous threat of Auschwitz always in the background, 'Gladiators' also suggests that the apparent stability of postwar European consumer society belies the fact that Europe's darker history is still present, just below the surface. In contrast to a novel like Georges Perec's *W or The Memory of Childhood* (1975), in which an entire society is based on the rigid lines of sport—an allegory of the attempt to turn interwar and wartime society into a grand barracks—Levi's vision is of a society not permanently mobilized, as under fascism, but nevertheless ready and willing to employ and enjoy violence.

Italy in the 1970s, when Levi wrote 'Gladiators', was a society scarred by the memory of fascism. In its most violent manifestation, the extreme-left Red Brigades (*Brigate Rosse*) sought to expose the 'objective' fascism of the modern state by provoking it into a clampdown, forcing a rightward shift. The idea was that this would reveal the state's real face, which it was hiding behind a façade of Christian Democracy. As with the Red Army Faction in West Germany at the same time, the Red Brigades were, unwittingly, doing the work of fascists for them; indeed, their immature psychological proclivities towards violence made them, despite their stated ideologies, heirs to European fascism in a complex way. In a time defined by both Eurocommunism and Eurosclerosis, the everyday chaos of postwar Italian politics meant that violence, corruption (most significantly with the 'state within a state' of the P2 masonic lodge), instability, and terrorism coexisted with historically unprecedented economic prosperity in the new, peaceful context of the EEC.

It is tempting to tell the story of Europe in the twentieth century in two halves: the first, a sorry, bleak tale of poverty, war, and genocide; and the second, a happy narrative of stability and the triumph of boring normality over dangerous activism and exuberant politics. This is not entirely unwarranted, especially if we stick to Eric Hobsbawm's 'short twentieth century' of 1914–89.[3] However, as the Italian example shows, whilst the extremes of the 'second thirty years war' did not return to Europe between 1945 and 1989, it behoves us to dig a little deeper and uncover some of the sub-plots of the redemptive narrative that is so appealing. Quite apart from the fact that Europe in 1944–5 could not feed itself—and therefore that the view from the early twenty-first century should avoid whiggish triumphalism—there were numerous fault-lines along which European politics, culture, and society split, sometimes very dangerously. Most obvious of these is of course the Cold War, which divided the continent in a way that defined it for forty years and whose after-effects are still evident. I will say more about the Cold War shortly, but it should not be taken as synonymous with the postwar period *tout court*, for this would lead one to overlook many other significant pressure points.

The impact of the Second World War, the largest and bloodiest conflict in world history, leaving so many dead that 'the very earth seemed to breathe',[4] did not end in 1945. Without understanding the nature of the Second World War, one cannot get to grips with what followed. The war was not just a classic territorial struggle that one can best understand in terms of military strategy; it was an ideological clash, in which a racialized vision of a Europe united under German domination fought, after 1941, against an uneasy alliance of liberals and communists (uneasy not only because of ideological differences, which paved the way for the Cold War, but also because until the Nazi attack of June 1941, the Soviet Union had been allied to the Third Reich). This war of ideologies, inspired primarily by Nazi chiliasm, gave the war its millenarian character, and accounts for the fact that in every state there was a mini-war going on, with large sections of the European population believing—with a peak in about 1941–2—that a Nazified Europe was an unstoppable reality. Military and ideological collaboration with Nazism meant that the viciousness of the fighting was akin to a civil war.[5] As the Italian fascist novelist Curzio Malaparte wrote:

all over Europe, a frightful civil war was festering like a tumour beneath the surface of the war which the Allies were fighting against Hitler's Germany. In their efforts to liberate Europe from the German yoke Poles were killing Poles, Greeks were killing Greeks, Frenchmen were killing Frenchmen,

Rumanians were killing Rumanians, and Jugoslavs were killing Jugoslavs.... While the Allies were allowing themselves to be killed in the attempt to liberate Italy from the Germans, we Italians were killing one another.[6]

In the Yugoslav context, renegade communist Milovan Djilas put it even more succinctly: 'A people was at grips with the invader, while brothers slaughtered one another in even more bitter warfare.'[7] The Liberation itself was a bloody and frightening process for millions of Europeans, from the citizens of Normandy whose towns were bombed by the Allies on and after D-Day, to the inhabitants of Nazi camps who were too dazed and weak to comprehend what was happening, and who continued to die in droves after being 'liberated'.[8] In the immediate postwar years, many millions of people—especially Germans—were displaced as borders were shifted and populations expelled or forcibly 'transferred', in the largest internal population migration in recorded European history.[9] As Mark Mazower notes, close to ninety million people were either killed or displaced in Europe between 1939 and 1948. 'We cannot hope to understand the subsequent course of European history', he writes, 'without attending to this enormous upheaval and trying to ascertain its social and political consequences.'[10] By the end of the war, the Allies were in effect promoting what the Nazis had advocated in the 1930s: 'ethnic homogeneity as a desirable feature of national self-determination and international stability.'[11] Purges of collaborators—often carried out by people who themselves had dubious pasts—resulted in tens of thousands of deaths before the return of governments-in-exile, most of which had sat out the war in London.[12] Even so, it is remarkable that, after the violence of the war, the retribution was not more terrible.[13] DP camps, especially housing Jewish survivors of the Nazi camps and of postwar antisemitic violence in Eastern Europe, were a blot on the Central European landscape until more than ten years after the war.[14] Violence and civil war continued in many parts of Europe. Communist authorities did not put down the last pockets of nationalist resistance in Poland until the early 1950s; civil war in Greece precipitated British withdrawal from Great Power status and permanent American intervention in Europe, in the shape of the Truman Doctrine and the Marshall Plan (the European Recovery Program). In the midst of the bloodiest war of European decolonization, in Algeria, France nearly succumbed to civil war in 1958, following a right-wing military plot. Decolonization in general was a great shock to European notions of superiority and power, which had long been taken for granted but which the experience of war had revealed as fallacious, as colonial powers were unceremoniously expelled from African or Far Eastern possessions. The leaders of the decolonization movements simply continued the struggles they had fought against the Japanese or in service in Europe during the Second World War against the colonial powers that sought to reassert their control after liberation. Even in the continuing arrangements of neo-colonialism and clientelism, which benefited the former colonial powers, decolonization brought new challenges: mass, non-white immigration into Europe, Third Worldism, and other political positions broadly associated with the 'New Left' that did not fit comfortably into paradigms which the establishment could understand. Dictatorships continued to exist in Spain and Portugal until the 1970s, as the Franco and Salazar regimes played on their supposed wartime neutrality and their anti-communist credentials to persuade the US and its NATO allies that in the context of the Cold War they ought to be tolerated. Twenty years after the end of its civil war, Greece fell prey to military dictatorship in 1967, a brutal junta that rose and fell over the question of Cyprus, itself one of the longest-running sores of postwar politics.

The Cold War itself—in the broader context of US–Soviet rivalry— obviously threatened not just the stability of Europe but of the world as a whole. The Cuban Missile Crisis of 1962 brought the world shockingly close to nuclear annihilation—it is impossible to read the transcripts of President Kennedy's discussions with EXCOMM (Executive Committee of the National Security Council) and the Joint Chiefs of Staff without one's palms sweating[15]—and the revival of the nuclear arms race in the 1980s not only re-awoke fears of Mutual Assured Destruction but understandably contributed to preventing the vast majority of Kremlin watchers from predicting the demise of communist Europe just a few years later. From the communist takeover of Eastern Europe in the immediate postwar years to the various Berlin crises, the establishment of NATO and the Warsaw Pact, the violent suppression of the workers' uprisings of 1953, the Hungarian revolution of 1956, and the 'Prague Spring' of 1968, the Korean War, the Vietnam War, and many other episodes, the global Cold War both influenced and was influenced by events in Europe.[16]

No book on postwar Europe can exclude the Soviet–American rivalry and the way in which it played out in and was in turn affected by developments in Europe. But the Cold War does not provide the only focus or conceptual framework for this study. Silvio Pons and Federico Romero write that the 'pervasiveness of the Cold War has often been used as an argument for studying it on its own terms: the bipolar system and its dynamics dominated all the nooks and crannies of the societies involved. But its very pervasiveness means that it was also porous, permeable and subject to myriad influences and transformative trends.'[17] In other words, one can show how the ubiquitous Cold War context shaped and informed all areas of life, not just politics in the narrow sense of international relations or military strategy. The Cold War, we are rightly reminded, 'was more than a high-political drama'.[18] Film, television, sport, gender relations, industrial relations, and technological development, to name just a few areas, were all affected by the basic fact of the division of Europe into two ideologically opposed camps. They were affected not only at an institutional level, in terms of funding or status, but also at the level of the imagination, as Cold War fears and insecurities crept, for example, into popular culture or family life. The reverse is also true: the way in which the Cold War was played out in international politics was also affected by gendered tropes, with Khrushchev's macho posturing and the phallic imagery of the space race being among the obvious ways in which cultural and social mores bled into the big political issues of the day.[19] Theodor Adorno wrote of Hitler's 'robot bombs' that they manifested 'world spirit' and, at the same stroke, refuted Hegel's philosophy of history.[20] It was perhaps even harder to be a Hegelian during the Cold War, in the face of nuclear annihilation.[21]

But if one can show that the Cold War as a phenomenon was porous, one should also note that it did not determine every area of postwar Europeans' lives. Certainly the focus on explaining the origins and course of the Cold War has tended to obscure the significance of the first two or three postwar years, in which the future was open and the formal division of the continent was by no means inevitable. But rock 'n' roll, the pill, and foreign holidays were all part of postwar Europe. Indeed, for many people, they were more so than the thought of nuclear destruction, which many preferred to box off in order to remain sane—and they can equally validly be the subjects of historical analysis. The many studies that have recently appeared on tourism, consumerism, family life, religion, industry, fashion and design, science and technology, art, architecture, music, film, the press, and photography all intersect with conventional narratives of the postwar period that take it as synonymous with the Cold War, but they also offer ways of understanding postwar society, culture, and economics that do not see those spheres of life as over-determined by the capitalism–communism rivalry.[22] All of these topics both slot into and cut across a standard chronological account of postwar Europe.

Moving away from high politics, many other spheres of life changed dramatically in the postwar period, so that simplistic notions of stability and normality cannot do justice to the complex realities of the period. In the field of gender relations and sexuality, the period was the first in human history in which women could take control of the reproductive process. Even if feminism and the 'sexual revolution' look somewhat jaded from the perspective of the twenty-first century, when the gender stereotypes against which feminists fought are being re-imposed, the phenomenon of women's rights (to equal pay for equal work, to initiate divorce proceedings, to protection from rape, especially in marriage, to contraception, and to abortion), backed by legislation, was still unprecedented in world history, and it is worth remembering that only a few generations of women in Europe have experienced them. Homosexuality was a subject that was not only unthinkable for most Europeans, but was certainly unmentionable in 'respectable' society in the 1940s; from the late 1960s onwards, gay rights (as opposed to the medicalizing terminology of 'deviants' or 'inverts'), though achieved steadily and unevenly, and sometimes in the face of violent opposition, made their appearance in West European law. The expansion of higher education, the rise of mass consumerism and tourism, the obsession with 'things', ownership, and wealth, the availability of cheap credit; all were phenomena of the postwar world. As one economic historian notes, 'the increase in material prosperity was probably *the* major characteristic of economic and social development in Western Europe since 1945'.[23] The same is true for Eastern Europe; even though standards of living were always sharply below those in the West, conditions were better than before the war for many and, importantly, the perception that improvements were possible became widespread. The bare economic indicators, indeed, seemed to suggest that in terms of wealth creation and technological advance, the communist half of Europe could hold its head high and compare favourably with the attainments of the West.[24]

In terms of wealth, health, technology, travel, and standards of living, postwar Europe after about 1960 marked a sharp break with the continent's previous history, as for the first time a large proportion of the population found themselves able to provide life's basic needs of food and shelter and still have money to spare. However, postwar phenomena were not all positive (even discounting, for the moment, the negative impact, on the environment or on community cohesion, of these 'goods').

In Western Europe, the postwar years also saw racialized understandings of immigration and decolonization, often resulting in riots and the rise of new far-right parties, sometimes with direct linkages to interwar fascism; terrorism of the radical left and right, as well as nationalist movements such as the IRA in Northern Ireland and Great Britain, or ETA, the Basque separatist movement, which operated in Spain and, less often, in France; the suppression of critical thought in the postwar period as old elites pushed with all their might for their rehabilitation at the expense of those with new ideas for antifascist grassroots politics. In Eastern Europe, the period saw the creation of police states backed up by powerful and all-pervasive secret police forces that were far more extensive than the Gestapo; the homogenization of living and working conditions; and the dominance of ideology over the private sphere, with sometimes tragicomic, sometimes lunatic results.[25] Indeed, if one compares Western or Eastern Europe in 1945 with Europe in 2000, in every sphere—political, economic, cultural, social, educational, and sexual— the difference between the start and the end of the period is so vast that probably no other comparably short period of European history has ever witnessed such remarkable change. Recognizing that fact and explaining it is the historian's task, and thus we can see that postwar Europe is fast becoming history. This process of historicization is being set in train in many ways, but clearly, comfortable notions of stability and progress are insufficient for the job. In his 1895 inaugural lecture at Cambridge, Lord Acton noted that 'there is far more fear of drowning than of drought' when encountering the sources for writing modern history—and that in an age when history writing was restricted to diplomatic history. Some clear-cut conceptual parameters are therefore required in order to make sense of this mass of material, encompassing every conceivable sphere of human activity.

My main conceit for understanding the period in this book is the rise and fall of the postwar European consensus. What this means is that the war precipitated the creation of an antifascist narrative both in Eastern and Western Europe—though vastly different in each sphere—which gave shape and significance to what might otherwise have appeared as the vast panorama of futility and anarchy that was the Second World War. In the east, this narrative was enforced, violently suppressing those who disagreed, and in the process permitting the destruction of the old social order in the name of constructing socialism. On the assumption that landowners, property-owners, businessmen, and professionals (a small minority, of course, of the population in Eastern Europe) were fascist collaborators or sympathizers, their property was 'redistributed' to 'the people', that is, to the state and its arriviste, often thuggish administrators and beneficiaries. The narrative was rooted in fact: the Red Army, albeit with American assistance, had indeed defeated fascism in Europe at tremendous cost to Soviet lives and society, and even those who were not natural communist supporters were forced to admire the achievement; most threw their lot in with communism, if not with enthusiasm then with a sense that it represented the future and that, if one wanted to get on, there was no option.

In the western half of the continent, 'antifascism' did not become state dogma as it did behind what soon became the 'iron curtain'. But a different sort of antifascism nevertheless held considerable sway over Western Europeans' lives. In Britain, pride at defeating Hitler was a commonplace sentiment across all classes for many years, contributing to the British sense of superiority where Europe was concerned and sustaining the fiction that Britain was still a major world power.[26] Britain's Labour government under Clement Attlee was more radical than most other Western European governments, which were dominated by centre-right Christian Democrats, but everywhere a new consensus was built which encompassed class cooperation, the welfare state of one variety or another, and the solid embrace of parliamentary democracy by parties of the right which had been hostile to mass electorates before the war.

In other words, antifascism became the basis of stability in postwar Europe. Some words of clarification are needed here: the term 'antifascism' is usually associated with communist ideology, and it is indeed a term that was instrumentalized by the Eastern Bloc regimes in order to justify their agenda for social 'reorganization'. This deployment of the term, as a guise for root and branch transformation of social relations, has been called 'antifascism as total ideology', and reminds us that the legitimacy of the communist regimes was always based on fact, but a fact that grew increasingly meaningless as the years passed and as those who had contributed to the defeat of fascism died, leaving their descendants with little but the officially endorsed narrative of victory over Hitler and the grim reality of the Eastern Bloc.[27] But, as another scholar notes, 'Antifascism cannot be reduced to a variation of Soviet Communism.'[28] There will be some who, not without good arguments, think that the term 'antifascism' is so freighted with historical misuse that it cannot be salvaged as a conceptual tool. However, my use of the term is meant to indicate that reducing antifascism to communist ideology is not only historically inaccurate where the phenomenon of antifascism is concerned—it would do a real disservice to the wide variety of antifascist individuals and groups to insist that they had been duped by or were patsies for communist manipulators[29]—but leaves one unable to see what is historically noteworthy about the years 1945–89.

By taking the notion of an antifascist consensus as the key to understanding postwar Europe, one can see more clearly that what the collapse of this consensus reveals is that the uneasy stability of the postwar period (1945–89) was an aberration in European history. As the meaning of Eastern European 'antifascism' has taken a battering following the collapse of communism, so too has the 'antifascism' of the West, which means an assault on the social democratic values that helped to build the first three postwar decades in Western Europe. These decades, which are still venerated as years of boom and unprecedented economic success, increasingly appear as aberrant in the sense that the values that they exhorted—democracy, class cooperation, good labour–employee relations, nationalization of essential services and utilities, high taxation to fund the creation of all-embracing welfare states— have come under fire by those who forget that they emerged as an antidote to the greatest catastrophe that Europe has ever brought upon itself.

The point is not just that the years in which the antifascist narrative held meaning and significance for Europe's people happened to coincide with the postwar period, 1945–89. The point is, rather, that the postwar years were structured and shaped by that narrative, and that in order to understand the post-Cold War period, one has to see that the concept of antifascism has been discredited, not only by those who were forced to live through its abuse at the hands of communists—for many of whom anything which smacks of antifascism, such as Holocaust commemoration, is distasteful, a problem which has unfortunate consequences, as we will see—but by many in the western half of the continent who are all too glad to see the old pieties obliterated. In other words, accompanying the argument about the rise and fall of the postwar consensus is the claim that this rise and fall must be understood in interplay with memories and interpretations of the Second World War.

I thus offer antifascism as a helpful conceptual tool not just for the sake of novelty. As I will explain shortly, there is no merit in pretending that the Cold War and the divisions and rivalries that it created was not the major structuring force of the post-1945 years. But there was more going on in Europe in the years after the Second World War than can be encompassed in a narrative of the Cold War which sees everything through the lenses of liberal democracy versus communism, or superpower rivalries. 'Antifascism', even when it is a term that the protagonists themselves would have abjured, helps one to explain why even Christian Democratic and other conservative parties, who dominated the politics of postwar Western Europe, embraced welfare states, corporatist labour arrangements, and the suppression of histories of wartime collaboration. Allied insistence on denazification in Germany and Austria went hand in hand with liberal nationalist narratives of antifascist resistance in France, the Netherlands, Italy, Scandinavia, and elsewhere in Western Europe, with the exception of the Iberian dictatorships—and even here the fiction of wartime anti-Nazism became important. Finally, the concept of antifascism needs to be rescued from the dustbin of history and shown to have been more than communist rhetoric, if some of the ideals which motivated the best aspects of the postwar settlement are not to be thrown out along with the worst.

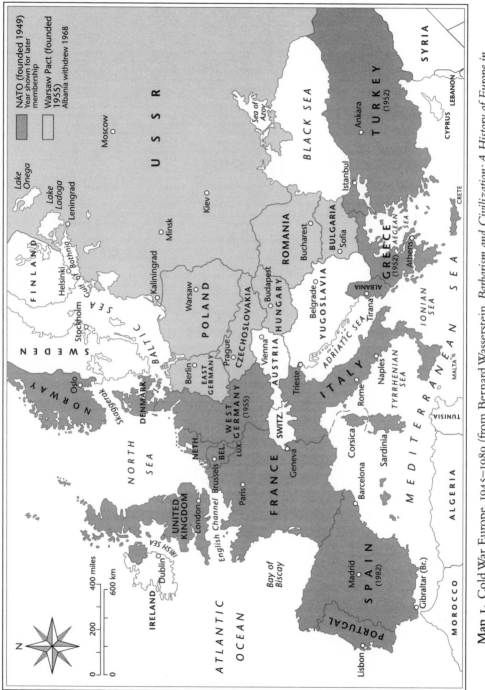

Map 1. Cold War Europe, 1945–1989 (from Bernard Wasserstein, *Barbarism and Civilization: A History of Europe in Our Time* (Oxford University Press, 2007), p. 426).

PART I

The Rise of the Postwar Consensus

I

Consensus Enforced

Eastern Europe, 1944–1953

The crisis of capitalism has manifested itself in the division of the capitalists into two factions—one *fascist*, the other *democratic*. . . . We are currently allied with one faction against the other, but in the future we will be against the first faction of capitalists, too.

Stalin to Dimitrov, 19 January 1945

. . . what had attracted me to the movement more than anything, dazzled me, was the feeling (real or apparent) of standing near the *wheel of history*. . . . we were bewitched by history . . . admittedly, in most cases the result was an ugly lust for power, but (as all human affairs are ambiguous) there was still (and especially, perhaps, in us, the young) an altogether idealistic illusion that we were inaugurating a human era in which man (all men) would be neither *outside* history, nor *under the heel of history*, but would create and direct it.

Ludvik, in Milan Kundera, *The Joke*[1]

Paths not taken?

Can one enforce a consensus? This oxymoron captures something of the complexity of Eastern Europe in this period, a complexity that was gradually suppressed and reduced—at least officially—to something quite simple. By the end of the war there was a multiplicity of peoples and groups fighting the Nazi occupier; some who fought for the Nazis, such as Ukrainian Trawniki men, Latvia's infamous Arājs Commando, or the tens of thousands of men in General Vlassov's army, many of whom chose to fight rather than face death by starvation in a corner of a concentration camp; regimes allied to the Third Reich in Romania, Hungary, Slovakia, and Croatia; not to mention whole groups of Ukrainians, Poles, Yugoslavs and other nationalities fighting each other. In other words, there were many competing understandings of what the 'nation' meant and what its future should look like after the war.

By contrast with this chaotic scene, the enforcement of communist rule meant the approval of just one version of events and just one simple, appealing message: antifascism had defeated Nazism, and that victory legitimized communist rule. As Stalin said in February 1946, 'our victory means above all that our social system has won and that the Soviet social system has successfully withstood the test of the fire of war and demonstrated its full viability'.[2] Whoever disagreed—those, for example, who had by no means been Nazi collaborators but who were anti-communists—found themselves labelled as enemies, as did those who were 'objectively' (i.e. from the Communist Parties' point of view) opposed to communist rule, such as businessmen or landowners, irrespective of their political opinions. This oversimplification of the enemy worked to the advantage of the communists, especially when dealing with insurgents who fought against communist rule, as some did in the border regions of the Baltic States, Poland, and Ukraine until as late as 1953. The communists' blanket and 'inaccurate perception of resistance as a class war eventually created precisely the opponents whom the Communists had expected to face, leaving them no option but to fight back'.[3]

But before the imposition of communist rule, which we will examine in detail shortly, the atmosphere in all parts of Europe, apart from the Iberian peninsula, was far more febrile than we often think. The immediate postwar period has been investigated in great detail by historians, mainly with the aim of explicating the origins of the Cold War. But by seeing these immediate postwar years as no more than precursors to the definitive Cold War settlement, the radical contestation and openness that characterized them can easily be overlooked. As Geoff Eley writes, the 'lasting framework of policy, reforms and dominant thinking that eventually solidified out of the intensely contested politics of 1945–46' have 'retroactively acquired a much stronger logic of inevitability', with the arrangements of 1947–8 being 'projected backwards onto the preceding moment of Liberation'. This retroactive determinism means that historians miss the possibility that existed in 1945 of a 'Third Way', a social vision 'situated somewhere between or beyond the starkly polarized options of Stalinism and the anti-Communist consensus of the West'.[4] This is a viewpoint shared by Mark Mazower, who notes that 'many former partisans and members of the underground were left with the feeling that they and their cause had been betrayed'.[5] Let us consider those first few years after the war in more detail and see in what ways possible paths to alternative futures were steadily closed off.

Until Stalin's perception that the USSR's security concerns were in contest with the actions of the Western Allies drove him to take the course of actions which resulted in the definitive communist takeover of the countries behind the 'iron curtain'—as Churchill called the border running from Stettin to Trieste in his famous speech at Fulton, Missouri, on 5 March 1946—there was some room for manoeuvre in the Eastern European countries. The contingent nature of these few years is most clearly illustrated by the lack of electoral success for the communists in Czechoslovakia and Hungary—not to mention the fact that elections were being held at all. And although—or perhaps because—the return of governments-in-exile put the brakes on really radical reform, the Eastern European states followed similar trajectories to their Western neighbours. In the same way that the 200,000 or so armed members of the French resistance were incorporated into the regular army with little difficulty, so in Eastern Europe the status quo was quickly reasserted. In Czechoslovakia, a Central Planning Commission was established by President Beneš in 1945, and in Poland, nationalization programmes introduced by (communist-dominated) coalition governments in 1946 indicated a turn towards state planning of investment that pre-dated the communist takeovers and shared many features with the planning mania that was sweeping the whole continent.[6]

At the same time as this reassertion of order, there were also outbreaks of violence, hardly surprising when one considers the chaos of the end of the war. Millions of people were on the move across a Europe whose infrastructure largely lay in tatters and which could barely feed its people. When one considers the purges of collaborators and revenge attacks that took place, what is noteworthy about them is that they were not more widespread and not harder to bring under state control. Besides, in certain cases, notably with respect to surviving Jewish victims of Nazi genocide, the violence that took place was instrumentalized—it was useful for the regimes seeking to establish themselves. In Bulgaria, for example, the Fatherland Front happily permitted, indeed even unofficially encouraged, attacks on those accused of being wartime collaborators, as this expedited the process of large-scale social change.

In Poland, revenge attacks on surviving Jews, most famously in Kielce in July 1946 when 43 Jews were murdered and many more injured, show on the face of it that the civil war-like conditions of postwar Poland had not yet been brought fully under control, revealing the limits of the antifascist narrative's reach.[7] In the aftermath of the pogrom, in a sign that their power was far from being consolidated in rural areas, the communist authorities appealed to a local antisemitic priest, Father Martuzalski, to co-sign a condemnation of the violence. His refusal indicates the lack of control that communists still had, outside of the cities and areas where the Red Army was stationed.[8]

Yet, contrary to what one might expect from a movement which espoused equality and had just defeated Nazism, it suited the Polish communists to permit, if not clandestinely to encourage antisemitism, as a way, first, of coordinating themselves with widely held views in Polish society and, second, of legitimizing the theft of Jewish property, by individuals and by the state. The end result, some twenty years later, was the communists' realization of the Polish nationalists' ambition of eliminating more or less entirely the thousand-year-old Jewish presence in Poland.[9] In Hungary, the opposite effect was the problem. Although Communist Party campaigns against black marketeers were often tinged with antisemitism, in the trials of Arrow Cross men or other fascist collaborators, the proceedings appeared, from the point of view of some Hungarians, to be there 'to compensate for, or to retaliate on behalf of, the Jewish victims'.[10] This false identification of Jews with communism would have unfortunate consequences later, as we will see.

But it was not only the Jewish presence in Europe that was being erased. In a process that President Wilson had begun in 1918, with his liberal support for national self-determination, then continued by Hitler, with his radical, racial approach to reshaping Europe's demography, the Allies authorized the attempt finally to eliminate the 'problem' of 'national minorities' in Europe. The Soviets, following Stalin's apparently paradoxical belief in the fixedness of national character, implemented the most radical demographic schemes.[11] In Poland, as elsewhere across the region, apart from the mass migration of over 11 million forced labourers trying to return home from the ruins of the Third Reich, and the Displaced Persons (DPs), many of them Jews, who were finding their way into camps—ironically, mostly in Germany and Austria—precisely in order to avoid going back to their places of origin in the Soviet Union or elsewhere in Eastern Europe, the most noteworthy phenomenon of the immediate postwar years was the expulsions of ethnic Germans into the new borders of the occupied German zones and the so-called 'population transfers' of other minorities. The policy almost worked.

Where, especially in the Eastern European borderlands, there had been a remarkable mix of polyglot peoples for whom, until it was forced on them by new, powerful regimes, the concept of nationality was meaningless, now this centuries-old history had come to an end, as Lithuanians, Belorussians, Ukrainians, and Poles were shunted from places where their families had lived for as long as they could remember, in order to place them in 'their' national boundaries. People who might once have identified themselves as 'peasants' or 'Orthodox' were now learning to be Ukrainian or Belorussian.[12] Some sizeable minorities did remain in place, for example Hungarians in Transylvania, which once more passed into Romanian hands—but here it suited the Hungarian communists to keep alive the question of Magyars outside the motherland as a way of legitimizing the regime. And the European minority which once again was entirely overlooked was the Roma, who, following their decimation at the hands of the Nazis—perhaps some 500,000 were murdered, mostly at the 'Gypsy camp' in Auschwitz-Birkenau—were returned to their traditional status as Europe's pariahs. But for the most part, the European map now looked very monotone, as the dream of ethnic homogeneity that united liberals, fascists, and communists had finally been realized.

With the ethnic cleansing of Germans from Eastern Europe and other expulsions—often euphemistically called 'resettlements' or 'population exchanges' in the same way that the Nazis used anodyne terminology to refer to deportation to death camps—a clear continuity with wartime violence can be seen in the years after 1945, only now sanctioned by the victorious Allies. Some 12 million ethnic Germans were expelled from the Sudetenland (Czechoslovakia), Romania, Hungary, the Baltic States, Poland, and elsewhere; and continuing its wartime policy of deporting 'enemy peoples' (including Chechens, Ingush, Greeks, Poles, Finns, Armenians, Balts, and other inhabitants of the Soviet Union's border regions), the USSR also authorized the 'transfer' of more than two million Poles from the USSR and some 700,000 Ukrainians out of south-east Poland into Soviet Ukraine between 1945 and 1947. At the end of the process, Poland, whose population before the war was comprised of only two-thirds ethnic Poles, was almost entirely ethnically homogeneous. This ethnic cleansing was presented by the Allies, including the US, as an orderly process, and preferable, as Herbert Hoover put it, to 'the constant suffering of minorities and the constant recurrence of war', but in reality it was a brutal process—some 1.5 million people were killed during the expulsions—and one which lent intellectual sanction to the notion of the 'unmixing of peoples', and thus implicitly to the racist notion that different peoples cannot live together.[13] It was endorsed even by liberal thinkers, such as the Hungarian historian and politician István Bibó, who argued in 1946 that finding a permanent territorial solution to the nationalities problem in Eastern Europe was preferable to Europe becoming the 'highway of the homeless masses'.[14]

As in Western Europe, there were of course officially organized trials in the lands east of Germany, following the brief period of unauthorized killings in the immediate aftermath of the war. But here, purges and trials were not only manifestations of justice, revenge, or the settling of scores, but also an opportunity to reshape society at large: 'throughout the territories under Red Army control, the trials and other punishments of collaborators, Fascists and Germans were always and above all a way of clearing the local political and social landscape of impediments to Communist rule.'[15] Certainly genuine war criminals were prosecuted, as in the Polish Supreme National Tribunal's trials of 49 major war criminals, which bears comparison in its legal methods and organization with the Nuremberg Trials; but in general the communists made use of the trials to facilitate the process of class 'reorganization' and to eliminate those who were 'hampering socialist reconstruction'.[16] Hence, whilst in the five years after the war the British tried more than 1,000 Axis nationals and the Americans more than 1,800, the Soviets tried far more. Exact figures are difficult to obtain, but in May 1950, there were 13,532 convicted war criminals in Soviet camps; in the Soviet zone of Germany there had been 12,177 convictions in the same five-year period.[17] Ultimately, apart from those whose records were too well known, the communists paid less attention to punishing card-carrying Nazis in the Soviet Occupation Zone of Germany or to fascist collaborators elsewhere in the region than they did to incorporating them into the service of the new regimes (in the same way that in the west, journalists, academics, and scientists, not to mention SS veterans—such as the Ukrainian Galicia division—often escaped prosecution because they were useful to the new regimes, provided much-needed labour, and, of course, had impeccable anti-communist credentials). In this they were very successful as, once they were invited in, many Nazis, Italian Fascists, and Hungarian Arrow Cross activists willingly opted to work for the communists.

All of these phenomena indicate how, immediately on the war's end, memories of the war were being shaped in the service of the present. If, as we will see, France styled itself a nation of resistors and Italy a country of antifascists, so too in Eastern Europe the process of 'selective remembering' which the communists adopted was already well under way as soon as the war was over. The same process that was occurring in Western Europe of constructing—from above and from the grassroots—narratives of the war which emphasized certain features at the expense of others, was also in train in Eastern Europe. Indeed, irrespective of whether communists were already in power (Yugoslavia, Albania, Bulgaria), were dominant forces in coalition governments (the Soviet Occupation Zone of Germany, Poland, Romania), or were biding their time (Hungary, Czechoslovakia), this mnemonic process was a necessary precondition for the rebuilding of a ravaged continent. But whereas in Western Europe the process was driven by governments but could be—within certain boundaries—contested in public debate, in the lands occupied by the Red Army the most noteworthy characteristic of the process of memory-building was the eradication of alternatives. Antifascist narratives predominated across Europe; but only in the communist countries did they become officially enshrined as the *raison d'être* of the state and the basis for social policy. When, for example, the SED (the Socialist Unity Party, East Germany's ruling Communist Party) refused to recognize any legal continuity between the Third Reich and the GDR (as the Soviet zone became in 1949), it not only heaped all the responsibility on to the 'reactionary' Federal Republic, but also—in a way that Austrian communists had refused to do, at the cost of their political fortunes—cynically incorporated many former Nazis, especially Gestapo and other policemen, into the new state's security apparatus, the Stasi. In this way, the GDR's leaders built a conspiracy of silence, forcing complicity and adherence to the regime, and incorporating a *ressentiment* which expressed itself in a brutal suppression of dissent.

In fact, the existence of the antifascist narrative pre-dated the rigidification of the communist regimes. Rather, it was this narrative, and the sense that accompanied it of being on the side of History, that assured Stalin that, no matter which tactic he chose, Eastern Europe would fall under his control and would be amenable to being Sovietized. Thus, the very takeover of Eastern Europe by the communists needs to be seen not only in the context of *realpolitik* and great power rivalry (that is to say, as the first manifestation of the Cold War), but of ideology and the communists' belief that the future was theirs. Many who were not (yet) communists found it hard to disagree— fascism had been defeated and whatever else was on offer had little leverage. This self-belief holds the key to understanding the fact that, contrary to the western Cold War claim that Stalin intended from the outset to install communists in government as quickly as possible, in fact the process was somewhat ad hoc, and was completed swiftly in 1948 only when changing circumstances made Stalin feel as though his window of opportunity might be closing.[18]

Sovietization

The Red Army's occupation of the lands between Russia and Germany, including eastern Austria, gave the communists confidence that Stalin's earlier territorial demands, of both Hitler at the time of the Hitler–Stalin Pact, and then Churchill from the time the Nazis invaded the USSR to the conferences at Yalta (February 1945) and Postdam (July–August 1945), could be realized. It would be naive to think that, having once occupied those countries, after fierce fighting and tremendous loss of Soviet lives, Stalin would abandon them. As Stalin supposedly said, in Yugoslav communist leader Milovan Djilas's famous quotation, 'this war is not as in the past; whoever occupies a territory also imposes on it his own system as far as his army can reach. It cannot be otherwise.'[19] Equally, Stalin's alliance with the US and the UK was by no means an impediment to the realization of his territorial ambitions; on the contrary, it legitimized them, as the famous 'Percentages Agreement' of October 1944 between Churchill and Stalin indicates. Here, on the back of a half sheet of paper, the British and Soviet future spheres of interests in the Balkans were hastily scribbled down by the former and just as hastily agreed to by the latter in a way that might appear apocryphal but actually corresponded quite closely with what came to pass—and with what, as Churchill may have calculated, he was in any case powerless to prevent. For example, Stalin did not demur when the British sought to put down the Greek Left (the communists there had in any case disobeyed Stalin's instructions to give up the revolutionary struggle), and nor did Churchill object when Stalin intervened in Romania in February 1945 to install a communist government there.[20] Sometimes historical myths generate reality. In any case, Moscow's cultivation of the Western Allies was thoroughly self-interested. 'It was to our advantage to preserve the alliance', as Molotov later remarked.[21] We might, in fact, better regard the division of Europe as 'a *solution* to the problem of how the two sides could get along, not as the *source* of that problem'.[22]

Nevertheless, there was, as one of the best historians of the Cold War notes, 'no straight line from Stalin's vision to the eventual partition of Europe as it took shape during the Cold War'.[23] In fact, although Stalin certainly never gave up the goal of Sovietizing neighbouring lands, as soon as the Third Reich invaded the USSR in June 1941 he ordered local communist parties across Europe to drop the revolutionary policy of overthrowing existing regimes, instructing them instead to engage in a gradualist strategy of obtaining power. By stressing the common threat, this new line brought allies to the Soviets, an alliance which remained no less useful after the war. This was the strategy of 'national fronts', or what communist ideologue Georgi Dimitrov called 'popular democracy', working with centrist and non-communist leftist parties as a way of levering communists into power whilst appearing to observe the rules of parliamentary democracy.

The 'national fronts' strategy, which replicated the 'popular fronts' of the 1930s, can be seen as simply a sham, a more cynical way of achieving the same end, engaging others and making them do the communists' dirty work. To the East German communists, for example, Stalin said in 1948: 'You should advance towards socialism not by taking a straight road but move in zigzags.' Or, more explicitly, as a letter of guidance from Moscow to the Polish Workers' Party (the Polish communists) put it in July 1944: the 'correct policy for a national front requires a series of concessions and compromises which will split our opponents without fundamentally altering our aim: satisfying the major demands of the masses and creating a situation favourable to our long-term plans.'[24]

Rather than just a sham, however, the strategy also reflected a sense that, with the immense prestige won by the Red Army—not to mention the apparent lack of credible alternatives—Stalin was genuinely relaxed about the method and speed with which communism would be installed. By replacing the revolutionary creed with one of peaceful integration on a national basis, Stalin signalled not so much that a twisted path to communism should be followed as a way of throwing its opponents off the scent, but that this approach really was better suited both to prevailing local conditions and to the maintenance of the grand alliance. As Stalin said in a January 1945 meeting with Dimitrov and Yugoslav and Bulgarian leaders, 'perhaps we are making a mistake when we think that the Soviet form is the only one leading to Socialism. The facts show that the Soviet one is the best, but it is absolutely not the only one.'[25] The Yugoslavs, having installed themselves in power without Soviet aid, disagreed, wanting, for example, to continue funding the Greek guerrilla struggle—a prospect which Stalin rightly identified as hopeless. This different approach to fomenting revolution was one of the key reasons for Tito's and Stalin's later split, which Stalin precipitated in June 1948 in annoyance at Yugoslavia's expansionist foreign policy in the Balkans.[26]

None of this means that Stalin would have let the countries occupied by the Red Army opt for capitalism. But it does mean that the Cold War was neither determined in advance nor consciously engendered by Stalinist bellicosity, and that 'the Western powers mistook his ability to use force for a determination to use it'.[27] Stalin wanted a weak Eastern Europe, but there were various ways of reaching that goal. The shape that the Cold War took by 1948 cannot simply be read off the state of Europe in 1944–5. Not only was Soviet decision-making in Eastern Europe opportunist, it was also reactive, driven largely by American decision-making—a fact that is often overlooked when the focus is on Stalin and his circle.[28]

In fact, Stalin had relatively few key demands for Eastern Europe, other than a desire to see it permanently weakened, even in preference to becoming communized. But these included several key territorial demands, notably on Poland and Romania. Here Stalin was insistent that communist rule should be swiftly captured, and by communists of the sort who were subordinate to Moscow. This prerequisite not only swiftly contributed to the eradication of communist leaders who had spent time in Western Europe; in the case of Romania with its tiny indigenous Communist Party (the clandestine RCP had, according to communist leader Ana Pauker, fewer than 1,000 members in 1944, including those in prisons and concentration camps; there were 80 RCP members in Bucharest in August 1944), it meant installing and maintaining communist rule by force—a stance easier to justify in Romania, given its history of ethno-nationalism and its alliance with Nazi Germany until very late in the war. Despite the RCP's tiny size, its members were convinced that they had history on their side and they 'acted accordingly'.[29] The RCP's rapid growth into a national mass party after the *coup d'état* of 23 August 1944 only confirmed this view.[30]

Stalin's eagerness to acquire control over these two countries had a simple basis: the need not so much to see the victory of communism as to have in place regimes which would recognize the new territorial realities. Poland had lost a vast eastern region (the *kresy*), and Romania had lost not just the part of Ukraine it had occupied during the war (Transnistria) but also Bessarabia (roughly today's Moldova), to the USSR. Poland and Romania were thus important buffer states between the Soviet Union and Central Europe, and with their traditions of anti-communism it was imperative from Stalin's point of view that friendly regimes be installed there as quickly as possible. By early 1947, the forced fusion of the socialists and communists (as in East Germany), the persecution and arrest of anti-communists, and the firm grip held by communists over key ministries and loci of state power, all indicated that communist control in these two countries had been firmly established. In Romania, rigged elections in November 1946 helped the National Democratic Front to hold on to the power it had seized in February 1945, ending the confusing period following Romania's switching of sides in the war of August 1944. As a popular quip had it after the first (and also fraudulent) parliamentary election in People's Poland in 1947, in which Stanisław Mikołajczyk's Polish Peasant Party won far more support than Stalin's placemen: 'What a magic ballot box! You vote Mikołajczyk and Gomułka comes out!'

In fact, Poland was a different case from the rest of the Soviet Bloc. For various reasons, its Sovietization process was incomplete. The settlement of formerly German territory in what now became western Poland (most notably in the major city of Breslau/Wrocław) by millions of refugees from the *kresy*, the continuing importance of the Catholic Church, and the failure completely to collectivize the peasantry were all phenomena which stored up trouble for later: Poland was the only country within the Eastern Bloc which repeatedly witnessed challenges to communist rule, in 1956, 1968, 1970, 1976, and 1980, and it was the last of these insurrections which gave birth to Solidarity, the movement which more than any other emboldened the people living under communist regimes throughout the region to take on their rulers. But this would all occur later; between 1946 and 1953, the traditional milieu and structures of Polish society were steadily eroded and power transferred to a Stalinist elite under Gomułka. When Mikołajczyk fled for his life in October 1947, no clearer indication could have been given of the shutting off of a democratic future for Poland.

This process had also occurred swiftly in the Soviet Occupied Zone of Germany. What became in 1949 the GDR is best understood as part of 'Eastern Europe', that is to say, as part of this process of the Sovietization of Soviet-occupied Europe, for here Stalin's intention was the simple one of neutralizing Germany as a future threat to Soviet security. Indeed, more than any other concern, preventing a revival of German power was the issue that dominated Stalin's mind—hardly surprising given the devastation wreaked upon the Soviet Union by the Nazis, with a loss of about 27 million Soviet citizens during the Great Patriotic War (1941–5). The replacement of communists who had been in exile in the west, such as the 'Mexicans' Paul Merker and Leo Zuckermann, with the 'Moscow' communists around Walter Ulbricht, indicated that here too, Stalin saw a supine and subordinate regime as absolutely necessary. Indeed, although the standard of living in East Germany was among the highest in the Eastern Bloc, it quickly became a tightly run ship with a vast network of informers supporting a massive security apparatus. Stalinization was forced through in an exemplary fashion here, with purges, the removal of industrial plant to Russia, and the firmly directed central control of the economy. By 1950, the GDR was—and remained—the most orthodox communist regime. And its Stalinist 'consensus' was based around an explicit reworking of the immediate postwar attack on fascism; by 1950, antifascism meant being opposed to West Germany and its NATO allies, and the East German supreme court (*Oberste Gericht*) convicted some 78,000 people of political crimes in 1950 alone.[31] Ulbricht explained the necessity of the national front by quite brazenly manipulating the message of antifascism so that it now meant less anti-Nazism than anti-westernism:

> Today, the measure of who is a peace-loving individual and who seeks German unity is not what party membership book they had earlier, and whether or not they belonged to the Hitler party. Rather, the only measure is: Are you for a peace treaty? Are you against the Atlantic Pact, as a result of which West Germany would be made into a base for war? Are you for the unity of Germany? Are you for the withdrawal of occupation troops following the conclusion of a peace treaty, or are you for a forty-year occupation and colonization of West Germany? Today, under these conditions, anyone who raises the question, 'Is this person a former member of the Nazi party or not' works against the formation of the National Front.[32]

As with Mikołajczyk's speedy departure from Poland, Ulbricht signalled quite clearly his willing subordination to Moscow and the death of any hope for democratic socialism in the GDR of the sort espoused by the 'western' communists, all of whom were now purged.

The cases of Romania, Poland, and the GDR bear out the claim that Stalin had a clearly defined goal which he realized as swiftly as possible. Since the partial opening of the Soviet-era archives, one can now defend the claim that 'Stalin had the intention, the means, and the ability to control the overall design, as well as the thrusts and parries of Soviet foreign policy.'

But, looking at Eastern Europe more widely, it is also clear that the Soviets wanted to divide the continent in 1944–5 *and at the same time* maintain good relations with the Western Allies, and that, for the first years after the war, the countries of what became 'Eastern Europe' had 'very different political constellations that, at least from the perspective of the time, might well have indicated diverse futures'.[33]

Stalin undoubtedly acted to secure the Soviet Union's new westward-shifted borders by installing friendly regimes in Poland and Romania. And as Averell Harriman, whose term in office as US ambassador to the Soviet Union had just ended, explained in a speech to the New York Union Club in March 1946, Stalin's principal object:

> was to cover her western borders with a screen of friendly countries. This...was in conformity with agreements reached in conferences with the British and the Americans; unhappily there was a wide difference between the American and the Russian interpretation of the term 'friendly'. For America it would connote an attitude something like that of Mexico, but for Russia, intolerant of opposition and used to liquidation as the sole means of dealing with opposition, it meant complete domination of the country before it is ready to regard it as 'friendly'.[34]

Yet it remains the case that elsewhere, notably Hungary and Czechoslovakia, Stalin was far more relaxed about the progress of communism.

In Hungary, for example, the Communist Party, which numbered a mere 4,000 members in February 1945, gradually increased its stranglehold on power through the use of what MKP leader Mátyás Rákosi called 'salami tactics'. This strategy involved the incremental acquisition of power by 'the cutting out of reaction in slices from the Smallholders' Party'. As Stalin put it, the goal was to 'isolate all your enemies politically', to 'resist the constant pressure from reactionary circles', and to pave the way for a 'decisive struggle against the reactionaries'.[35] In other words, the imposition of communism in postwar Hungary did not proceed in one fell swoop, but was 'the result of changes which came about one after the other.'[36] The Smallholders' Party won the (genuine) election of November 1945, and forced the communists onto the back foot. A slow process of building up a political police force, with Soviet assistance, was key here to the communists' ability to regain control over the 'popular front' government by the summer of 1947. Following the expulsion of French and Italian communists from government in May 1947, Moscow finally permitted Rákosi to move against ministers in the coalition from the Smallholders' Party (most significantly

Prime Minister Ferenc Nagy) and to end the process of 'peaceful transition'. By 1948, Rákosi had eliminated all representatives of the national road to socialism, such as Imre Nagy, which was condemned as a 'right-wing deviation'. By even exceeding Moscow's demands, attacking the Catholic Church, announcing the nationalization of industry, and attacking individual farmers as kulaks, Rákosi saved his own skin (his friendliness with the Yugoslavs was on record), and ended the period of Hungarian gradualism.[37]

In Czechoslovakia, the Communist Party, as elsewhere, played a role in the new coalition government, overseeing land reform and other measures, such as the nationalization of banks and large industrial enterprises. Indeed, there was considerable support for major reform among Czechs at the end of the war, such that President Beneš could talk of creating a 'socializing democracy'.[38] The Red Army had withdrawn in November 1945, and Stalin did not concern himself with the country, where communist leader and Prime Minister Klement Gottwald assured his supporters that communism would triumph through a 'Czechoslovak road to socialism'. So although there was a coalition in power, in the May 1946 elections, the Czechoslovak Communist Party, which already had over 1,000,000 members, won 38 per cent of the vote (40.2 per cent in Bohemia and Moravia), a clear victory; with its ally, the Social Democratic Party, the coalition held a majority of the vote. Nevertheless, Gottwald was content to allow a 'gradualist' approach to the Sovietization of Czechoslovakia—for example, in not resolving the Czech–Slovak national question—for which he was censured by the Soviet authorities. When the Cominform was established in Szklarska Poręba in September 1947, it became clear that the 'national road to socialism' was no longer acceptable to the 'Moscow centre', and that rather than worry about obtaining a majority in the forthcoming May 1948 elections, the communists should act more decisively. Their chance to do so came with the resignations of the communists' coalition partners and the coup of February 1948. This did not mean that the Czechoslovak road to socialism came to an abrupt end; it took another year or two for it to be transformed into Czechoslovak Stalinism. But having obtained total power, the communists, shocked as they were, held on to it. Here nothing like a long-term plan to take over the country can be deduced; as dissident author Ludvík Vaculík later wrote, 'I frequently wonder how it is possible that this entire collapse, this national disaster, started with several seemingly decent, from a political point of view understandable and voluntary resignations.'[39]

Following the condemnation of Yugoslavia in June 1948, the Czechoslovak regime committed itself finally to fully-fledged Stalinism, which was in place by the time of the CPCz's Ninth Congress, in May 1949. The purges of 1951–3, most famously of former Foreign Minister Vladimír Clementis and deposed General Secretary of the CPCz Rudolf Slánský, rid the regime of 'Titoist agents' and 'Zionists'. By contrast, and partly as a consequence of western intervention after the Prague coup, Finland was exempted altogether; with the signing of the Friendship Treaty of April 1948, Finland was spared the Finnish People's Defence League—the local version of the communist-dominated national front—coming to power. As one historian notes, had Stalin been willing to permit the (admittedly unlikely) 'Finlandization' of the rest of Eastern Europe, 'then the West would have been much less alarmed'.[40] But such could not be the case. Nevertheless, when one examines the Sovietization of Hungary and Czechoslovakia, one sees a different process from the one that took place in Romania, Poland, and the GDR, and one gets a sense of the greater urgency that intra-communist and international events were imposing on the unfolding of events. The creation of Stalinist 'consensus' in these countries was a counter-revolutionary process in which alternative versions of socialism or radical social change were eliminated in favour of the 'security' model espoused by Moscow.

Only in 1947, with the failure of the Council of Foreign Ministers in both New York in 1946 and Moscow the next year to agree terms of a German peace treaty, the declaration of the Truman Doctrine to defend 'free peoples', the announcement of the European Recovery Program (Marshall Plan)—which was also offered to the Eastern European countries, but which Stalin pressurized them to turn down—and the exclusion of communists from government in France and Italy, was Stalin motivated into decisive action. The result was the coup in Czechoslovakia in February 1948 which brought the communists to power there, and the creation of the Cominform in September 1947, partly out of a desire to imitate the Marshall Plan, partly in order to provide the Eastern Bloc with a coherent focal point, firmly under Soviet control.[41] Ironically, the creation of the Cominform also meant the end of the 'national fronts' strategy, though this by no means indicated a newfound agreement with the Yugoslavs; to the contrary, at the same time as reining in revolutionary impulses, the Cominform was designed to be at the forefront of the struggle against Tito and to make one thing clear: the dominance of Soviet state interests over the wishes and impulses of local communist parties: 'the strategy of discipline prevailed over the strategy of mobilization.'[42] So if it is true that Stalin aimed neither to divide the continent at the end of the war nor to force all countries in the region into the same straitjacket, he did foresee the eventual Sovietization of them all; even more strongly, he foresaw this process as being centrally directed by Moscow.

Thus, although one can trace its origins back to the Bolshevik Revolution, and tensions between the Allies began shortly after the German invasion of the USSR in June 1941, the Cold War did not begin in earnest until 1947–8, with the Marshall Plan the key moment. Despite some initial enthusiasm for the plan, the Soviets soon boycotted it, seeing the ERP as a western attempt to divide Germany and thus Europe.[43] Following the Prague coup, the French-occupied zone of Germany was merged with the British-American 'Bizonia' (itself created on 1 January 1947), the Soviets blockaded Berlin's Western Sectors, culminating in the Berlin Airlift, and within a year the Federal Republic of Germany and the German Democratic Republic had been born, ironically normalizing German statehood and permitting Adenauer (though not the SED to the same extent) to act as the head of a sovereign nation. The Treaty of Brussels created a military alliance in Western Europe, aimed at defending the region from the Soviet Union rather than from Germany, and within a few years the new Germanies, which lay at the heart of Cold War Europe in all senses, had been relieved of their very short period of denazification purdah and, now functioning as independent states, were willingly incorporated into NATO and the Warsaw Pact.[44]

What is clear is that, irrespective of whether Stalin set out with a great plan in 1944 to create communist dictatorships across Eastern Europe, as historians have traditionally assumed, or whether, as seems more likely, he was willing to use different tactics in different locations, he always intended that the end result would be the Sovietization of the countries that the Red Army had liberated from Nazism. That this goal was achieved so fast was less a result of Stalin's policies alone than of their interaction with western policies and, in particular, of mutual misunderstanding. Across Europe, local communist parties were as suspicious of parliamentary democracy as non-communist parties were of the communists' motives. 'Popular democracy' was not so much a cynical manoeuvre as one approach to the transition to Sovietization whose presuppositions in 1945—especially the belief that the process could take up to ten years—no longer held three years later. By then the situation was quite changed, following the split with Tito and the concomitant need to hold on to the remaining Eastern European satellites, the economic pressure being

applied by the west, and, most importantly, the fact that the appeal of a com-
munist-led popular front government was, with the exception of Czechoslovakia (and here, only in the Czech lands, not in Slovakia), only ever supported
by an electoral minority.[45] With Stalin increasingly fearful of conflict with the
west (the Berlin Crisis of 1948 and the Korean War of 1950 led him to fear war
in Europe itself), industrialization was geared not to the needs of the people
of Eastern Europe but to the Soviet Union's foreign policy and security. What
is also thus clear is that, by the early 1950s, after the break with Tito, a crash
course in industrialization, massive military expansion, a liberal use of terror,
and purges of the police, armies, and the 'wrong' sort of communists (those
accused of being involved in the 'Titoist conspiracy', like Kostov, for example),
all of which secured obeisance to Moscow, Soviet control of Eastern Europe
reached a peak which it never again achieved.

Stalinism as a civilization

The Sovietization of Eastern Europe was primarily driven by the needs of
the Soviet Union. But it should not be viewed solely as a top-down process,
for this would be to miss the involvement not just of local communists but
of Eastern European societies, which adapted to the new reality with varying degrees of enthusiasm and spontaneity. In the rest of this chapter, we will
examine how communism became part of the fabric of everyday life,
through the changing nature of work, through access to resources, through
the pressures to conform both real and imagined (the fear of terror), and
through the cultural production of communism as a lived reality. The point
here is that Stalinism was not just imposed on an unwilling population; it
was more than a political vandalism, but insinuated itself into every realm of
life, public and private. Stalinism was a civilization, and therefore needs to
be understood as part of social and cultural life, for if one remains at the
level of high politics and the international machinations which brought
about the Cold War, one misses something fundamental about the nature of
life in Eastern Europe, especially in the years 1945–53 when that new civilization was being built, not just in the client states behind the iron curtain
but in the western areas of the Soviet Union that had been newly annexed
from Poland, Ukraine, and the Baltic States.[46]

The concept of Stalinism as a civilization is most evident within Russia
itself, with the building of cities such as Magnitogorsk, dedicated to the

dream of industrialization.[47] The creation of *Homo Sovieticus* was the intended result of a whole complex of 'institutions, structures and rituals' that included 'Communist party rule, Marxist-Leninist ideology, rampant bureaucracy, leader cults, state control over production and distribution, social engineering, affirmative action on behalf of workers, stigmatization of "class enemies", police surveillance, terror, and the various informal personalistic arrangements whereby people at every level sought to protect themselves and obtain scarce goods'.[48] High politics can account for the policy decisions that drove the Stalinization process, but in order to understand how that process was realized, one needs to consider the actions of local communist representatives and the behaviour of ordinary people in attempting to accommodate themselves to rapidly changing realities, in many places very soon after they had adapted to fascist rule.

In the first instance, one has to take into account the prestige of the Soviet Union in general, and the Red Army in particular in defeating Nazism. This fact generated immense feelings of pride and patriotism in the USSR itself, where the Great Patriotic War became *the* key component of communist legitimacy. And apart from the fact that in many parts of Eastern Europe, support for communism was generated by the brutal nature of the Nazi occupation, at the end of the war it made sense to assume that the future lay with the communists who, despite their massive wartime losses, had at their disposal the largest military force that had ever existed in Europe, with 11,365,000 troops. The Western Allies, too, felt that the Soviets had earned the right to exercise power over the lands they had conquered and, in this sense, the onset of the Cold War was also not inevitable—many American policy-makers, for example, felt that the wartime alliance with Stalin had a postwar future, at least until George Kennan's 'long telegram' of 22 February 1946, which first set out a statement of 'the Kremlin's neurotic view of world affairs'. Once Hitler had been removed from the scene, there was only one power in the region, and it made sense for many people to throw in their lot with Stalin, for with him, they felt, lay their future prosperity.

Thus it should come as no surprise to learn that in some cases, local communists were startled to be reined in by Moscow, in case a too-rapid transition to communist dictatorship should alienate larger swathes of the population than was necessary. In Bulgaria, for example, where the Father-land Front came to power on the back of Soviet liberation in September 1944 at the height of the 'national fronts' strategy, the local communists, who numbered only 8,000 members, had to be held back by Moscow from establishing too quickly a communist dictatorship that would exclude other antifascist forces who could be used in the building of a popular government. This was a period that did not last long—Bulgaria was more swiftly brought under communist control than any of the other countries here under discussion—but it is still worth noting that in March 1945, Traicho Kostov, one of Bulgaria's leading communists, said that only a few months earlier, in autumn 1944, 'the Red Army would have put an end' to any attempt 'to establish Soviet power'.[49] The same was true in Hungary, where underground communist activists who remembered the short-lived Soviet Republic of 1919 were astounded by the MKP's reluctance to instigate a full-fledged takeover of power at the war's end. Again, directives from Moscow kept in check the most radical versions of communism, until the centre decided that its own security necessitated unleashing these forces—as long as they were not acting independently from Moscow.

As far as the social history of communist takeovers is concerned, then, the transition 'from authoritarian backwardness to Communist "popular democracy" was a short move and an easy one'.[50] But this claim does not tell us much either about how communist parties transformed themselves from tiny underground cells into mass parties with such speed, nor about how ordinary people experienced the transition. It certainly does not explain why, in Hungary, Poland, Czechoslovakia, and elsewhere, in 1945–6, 'a strikingly large number of voters freely went to the polls and elected Communists'.[51]

The war itself had transformed the region. Traditional social structures were broken down; with some exceptions, such as Polish coal and Romanian oil, economies were fleeced and infrastructure demolished under Nazi occupation; most important, whoever was in power, during the war industry and enterprises came increasingly under state control. This was a significant development, one which helped pave the way for the measures that would be introduced by the communists. Where the political history of transition to communism suggests a radical break with the past, 'a social history approach unveils an ongoing process'.[52] With traditional elites and ethnic minorities murdered by the Nazis, and with the state assuming control over ever-greater areas of life, the communists were pushing at an open door. Guilt and resentment over wartime activities could be translated into grudging support for communism, and central direction permitted people to believe that they were powerless to resist the march of progress.

For ordinary Eastern Europeans, then, the years 1945–8 required a gradual coming to terms with communism. This process is nowhere better illustrated than in fiction. Czesław Miłosz's *The Seizure of Power* (1953) and Jerzy Andrzejewski's *Ashes and Diamonds* (1948) are perhaps the most compelling ways to understand the negotiations and struggles that ordinary people went through in order to come to a *modus vivendi* with communist rule. The fact that Andrzejewski's book could be published in Poland in 1948 whereas Miłosz's could not in 1953 (it first appeared in France, in French translation) is itself revealing of the success of Sovietization in Poland.

The Soviet takeover was by no means confined to the political sphere. Rather, as Andrzejewski's and Miłosz's novels indicate, the *pax sovietica* aimed to encourage people to play the parts that had been assigned to them in the communist script. The communists wanted control over the Eastern European countries and, after 1948, they wanted absolute control in which local leaders fulfilled Moscow's requirements. But they also wanted local people to appreciate the USSR's achievements and to win over support for the new regimes. Political takeovers went hand in hand with the 'symbolic appropriation of these territories'.[53] 'Consensus' would certainly be enforced, but the regime wanted adherents, and it wanted popular legitimacy. And to some extent, it achieved it, especially in factories and other sites associated with the industrial working class.[54] The Soviet monuments that were built across the region not only commemorated the war dead but, in their vastness, reminded locals of the sacrifices that had been made by the Soviet Union to liberate Europe from fascism. The power of these monuments, such as the memorial complex at Treptow Park in Berlin or on the banks of the Vistula in Warsaw-Praga, consisted not only in their overwhelming physical presence, which constituted a stark, Ozymandias-like reminder of the might of communism, but in what they implied: that rejecting their message made one guilty of supporting defeated regimes and thus of withstanding the force of History. The cult of the Great Patriotic War was no mere cynical tactic, designed to remind subordinate Eastern Europeans of who their new masters were; it represented a sincerely held belief that communism had unlocked the secrets of the direction of History, and that if one wanted to ride the crest of the wave of human progress, one had better be on board with the new regimes. Whilst Stalin's foreign policy was in many respects indistinguishable from that of the tsars, the Soviet Union's victory in the Second World War transformed Russia's standing in the world. Even with respect to the Soviet Union's self-perception, the war dramatically transformed communism's myth of origins, with the cult of the Great Patriotic War largely supplanting even the cult of the October Revolution.[55]

Like antifascist monuments, large rallies were another popular manifestation of the communist takeover. Although usually instigated by the authorities, they brought onto the streets thousands of people. At the time of the communist takeover in Romania, for example, a call by communist leader Gheorghiu-Dej, condemning the Sănătescu government (the first to succeed wartime leader Ion Antonescu), for failing to purge the administration of fascists, succeeded in mobilizing rallies at factories and on the streets in support of the National Democratic Front. Attendance at the rallies was certainly helped along by veiled threats of unemployment for non-attendance, but the sight of thousands of workers bearing banners proclaiming their support for the NDF, accompanied by the communist press's promises of a better life for workers and accusations that the historical parties had sabotaged the war effort, was undoubtedly persuasive.[56] Although the NDF actually commanded less than 10 per cent of the vote, its unassailable advantage was to be backed up by the Soviets (in the guise of the Allied Control Commission). Thus, whilst they delayed the takeover process, the final takeover of March 1945 which saw Petru Groza installed as Prime Minister was not just a backroom procedure, but accompanied a large-scale attempt to mobilize popular opinion and to destabilize the country. As the National Peasant Party, one of the largest Romanian parties, communicated to the American Embassy, 'After the public forces were disarmed the NDF, with the aid of armed guards occupied the Public Institutions. They also compelled the workers to help them by demonstrating.'[57] Only days earlier, the Soviet-controlled newspaper *Graiul Nou* had explained the situation as it saw it: 'The Representatives of the Red Army, which is bearing the main burden of the war against Hitler's Germany, are entitled to request that calm, a working atmosphere and the democratic order reign behind its lines, which is so necessary for the front, are expressing the hope that the new Romanian Government will be ready to apply the Armistice conditions.'[58] In other words, the Soviets required a 'friendly' government in Romania, 'friendly' meaning 'an unquestioning acceptance of the armistice terms and all-out support for the Red Army and the Romanian army on the fighting front, a thorough purge of the army and police of pro-German and "fascist" elements, the absence of public criticism of the Soviet Union in the press, an agrarian reform to break up the big landed estates, and a reorientation of Romanian trade policy away from the West and toward the Soviet Union'.[59]

In 1944, 'friendly' did not necessarily mean Sovietized, but by 1945 this had changed: the failure of the Sănătescu and Rădescu governments to implement the armistice agreements gave force to the RCP's appeals to Moscow to come to their aid. Compulsion and Soviet force aside, it was also the case that the RCP's promises, especially of land reform and support for the poor, 'contributed to an attenuation of popular distrust of a party long perceived as lacking national roots'.[60]

The message that communism was on the side of History was continually reinforced, not just by the monuments themselves or by new school curriculums, which were forced to conform to Marxist–Leninist tenets, thus interpreting the war as a struggle of antifascist proletariats against fascist barbarians, and which saw compulsory Russian as standard (except later, in Romania, following Ceauşescu's 'independent line'). The message was conveyed in an emotional way through the commemorations which took place at these monuments and at other sites associated with the defeat of Nazism, such as the former concentration camp at Buchenwald, or rituals such as the 'uprising days', on which the start of the Partisan struggle in each of Yugoslavia's republics was recalled. At such commemorations, the rituals which built the antifascist community were performed and the communist consensus powerfully seared itself into the participants' emotions. Adherence to communism for the generation which lived through the war was very hard to break, even when the system became ossified and bankrupt of ideas, precisely because the antifascist narrative resonated so clearly with their experiences, and justified their struggles. That it also became a bludgeon with which to beat and accuse the coming generations, who felt no such affective or instinctive ties to the Soviet victory, was just one more nail in the coffin as far as those generations were concerned, who learned to mouth the slogans as soon as they could speak, but for whom their words held little significance.

At the start of the period, however, reshaping society and promoting antifascism went hand in hand, and the latter was no opportunist ploy but a serious-minded attempt fundamentally to change how Europeans thought. Among the earliest-founded organizations in the Soviet Occupation Zone of Germany, for example, was the Central Authority for the Victims of Fascism (*Hauptausschuß für die Opfer des Faschismus*, OdF), established in May 1945. At its head was one Ottomar Geschke, a communist who had spent most of the Nazi years in the Sonnenburg prison and some time in Sachsenhausen concentration camp. Among its earliest activities was an event

Figure 1. Soviet memorial, Treptow Park, Berlin (built 1949).

entitled 'We accuse!' on the occasion of the start of the Nuremberg Trials (20 November 1945) and, one year after their liberation, commemoration ceremonies at Ravensbrück and Sachsenhausen, on 12 May 1946. Because the latter was now in use as a 'special camp'—that is, it was being used by

the Soviet/German communist authorities to imprison political enemies—
the event took place in the nearby town of Oranienburg rather than at the
camp itself. The OdF's mission was set out very clearly by Karl Raddatz,
head of the Berlin section, on the occasion of its foundation:'You should be
the great political educator of the German people [Volk]...become flag-
bearers of the new Germany, which must win back its place among the
nations through a complete overcoming of Nazism's false doctrine.' And
later:'We want to praise the valiant forms of the fight against fascism, those
workers, priests, scholars and officers who fought without fear against the
Nazi regime.'[61] The OdF recognized at first that Jews, and not just communists, had been persecuted by the Nazis, but Raddatz and others drew a
distinction between active 'fighters against fascism' and 'victims of fascism',
a term which unmistakably carried a pejorative implication of passivity.[62]
This made it easier after 1948 to de-emphasize 'racial' victims and to focus
on communist resistance, thus rendering the antifascist message univocal.

When the OdF was merged into the newly created VVN (Association of
Those Persecuted by the Nazi Regime, *Vereinigung des Verfolgten des Naziregimes*) in 1947, along with committees representing survivors of several concentration camps, the focus became even clearer: establishing the history of
the antifascist resistance, making the communist element of the story pre-
dominant. And with the founding of the GDR in 1949, propounding and
explicating this narrative was made a central plank of the regime's operations, as a powerful legitimization strategy. Thus began the building of monuments at the concentration camps that lay inside the GDR, with particularly
noteworthy sculptures at Buchenwald, Sachsenhausen, and Ravensbrück,
which became the 'GDR's national memorial complexes [*Gedenkstätten*]'.[63]
These sites were now under the direct control of the state; accordingly, the
VVN was disbanded in 1953 and replaced with the Antifascist Resistance
Fighters' Committee (*Komitee der Antifaschistischen Widerstandskämpfer*), a
state-controlled body tasked with 'establishing the antifascist tradition on a
broader basis'. In practice, this meant downplaying the extent of Jewish suffering under the Nazis, and making the history of the communist resistance
the centrepiece of its work and thus, the KAW intended, of East German
collective memory.[64] By contrast with the establishment of the GDR as the
site of the 'better Germany', no opportunity was missed to condemn Adenauer's West Germany as 'a continuation of reactionary militarist and anti-
humanist traditions'. This transition from grassroots committees to
state-directed 'memory projects'—culminating in Sachsenhausen in the

1961 opening of the Museum of the European Peoples' Antifascist Freedom Struggle[65]—illustrates the way in which the antifascist consensus was driven primarily by the concerns of the Sovietizing state. As with the takeover of the political sphere, the cultural life of the Eastern Bloc states fell under increasingly centralized control, a process that on the official level was largely complete by 1953. 'The building of socialism in our homeland' and 'pride in the achievements of the War of National Liberation' were inseparable, in the words of one Yugoslav school curriculum.[66]

This control took many forms, from the control of education and sporting events to the press and religion. In work, agriculture was largely collectivized. In factories, as in economic matters generally, power passed to Moscow, which, through Comecon (the Council for Mutual Economic Assistance), founded in 1949, sought to direct the division of economic labour among the communist states (including, later, Vietnam, Cuba, and North Korea, which did not help the efficiency of the system). Factories, as of 1949, were subjected to five-year plans, which distorted the production process in many ways: not just shortages of some materials and excesses of others, but a tendency to massage figures or to over-fulfil quotas irrespective of demand. In Czechoslovakia, Soviet intervention meant that the previously competitive and effective Škoda-AZNP automobile plant not only had to change what it produced, so that henceforth only one model of automobile would be built in the country; it also changed working patterns, with 'rationalization', as it was called, tightening the discipline of the workforce but without providing the workers with the technology to produce quality goods. This one case typifies the situation across the region, whereby the Soviet insistence on economic uniformity rode roughshod over local working traditions, imposing targets, and managerial and administrative regulations which clashed with the knowhow and skills of the workforces.[67] What was deemed 'rational' often bordered on the surreal.

Perhaps the most visible manifestation of the 'popular' support for communism—or rather, the communist infiltration of daily life—came in the shape of the leadership cults that were such a ubiquitous characteristic of communism throughout the twentieth century, whether in Europe or elsewhere (North Korea or Cambodia, for example). At May Day parades, which across the Eastern Bloc became a national holiday designed to celebrate the regimes' achievements in building the road to socialism, routes were designed which took marchers past new buildings which reminded them of the construction of socialism that had taken place since 1948.

And most important, the marches and parades celebrated above all the successes of individuals, the revered leaders.

In the case of Hungary, for example, following the example of the Stalin cult in the Soviet Union, the image of Mátyás Rákosi became ubiquitous, as did his name. Eulogized as the father of socialism, the man who was providing Hungarians with their basic needs and developing the nation, Rákosi rapidly took on a 'sacred' aura after 1948. National iconography, ritual, and even the calendar itself were reshaped along the Soviet model, with Rákosi at its centre, for example at 4 April (Day of Liberation) and 1 May celebrations on Heroes' Square (*Hősök tere*), a symbolically laden site of Hungarian national consciousness which was refashioned along communist lines.[68] The Party even authorized particular images, as well as issuing guidelines for their placement in factories, schools, homes, and police and military offices. They were issued and sometimes sold in the millions.

But there were limits to the Eastern European leader cults. Although Rákosi, like Bierut (who succeeded Gomułka), Gheorghiu-Dej, Gottwald, Ulbricht, and Dimitrov, were all made the focus of such cults, which placed them at the 'sacred centre' of the nation, the panegyrics to them never reached the same level of obsequious absurdity as did the cult of Stalin. Where Stalin was regularly deified, an explicitly religious imagery and vocabulary was less often used for the mini-Stalins in the satellite countries. Where Stalin's image often took the place of icons in Russian homes, the adoration of images of the Eastern European first secretaries was rare, and not only because the period of Stalinization was quite short. Only later, with the cults of Ceauşescu in Romania and Hoxha in Albania, did something comparable—and possibly even more extreme—occur, when these countries resisted the destalinization process that their neighbours experienced. By contrast, in Yugoslavia and Albania around 1950, the cults of Tito and Hoxha enjoyed genuinely popular support, thanks to their status as war leaders, and here the leadership cults owed little to Soviet manipulation.

The leadership cults meant that there was little resistance to some of the more absurd and pernicious aspects of the Sovietizing regimes. The true communist was supposed to be vigilant, not so much against counter-revolutionary enemies—this was taken for granted—but primarily to enemies within. The purges that accompanied the Stalinization of Europe drew strength from the tightly organized hierarchical structure of the parties. The fact that the charges against committed and intelligent communist leaders who had been active in the anti-Nazi underground and had worked tirelessly to bring communism to their countries were purely fictional was precisely the point: the good communist had to believe what was being set out, no matter how improbable it seemed. When Rákosi detected the plot against the Party being supposedly undertaken by László Rajk, who was accused of conspiring with Tito, or when Gheorghiu-Dej unveiled Lucrețiu Pătrășcanu's 'hidden conspiracy' in 1948, which ended with his trial and execution in 1954 after he was shown to be a 'Titoist-fascist' agent and a spy working for western intelligence, the real face of Stalinist terror became clear.[69] These men were among the most dependable communist leaders; their trials were therefore all the more significant for impressing on the population that what was required of them was absolute submission to the will of the Party. Leaders who had in fact led the Sovietization process—Kostov, Gomułka, Czechoslovak Party Secretary Rudolf Slánský, and Albanian Interior Minister Koçi Xoxe among them—now found themselves ousted, on the basis that as 'home-grown' communists they were supposedly less bendable to Moscow's will than were those communists who had spent the war years in the USSR. Publicly, however, the charges against them were treason, 'cosmopolitanism', and espionage; as George H. Hodos, a survivor of the Rajk trial, noted, the trials also 'attempted to brand anyone who displayed differences of opinion as common criminal and/or agent of imperialism, to distort tactical differences as betrayal, sabotage and espionage'.[70]

Perhaps the most extreme version of this trend towards using serious charges as a way of masking power-play after the changes initiated by the founding of Cominform, however, came in 1952 with the Slánský trial in Czechoslovakia and in 1953 with the so-called 'Doctors' plot' in the Soviet Union. In fact, the former was a kind of preparation for the latter, being entirely driven by Moscow's demands for a show trial. Many of the show trials that took place in the late 1940s and early 1950s had a clear antisemitic basis; Jews were purged from government and party positions in Romania, Poland, and East Germany. In Czechoslovakia, the Slánský trial was explicitly founded on charges of Zionism as well as Titoism, and of the fourteen defendants, eleven were of Jewish origin (though presumably Judaism was not that significant to them since they were devoted communists). The prosecutors, witnesses, and judges, and the press, continually emphasized the defendants' Jewishness—they were, in the words of Prague daily *Rudé Právo*'s editorial, 'cynical Zionists, without a fatherland . . . clever cosmopolitans who have sold out to the dollar . . . guided in this criminal activity by Zionism, bourgeois Jewish nationalism, racial chauvinism'. After the week-long trial (following a year of torture and the extraction of 'confessions'), eleven of the accused were executed and the remaining three (all Jews, intriguingly, suggesting that antisemitism alone was not the motivating factor) were sentenced to life imprisonment. Gottwald—fearful for his own position, given his friendship with Slánský—even had the temerity to insist that the Party's 'repulsion at antisemitism and our respect for the suffering of the Jews' had permitted the unlikely scenario whereby a group of bankers and former kulaks had managed to get into the Party's high ranks.[71]

Following the Slánský trial, and as a consequence of its 'success', Stalin ordered the arrest of a 'Zionist terrorist gang' of nine doctors, six of them Jews, at the Kremlin polyclinic. Their plot against the Soviet Union, which included murdering key Soviet leaders, such as Zhdanov, was revealed in *Pravda* on 13 January 1953, which described the doctors as 'monsters in human form'.[72] Its interest lies primarily in the fact that the trial of the doctors appears to have been—and was certainly believed at the time by the panicked Soviet Jewish community to be—preparatory to a mass round-up of Soviet Jews which would have seen them deported to Birobidzhan, the Yiddish-speaking Jewish 'homeland' in the Soviet Far East. Thanks to Stalin's death on 5 March 1953, the trial did not take place. But the Doctors' plot and the Slánský trial tell us a great deal about Stalinist Eastern Europe: power rested on the exercise of terror and the absurdity of the charges against committed communists clearly served the purpose of 'encourager les autres'. 'The public', as Judt notes, 'were not being asked to believe what they heard; they were merely being trained to repeat it.'[73] In these two cases, the outer limits of the Stalinist parties' irrationality is clear.

By 1953, then, the communist regimes had attained, if not legitimacy, at least mass compliance.[74] The antifascist consensus had been created in the sense that a minority adhered to it out of conviction and a large majority was too cowed into submission to resist it. This compliance came at a cost. Although local communist parties had been successfully subordinated to Moscow and the Warsaw Pact countries had become miniature versions of the non-participatory, industrialized communism pioneered by the Soviet Union under Stalin, by 1953 the regimes were also—and as a direct result of these policies—in crisis. In the words of Agnes Heller, with specific reference to Hungary, 'the regime, after its Stalinist turn, became merely a bloody tyranny in the service of an alien power. To make matters worse, it also showed a great capacity for irrational decision-making, as it destroyed its own supporting basis.'[75] Excluding 'the people', whom communism was meant to represent, from the political process and implementing the industrialization and collectivization drives led to cuts in real wages, food shortages, and labour unrest. All of which meant that although 'state socialist regimes emerged consolidated from the crisis that followed Stalin's death in 1953, the political project it rested on was ossified' and that the regimes 'sat on a cauldron of frustrated expectation'.[76] This frustration would burst into the open after Stalin's death.

2

Consensus of Silence

Western Europe, 1945–1953

But what if the project which lies behind the Atlantic Charter 'comes off'?
What if there is no socialist revolution in Germany and Europe in general?
What if, instead, there is a respectable conservative government in Germany,
governments with varying degrees and kinds of capitalist reaction in most
other European countries, a network of sovereign States on the old model,
and the whole dominated by and dependent on Anglo-Saxon capitalism?
What then?

Victor Gollancz, 1942

The ruins which the Nazis leave behind them will not be merely those of
the scorched earth and of its burnt and bombed cities; if they were, the
problem of reconstruction would be a comparatively simple one; the real
problem will be the ruin and wreckage of human life, of civilization itself,
of millions of individuals all over Europe weakened by under-nourishment
and disease and threatened by starvation and disease. These people are the
real ruins and wreckage of our civilization which the Nazis and war have
wrecked and ruined.

Leonard Woolf, 1943[1]

When the American reporter Percy Knauth entered Buchenwald after
its liberation, he could barely comprehend what he saw. 'Numbly,
I saw death now', he wrote, 'and before I left the camp that evening I saw it
reduced to such ordinariness that it left me feeling nothing, not even sick-
ness at my stomach.'[2] Of the survivors of Gunskirchen camp in Austria, one
American private wrote that their 'only similarity to human beings is, they
were standing'.[3] Thirty-five years later, the rawness of these emotions was
still in evidence. In 1981, a conference took place in Washington DC,
bringing together liberators and survivors of the Nazi camps. One Dutch

survivor of Auschwitz and Mauthausen, Anthony F. Van Velsen, said that for many survivors, 'Their liberation was only a physical one. In the psychological sense, they were not liberated and will never be liberated.... For them is not the peace they longed for.' He ended his address by asserting that 'The political weakness that paved the way for Nazism and, therefore, for the Holocaust is still there in our world of today.' The next speaker, Benjamin Meed, a survivor of the Warsaw Ghetto, concurred, adding that he did not need to prepare his talk because 'I am still in the Warsaw Ghetto, 38 years later—and I don't think I ever left the Ghetto.' This feeling that the survivors had that their experiences would not simply disappear with the end of the war was intimately connected to the manner of their 'liberation':

> How does one answer today how he felt the day after the liberation? As far as I can remember, this was not a day of joy. Maybe it should have been a day of joy, but it was not.
> When liberation came, I remember feeling and thinking that the whole world was destroyed, not only our loved ones, but the whole world, a whole civilization had been lost. I felt then, and I'm feeling today, that something we left had been taken out of us and that the wounds will never heal.[4]

Most of Europe was oblivious to these feelings of the Nazi camp survivors. There were simply too many other constituencies of suffering, too much widespread distress that urgently needed alleviating for fine distinctions to be drawn between different groups of victims of war. As this chapter will show, this was in many respects an understandable response; indeed, it was one of the conditions for economic growth and stability. At the same time, the political consensus that accompanied and facilitated this new stability and prosperity was built on a societal consensus of silence. This silence meant that those who did not experience 'the peace they longed for' had their experiences subsumed into broader narratives of national heroism and resistance; their suffering was instrumentalized in the cause of national unity in order to facilitate and ease the process of rebuilding, a process that involved not asking too many questions about precisely who had done what or suffered what during the war years.

None of this is to say that in the early postwar years the murder of the Jews, and even less the sufferings of forced labourers, political prisoners, or the populations who endured the deprivations of war, were forgotten, or not discussed. Quite the contrary is true. What later became known as 'the Holocaust' was well known, and could be referred to in a gesture, a shudder or shake of the head, or a widely shared reference—a tattooed wrist, for example. But outside of small numbers of scholar-survivors and the remnants of the Jewish communities, the Holocaust was not the subject of scholarship, commemoration, or cultural interest in the ways that would become common in later decades. And the war itself, although in many ways—and obviously—ubiquitous in the public sphere in the late 1940s and early 1950s, was discussed in selective terms. In the same way that the imposition of communist rule in Eastern Europe saw an officially endorsed narrative of the war go hand in hand with social reorganization, so in Western Europe the new shape of politics was accompanied, and to some extent legitimized, by a selective understanding of the recent past. This understanding can be summarized as a consensus of silence, in which certain aspects of the interwar crisis and the war were emphasized at the expense of others. The crisis of Western European politics and societies as of the mid-1970s, would accordingly see the simultaneous unravelling of this narrative, not by coincidence but as a necessary component of the process of change.

Liberation and its aftermath

The Western Allies liberated most of the concentration camps in the *Altreich* itself (Germany within its 1937 borders), whilst the death camps of Auschwitz and Majdanek had been discovered by the Red Army. Hence, although there was some reporting of those camps in the western press, in Western Europe the more familiar names of Dachau, Buchenwald, and Bergen-Belsen were to become, for several decades, synonymous with Nazi crimes. The famous images of British bulldozers moving mounds of corpses at Belsen were seared into people's consciousnesses in 1945, and paved the way for the demonization of Nazism that would be compounded by the Nuremberg Trials and the denazification programmes. But those images and their reporting failed to grasp the facts: that the vast majority of Jews were murdered in death pits, ghettos, and extermination camps in Eastern Europe; that Belsen, Buchenwald, and Dachau were places of horror in 1945 because of the Nazi death marches from the emptied eastern camps; and, most significant, that there were distinctions in the Nazi world view between categories of prisoners. Faced with mountains of corpses, Western European reporters blurred all of these distinctions, and few took note of British Chief Rabbi J. H. Hertz's letter to *The Times* of 28 May 1945, in which he wrote that whilst the Archbishop of Canterbury was correct to note the horrors of the concentration camps, 'there are Nazi horrors far vaster and more unspeakably foul, and these have not been brought home to the larger British public. It is therefore not generally known that the Nazis have exterminated 5,000,000 Jews—and millions of non-Jews in monster crematory and asphyxiation halls, by machine-gunning, clubbing to death, and mass drownings.'[5]

The remnants of these horrors now found themselves washed up in Central Europe. What to do with them—how to feed them—was a problem that cannot be underestimated, as one commentator foresaw in 1943:

> The biggest human problem with which we shall be faced in re-ordering the world after the end of the war will probably be that of re-establishing the peoples who have been displaced from their homes and localities for one reason or another. The magnitude of the problem is such as to cause the heart to sink and beside it the re-organization of the world's economic life may well seem a simple matter.... There have been vast migratory movements before in the world's history but never one which has taken place under such conditions.[6]

This was so not just because of the enormous figures involved, but because of the seemingly intractable political problems. Of the 5,800,000 Displaced Persons (DPs) in Germany at the end of the war, 2,326,000 had been returned to their countries of origin within months. And there were millions more, who could not be classed as DPs, including Soviet nationals. By 1953 some five and a half million of the latter, according to the terms of the Yalta agreement, were forcibly repatriated. But there remained tens of thousands for whom such an option was not just undesirable, but which they fiercely resisted, which is hardly surprising when one considers, as Tony Judt reminds us, that one in five Soviet returnees were either shot or deported to the Gulag.[7] These were the so-called 'non-repatriable refugees'. They included many Poles who refused to return to a Poland that was being taken over by communists. And many Jews found that they were unwelcome in their pre-war homes in Eastern Europe; although not technically DPs, some 220,000 Jewish refugees from Eastern Europe 'infiltrated' their way into the DP camps, swelling their numbers substantially in the first two years after the war.[8] Coupled with a widespread desire among Jewish DPs to emigrate to Palestine, a desire that was resisted by the British mandate authorities, this all meant that what were originally conceived of as places of temporary shelter turned out to be long-term homes for the war's displaced. It is one of the great ironies of the Holocaust that many of its surviving victims spent the next years of their lives in camps in the lands of the perpetrators; in some cases in the immediate aftermath of the war they even shared the camps with imprisoned Nazi perpetrators and, in the case of German-Jewish DPs, were regarded as 'enemy DPs' and subjected to the Allies' non-fraternization policy.

The ambivalence of the Allies' policies towards DPs is striking. Whilst many thousands of Eastern Europeans obtained entry visas to the labour-short United Kingdom or the United States, especially Balts, who were recruited because of a widespread belief in their 'good racial stock',[9] Jews were for the most part left languishing behind, once again unwanted, in an echo of the pre-war reluctance to accept Jewish refugees from the Third Reich. The fact that among the Eastern European DPs were to be found 'collaborators and former members of Waffen-SS and other German detachments' was no bar to obtaining entry.[10] The Allies engaged on the one hand in massive efforts to house, feed, and clothe DPs, no mean feat at the end of the war when resources were extremely scarce and when Europe was in such a desperate state that it was unable to feed itself (as a German joke had it, 'Better enjoy the war—the peace will be terrible'). At its height, in September 1945, the United Nations Relief and Rehabilitation Administration (UNRRA) was caring for or arranging the repatriation of 6,795,000 liberated United Nations civilians (that is, not including citizens of former Axis countries), an extraordinary effort of international ambition and enterprise.[11] On the other hand, the Allies displayed, at least at the start, little understanding of what DPs had gone through, with the result that they were sometimes treated callously; American war hero General George S. Patton famously earned himself his dismissal when he referred to the Jews in DP camps as 'lower than animals'.[12] Only in August 1945 did an American report clarify that housing Jews together with their former persecutors was 'a distinctly unrealistic approach to the problem. Refusal to recognise the Jews as such has the effect... of closing one's eyes to their former and barbaric persecution,' leading President Truman to announce that Jews would be given separate facilities.[13] Further policies, especially on the part of the British, certainly had the effect of thwarting the aspirations of DPs to move on either to the US or to Palestine. It is no surprise that as time passed, relations between the DPs and the Allies, especially in the British zone, became strained. The British, for their part, faced the dilemma of widespread public sympathy for the surviving Jews and dealing with an increasingly strident Arab anti-Jewish settlement sentiment and a violent Jewish terrorist threat in Palestine itself—which led, at its height, to the murders of British officers and to anti-Jewish riots in the UK in the summer of 1947.[14]

The founding of UNRRA (1943) and its replacements the International Refugee Organization (IRO, 1947) and the United Nations High Commission for Refugees (UNHCR, 1951) meant that DPs were cared for at the expense of the US, Canada, and Britain; it also institutionalized their care, thus prolonging it. After the founding of the state of Israel in 1948, Jewish DPs were free to go there; the continued existence of a minority of the Jewish DP population in Germany after 1948 gave the lie to the Zionist claim, dominant in the DP camps and, most significantly, among those who made their voices heard most loudly in negotiations with the Allies, that all the Jews wanted to go to Palestine.[15] Only by the mid-1950s, when it became too embarrassing in the context of the Cold War to be reminded of Germany's role in the Second World War, did the remaining DP camps, still housing 177,000 people, close, the last being at Föhrenwald in Bavaria in 1957.

Those who were still in DP camps a year or two after the end of the war could, then, be regarded as 'the real ruins and wreckage of our civilization'. Children, in particular, were 'all equally thirsty for caresses and attentions, more so than normal children', as one relief worker noted.[16] But the DP camps flourished. They had the highest birth rate anywhere in Europe as Jews remarried and sought to rebuild their communities. They had schools, synagogues, and other communal institutions working in Yiddish and Hebrew as well as the languages of Europe. It is hardly surprising to find, for example, that on the site of one former concentration camp a social experiment known as Kibbutz Buchenwald began, preparing its members for life in the future Jewish state.[17] DPs may have been pawns in the superpowers' games, but they lived their own vibrant lives and their decision-making abilities were not totally constrained by states and their representatives. The self-designated 'she'erit hapletah' (saving remnant) keenly felt their role as seeds of a future Jewish presence in Europe, Palestine, or further afield, all the more so given that they were all too aware of the negative impressions of them often held by the Jews of the *Yishuv* (the Jewish community in pre-1948 Palestine).[18]

The DPs, however, were just one of the many problems facing the occupiers of Germany. Germany itself, with the loss of its eastern territories to

Figure 2. Purim celebrations in Landsberg DP Camp, 1946.

Poland and its division into western and Soviet spheres of occupation, was faced with mountainous challenges: the after-effects of Nazism had to be faced, both by the occupation forces and the German people themselves; some 12 million refugees, or *Heimatvertriebene* (a term which is more resonant of the loss of homeland), had to be accommodated; and the country needed rebuilding, especially the major cities. For most Germans, the biggest problem at war's end was not coming to terms with the moral enormity of Nazi crimes but finding food and shelter: 'Erst kommt das Fressen, dann die Moral' (first comes eating, then morals) was the slogan of the day.[19]

Hence, many Germans brushed off the International Military Tribunal (IMT) at Nuremberg as 'victor's justice' and objected to the denazification programmes, to which they responded with resentment. Besides, there was some irony in the Allies' attempt to instil peaceful, democratic values by force, in a country swamped by an overwhelming military power. Nevertheless, the accomplishments of the Nuremberg Trials were considerable. Many Germans were expecting to be treated the way the Nazis dealt with their vanquished, and to become the victims of summary justice. Indeed, after the firebombing of Dresden, the brutal experience of the Red Army's westward advance through the Reich, and Allied statements which suggested that Germany would be 'pastoralized', such notions made sense. Yet the Allies spent large sums and used scarce resources to ensure that the leading Nazis were treated according to the rule of law, all the more strongly to emphasize how such markers of civilization had been abandoned by the Nazis. As Justice Jackson said in his opening address:

> The real complaining party at your bar is civilization. In all our countries it is still a struggling and imperfect thing. It does not plead that the United States, or any other country, has been blameless of the conditions which made the German people easy victims to the blandishments and intimidations of the Nazi conspirators.[20]

As Jackson's statement implied, the trial of the 22 major war criminals, which opened on 20 November 1945 and lasted nine months, centred on the charge of conspiring to wage 'aggressive war'.

Yet, this notion of the 'common conspiracy' was also a problem, one which subverted the good intentions and the remarkable achievements of the IMT's organizers. First, the judicial procedure being used, even if one sees its validity as being based on natural law or on justified retrospective legislation, was unable to take the measure of what the Nazis had done, as the exiled German-Jewish political philosopher Hannah Arendt noted:

> The Nazi crimes, it seems to me, explode the limits of the law; and that is precisely what constitutes their monstrousness. For these crimes, no punishment is severe enough. It may well be essential to hang Göring, but it is totally inadequate. That is, this guilt, in contrast to all criminal guilt, oversteps and shatters any and all legal systems. That is the reason why the Nazis in Nuremberg are so smug. They know that, of course.[21]

Second, the suggestion that the German people had been victims of a Nazi conspiracy was one which signalled a swift turnaround from wartime statements about German collective guilt and, most important, one which left open a window of opportunity for the rehabilitation of Germany, or rather, for the western zones. By suggesting that the German people had been led astray by an evil clique, the tribunal passed over the question of how widespread popular support for Hitler's regime had really been.[22] It therefore encouraged a postwar atmosphere in which the message that Germans had been victims could flourish at the expense of the Nazis' actual victims.

Perhaps the most egregious example of this phenomenon was the widespread belief in the 'clean Wehrmacht', the idea that criminal actions had been carried out by the SS (part of the 'conspiracy') but not by the regular army. This myth was happily propagated by the British authorities, who, as

a result, prematurely released Erich von Manstein, one of the Reich's leading generals heavily implicated in the transmission of criminal orders from
Hitler to the army before Operation Barbarossa. What was happening was
clear: a widespread belief that the soldiers had not really done anything
wrong was helping to ensure that the ambition to eradicate Nazism was
already, in 1946, beginning to give way to a vision of a renewed Germany
that would be a useful ally against the Soviet Union. Indeed, Manstein
himself returned to office in 1956, to advise the Federal Republic on the
creation of its new army, the *Bundeswehr*.[23] And by 1957, the last war criminals had left the British prison in Werl, as was the case at the Americans'
Landsberg prison a year later. Dissenting voices were only rarely heard, as in
the case of a German veteran who suggestively noted that: 'it must be supposed that the majority of German soldiers who could contribute factual
proof against the war criminals are either dead or prisoners of war; again,
that a not inconsiderable number of them dare not speak.'[24]

The first, quadripartite, internationally organized trial was thus also the
last. From the outset, the Soviets were the most reluctant to devote time and
energy to a procedure based on the normative rules of law. Hence, the
twelve so-called 'Subsequent' trials of the Nuremberg Military Tribunals
(NMT)—including of medics, of industrialists, and of the heads of the Nazi
Einsatzgruppen (or special killing squads)—were organized on a national
basis, by the Americans. The Soviets took matters into their own hands, too,
in their sphere of Europe. These trials, though less well known today, were
nevertheless significant in exposing to the wider world the fact that the
perpetrators were not 'monsters', but human beings, and opening up an
awareness of the scale of the crimes committed, including introducing the
term 'genocide' to international law.[25]

Apart from the Nuremberg Trials, the major Allied programmes for postwar Germany were the interconnected ones of denazification and re-
education. These had been planned since several years before the end of the
war, and much ink had been spilled amongst exile communities, intellectuals, and civil servants on 'what to do with Germany' on war's end.[26] The
most prominent and radical visions were Henry J. Morgenthau's and Robert
Vansittart's plan for the 'pastoralization' of Germany, that is, stripping the
country of its heavy industrial capacity, thus ensuring its inability to wage
war on its neighbours. Whilst the alliance with the Soviet Union held, this
seemed attractive to those who thought the key to the peace was to be
even more punitive than after the First World War. But even apart from the

worsening relations with the USSR from 1944 onwards, many objected that to treat Germany so harshly was to engage in the kind of 'group thinking' that was no different from how the Nazis comprehended the world. The publisher and campaigner Victor Gollancz, for example, who had been trying to draw the world's attention to Nazi persecution from 1933, was outspoken in his attack on this sort of group thinking, arguing that it would be ironic and shameful for the 'shoddy emotional vulgarism' that had characterized the Nazi regime to be adopted by those claiming to represent better values.[27] In his pamphlet *What Buchenwald Really Means* (1945), Gollancz made the simple point that the attack on 'the Germans' overlooked the fact that some of those being liberated from Nazi camps were themselves German, and thus that there were German traditions and values other than Nazism. And in his attack on Vansittart, penned as early as 1942, Gollancz set out his belief that to win the peace, a socialist revolution would have to succeed across Europe that could resist both Sovietization and 'monopoly capitalism'; in his view, Vansittart's plan for Germany would exacerbate the very problems it was designed to solve, simply because it would leave in place the international competition and hatred that led to war in the first place: 'If this mood of revenge and hatred for the whole German people were to spread to the point of becoming decisive, it would be impossible to contemplate the future without despair.'[28]

The Allies dropped the Morgenthau plan in 1944, and the British Foreign Office never endorsed Vansittart's; nevertheless, it did alter its own plans as the end of the war loomed. What changed the Allies' plans were not the consciences and fine words of intellectuals such as Gollancz. As with the change in the Nuremberg paradigm, the *volte face* was engendered by *realpolitik*. Thus, instead of a notion of collective guilt, the Allies opted to criminalize the SS; instead of the working assumption that Nazism was deeply rooted in German ways of thought, institutions, and structures, they sought instead to impugn the most obviously tainted individuals and organizations, and to limit the damage of the attack by painting a picture of Nazism that accorded with the Nuremberg concept of a conspiracy: Nazism was shown to be an 'evil' with no connections to the great German cultural traditions or to 'Europe' in general. During the war, on 27 May 1943, the MP for Marylebone, Alec Cunningham-Reid, could comment that 'it would be much easier to educate 80 million baboons' than to teach the Germans the ways of democracy and reason. But within months of the end of the war, as the Sovietization of the Soviet zone and the rest of Eastern Europe

proceeded apace, the emphasis changed so that now it lay firmly on winning German support:

> Instead of the 'collective guilt' of the German nation, and 'there are no good
> Germans', which had until recently been the *leitmotiv*, the German people's
> guilt in the Nazi regime and the war was to be presented in terms of cause
> and consequence, a workable means of creating the new Germany.[29]

The denazification programme, then, used as its main weapon a questionnaire
(*Fragebogen*), on which individuals had to set out their activities and organizational affiliations during the war. The practice was far more energetically
pursued in the American zone than in the French or British (where a policy
of re-education was preferred to aggressive denazification) and, even without
the loss of enthusiasm that came with the changing political circumstances in
Europe, it would have been an impossible task to carry out the denazification
process thoroughly across the whole of Germany. Even so, the programme
was wound up far quicker than originally intended, as expediency triumphed
over morality, and the Allies realized that maintaining a strong and compliant
West Germany was vital for Western European security.

Criticism of the programme was therefore not hard to come by. One
commentator claimed in 1948 that denazification, 'which began with a
bang, has since died with a whimper'.[30] The proof was the high numbers of
implicated professionals still in office: 40 per cent of civil servants and 76 per
cent of Bavarian public prosecutors, for example. The author's dark conclusion was that Germany was 'in the process of being "renazified" in all spheres'
and that the process of entrusting Germans to vote and to hold office had
'simply delivered the fragile new democracy to the tender mercies of its
enemies'.[31] This was an exaggeration, of course, but what did happen was
that, in a German counterpart to events elsewhere, the failure to see through
the denazification process permitted the re-establishment of former elites at
the expense of grassroots democratic initiatives. It was easy to lie on the
forms and there were insufficient resources for checking people's statements.
'Big' Nazis often escaped justice thanks to networks of assistance, and 'little'
Nazis could lie low or move between zones. As the (exiled) German philosopher Karl Jaspers explained:

> However incriminated, the denazified received a paper that spared them any
> further interrogation or investigation. The piece of paper was regarded as
> proof. Even against better knowledge, a government agency could appoint an
> official, citing this paper and feeling relieved of personal responsibility.[32]

This was the famous *Persilschein*. The whitewashing was the result of a coincidence of wants: the German people's to be rid of the denazification mechanism and the Allies' to have the Germans on side as the Cold War set in.

Just as the problem of what to do with Germany was the major question facing the Allies at the end of the war, so Germany would remain the focus of the Cold War in Europe; the second half of the twentieth century would be as much the 'German century' as the first half. Indeed, many of the characteristics of Germany replicate those elsewhere in Europe, only writ larger. For example, whilst grassroots movements all over Europe were disappointed that their visions for the future were submerged by the reappearance of old elites, in Germany, where the starting point was so much lower in terms of moral and political chaos, not to mention the gulf between the left-wing 'antifas' and most of the population, the restoration of the old order, in the shape of Adenauer and the Christian Democrats, was perhaps not so surprising. As Stig Dagerman, a Swedish journalist sent to Germany in the autumn of 1946 to report on the state of the country, reported:

> there is in Germany a large group of honest anti-fascists who are more disappointed, homeless and defeated than the Nazi fellow-travellers can ever be: disappointed because the liberation did not turn out to be as radical as they had thought it would be; homeless because they did not want to associate themselves either with the overall German dissatisfaction, among whose ingredients they thought they could detect far too much hidden Nazism, or with the politics of the Allies, whose compliance in the face of the former Nazis they regard with dismay; and, finally, defeated because they doubt whether as Germans they can hold shares in the final victory of the Allies while at the same time they are equally unconvinced that as anti-Nazis they can be partners in the German defeat. They have condemned themselves to complete passivity because activity means co-operation with the dubious elements which in the course of twelve years of oppression they have learned to hate.[33]

The expellees were no less problematic than the DPs; indeed, as Germans (some of them only loosely so), the expectation that they would fit into the population at large only added to the pressure. Dagerman noted that 'The refugees from the east speak bitterly about the Russians and the Poles, but are regarded as intruders and end up living in a state of war with the people of the west.'[34] His assessment was correct, for there are numerous reports along the lines of this landowner from Eversen in north-west Germany, who complained that the refugees were 'hostile to family and to work, and...shatter the uniform character of our villages and farms', a statement which reveals the extent to which Nazi propaganda about 'the east' influenced even perceptions of ethnic Germans.[35] Their integration was facilitated no less by films such as *Grün ist die Heide* (*The Heath is Green*), about a Pomeranian landowner who loses everything and starts a new life on the Lüneberg Heath, than by the economic boom, but these economic and cultural conditions would only come after the currency reform of June 1948 and the formal creation of the Federal Republic in 1949.

The conservative reassertion

The immediate postwar years in the western zones of Germany saw an astonishing transformation, from devastation and denigration to reconstruction and newfound Western Ally. The centrality of Germany to the shape of Europe would come even more sharply into focus with the politics of the Cold War, as we will see.

Elsewhere, much of Western Europe also went through a period of volatility after 1945. But what is perhaps surprising about the re-establishment of order in France, Belgium, the Netherlands, Denmark, Norway, Italy, and elsewhere is that it was achieved with remarkably little chaos; the level of bloodshed, though high, could easily have been worse. In Italy, after the initial wave of unorganized purges, some 10,000–15,000 were killed between 1943 and 1946; and in France some 25,000 civil servants were punished and there were nearly 10,000 official executions.

The impressive fact is that official control of the purge process worked: the numbers killed in spontaneous, revenge attacks were relatively small. Indeed, what is striking is not that so many people were killed in revenge but that so few were killed, a claim that takes on meaning when one considers the numbers murdered by Nazi firing squads, the villages destroyed across Europe, and the populations uprooted as a result of the war. The image of a shaved French woman, accused of 'horizontal collaboration', being forced to march down the street is a powerful one, resonant with shame, but it does not conjure up visions of mass-murder.[36]

This official control was given added impetus with the return of governments-in-exile from London to their countries, coming back with the desire to implement the rule of law and to expedite a return to normality. By the time the Western European (French, Belgian, Dutch, and Norwegian) governments-in-exile returned, the worst excesses of the wild purges were already over and formal, state-controlled judicial systems were taking over. What this meant in practice was that, in the broader interest of maintaining internal stability and international cooperation, large numbers of collaborators were not tried. Court action against collaborators was brought to a swift end with the onset of the Cold War.

How was this restoration able to take place so rapidly? One answer is that the Western European governments-in-exile were able to return home 'not as reviled *fuyards* but as custodians of the national honour and highly convenient retrospective incarnations of unwavering opposition to Nazi Germany'.[37] With the exception of the Belgians, under Hubert Pierlot, they had more or less successfully managed to convince internal Resistance movements that, given the brutality of Nazi occupation regimes, London offered the best prospect for guarding their interests. Their careful planning for liberation thus paid off, as they were welcomed back as legitimate representatives of the nation.

But their moment of triumph did not last long. Actually, the exiles had very little impact on shaping their postwar states, apart from preventing a power vacuum at the end of the war. They had barely planned for the process of rebuilding, focusing their energies on choreographing the liberation and preventing chaos. And they quickly lost ground to new governments whose members were drawn from those who had been in the occupied countries during the war, and who were therefore received as less patronizing when addressing their compatriots, who felt instinctively that such people understood what they had gone through in a way that the 'Londoners' did not. Following the euphoria of liberation, the various political forces who had swallowed their differences during the war in order to support the exiled representatives of the nation no longer felt the same obligation to maintain such unity, and politics as normal soon resumed, with most of the exiles swiftly becoming its victims. One of the few exceptions was Belgium's Paul-Henri Spaak (who, it might be noted, did not speak a word of English until he arrived in London in 1940), who survived the collapse of the Pierlot government in February 1945 and went on to become one of the prime movers of European integration. But most others in power by the end of the decade had not been in London during the war. Nevertheless, there was still a remarkable continuity in power, contrary to what one might expect after the great cataclysm of the Second World War. Nothing like the shifts in control that took place after 1918 or after 1968 took place in 1945 in Western Europe: in 1948 the generation in power was the same as in 1938, and often that meant the same people. Most of these politicians were Christian Democrats; the period of radical possibilities closed very quickly in Western Europe, and not just because of the Cold War. Groups such as the Laski Group in London, which published the International Socialist Forum, or the Stockholm-based International Group of Democratic Socialists lost ground to locally based politicians and, especially, to parties which rejected non-communist varieties of socialism.[38] The exception, of course, was the British Labour Party, but it quickly distanced itself from anything which smacked of international socialism.

Why, with the exception of Britain and Scandinavia—the latter of which was in any case merely another example of continuity across the wartime period—were the Christian Democrats more able to win popular support than the Social Democrats in Western Europe? One answer has to be confessional: the church, especially the Catholic Church in Western and Southern Europe, remained a key source of authority for several decades after 1945. On 10 February 1948, a woman reported seeing the statue of the Virgin Mary on the church of Santa Maria degli Angeli in Assisi move her head from side to side and sigh heavily, 'as if she were in deep pain'. This and many other Marian apparitions in the run-up to the 1948 elections in Italy 'reflected both an individual and collective search for meaning, order and protection on the part of ordinary Italians who worried about the implications for the faith and for the country of the Popular Front's bid for power'.[39] The Madonna helped to defeat Marxism at the polls. In West Germany, the 'existential dissonances' of the 1950s meant that just below the surface of consumer society and rationally planned labour regulations lay 'powerful undercurrents' of mysticism, Marian apparitions, and religious visions.[40] Second, it may no longer have been logical to portray the centre left as an 'icebreaker' for communism, especially after 1948 when Western European socialist parties expelled the eastern parties from international socialist organizations for their role in facilitating the communist takeover. But this fear still excited the minds of many middle-class Western Europeans, a class which was growing thanks to the rapid expansion, for the first time in European history, of a substantial section of the population with a disposable income. The conservative political governments of Western Europe oversaw a consumerist boom that encouraged personal consumer choice but social and cultural restraint—a contradiction that would unravel (at least on the face of it) when a new generation came of age in the late 1960s. It was one which successfully seduced even those who tried to resist it; as Bianca

Secondo, communist and worker on feminist magazine *Noi donne*, recalled, the PCI had to face up to the fact that Party women were 'sighing outside the [boutique] windows of Via Roma'.[41] Third, and related to the former point, for the most part Christian Democrats were so successful in Western Europe because they employed a vocabulary that transcended traditional class divisions and allowed all strata of society to feel that they had a stake in renewing the political process. This they achieved in a way that the centre-left parties were unable to replicate. In West Germany, for example, the CDU more successfully widened the appeal of its conservative, Catholic base than the SPD did in attracting a broader constituency. Both parties aimed at becoming 'people's parties', but by defending private property whilst anchoring this defence in a concept of 'social justice and public welfare', the CDU's offer of secure support for the individual was more favourable to the electorate than the SPD's democratic socialism.[42] Christian Democrats spoke to the masses whose instinctive reaction to the shock of the war was not to set about planning to reshape society, but to 'return' to peace and quiet—an innately conservative agenda, therefore, which the CDs effortlessly represented despite the SDs' attempt to make these same masses realize that their proposals were more likely to be in their interests.

Finally, despite the pretensions of the exiles, the people who really made important policy decisions in the immediate postwar years were those with Atlanticist outlooks and American connections. De Gaulle's resignation in 1946 indicated the rise of planners such as Jean Monnet and Robert Schuman, whose visions differed markedly from those of the exiles or the resistance. The Monnet Plan (1946) was just one of a raft of suggested measures designed to create economic and military interdependence between the states of Europe; it did so not by aiming at state-directed economic planning (as in Britain under Attlee) but by encouraging state investment in certain areas, thereby kick-starting their recovery. Where these schemes were most successful, as in the Marshall Plan, they also tied the US to Europe, justifying Geir Lundestad's famous notion of America's continued involvement in Western Europe after the war as constituting a form of 'empire by invitation'.[43] The main exception is Altiero Spinelli, the founder in Milan in 1943 of the Movimento Federalista Europeo, whose *Manifesto di Ventotene* constituted perhaps 'the most powerful vision of continental unity to emerge from the European resistance'.[44] Spinelli is one of the rare cases of a resistance fighter who went on to a successful career in the EEC, as the father of the European Parliament. But in general, what is so striking here is the continuity in political values, institutions, and personnel across the period 1938–48: capitalism, albeit now softened by substantial welfare measures; defence of traditional institutions, the church, army, state, and family; and, after 1947–8, a firm rejection of communism across the political spectrum. When de Gaulle returned to politics in 1947, he already found that his vision of a strong presidency had been overtaken by a parliamentary system which even he could not trump, and in 1953 he withdrew from politics again. The 'Third Force' governments that ruled France from 1947 were comprised of the socialists, the Christian Democratic MRP (Mouvement Républicain Populaire), and the Radicals, which tempered the Christian Democratic dominance that characterized France's neighbours; but in practice, the policies of the 'Third Force'—which was held together by its equally strong rejection of communism and Gaullism—did not differ significantly from countries where Christian Democrats had a firmer grip on power.

Above and beyond these continuities and the supremacy of Christian Democracy, Western Europe's postwar recovery also owed much to a widely shared antifascist narrative. This was entirely different from that prevailing in the eastern half of the continent, for this was an antifascism that owed little, if anything, to Moscow's insistence that fascism had been defeated by working-class resistance. It was an antifascism based not on the celebration of what the victors had done to defeat fascism, but on remembering what fascism had done to the people of Europe and the determination that they (whoever 'they' were) should not have the chance to do it again. Thus, even though the concept might seem out of place in a Christian Democracy-dominated political scene, actually this shared position was ultimately more significant to creating the postwar consensus in Western Europe than anticommunism or an acceptance of welfare capitalism by former socialists or liberals. In Western Europe, this antifascism meant not the celebration of brave partisans overthrowing fascist barbarism with the aid of the Red Army, but an anonymous narrative of victory over 'evil' and silence over the substantial levels of support for fascism/Nazism in former Axis countries (West Germany, Austria, Italy) and over the substantial levels of collaboration of individuals, institutions, or states in all other countries. Thus, while an official antifascist narrative was not imposed in the west in the same way as in Eastern Europe, nevertheless, the rebuilding of Western Europe also took place thanks to the suppression of open discussion of what the Second World War had really been about, a process that was facilitated by the emerging Cold War division of Europe.

This version of the recent past rested largely on narratives of heroism and national glory. First of all, contrary to today's emphasis on the Holocaust, based on an understanding of the particular venom with which the Nazis targeted the Jews, at the end of the war, survivors of the Nazis' 'racial persecution' were grouped together with other 'deportees' who had been targeted, in far greater numbers, for other reasons: forced labour primarily, but also voluntary workers in the Reich, POWs, and captured members of the resistance. Other victims, even including collaborationists who had fled to the Reich to escape revenge attacks, were also intermingled in the generalized understanding of 'victims' that prevailed by the later 1940s and early 1950s. In order not to bring about a situation in which the competing memories of these groups would be set at war with one another, Western European states immediately began constructing 'patriotic memories' which acted as a kind of social glue and permitted amnesia to settle over the various groups' disparate experiences. The notion of *resistancialisme*, which, by incorporating the 'sword and shield' concept of Vichy, encompassed a far wider section of society than 'la Résistance', like similar, triumphalist notions of the role played by the Dutch Union or the Belgian secretary-generals under the Nazi occupation, generated a 'collective self-image of the liberated societies' which 'required an active denial of the actual experience of the occupation'.[45] This meant the incorporation of Jewish victims into a generalized narrative of deportation and resistance, a narrative that accompanied the Gaullist rise to power in France and sustained Catholic support for the 'Government of the Resistance' in Belgium between August 1945 and March 1947 (when communist ministers left the government). In the Netherlands, a 'policy of forced consensus' meant the suppression of any discourse which sought to elucidate the different categories of victims, on the spurious grounds that since the Nazis had gathered all types of people together in their concentration camps, to lobby on behalf of any particular group could only be to make 'claims for special benefits or political manipulation, since they are not in any way united by a common action or ideal', as the official line had it.[46] In Denmark, the stress was on 'national unity', with an official narrative promoted and widely accepted, which stressed that all Danes had been victims of the German occupation.[47]

The consensus of silence did not therefore mean not speaking about the war; it meant highlighting only those aspects of it which spoke to a sense of security and wholeness, and ignoring those which might have engendered dissensus, discomfort, or renewed social disintegration. By contrast with the

antifascism of the immediate postwar years, which recapitulated the Popular
Front's demands for social change, the antifascism of the Christian Democratic ascendancy rested on the preservation of social order and traditional
institutions, blaming the downfall of European civilization not on untrammelled capitalism but on the lack of respect for tradition. Both narratives,
which aimed at rebuilding the nation on different lines, 'systematically
obscured the specificity of the genocide' of the Jews, for its victims were
neither suitably heroic nor representative of national glory.[48]

Building consensus in Western Europe was eased thanks to these patriotic narratives. But narratives alone would of course not suffice; new structures also had to be built, such as corporatist arrangements in industry, labour
relations based on cooperation, a system of welfare that supported families,
and so on. But that begs the question—why was it possible to build these
structures? If the years up to and during the early Cold War saw the reassertion of conservative values throughout Western Europe, what were the bases
on which they rested?

First, the right's interwar position was discredited, as notions of national
autarky and protectionism no longer held sway. Wartime planning fed into
the organization of international trade and security arrangements; and, even
if the most striking fact about postwar economics was the swift return to a
form of market-driven capitalism with little state intervention or 'rational
planning', still right-wing parties felt the necessity of at least directing some
sort of welfare capitalism and nationalizing certain key industries and natural monopolies. In Italy, for example, although the focus of policy was always
the individual and the family, reforms of the tax system and of the technocratic body that governed Italy's state-owned companies, the Institute for
Industrial Reconstruction (IRI), helped smooth the Christian Democrats'
passage to victory in the 1948 election on the basis of its myth of 'self-
generating prosperity' (mythic because Italy's prosperity was actually based
on its new integration into Western European trade structures, beginning
with the Marshall Plan).[49] In West Germany, Adenauer's ascendancy within
the CDU was strengthened in 1946, when in various key speeches he set
out a vision of economic planning which had remarkably little role for the
state as such (and not just because at this point the state was under Allied
control), putting the onus instead on autonomous employers', employees',
and consumers' institutions.[50] By 1948, when Adenauer's liberal-conservative
wing of the CDU was firmly in control, the party's programme was one of
anti-monopolistic capitalism with a strong social policy element built in.

In Britain, the Attlee government introduced the NHS in 1948, and before that the 1942 Beveridge Report had played a key role in focusing nascent Western European political movements preparing for the new postwar arena. Outside of Britain, they favoured Catholic welfare organizations and other civil society options rather than a state-directed, British model, but that still meant the state underwriting and protecting the right to some sort of welfare.

On the left, interwar socialist parties were increasingly turning, after the war, into social democratic ones, not just accepting the market economy but tempering it with welfare and interventionist measures aiming at wealth distribution, but, even more important at this time, firmly rejecting communism. After the exclusion of communists from government in France and Italy in 1947, and having witnessed the charade of the 'national fronts from below' strategy in Eastern Europe, social democrats turned decisively and permanently to face the centre, and to make peace with the anti-communism of the day. Kurt Schumacher, the leader of Germany's SPD, who, having spent twelve years in concentration camps (including eight in Dachau), had impeccable anti-Nazi credentials, typified this trend, when he spoke of the Nazis, following the Nuremberg example, as a 'group of clever thieves', and blamed their rise to power not only on 'the failure of the bourgeoisie' but, more notably, on 'those Communist parts of the working-class movement which did not recognize the value of democracy'.[51] The culmination of this trend came in 1959, when, at its Bad Godesberg congress, the SPD famously rejected its Marxist heritage. Declaring itself to be a 'party of the whole people' rather than of the working class, its new slogan was now: 'As much competition as possible, as much planning as necessary'. The West European non-communist left had accepted the terms of the debate set for it by the conservative majority. By doing so, they effectively entrenched a conservative hegemony in Western Europe.

There were, however, exceptions. Portugal under Salazar and, especially, Spain under Franco had survived the war with their authoritarian, if not fascist regimes still firmly in place. Where antifascism provided a new narrative of national unity for most of Western Europe, in Iberia (and Greece), ultra-nationalism was the major source of regime legitimacy, providing the collective memory of the victorious elite and eliciting the complicity of the majority of the population. On the face of it, these regimes appear anomalous, for they 'were partners in the western alliance against communism, but they were "uncomfortable" and awkward ones. Not only did they fail to fit the mythic grand narrative of a "national resistance to fascism as generator of parliamentary democracy" that proved so useful for nation-building in post-1945 Western Europe, but these three regimes replicated the structural violence and coercion of the Cold War enemy, which meant they actively undermined the idea of western political superiority and civility.'[52]

Salazar had hedged his bets during the war. Despite some trappings of fascism, Salazar's 'collaborationist neutrality' during the war was turned more towards the Allies than the Axis. Portugal's empire was an outlet for those with fascistic ideological leanings, and the metropole itself remained a fairly quiet outpost of Catholic authoritarianism. There was torture and repression, but not on the scale of Spain's. It was thus relatively unproblematic to provide Portugal with Marshall Aid and to bring it into NATO in 1949.[53]

Spain was a different case. Here there was no need for a conservative reassertion, for all opposition had been ruthlessly put down. Following the civil war, Franco's regime had brutally suppressed those it deemed to be the enemies of 'eternal Spain', in a process which makes Spain central to the story of twentieth-century European violence.[54] This was not just the suppression of combatants, but an attempt to demonize whole sections of society who, Franco supposed, were 'natural' opponents. The result has been termed the 'Spanish Holocaust'.[55] By the end of the 1940s, the regime had murdered more than 130,000 people. In forging the Spanish equivalent of the Nazi *Volksgemeinschaft* (national community), about a million people experienced some form of incarceration or punitive measure; this long period of regime-led violence was a process that brutalized and bound to the regime a generation of perpetrators too, building into the system a fear and resentment that contributed to its longevity. During the war, Spain, like Portugal, was officially neutral, but leant quite clearly towards the Axis. As a result, in the immediate postwar period, Spain found itself isolated from the trends described above, and excluded from the new international structures, such as the UN, OEEC, and the Marshall Plan. Since autarky was still the basis of Spain's economic policy at this point, these exclusions were not felt so keenly, until after 1951 when growing demands were made within the regime for a liberalization of the economy and thus for an engagement with the international community.

Having successfully negotiated the war, however, Franco was quite capable of capitalizing on the changing international situation in order to reverse Spain's status as international pariah. After 1948, the US began to regard

Spain as geopolitically useful and heard Franco's anti-communism with ever more receptive ears. Franco made great play of this anti-communism, as in these words of 1952: 'Spain is self-confident and knows that it could not be attacked without offering resistance.... The American people should know that if Spain had refused to sacrifice itself, or if after victory she had gone back to the wretched pre-war regime, she would have ended in communist chaos.'[56] It did not take long for the US and other Cold War allies to renew diplomatic relations with Spain and, within a few years, the US was providing Spain with its own aid package (1953) and Spain had joined the UN (1955), the International Bank for Reconstruction and Development, and the International Monetary Fund (1958) and the OEEC (1958). The Spanish 'anomaly' was perpetuated by the same international organizations that reconstructed Western Europe as much as by the strength of the Franco regime itself.

In the few years between the end of the war and the hardening of the Cold War into a seemingly permanent division of the continent, the Western European states outside of the Iberian peninsula had more in common with Eastern Europe than they did with Spain and Portugal (and to some extent Greece, with its semi-authoritarian, right-wing government). This short period was one of experimentation and openness to new ideas across Europe. Or rather, of a kind of continuity of old ones, as an antifascism reminiscent of the Popular Front days of the mid-1930s reappeared, with communists and trade unionists uniting with centrist parties to promote grassroots democratic politics. In 1947, with the announcement of the ERP and the Truman Doctrine, and definitively in 1948, with the Prague coup and the exclusion of communists from government in France and Italy, that short, volatile period came to an end. Antifascism would remain the order of the day, only now as an officially endorsed position, often propounded by political parties and institutions who were themselves not always as free of the taint of fellow-travelling as they wanted to appear.

The most striking turnaround of political parties' positions occurred in the western zones of Germany/FRG. In the summer of 1945, the Free Democratic Party (the liberals) declared that 'in clear recognition of the crimes committed by Hitler', it would 'work for an honest reconciliation and compensation'. By January 1946, this had changed so that the FDP was now signalling its readiness to fight socialism of every sort, 'be it National or Inter-National Socialism'. Likewise, the CDU (Christian Democratic Union) diluted the message of its October 1945 *Cologne Guidelines*, which stated that Nazism had 'covered the name of Germany throughout the world with shame and dishonour', when, in January 1946, it announced: 'We demand that Christians recognize the fact that they made one of the greatest sacrifices in Hitler's Germany and that they contributed decisively to the defeat of National Socialism.'[57] The CDU, in fact, built its post-1945 shape on the pre-war structures not just of the Centre Party but the ultra-nationalist DNVP (German National People's Party). Here 'antifascism' meant the official repudiation of Hitlerism, but the survival of authoritarian structures, the promotion of anti-communism, and a focus on Germans' suffering and victimization, as dupes of Hitler, of the Eastern Front, and, after the war, of expulsion, rape, and the imprisonment of POWs.[58] Nothing facilitated this drift away from denazification and a reassertion of German traditionalism more than the Western Allies' decision to treat West Germany with kid gloves, and to bring it back into the fold, as the Cold War took shape.

The transitions in the spheres of culture, politics, and society that took place in the years 1944–8, then, were ones that accompanied the steady rise to ubiquity of the Cold War. The shift, from antifascism to anti-communism, from contrition to strident self-glorification, and from incipient grassroots democracy to the reassertion of the old order, were all markers of the preparation of a Western Europe ripe for incorporation in the alignments of a bipolar world system. As in the Sovietization of Eastern Europe, this transition took place under the sign of geopolitics.

The unfolding of the Cold War in Europe

No matter how compelling the evidence for the brutality of Stalinist rule in Eastern Europe, historians cannot conclusively demonstrate that a deliberately orchestrated strategy of Sovietization was the root cause of the Cold War.[59] In 1945, Europeans could envisage many different futures from those retrospectively imposed by historians, which restrict the choice to either market liberalism or Sovietization.[60] Besides, the division of Europe and the Sovietization of Eastern Europe are two separate though related matters; the former was a logical result of the Soviets and Americans recognizing each other's legitimate spheres of interest, the latter the end result of Stalin's aims for his sphere, which he hoped would be understood by the western powers. Yet, as we have seen, many immediate postwar problems were 'solved' (or swept aside) one way or another by the intrusion of the new realities created by the Cold War. The NMT and the denazification programmes ran out of steam as the rearming of Germany became a more urgent matter; the need to close DP camps seemed more pressing when West Germany was needed as an ally against communism. Indeed, whilst historians are correct to stress the numerous alternative paths that could have been taken in the years 1945–8, the Cold War (and not just historians' reconstruction of it as a historical necessity) really did radically circumscribe states' and organizations' actions and choices. However, what historians now understand, in ways that contemporary commentators could not, was that the Cold War framework of two superpowers facing off across the globe offers insufficient understanding of the origins and unfolding of the Cold War in general, and in Europe in particular. Rather, during the years 1948–53, the institutions that Western European leaders and peoples created were as much responsible for the way the Cold War unfolded as they were reactions to rapidly developing and hardening international tensions.

Traditionally, the Cold War has been understood as the final stage in the breakdown of the wartime alliance, driven by Stalin's paranoid personality and Soviet aggression, with the US reacting to contain this expansionism. The classic moments of this US response are George Kennan's 'long telegram' (22 February 1946), which advised US commitment to resisting the spread of communism, the announcement of the Truman Doctrine (March 1947) and the Marshall Plan (June 1947), the Berlin blockade and airlift (June 1948–May 1949), and the establishment of NATO (4 April 1949). Of no less significance are the US–Soviet clash over Iran at the United Nations and Churchill's 'iron curtain' speech at Fulton in February 1946. This view has proven to be durable and, although we can now understand the Cold War through the lenses of economics, consumerism, and 'culture' in the broadest sense to include art, film, gender relations, or technology, the traditionalist version still prevails.[61] Although 'revisionists' put forward arguments to suggest that the US rather than the USSR was the key aggressor, the direction of the interpretive wind since 1989—when Eastern European documents became available in far greater quantities—has been towards Moscow.

Certain factors are missing in these grand histories of international relations. Not least among them is the role played by Europeans themselves, such that the old view of the Cold War as 'two dogs chewing on a bone' now looks inadequate. The Cold War not only had a European dimension—albeit an important symbolic one by comparison with the real wars fought in Korea, Indochina, and elsewhere—but was, to a larger extent than contemporaries realized, driven by Europeans and the decisions they made. In 1945–6, one could even argue that 'the main antagonists were Britain and the Soviet Union, not the United States and the Soviet Union' and that only by the end of 1946 did the UK and US share a unified view.[62] The cultural and social history of the Cold War is no less important than the high politics of diplomacy in understanding how the division of Europe was played out in each European country. In particular, narratives and memories of the war shaped the different attitudes of the superpowers towards European states and determined the ways in which local politicians and people at large responded in turn. The American and British focus on Germany indicates how postwar plans were guided by the war. For the Soviets especially, their wartime experience at the hands of Germany was the decisive factor in determining postwar foreign policy.

At the end of the war, the Americans, and parts of the British civil service especially (despite longstanding, pre-war misgivings), were still remarkably pro-Soviet, and their assumption was that the Soviets wanted to maintain the Alliance.[63] The Western Allies were aware of the danger of the 'Bolshevization' of Eastern Europe, but they did not regard it as an inevitable outcome; indeed, British diplomats—in contrast to the army—believed that Soviet policy would in no small measure be determined by Britain and America, as Sir Nigel Ronald wrote in May 1943: 'The way in which the Soviet Union will behave towards us and those in whom we profess to be interested after the war will, anyhow to some extent, be conditioned by how *we* behave towards her now and then.'[64] This fear of 'Bolshevization' did not mean that the British would object to the spread of Soviet influence in Eastern Europe, for that would not necessarily contradict either the Atlantic Charter or British interests in the Balkans. Similarly, the Americans, despite some vacillations in policy over 1945–6, ultimately accepted that the Soviets could have a free hand in Poland, Romania, and Bulgaria since this did not directly challenge US interests, rhetoric notwithstanding.[65] France may have had more interest in Eastern Europe, thanks to its historic links with the region, but even though the country maintained a cultural dialogue with Eastern Europe, it was too reliant on the US and the integration of Western Europe to have a decisive influence on events there.[66]

This acquiescence to *realpolitik*, or a desire to prevent a clash of ideologies spilling over into actual warfare, appears to make the rapid deterioration of relations in 1946–7 all the more puzzling. But the fact is that the Soviets, as we saw in Chapter 1, held a different definition of 'friendly' from the Western Allies, and Stalin was only satisfied once regimes led by communists who were totally in the pocket of Moscow were in place. In the cases of Poland, Romania, and Bulgaria, the Western Allies might have spoken out in favour of free elections, but in reality they accepted that the Soviets had legitimate claims. But the Sovietization of those states (as opposed to their merely being brought into the Soviet sphere) was enlightening for the west. Thus began the process of 'containment' which led to the downward spiral of each side outbidding the other in the aggression of its actions: the Truman Doctrine and the policy of 'rollback', beginning with the banning of the Communist Party in Greece in 1947; the Marshall Plan and the Soviets' rejection of it, leading to the Sovietization of Hungary and the Czech coup; the objection of Togliatti, the Italian communist leader, to the terms of the Marshall Plan and thence to the exclusion of French and Italian communists from government; the creation of the Cominform; the defeat of the Italian communists in the 1948 election; and the Berlin Crisis. By 1948, with the creation of the Western Union and the unification of the three western occupation zones of Germany, the wartime alliance was dead.

The involvement of the Western European states in this dynamic of belligerent misunderstanding cannot be underestimated. The first key moment was the British announcement on 21 February 1947 that it would be pulling out of Greece, which left the monarchist government vulnerable to communist guerrillas and the renewed threat of civil war. This was the occasion for Harry S. Truman's famous 'Doctrine'. Here was the chance for American officials to prove to their people that the US needed to remain committed to Europe, in order to keep the threat of Soviet aggression at bay. In his speech in Congress on 12 March, Truman argued that the US must take the lead in the coming world struggle between free societies and totalitarian dictatorships: 'It must be the policy of the United States to support free peoples who are resisting attempted subjugation by armed minorities or by outside pressures,' as he put it.[67] Coming at the same time as the meeting of the Council of Foreign Ministers in Moscow, this was a direct challenge to the Soviets.

The challenge was compounded by the almost simultaneous announcement of the ERP.[68] In his speech at Harvard University on 5 June 1947, Secretary of State George Marshall launched the plan that sought to prevent 'the dislocation of the entire fabric of European economy'. Marshall was eager to get his point across that the policy was 'not directed against any country or doctrine but against hunger, poverty, desperation, and chaos'. And he stressed that 'Any government that is willing to assist in the task of recovery will find full cooperation, I am sure, on the part of the United States Government.' It is hard to believe that the USSR could have been included here—neither the US nor Foreign Ministers Ernest Bevin or Georges Bidault was going to fund communism—but Marshall Aid was certainly on offer to the Eastern European states, at least for the purposes of taking the diplomatic offensive. Marshall also stressed that aid would be given to projects that involved European countries working together, and that the initiative for how money should be used should come from the Europeans themselves; the US would not engage directly in drawing up detailed programmes. Unsurprisingly, the Soviets forced the Czechs and Poles, who wished to take up the offer, to change their minds.

Clearly, the Marshall Plan envisaged both European economic recovery and, as a consequence, Western Europe's commitment to the market and thus to anti-communism. Yet although the Marshall Plan has been criticized for being a tool of US commercial and geopolitical imperialism, it is perhaps best described as 'Enlightened self-interest', as one early commentator put it.[69] Besides, the Americans were knocking at an open Western European door. The economic gain for the US economy was certainly relevant, and the deal committed the US to a long-term presence in Europe, but the contribution of the Marshall money to Western Europe was immense, both financially and psychologically, and it achieved its goal—and that of Western European elites—of keeping communism at bay. The Soviets recognized this too; at a speech to the UN in September 1947, Soviet Deputy Foreign Minister Andrei Vyshinsky stated: 'It is becoming more and more evident to everyone that the implementation of the Marshall Plan will mean placing European countries under the economic and political control of the United States and direct interference by the latter in the internal affairs of those countries.' He added, ominously, that 'this plan is an attempt to split Europe into two camps and, with the help of the United Kingdom and France, to complete the formation of a bloc of several European countries hostile to the interests of the democratic countries of Eastern Europe and most particularly to the interests of the Soviet Union'.[70] Both sides had reached the stage of accusing the other of exactly what they themselves were doing.

The sums involved in the ERP were large, but not so large that they can be said to have been decisive: before 1947, the US had already pumped about

15 million dollars worth of aid into Western Europe, and between 1948 and 1952, the life of the ERP, an additional 13 billion dollars of US government grants was made available. No doubt the ERP expedited a process of rapid economic growth that was already in train and, together with the Bretton Woods Agreement of 1944, helped to set the scene for economic stability. Bretton Woods, which established the IMF and IBRD, was originally intended to be more than a mechanism for controlling currency exchange, but this was where it was most successful; even though the Bretton Woods system as a whole did not come fully into operation until 1959 (by which point it already required a major overhaul), by pegging the IMF system to gold, the dollar, and sterling, and allowing only 1 per cent fluctuation, international trade was able to function more predictably. Yet the agreement also gave rise to a shortage of US dollars as countries rushed to convert their savings into that currency, and the UK especially suffered from a run on sterling. GATT, initially conceived as a short-term stop-gap for the failed ITO, was designed to boost world (as opposed to purely European) trade, but only achieved limited tariff reductions overall, principally in high-value-added goods.[71] So by bringing in the Americans, the Marshall Plan provided more of a psychological than financial boost.[72] Never intended as a long-term development programme (most physical reconstruction was already complete before it began), the ERP, even if it did not attain the results envisaged for it by the US, did achieve the goals of forcing European states to cooperate, through the agencies set up to administer it: the Organization for European Economic Cooperation (OEEC, later OECD) and the European Payments Union (EPU).[73] Its major role was thus to smooth the passage of economic growth by altering the framework within which that growth was taking place, producing a more integrated Western European economy with stable prices and exchange rates, and a liberalizing economy that overcame the problem of national trade deficits. The Marshall Plan 'solved the catch-22 of having to export in order to pay for imports but being unable to produce for export without first importing materials and machinery'.[74] By tipping Western Europe decisively towards a liberal market economy, it also helped to solidify the centre-right dominance over the political process. Western Europe went on to create 'mixed economies', which combined the market with social safeguards, but the Marshall Plan ensured that these economies would be 'superimposed on a private-ownership economy'.[75] It left Western Europe firmly anchored in the American-led capitalist world, as Bidault, de Gasperi, Spaak, and the rest of the Christian Democrat elite had intended.

If the Marshall Plan had engendered a sense of the permanence of the division of Europe, then confirmation of that state of affairs followed soon afterwards, with the failure of the London Council of Foreign Ministers in December 1947 to agree terms on Germany, reparations, and peace treaties with the Eastern European states. Germany held the key to any possibility of cordial relations, for its economic potential was crucial for future European development. The formation of 'Bizonia' out of the American and British occupation zones in late 1946 set the scene for the flow of Marshall money the following year, and confirmed the Soviets' already hard-line position on their zone of occupation. Had the four powers agreed to the permanent disarmament and neutrality of Germany, perhaps the dynamic of distrust in Europe could have been averted; Germany, however, was not a sideshow, like Finland, or even Austria, but was the heart of the problem.

Stalin's key aim in Europe was to prevent a rejuvenated Germany from threatening Soviet security. That meant preventing the western zones from becoming part of a Western European security framework, and most of all stopping German rearmament. The Soviet response to the events of 1947 and early 1948 was to challenge the Western Allies over Germany, and to implement a blockade of all road and rail routes into West Berlin, thus precipitating the Berlin Airlift (*Luftbrücke*). Bevin voiced a widely shared view when he wrote to Attlee in July 1948, just after the start of the blockade, that a 'prosperous and contented Germany, built on sound democratic principles, is the best guarantee for the safety of Europe'. Bevin's perception was that the future of Europe would be determined by what happened to Germany: 'If our policy succeeds, Western Germany, forming part of the Western Defence System and contributing to the ERP can become a most effective barrier against the spread of communism across Europe. On the other hand, if we fail, the only alternative is Soviet control on the whole of Germany and therefore Europe.'[76] Thus, whatever Stalin's real intentions in April 1952, when he offered a deal to exchange German unification and the withdrawal of foreign armies for the country's neutrality—historians argue over whether this was sincerely meant or just a propaganda stunt[77]—it is hardly surprising that the Allies, and the West Germans themselves, opted for continuing the policy of integrating the newborn Federal Republic (1949) into the economic and security structures of the west. This was a circular process: 'The Cold War made West Germany a necessary component of non-Communist Europe. But in turn the need for German participation made a new level of intra-European institutional development necessary.'[78] As George Kennan wrote in a memorandum of March 1949, 'There is no solution of the German problem in terms of Germany; there is only a solution in terms of Europe.'[79] Indeed, a top secret US State Department paper of the same date confirmed that fitting Germany into a Western European community required that 'such a community must exist, and must be adequate to handle the German problem'. It argued that 'the most important steps in this direction have been ERP, including the formation of the OEEC, and the North Atlantic Treaty'.[80] And this understanding of the necessity of integrating Germany into wider frameworks applied in both east and west, where the blocs were in some ways centred on the question of what to do about their slice of Germany.

Economic growth and geopolitical security concerns thus went hand in hand. The bodies set up to administer the Marshall Plan, notably the EPU and the European Cooperation Administration (ECA), stimulated economic planning, national income accounting, and investment and growth. These bodies operated without much American intervention: there is a striking contrast between US 'colonial' administration in Greece (in dealing with hyperinflation after the civil war) and hands-off, technocratic supervision in northern Europe, and the US enjoyed only limited leverage over local and even national levels in Italy and elsewhere.[81] Italy may be something of an exception, but the day-to-day workings of the Marshall Plan here are not untypical of the programme's operations elsewhere: even if the reforms that did away with the legacy of fascist autarky were the order of the day, this still left plenty of opportunity for the continuation of older traditions favoured by elites. Marshall Plan 'propaganda' was especially important in Italy, in the form of travelling exhibitions and the like.[82] Yet one American official could still complain that Italian industrialists refused to countenance German-style 'co-determination' in industry or improvements in industrial productivity; rather, they were only interested in 'perpetuating the myth that there is no alternative between communism and their capitalistic model based on monopolies, low salaries, limited production, high costs and high prices'.[83]

But apart from the technical controls that the ERP encouraged, security concerns also played a key role, most notably in 1949–50, when rearmament became important for economic growth. 'If we consider the period 1947–54 as a unit', writes Charles Maier, 'the major watershed within the period was the rush to rearmament in 1949–50.' The Soviets' nuclear test of 1949 led to Truman's decision to build a fusion bomb and intensified the security paranoia in the US that led to the excesses of McCarthyism.[84] The cooperative frameworks and institutions established by the ERP now assumed a military role: the ECA segued neatly into the Mutual Security Administration and NATO as military necessities facilitated institutional cooperation and integration, and assisted in persuading the Americans to become involved in Indochina. NATO itself was the beneficiary of the French decision to abandon their original proposal to set up a European Defence Community (1954); the French aims of agreement but with firm control over Germany were met with the creation of a France- and NATO-oriented West Germany, as France's weakness on the international stage forced it to work within larger, US-led structures.[85]

The Marshall Plan may have acted as the primary cause of the growing division in Europe,[86] but it also stimulated Western European cooperation and integration. The Resistance movements had spoken of creating a federal Europe which would abandon petty nationalisms; this ideal remained, but what helped it become reality was precisely the showdown with the Soviet Union over Germany. Here was the chance for a coincidence of wants between those, like Spinelli, who had dreamed of a united Europe (albeit a socialist one) and those like Monnet, who wanted to submerge Germany in international structures, thus providing stability and prosperity in Western Europe and simultaneously ensuring France's security. The signing of the Treaty of Paris in April 1951, which created the European Coal and Steel Community (ECSC), was to some extent the realization of the dream of European unity, but restricted to the level of trade and economics. The subsequent development of this integration process, through the EEC, would continue to give prominence to national interest, even if that should not be understood as necessarily in competition with the integrationist ambition.

The Resistance movements had dreamt about a world in which the 'maintenance of freedom and security on the entire continent should be solely in the hands of the European federation and its executive, legislative, and judiciary organs'.[87] Robert Schuman (the MRP's Foreign Minister) clarified what was really going on in his speech that initiated the ECSC: 'The solidarity in production thus established [by joining coal and steel production] will make it plain that any war between France and Germany becomes not merely unthinkable, but materially impossible...this proposal will build the first concrete foundation of a European federation which is indispensable to the preservation of peace...'[88] However, this is not to say that the great powers 'did nothing more than arrange for the restoration of the system of national states', as one admirer of the Resistance movements claims.[89] The move towards the pooling of resources and the creation of a common market in the Treaties of Paris (1951) and Rome (establishing the European Economic Community and Euratom, 1957) was driven by national interests. But national interest at this point, for France, Italy, West Germany, and the Benelux countries, meant precisely entering into a sharing of resources and an integration of economic and military structures. For the West Germans, in particular, a sharing of resources was the *sine qua non* for their national aspirations, as Adenauer admitted to Monnet in 1950: 'I have waited 25 years for a move like this. In accepting it, my government and my country have no secret hankerings after hegemony. History since 1933 has taught us the folly of such ideas. Germany knows that its fate is bound up with that of Western Europe as a whole.'[90] The Schuman Plan, the basis of the ECSC, could emerge and make political sense in the framework for cooperation established by the Marshall Plan.

The Marshall Plan thus stimulated European economic and military cooperation in equal measure. If by 1948 the wartime alliance was dead, this mortification was confirmed first by the establishment of the Western Union in 1948, a European initiative, and then, growing out of it, of NATO in 1949.[91] The Soviets (and Togliatti) predictably objected, on the basis that NATO constituted an act of aggression against the Soviet Union. As they had done in response to the Truman Doctrine and the Marshall Plan, the Soviets claimed that NATO also represented a breach of the UN Charter. Within a few years, the wartime alliance had been replaced by the North Atlantic alliance, the Eastern Europeans had rejected Marshall Aid, Italy had made its 'Western choice', and the division of Europe now looked set in stone.

The shadow war

On one level, the emergence of the Cold War seems to indicate that the Second World War was rapidly consigned to the past. Events overtook the possibility of dwelling on the past, and a new world order took over. But on another level, the Cold War incorporated the 'lessons' of the Second World War and, furthermore, facilitated social unity in Western Europe because it fostered a new version of 'enemy-thinking'. With the exceptions of Spain and Portugal, Western European states revelled in their myths of wartime resistance to fascism, and put those myths at the service of fighting communism, or 'red fascism' as it soon became known in conservative scholarly circles. From the 'lesson' of appeasement, which justified 'rollback', to the 'need' for a nuclear deterrent, strategic planners were often fighting Hitler when they were containing Stalin. It was no coincidence, for example, that the 'lessons of Munich' were applied to the 'lessons of Prague', and that the British played a major role in creating the Western Union just days after the Prague coup in 1948.[92] This became especially clear during the culture wars of the 1950s, as we will see in Part II, when the Soviet Bloc accused the western states of harbouring fascists, or indeed of being *in toto* a new variant of fascism, and when the west spoke of the communist world as trapped under 'totalitarianism', a term which amalgamated the Third Reich and the USSR. Certainly, when the silence about what had actually gone on in Western Europe during the Second World War was broken, when rare voices of dissent cracked through the carapace of the resistance myth, the effect was like a shard in the Cold War's flesh. But these voices were rare indeed before the mid-1950s: Primo Levi failed to find a publisher for his memoir of Auschwitz, *If This Is a Man*, after the first print run of 2,500 in 1947; Levi himself mused on the possibility that this lack of interest perhaps arose 'because in all of Europe those were difficult times of mourning and reconstruction and the public did not want to return in memory to the painful years of the war that had just ended'.[93] The book was not reissued until 1958. Hans Keilson's remarkable psychological dissection of Nazism, *The Death of the Adversary*, quickly went out of print and was only rediscovered half a century later. Western antifascism rapidly took on the air of a defence of conservative heroes, such as Stauffenberg and the resistance to Hitler. Soviet antifascism was condemned as shrill and retributive, such that the kernel of truth behind it got lost.

According to the former member of the Spanish Communist Party, Fernando Claudín (expelled in 1965), western historians and politicians who turned against Stalin for his 'trickery' in obtaining Eastern European satellites showed 'not only a lack of objectivity but also ingratitude'. Western Europe, in this reading, was only in a position to praise Roosevelt and Truman for championing the 'free world' because of what the Soviet Union had done first: 'If the "free world" did not lose some of its finest flowers in the crisis, there can be no doubt that it owes this to Stalin.'[94] And Eastern Europe, in this reading, was the fair price for this Soviet sacrifice. Perhaps the origins of the Cold War lie here, in the context of competing understandings of the war, just as much as in exclusively geopolitical or diplomatic explanations. Stalin could not understand why he should not have a free hand in countries like Romania, which, until its opportunistic switch of sides in 1943, was one of Hitler's staunchest allies and contributed far more troops to the invasion of the USSR than any of the Wehrmacht's other sidekicks. And he certainly could not understand why the west cared about what happened there, as it did not threaten their interests. Indeed, he might have been forgiven for thinking that the anti-fascist alliance had a future in 1944–5. But the rapid Sovietization of Eastern Europe rattled the Western Europeans, who quickly bound themselves together and to the US in military and trading alliances that had jointly reinforcing aims of reconstructing Western Europe's economies and keeping communism at bay—based on their (mis)perception that Stalin wanted to unleash revolution in Western Europe at the first opportunity. No wonder that Stalin saw this as the capitalist world turning bandit: having used the USSR to solve its own crisis and to defeat Germany, it now turned against its erstwhile ally. No wonder too that Stalin, who did not want to break the wartime alliance, was driven to do so by his own perceptions of Soviet security; as we are well reminded, 'Without an understanding of the phenomenon of the war as it entered the flesh and blood of that generation, postwar history and social behaviour are incomprehensible.'[95] Of course, the Western Allies themselves saw the situation differently, and regarded moves to rebuild Europe's economies, to rearm West Germany, and to create NATO as largely defensive measures. But in order to understand Stalin's mindset, and thus the emergence of the 'unwanted Cold War',[96] we have no choice but to consider the massive Soviet contribution to Hitler's defeat, and Stalin's understanding of the Second World War as a product of the capitalist system. The history of the Soviet Bloc after 1953 is a history not just of competing with the west, but of trying to maintain and inculcate the values of the antifascist consensus.

PART II

Boom to Bust

3

Golden Years?

Western Europe, 1953–1975

The necessity of negotiation is, I believe, undisputed. World Powers primarily, but not they alone, are under extreme objective pressure to create a certain amount of order if they are to prevent the collective suicide of the human race.

Willy Brandt

The events and decisions of the next ten months may well decide the fate of man for the next ten thousand years. There will be no avoiding those events. There will be no appeal from these decisions. And we in this hall shall be remembered either as part of the generation that turned this planet into a flaming funeral pyre or the generation that met its vow 'to save succeeding generations from the scourge of war.'

John F. Kennedy[1]

Introduction

Historians conventionally talk of the years 1945–75 as the thirty glorious years, *les trentes glorieuses*. And with good reason: until the oil crisis of 1973 and the return of the business cycle, economic growth in Western Europe ran at unprecedented levels for so long that economists and politicians, not to mention 'ordinary people', began to think that the days of bubbles and recessions were gone and that the future consisted of nothing more than managing the levels of Keynesian counter-cyclical state investment. That is to say, the triumph of economic planning combined with welfare capitalism meant that the administration of the state was a merely technocratic measure; events such as the Great Depression would not occur again. Although differences between parties of the left and right continued to exist, so this viewpoint ran, all mainstream parties working within the rules of parliamentary democracy accepted the value of one or other variety of the welfare state and agreed that capitalism, to whatever extent they enthused about it, needed to be tempered. Indeed, politicians recognized that capitalism benefited from social stability and widespread prosperity, for these conditions allowed for flourishing growth without, apparently, the threat of recession or stagnation.

This chapter focuses on only twenty years, because whilst economic growth was strong during the initial period of reconstruction, it took until the mid-1950s before the new system was entrenched and bedded in. With the OEEC and EPU set up to administer the Marshall Plan, and the ECSC, Brussels Pact and NATO providing frameworks for political, military, and economic cooperation and integration, the first ten postwar years were as much about providing the context for economic growth as about growth itself. By the mid-1950s, with the end of austerity in Britain and a sense across Western Europe that the most obvious physical reminders of the war had been removed, one can sense a new era beginning, an age of consumer confidence and great social change. This was also an age of intense Cold War activity—the hottest moments of the whole Cold War occurred in the middle of the period, as did the first steps towards détente—as well as of other major changes in world history: the European empires definitively collapsed; British pretences to great power status were exposed as a sham over Suez, at the same time as anti-Soviet uprisings were taking place in Hungary and Poland, and as the EEC was being constructed; West Germany re-emerged as a major power in Europe, and began diplomatic overtures towards the GDR with its *Ostpolitik* (eastern policy); generational change brought about the rise of civil rights and other new social movements across the world, including the New Left, feminism, the green movement, and gay rights, with the most explosive events pertaining to these movements occurring in the tumultuous year of 1968. Finally, the presumptions of the technocrats regarding the economy were to prove dreadfully wrong. The 'golden age', as Eric Hobsbawm called it, came crashing to a halt, and only a decade and more of painful restructuring of the Western European economies eventually brought the region out of the economic doldrums—at least until the financial crisis from 2008 onwards.[2]

The widespread use of a term such as '*les trentes glorieuses*' is understandable enough, when one considers the extent of economic growth and the improvements in Western Europeans' lifestyles, not just in terms of access to consumer goods but of healthcare provision, life expectancy, access to work and leisure—even if all of these things became available to the mass of the population more slowly than the popular imagination likes to recall. But why should Hobsbawm, one of the most famous Marxist historians, have been tempted to speak in these terms, when the age saw the rebirth of a self-consciously anti-communist capitalism and not, as many of the Resistance manifestos foresaw, a resurgence of socialism in a reinvigorated, politically integrated Europe?

The answer is that the capitalism of the 1950s and 1960s was, we can now see, 'an exceptional moment in the several-centuries' history of industrial capitalism'.[3] In marked contrast to the nineteenth-century and interwar periods, when one can hardly speak of 'labour relations' in any meaningful sense, or of the late twentieth and early twenty-first centuries, when deindustrialized and de-unionized labour has again been squeezed by global big business, the mid-twentieth century witnessed an unprecedented rise of organized labour. The successful corporatist arrangements in place throughout much of Western Europe provide one of the clearest indications of the meaning of the postwar consensus: welfare capitalism as 'reward' for the sufferings of working people and as a way for elites to stave off rejectionist political ideologies; but also an incorporation of antifascism in the sense that if fascism is understood as an outcome of capitalism in crisis, then regulating the capitalist economy so that all sections of society have a stake in it and benefit from it can be understood as a way of responding to the disaster wrought by fascism, preventing its repeat.

In another, more radical sense, this framework was a way of *not* addressing fascism and its links with either capitalism in the narrow sense (in the way that Marxists, and especially the official Marxism-Leninism of the Eastern Bloc, understood fascism as 'crisis capitalism with a cudgel') or with liberal democracy more broadly—the failure of 'liberal' elites at best to prevent the rise of fascism and, at worst, to accommodate it in the belief that their own power would be safeguarded. In the 1950s, the best example of this criticism came, for obvious reasons, from West German intellectuals.

Centre-right governments in power and the institutions that took shape in the 1940s and 1950s gave a very conservative cast to Western European political culture, as we have seen in Chapter 1. Stability through parliamentary democracy was certainly one result of the right's newfound commitment to democracy—though not in Southern Europe—especially since it came nicely wrapped in shiny consumer goods. Consensus about the state

and its duty to its citizens gave postwar European polities (if not governments, as Italy proves) a solidity and longevity that few had enjoyed between
the wars. This consensus lasted for over two decades, 'subsisting on the doubled memories of war and Depression'.[4] There is nevertheless something
startling about a situation in which large numbers of former Nazis could
still be working as teachers, judges, and policemen, or in which representatives of political parties that (in the most charitable reading) had failed to
prevent the slide into the apocalypse were once again at the helm, not ten
years after the war. The philosopher Theodor W. Adorno was being dramatic, but when he penned his essay 'The Meaning of Working Through the
Past' (1959), it was not entirely hyperbolic to write: 'I consider the survival
of National Socialism *within* democracy to be potentially more menacing
than the survival of fascist tendencies *against* democracy. Infiltration indicates something objective; ambiguous figures make their *comeback* and
occupy positions of power for the sole reason that conditions favour them.'[5]
Although he was speaking explicitly of West Germany, Adorno's claim
applied no less forcefully to Austria, which, after the State Treaty of 1955
delivered full independence in return for neutrality, officially peddled the
obfuscation that it had been the 'first victim of National Socialism' and
where local commemorative rituals kept alive a counter-narrative which
celebrated the bravery of the Wehrmacht in the defence of the *Heimat*.[6]

The best (worst?) examples were indeed spectacular proof of Adorno's
claims about the survival of Nazism within democracy: Hans Globke (1898–
1973), who as a fairly high-ranking civil servant in the Reich Ministry of the
Interior had been co-author of a legal commentary on the Nuremberg race
laws of 1935, went on, after being employed by the British occupying
authorities, to become Adenauer's *éminence grise* in the 1950s. The fact that
he had not provided full disclosure about his activities during the Third
Reich in his denazification questionnaire was only exposed in the 1960s
when the East Germans released incriminating documents about him which
made his contribution to the Nazi state appear graver than had really been
the case. Globke was just the most celebrated example of a very widespread
phenomenon: incorporating civil servants who had worked in the Third
Reich into the new West German state because, the argument ran, it was
better to make use of them than to exclude them. Such people survived if
they adopted the right tone and employed it consistently.[7] And many did so
successfully: in 1952, one third of Bonn's Foreign Ministry officials had been
a Nazi Party member.

Adenauer himself, though he did speak of Jewish victims of Nazism, did not explicitly speak about German perpetrators. Compensation for Eastern European victims of Nazism was ruled out as a matter of course, a stance encouraged by the Cold War context; victims of Nazism in what were now communist countries were directed from Bonn to East Berlin. It was perhaps not surprising, then, that although Adenauer agreed a package of compensation to go to Israel in 1952 (the Luxembourg Agreement), bilateral negotiations to agree compensation packages with Western European states were drawn out and acrimonious. When they were finally concluded in 1965, Chancellor Erhard declared that the postwar era had come to an end.[8] Additionally, West German culture in the 1950s and early 1960s was suffused with images of German suffering, and whilst West Germany was effectively an American protectorate there was little reason for a more self-critical impulse to develop. Thus, Adenauer's brand of Christian Democracy was regarded suspiciously in some quarters less as proof of West Germany's newfound turn to democracy than as a threat to it. His famous firmness (to put it mildly) helped to entrench the CDU's power by besmirching not just the opposition SPD—relatively easy to do until its reforms of 1959—but his own colleagues.

An even more compelling case of what we might politely call 'directed democracy' was to be found in Italy, where the Christian Democrats introduced an election law in 1952 which aimed to give any coalition winning more than 50 per cent of the vote two-thirds of the seats in parliament, thus ensuring a permanent majority. No wonder it was dubbed the *legge truffa*, or 'swindle law'. With 49.85 per cent of the vote in the next election, the Christian Democrats' machinations narrowly failed (by 50,000 votes) to establish this quasi-dictatorship, but, under party secretary Amintore Fanfani, they did not fail to entrench themselves and their network of patronage deeply into the Italian state, creating 'a syndicate of provincial political machines' that ensured grassroots support. As *La Stampa* journalist Vittorio Gorresio sarcastically observed, 'one should give' the DC party bosses who wished to create a closed power system under their domination 'their due for having operated to the best of their abilities for the sanctifying goal of the demochristianization of Italy'.[9]

Indeed, elections are only one marker of the success of the centre right in postwar Europe in entrenching itself as the 'natural' party of government. Christian Democrats succeeded where socialist parties did not in creating some cross-class participation.[10] This was ruefully acknowledged by Togliatti, who observed in a speech in Florence in October 1944 that Catholic organizations had been able 'to exist legally...for nearly twenty years under the fascist regime, and therefore have many cadres who are at this moment going back into political life and are able to work to organise a large party quickly', a party which would include not only the middle classes but also 'working people, even workers, but most of all peasants'.[11] If de Gaulle's reign looked, as one commentator puts it, increasingly 'like a presidential dictatorship', it also 'ensured a level of political continuity and stability unknown under the previous Third and Fourth Republics'.[12] Even so, these conservative parties reaped the benefits of a system that was essentially prepared and acquiesced in by social democrats. In other words, the pressures of the Cold War—especially anti-communism and the drive for economic growth—pushed left and right towards the political and economic centre ground. The same pressures meant that the right, in its new guise as protector of western democracy, convinced most Western European electorates to entrust it with power, as long as they subscribed to this essentially social democratic framework created at the end of the war. This was an antifascism that shared obvious characteristics with the communist variant—the postwar generations' prosperity was regularly held up as the outcome of their parents' wartime sacrifices—but one which was future-oriented, in which the nostrum of economic growth and full employment took precedence over asking too much about what had happened in Western Europe under Nazi occupation.

Integration

Nothing signified the new direction in postwar Western Europe better than the process of integration. Although there had been plans for and visions of European integration before and during the Second World War, only the postwar conditions made what seemed a utopian goal anything like realizable—even if what was realized bore little relation to many of the Resistance movements' dreams of a 'United States of Europe'. From the six states (France, West Germany, Italy, the Netherlands, Belgium, and Luxembourg) that joined together in the European Coal and Steel Community (1951) and the European Economic Community (1957), to the enlargements to nine, ten, twelve, fifteen, and finally twenty-seven countries, the integration process has signalled mobility, the free market in goods, services, and capital, free movement of people between the member states (as of July 1968), and, above all, economic prosperity. That economic success is what has drawn other countries into the orbit of an integrated Europe. The picture of the British, who merely fifteen years earlier talked of being, with 'mighty America', 'the friends and sponsors of the new Europe',[13] coming cap in hand to ask for entry, is proof of the rapidity with which the EEC outperformed its rivals in wealth creation. The European Free Trade Area (EFTA), established by the British in 1959, was simply a customs area incorporating smaller, peripheral European economies, and lacked the clout of the EEC's much larger market.[14] There have always been critical voices—many of them justified, as we will see later—but the perception that economic success rested on a 'return to Europe' has persuaded most Europeans, and certainly most European statesmen, that joining the EEC/EU was their best hope. The states that have stayed out, notably Norway and Switzerland, have been fortunate enough to have their own sources of independent wealth and have been able to trade with the EEC without needing to join it. The so-called 'democratic deficit' within the EEC was tolerated whilst times were good. Only in the last few years has that picture really come under threat, as the financial crisis has strained the credibility not just of the euro but of the EU's operating procedures—its slowness, Kafkaesque bureaucracy (this is something of an unfair caricature), and technocratic elitism. That the EEC was also intended to be more than a customs union, but a new venture in European history that would end Franco-German antagonism and make war in Europe unthinkable, has gradually been forgotten, as one defender of the project notes:

> The EU itself has always been a peculiar kind of monument to the Second World War—not a monument that commemorates battles, but an institutional edifice whose foundations contain the very lessons learnt from the experience of totalitarian war, subjugation and European-wide genocide. It is not simply starry-eyed pro-European propaganda to say that the European Union was constructed as a result of the memory of the war, which animated the likes of Robert Schuman, Konrad Adenauer and Alcide de Gasperi. Nor is it empty rhetoric to point out that politicians such as Helmut Kohl pursued a fusion of European interests on the basis of memories of large-scale violence and atrocity. The fact that these memories often remain hidden behind the language of technocracy and economic benefits does not detract from the actual motives of the founders (and subsequent re-founders) of the European Union.[15]

The history of European integration, however, is more than a unidirectional story of ever closer union and enlargement as more and more states saw the benefits of membership. Rather, if one examines the key moments in the process, they were always given added impetus by something else, something external to the process of European integration in the narrow, technical sense. Where the creation of the Council of Europe (1949) was relatively straightforward, establishing the European Court of Justice, anything involving a pooling of economic or, especially, political resources was bound to be more hotly contested.

Indeed, 'ever closer union', as the preamble to the Treaty of Rome establishing the EEC had it, was a phrase that rapidly got dropped from Community documents, as did the embarrassing name of the High Authority, the supranational body which administered the ECSC. Such suggestions of elite technocracy or the signing away of sovereignty engendered antagonism, not just on the part of de Gaulle, but amongst Europeans in general. So even if the idealists of political federalism, from Jean Monnet in the 1940s and 1950s to Jacques Delors in the 1980s and 1990s, have believed that economic integration would 'spill over' into political union, in actual fact the EEC and even the EU have tended to succeed best where they have permitted the national interests of Europe's nation-states to flourish in concert with one another. The EEC prospered in the context of the economic boom—indeed the boom, the Marshall Plan, and the frameworks established by the ECSC and EEC were mutually reinforcing—and, until the period of Eurosclerosis in the 1970s, no one worried about the fact that the only really integrated common policy was that for agriculture, or about the fact that the Common Agricultural Policy (CAP), finally agreed upon in 1967 after protracted negotiations, was expensive and weighted overwhelmingly in French interests.[16]

What then have been the factors external to the process itself which have worked as the engines of integration? The first and, from today's perspective, most readily overlooked, was fear of war and, in particular, fear of Germany. All the key moments of the EEC/EU's creation and expansion have coincided with crucial moments in the second half of the 'German century'. At the very start of the process (1945–50), when early schemes for integration looked like coming to naught, the issue that 'more or less at the last moment, blew away the fog on the landscape was the reappearance of Germany on the political scene. It was the calendar of German revival that concentrated neighbours' minds and fixed the European breakthrough in May 1950 and not before.'[17] As Sir Oliver Harvey, British ambassador to Paris, observed, the Schuman Plan seemed to the French 'the only chance of preventing exclusive German control of the Ruhr, which to their minds still represents the greatest potential danger to French security'.[18] The negotiations leading to the ECSC took place at the same time as the FRG's creation and debates about whether and how best to permit the rearming of West Germany; the Treaty of Rome came hard on the wars in Suez, Indochina, and Algeria, which heightened the French desire to tie the country more closely to German primary resources; the admission of Britain finally broke de Gaulle's resistance to anything other than an *Europe des patries* based on intergovernmental cooperation (with the exception of the CAP) and led to his reaffirmation of Franco-German unity, a stance continued by Pompidou even as he looked to the UK to temper the new risks associated with *Ostpolitik*; the years of stagnation of the 1970s and 1980s were broken thanks to the Kohl–Mitterrand relationship; and the introduction of the Single European Act at Maastricht (1991) coincided with German unification and new fears of German power at the heart of Europe. Memory politics not only helped to bring about the EEC; they have sustained it ever since—including during its recent crisis, when vituperative echoes of German wartime occupation have been heard in more desperate quarters.

The integration process worked for the Germans too. Not that there was any lack of commitment to the ideal of *Westbindung* (being tied to the west), but the FRG's leaders willingly subscribed to the ECSC and EEC because, more than anything else, doing so legitimized the new state itself. 'Accepting the Schuman Plan and signing the Treaty of Paris', as one historian puts it, 'was the only way to commence their national rehabilitation as an independent sovereign state.'[19] West German enthusiasm for the EEC depended on an equal response from the French, hence Walter Hallstein, first president of the European Commission, saw many of his federalist hopes dashed thanks to de Gaulle. But at this stage, the Commission, which was established to defend the EEC's interests, had no source of funding apart from nation-states', and it was beholden to the Council of Ministers, where real power lay. And this was a body comprised of ministers (usually foreign ministers) from the member states, rather than non-elected supra-governmental representatives. Thus, the early EEC undoubtedly had some federalist foundations, but the significant, visible architecture was provided by the member states, who worked together to protect their own interests. A community which emerged on the back of visions of political integration became reality and achieved success on the basis of economic integration.

It would be strange to explain the readiness of states to enter into this sort of multilateral, international agreement if notions of federalism were

wholly irrelevant.[20] Transnational networks of Christian Democratic elites
were crucial in realizing the ECSC and EEC, with the express aim of
Franco–German reconciliation through political integration.[21] Nevertheless, national interests concretized the plans, and national interests have sustained the EEC/EU ever since, which, despite Schuman's talk of 'European
federation', remains an economic rather than a political union (the response
to the 2011 financial meltdown suggests that some of the EU's elites would
like to use the opportunity to argue that economic union can only work
together with political union, but it will be hard to convince national electorates). The key moments of the union's development, from the creation
and renegotiation of the Common Agricultural Policy to the Maastricht
Treaty and the post-communist accessions, have been driven by national
interests, especially French fear of a newly powerful Germany, far more than
by federalism. From the start, the West Germans, for their part, enthusiastically participated in the European integration project as a way of pouring
'psychological oil on a wounded soul', that is to say, of feeling that, by sitting
at the same negotiating table as one of the victors (albeit only a victor *hon-
oris causa*), West Germany was being readmitted into the family of nations.
For Egon Bahr, later Willy Brandt's foreign policy adviser and one of his
closest collaborators, this newfound acceptance opened up possibilities for
the West Germans that were of far greater significance for the Germans
than for the French.[22] The 'founding fathers', Monnet, Schuman, Spaak, de
Gasperi, and so on, might be cheered by the fact that the union has contributed to keeping Europe in a state of peace since the Second World War
(with the admittedly rather significant exception of Yugoslavia in the 1990s),
but they would soon see that it is economic interdependence that holds
Europe's nation-states together in the EU. Political power in the EU,
throughout the twentieth century and into the twenty-first, resided not in
a supranational European 'state' but in the context of the Council of
Ministers, which means a voluntarily entered into sharing of sovereignty. A
'state' that has a toothless parliament and a shared currency but that cannot
raise taxes or make war is unlikely to replace the European nation-states any
time soon, unless the euro crisis precipitates the EU into the unexpected
zone of fiscal union.[23] This was already clear by the end of the 1960s, when
the closest thing to federalism that one can identify is a renewed commitment to intergovernmental links (as opposed to supranational ones) and,
with the 1970 Werner Report, the establishment of a timetable for economic and monetary union (EMU).

Most histories of European integration are written in isolation from histories of the Cold War, as if the two were in reality entirely separate phenomena. Where the two seem to meet—in the Marshall Plan and the EDC—the failure of each to bring about the kind of supranational arrangements envisaged by the Americans appears to justify their continued separation by scholars.[24] The road to the EEC seems to have had little to do with the early Cold War, just as the European role in working with the Americans, pushing them to maintain a strong presence in Europe, is usually discussed as though it owed little to the discrete history of early moves towards European economic integration.[25]

Yet the two trajectories were not sealed off from one another in this manner. Particularly in the 1960s, when the Western European countries felt firmly established in their newfound prosperity and stability, a good deal of interplay between ostensibly 'European' and 'Cold War' matters is clearly visible. The Dutch, for example, were staunch adherents of Atlanticism, and strongly resisted French moves to coordinate European foreign policy, especially the so-called Fouchet Plan of 1962, which Dutch Foreign Minister Joseph Luns saw as an attempt to disregard the wishes of the other member states and to arrogate some of NATO's responsibilities. They only softened their stance on the occasion of Britain's entry to the EEC in 1973, because the presence of the British would, the Dutch believed, reduce the chances of any shift in policy away from the US. The British decision to try for a second time to join the EEC was itself partly a result of de Gaulle's decision to withdraw France from NATO's command structures in 1966, itself an echo of the 'empty chair' crisis in the EEC of July 1965 to January 1966, when de Gaulle withdrew France from EEC decision-making on the grounds that too many moves towards supranationalism were afoot under the pro-US Hallstein's leadership of the Commission.[26] Indeed, at a press conference on 9 September 1965 de Gaulle accused Hallstein, not without reason, of seeking to create a European super-state and called him the grand master of an 'areopagus of stateless technocrats'.[27] Washington and London came to the conclusion that British membership of the EEC would help to hold the pro-Atlanticist line in Western Europe and mitigate France's obstreperous posturing (that they were right was proven by de Gaulle's 'veto' of British membership for a second time, in 1967). As one West German Economics Ministry official put it, rather hyperbolically: 'If the old rift between the EEC and EFTA reappears and on top of this a new fracture between the Six and America is allowed to develop, the situation can produce only one winner: Khrushchev.'[28] In general, what these examples show is that whilst the Six were increasingly free from dependence on America in the economic sphere, they were not—nor did many want to become so—in the military-security sphere. From the opposite side, the Soviets regarded the EEC as a tool of capitalist aggression and feared the empowerment of West Germany. Even if the EEC's own institutions remained divorced from direct involvement in the Cold War, the very environment in which the notion of Western European integration could take root and flourish was shaped by the east–west conflict. Indeed, the larger framework within which integration developed, that is, the Cold War, may even have smoothed the passage of that process.[29] Crucially, the EEC's commitment to free trade and to economic integration pushed it into the American orbit, with full US support.

The height of the Cold War

Historians have tended to take it for granted that the Second World War was good for Western Europe, and good for Britain especially, in that it brought people together and ushered in the welfare state and the age of prosperity. Yet Europe after the war was at the heart of the Cold War; one cannot explain the rise of welfare capitalism without also seeing it as part of the process whereby Western Europe was tailored to 'fight' for the values of the democratic west. Focusing on the welfare state alone means missing the fact that Western European states, Britain especially—perhaps unsurprisingly, the country where the narrative of the war being good for creating the welfare state is strongest—were also *warfare states*.[30] This period saw the build up of nuclear arms in the UK and France and the stationing of US troops across Western European territory, from Greenland to West Germany. If Britain's postwar welfare state is more accurately labelled a 'military-democratic state' in which 'welfarism went with a particular form of mass warfare',[31] so across Western Europe the political integration of states into the Western Union and then NATO required social democrats as much as Christian Democrats to sign up to continued spending on the military at rates which meant that the military and the industries supporting and supplying it accounted for a considerable portion of GDP.

This large spending on defence should come as no surprise when we consider that the years 1958–63 constituted the 'hottest' phase of the Cold

War. The question is whether defence spending, on nuclear weapons in particular, was a cause or consequence of the Cold War.[32] Certainly that spending, even on the part of leaders such as Eisenhower who aimed to cut military expenditure, or Khrushchev, who in 1960 sought to reduce the size of the Soviet army by 1.2 million men, emboldened the aggressive rhetoric which almost took the world to nuclear disaster. At the same time, NATO's perception that it could not confront the USSR with conventional weapons, especially in the Far East, and the Soviets' similar attitude towards defending Cuba indicates a genuine sense that limited nuclear strikes were regarded as possible options. This shared 'exterminism'—Mutual Assured Destruction—brought the superpowers together in a project that bound them to the 'military-industrial complex', as New Left critics had it. It meant too that whilst ratcheting up the rhetoric could be done carelessly, without consideration of how tactical nuclear strikes could be prevented from escalating into general nuclear war, backing down or calming relations required skill and composure.[33]

The need for such statesmanship soon became apparent after Stalin's death. Despite hopes that a new era might dawn on relations between the two blocs, the arms race, continued Soviet fears of a rearmed West Germany, and intra-bloc conflicts between the Soviets and the Chinese among other factors all conspired to prevent such a pleasing outcome. Instead, in 1958, Karl Jaspers's warning that 'An altogether novel situation has been created by the atom bomb. Either all mankind will physically perish or there will be a change in the moral-political condition of man' looked to be terrifyingly prescient.[34] Resolving first the Berlin Crisis of 1958–61 and then the Cuban Missile Crisis revolved around brinkmanship which, rhetorically in the former, in actuality in the latter, brought the world teetering to the edge of annihilation.[35]

In terms of the Cold War in Europe, the centrality of Germany was no coincidence. Once again, Soviet concerns about security from German aggression were at the fore, this time wrapped up in suspicion about the motives of the 'reactionary bourgeois' forces of NATO. The postwar antifascist settlement seemed to be under grave threat, especially from the Soviets' perspective, and the height of the Cold War turned on what to do about Germany. By the end of the Second Berlin Crisis, with the building of the Berlin Wall, a new order was in place: the two Germanies were recognized as sovereign states fully incorporated into their respective blocs, and the Soviet dream of a unified, demilitarized Germany had been abandoned.[36]

Willy Brandt, who became Chancellor in 1969, signalled a possible way out of this impasse with his *Ostpolitik*, or turning towards the east. Since 1962, the FRG's basic position with respect to the GDR was represented by the Hallstein Doctrine, which said that the recognition of the GDR by any nation other than the USSR would be regarded as an unfriendly act towards the FRG, which would as a result sever diplomatic links. This doctrine had been in place since 1955, when there were still hopes of unification. Over time, it became something of a burden, as it limited the FRG's contacts with other states, and could also be used as a means of retaliation as, for example, when Arab states punished the FRG for recognizing Israel by severing diplomatic links and establishing them with the GDR instead. The US too pushed for a more flexible approach towards the Eastern European states. When the Berlin Wall went up in 1961, the West German leadership realized that its policy of ignoring the east had been rewarded only by failure, and that, if it were to assist the people of the GDR, it would need to deal with the East German regime. As Egon Bahr later said, there should be a Prague Spring in Moscow.

Brandt's policy, initiated on the basis of Bahr's advocacy of 'change through rapprochement', which he had been promoting since 1963, culminated in the signing of the Treaties of Moscow and Warsaw in 1970, which (thanks primarily to Gomułka's fear that the Warsaw Pact's hard-line stance towards the FRG had been compromised by the new policy of openness to the west[37]) recognized the Oder–Neisse Line as Germany's border with Poland, the Treaty of 1971 on Quadripartite control of Berlin, and, most important, the Basic Treaty (*Grundlagenvertrag*) of 1972 between the two Germanies.[38] This established diplomatic ties between the FRG and GDR and promoted cultural and other contacts. Furthermore, it allowed both states to join the UN and led to the establishing of diplomatic ties between the GDR and many western nations, starting with Australia in 1972. This was indeed proof of Kennedy's paradox that in order to change the status quo one first had to recognize it.

Ostpolitik's success was proven by the fact that the policy was maintained by Helmut Kohl and Franz Josef Strauss when the former became Chancellor in 1982 and when the latter, like most of the CDU/CSU opposition, a fierce opponent of the treaty when it was being negotiated on the basis that it constituted a 'capitulation to Moscow and the final acceptance of the division of Germany', approved a loan of 3 billion deutschmarks to the GDR in 1983.[39] Its success in asserting the FRG's autonomy also precipitated the

French change of heart regarding British membership of the EEC, as fears that the Franco-German axis would be sidelined in favour of cooperation with the communist countries made British participation in Europe seem attractive. Britain, for its part, reluctantly accepted the German initiative, with Edward Heath observing that 'Close relationships between Germany and the Soviet Union had seldom been to our advantage in the past.'[40] The Basic Treaty has been credited with beginning the process of disintegration in the GDR which culminated in the events of 1989; whilst, as we will see, other factors played a more significant role in the collapse of communism across Eastern Europe, including in the GDR, nevertheless, the GDR's engagement with West German—and by extension Western European and American—ideas, values, and goods, certainly helped to undermine communism's authority, as the gap between rhetoric and reality became ever harder to disguise. No less important, when Brandt famously fell to his knees in Warsaw on the site of the former ghetto, *Ostpolitik* joined up the politics of the Cold War with dealing with memories of the war, and both *Ostpolitik* and the *Kniefall* were gestures which frightened as many Germans as they enthused. This is why after the turmoil of the late 1960s, the West German

Figure 3. Willy Brandt's *Kniefall*, Warsaw Ghetto Monument, 7 December 1970.

elite changed the focus of *Ostpolitik* 'from a call for open politics to a form of domestic containment'.[41] What is not in doubt is their significance; as the US ambassador to Bonn, Kenneth Rush, claimed: 'The change of government, with the new *Ostpolitik* of the Brandt government, along with Germany's new approach to the West, and her also very important new steps in domestic policies, have created an atmosphere of change and excitement even greater than that of the New Deal thirties in our country.'[42] Perhaps most important, Brandt's gesture made the communists' claim about the Federal Republic being a revanchist, fascist state much harder to sustain.[43]

This uneasy truce between the two Germanies was facilitated by the ending of the Cuban Missile Crisis, which showed the value of negotiation, just as Kennedy had said in his speech to the UN on 25 September 1961. Settling the crisis ushered in a period of détente, in which both sides recognized the other's legitimacy and tacit agreement was reached not to engage NATO and Warsaw Pact forces directly in war or to use nuclear weapons. One could even say that the shock of 1962 brought Moscow and Washington to their senses, and helped to bring about the apparently permanent situation in which the superpower clash 'had been transformed into a non-antagonistic one, a mutually profitable system, to put it bluntly, of hegemonic control over the two halves of Europe'. One can see that, with proxy wars being fought in the Third World, the 'Cold War proper was thus over in its European context'.[44] That did not mean that the threat of mutual assured destruction disappeared altogether; in fact, two decades after the Cuban Missile Crisis, and despite the Strategic Arms Limitation Treaties (SALT I and the draft of SALT II), which called for the dismantling of ICBMs, the world came perilously close to nuclear armageddon, thanks to a little-known crisis of 1983, as we will see in Chapter 6. But from the mid-1960s on, in the narrower, European context, the Cold War was fought more by soft power, especially through cultural means, than through the threat of direct military confrontation. Nothing illustrates this claim more clearly than the crushing of the Prague Spring in 1968, when neither side worried that the other would detach itself from the détente process then in train as a consequence of the invasion.

The process of détente focused on arms limitations and 'confidence-building' between the two sides, and was realized primarily at the talks known as the Helsinki Process. In July 1973 the Conference on Security and Cooperation in Europe (CSCE) opened in Helsinki with all the protagonists except Albania represented. After two years of discussions aimed at improving east–west relations, the original aims of *Ostpolitik* were writ large in the Helsinki Final Act, signed in August 1975. Apart from recognizing the postwar map of Europe, it appeared that the Soviets were the primary beneficiaries of the accords. Although, as has been insightfully pointed out, the only country that had invaded another state involved in the Helsinki discussions was the Soviet Union—twice, in fact, in 1956 and 1968—the Soviets were very keen to include the clause specifying that 'all armed intervention or threat of such intervention against another participating state' should be forsworn.[45] What this indicates is not so much a lack of self-awareness on the part of the Soviets as a belief that the Western Allies had sold them out and reneged on the postwar settlement, especially by rearming West Germany. Indeed, the US and its allies signed in order to reassure the Soviets that they were not about to invade them.

But what both sides had not predicted was that other, apparently less-important clauses in the accords would come to assume vital significance. After Moscow reluctantly signed up to the human rights clauses of the Helsinki Final Act, the unexpected effects of doing so contributed powerfully to consciousness-raising not only among intellectuals and dissidents but also 'ordinary people' and communist elites. The principle of respect for human rights first appeared as Principle 7 of Basket I's ten basic principles.[46] It was then expanded on in 'Basket III', where the relevant clauses enjoined the signatories to respect 'human rights and fundamental freedoms, including the freedom of thought, conscience, religion or belief' and to reaffirm the 'equal rights and self-determination of peoples'. They went further, and asserted the 35 states' commitment to 'promote and encourage the effective exercise of civil, political, economic, social, cultural and other rights and freedoms' and to 'recognise and respect the freedom of the individual to profess and practice, alone or in community with others, religion or belief acting in accordance with the dictates of his own conscience'.[47] Such words, considered empty sloganeering by the signatories themselves, were soon picked up by citizens of the communist countries, who pointed to them as evidence that the communists' ideals were some distance from the reality of the states over which they presided. They were, indeed, 'hoist by the petard of their own cynicism' and, in a moment of carelessness, or believing that they were immune to such vulnerabilities, had 'inadvertently opened a breach in their own defences'.[48]

The Final Act might on the face of things have legitimized the status quo, but it 'left open the possibility of domestic and international change'.[49]

Groups sprang up whose aim was to monitor the communist states' adherence to the principles to which they had signed up, including the Moscow
Helsinki Watch Committee, Charter 77 in Czechoslovakia, and the Workers'
Defence Committee (KOR) in Poland, a forerunner of Solidarity. Such
movements were initially suppressed, yet, as Iurii Andropov, the head of the
KGB, admitted in 1976, 'the enemy who does not take note of his failures
constituting an "internal opposition", continues to pursue his action in the
same fashion', particularly with the intention of 'put[ting] pressure onto the
Soviet government concerning the implementation of the Helsinki
accords'.[50] The result was that the ideals of the Helsinki Final Act gradually
seeped into the consciousnesses of the communist rulers themselves as their
failure to live up to the accords' demands left them hostage to criticism; and,
a little later, they would play a key role in the formation of Mikhail Gorbachev's reformist mindset.[51]

The impact of human rights ideas on the internal politics and external
reputation of Eastern European communism—the aptly named 'Helsinki
effect'—reminds us that ideas were as crucial to the Cold War as were
nuclear weapons, international treaties, and politicians' grandstanding.[52]
Ideas do not float freely, but are anchored very firmly in real life and one
cannot easily separate out 'ideas' from their 'effects'. The idea of 'mutual
assured destruction' (MAD) was more real for most Europeans than actual
weapons, with which most citizens had no contact; and more or less propa-
gandizing representations of the 'other side' were instrumental both in
demonizing and, for more critical minds, intriguing ordinary people as to
the reality of life in the other, mostly inaccessible half of the continent. Thus,
we should not be surprised to find that the Cold War was very much a war
of ideas, and that it was fought on the cultural front as much as, if not more
than, the diplomatic or military front. Since real war in an age of nuclear
weapons would have been disastrous, the role of the propaganda war assumed
even greater shape. Indeed, the point where the purely 'military' ends and
where the 'cultural' begins is hard to discern, for all aspects of the Cold War,
from its beginning to the processes of détente in the 1970s to its ending,
were based on 'intelligence' and often wildly off the mark ideas about the
nature of the enemy.

That said, a great deal is now known about what has come to be called
the 'cultural Cold War'. The height of the Cold War coincided with the
emergence of the age of mass communication, especially via film and television, as well as older mediums such as radio. 'Virtually everything', therefore,

'from sport to ballet to comic books and space travel, assumed political significance and hence potentially could be deployed as a weapon both to shape opinion at home and to subvert societies abroad.'[53] From the Soviet side, Agitprop and the Cominform were used to try and promote communist ideas in the west, whilst the major sources of explicitly political western propaganda came from the Americans, with institutions such as the Voice of America or Radio Free Europe radio stations.

Among the best known of such institutions was the Congress for Cultural Freedom (CCF, founded 1950), a body which exemplifies the Cold War's intellectual battlegrounds. It fought against Stalinist propaganda and advocated liberal democracy and, most infamously, it was funded by the CIA.[54] Founded by the author Arthur Koestler and the journalist Melvin J. Lasky, it counted among its members such luminaries of European liberalism as Raymond Aron, Daniel Bell, Ignazio Silone, Stephen Spender, Karl Jaspers, and Willy Brandt, and its journals, such as *Encounter*, *Quadrant*, and *Cuardernos*, were widely read and held in high regard across the world. For such intellectuals, their anti-communism followed naturally from their antifascism, and they therefore tended to admire the notion of totalitarianism which was such a powerful tool of Cold War historical and political analysis.[55] Their key aim was to persuade the non-communist left to align itself with mainstream European liberalism as represented by Christian Democratic and conservative parties. It did so by advocating an American-style liberal-progressivism which could easily encompass the main facets of the postwar social democratic consensus. And, most importantly, it sought to expose the myths of communist egalitarianism, as in the book *The God That Failed*, edited by Labour MP Richard Crossman in 1950, in which former communists such as Koestler explained how they came to the realization that the faith-like structure of Stalinism had blinded them for so long to the brutal and hypocritical realities.[56] Whilst it is hard to measure the CCF's success directly, it seems to have influenced the SPD's decision to adopt its Bad Godesberg programme in 1959, C. A. R. Crosland's important work of socialist revisionism, *The Future of Socialism* (1956), as well as helping to develop a pro-Atlanticist stance across Western Europe. Nevertheless, the CCF 'could not present a playwright better than Brecht, a composer as popular as Prokofiev or Shostakovich, a ballet company superior to the Bolshoi, instrumentalists more skilled than Richter, Oistrakh, or Rostropovich, ensemble acting more subtle than the Moscow Art Theatre's, or, with the single exception of Bobby Fischer, chess players to compete with the

Soviet grandmasters'.[57] 'Culture' on its own cannot explain the course of the Cold War.

Other organizations were led by the Europeans, at least in the initial stages of the Cold War, such as Britain's Cultural Relations Department, the World Assembly of Youth, or the international Bilderberg Group. These tended to be reactive, established in response to Soviet initiatives which already existed. They also tended to have a different focus from American initiatives. But Americanization in the broader sense was far more important for developing the Western European sphere, in particular in making its attachment to the US into an emotional bond based on shared notions of freedom, consumerism, and lifestyle symbols, than was American proselytizing to the Eastern Bloc. And whilst high art in Western Europe could come dressed in a patrician anti-Americanism, especially in France, in fact high culture (music, opera, art, and theatre) was also an important site of more or less overt intervention, although here we see the limits of state interference.[58]

The Vietnam War to some extent reduced American influence in Western Europe, with the CIA itself recognizing that its policies in Vietnam 'will plague us for many years to come' where American standing in Europe was concerned.[59] Indeed, it was at the same time, when its reputation was at its nadir, that the CIA came to realize that offering financial support to cultural movements was inherently problematic. The demise of the CCF, for example, came in 1966–7 when *Ramparts*, a New Left magazine, and the *New York Times* both revealed that it had been bankrolled by the CIA. Nevertheless, American goods and products were just as fundamental in reshaping Western Europe, and in shaping Eastern Europeans' aspirations, as were American values, irrespective of whether the US itself upheld or was believed to have upheld them.

Decolonization

The wider context for Vietnam protests was the rise of the New Left, the Civil Rights Movement, and the generational shift that brought a critical gaze to bear on the baby-boomers' parents. The appeal of this intellectual package should not be exaggerated—far more youngsters were interested in cars and fashion than in critical theory—yet it did mobilize quite large numbers and it undoubtedly had a profound effect on the cultural milieu.

Particularly prominent in this set of ideas was a 'third-worldism' which looked for inspiration less to the canon of western Marxism (Marx, Engels, Lenin) than to the anti-imperialist communist leaders Che Guevara, Fidel Castro, and Mao. The idolization of such men was deeply problematic, and many affluent young radicals in the west presumably had little sense or real understanding of the disasters that Mao in particular was perpetrating on his countrymen in the name of progress (as later with Pol Pot, whose 'communism' was blended with elements of Nazism). But the wider message of anti-imperialism was one which resonated deeply, and lent support to indigenous national liberation movements across the European empires. And in understanding decolonization, it was the force of these movements, not support for them from newly empowered leftist movements or the decisions made by European governments, which was to prove really decisive.

Adorno's warning about the continued existence of Nazism was startlingly echoed in the writings of anti-colonial thinkers such as Aimé Césaire, Frantz Fanon, and Albert Memmi. Although many of the overseas colonies, such as Singapore, Malaya, and the Dutch East Indies, were occupied during the war, the European powers considered it their right to reassert their rule at the conclusion of the conflict, albeit within new frameworks such as the 1942 Dutch Commonwealth, announced by the Dutch government-in-exile in London, or the 1946 French Union, which admitted the need for a more sensitive handling of colonial subjects. But the fine words were not matched by deeds; in fact, the postwar colonial state was 'one that claimed to be liberal while deploying force to defend what were seen to be key geostrategic interests'.[60] Unsurprisingly, then, newly empowered colonial subjects objected and, in one of the more remarkable phenomena of postwar history, the decolonization process became an unstoppable force. Where Adorno saw the persistence of Nazism within democracy as especially threatening, anti-imperialist critics saw the survival of empire in an age of antifascist democracy as equally troubling. It presented a paradox no less severe than the American one of defeating fascism in the name of democracy, but with segregated troops. Decolonization had taken place before the Second World War (Brazil in 1830, for example, or the creation of the United States), but the year 1960 brought European colonial history—barring a few exceptions—to a close, at least in the formal sense (informal empire and exploitative relationships did not end). In the process, the West European self-image as civilized, progressive, and modern was severely tried, and West European confidence in its military prowess was shattered.

The British decolonization process was neither as peaceful nor ordained from above as the official (and popular) narrative would have us believe. The dirty wars in Malaya and, especially, Kenya, in both of which the police and army employed methods that had been used to combat Jewish terrorism in Palestine, and the aftermaths of empire in India/Pakistan and Palestine give the lie to the notion that the British exit from empire was a 'graceful' process. Instead, it suggests that the majority of colonized peoples resented their position, that the British were reluctant decolonizers, and that underhand and at times illegal tactics which British commentators would have regarded as 'foreign' (that is, unpleasant and brutal), were widely used.[61] Still, the shameful abandonment of the Belgian Congo (Zaire) in 1960, and the wars in Indochina and, especially, Algeria, were of a different order from the active role played by the British in their decolonization processes—if one leaves to one side violence that resulted from but was not directly committed by the British, such as that which accompanied the Partition of India.

In some cases, decolonization was spurred on by wider international developments. At the end of the war, for example, the Dutch sought to reimpose control over the Dutch East Indies, sending 170,000 troops to achieve that aim. Following the ravages of the war, most Dutch policymakers now foresaw a new colonial relationship along the lines of a more harmonious commonwealth.[62] But believing that their actions were enhancing Soviet prestige in the region, the Truman administration pressurized the Dutch—by threatening to withhold Marshall Aid—into abandoning their recolonization project. Unable to resist, the Dutch conceded, and Indonesia became independent in 1949. Indonesia would go on to host the Bandung Conference in April 1955, at which 23 countries—'the underdogs of the human race', as Richard Wright called them—proclaimed their membership of the 'non-aligned movement', an attempt to step out of the Cold War framework.[63] Most significant, as we will see, the conference also made a strong analogy between colonialism and Nazism, and stressed its support for France's North African colonies in their aspirations for independence.

Elsewhere, colonial powers proved more reluctant to let go of their possessions. Belgium saw the Congo—despite talk of a 'Belgian-Congolese Federation'—as a cash cow that would prop up Belgium's feeble postwar economy and invested heavily in mining in the 1950s. The rapid abandonment of the country in 1960 only occurred when the Belgians accepted that they could ill afford to sustain the kind of all-out warfare that would be required to hold on to a territory the size of Western Europe. The British and French, in league with Israel, failed spectacularly to retake the Suez Canal, following Nasser's annexation of it in July 1956, although this result occurred thanks to American pressure more than military deficiencies. It was after Suez that Harold Macmillan accepted that Britain's remaining colonies were a drain on resources, and led to his famous 'Winds of Change' speech in South Africa in February 1960. The French, although they were more willing in some cases than others to untie the strings, proved fiercely tenacious in the cases of Indochina and Algeria.

When the French army surrendered at Dien Bien Phu in May 1954, and lost Indochina after five years of war, Algeria was the only remaining colony of significance for the French. In fact, it was not formally a colony at all but part of metropolitan France, split into three Departments (Oran, Algiers, and Constantine) and returning deputies to the National Assembly in Paris. Thus, it was all the more galling that the Algerians rejected the benefits of French civilization. This rejection was partly based on cultural differences but, above all, the vast economic disparities between *colons* (French settlers) and Algeria's Muslim population were to blame for alienating and enraging Algerian families and driving them into the arms of the FLN and Messali Hadj's MNA (*Mouvement National Algérien*).[64] The FLN itself cleverly exploited the opportunities offered by the emergence of the non-aligned movement, by announcing in September 1958 the creation of a government-in-exile, accredited by Tunis and Cairo.[65]

The 'war' was truly a dirty war. Even when the centre left under Guy Mollet was in power (1956–7), the level of aggression was ratcheted up, with nearly half a million conscripts being sent to Algeria and their tasks becoming ever more ruthless. The war saw the use of torture—the army was condemned as 'your Gestapo in Algeria' (*Votre Gestapo d'Algérie*) as early as January 1955 by Claude Bourdet in *France-Observateur*—and Hubert Beuve-Méry, editor of *Le Monde*, asserted that 'From now on Frenchmen must know that they no longer have exactly the same right to condemn in words identical to ten years ago the destroyers of Oradour and the torturers of the Gestapo.'[66] Although such hard-hitting claims did not immediately resonate with the broad public, the sensational publication of communist activist Henri Alleg's experiences at the hands of the French army in his book *La Question* (1958) made the comparison between the army and the Nazis harder to brush off as the typical hyperbole of Trotskyites.[67] Indeed, Jean-Paul Sartre's preface to Alleg's book insisted that torture was by no means the incidental result of a few sadists; rather, '[t]orture is imposed by the circumstances and required by racial hatred; in some ways it is the essence of the conflict and expresses its deepest truth.'[68] As Francis Jeanson, one of the *porteurs de valise*, the French runners for the FLN, put it, 'It was France which betrayed its own values.'[69]

Most significant, the war precipitated a crisis in the Fifth Republic when the OAS (*Organisation de l'Armée Secrète*), which thought of itself as a 'national resistance' and which therefore believed torture to be quite justified, twice came close to unleashing civil war in France, in May 1958 and in April 1961. In the first instance, new Prime Minister Pierre Pflimlin's call for negotiations led to insurgents seizing power in Algiers and invading Corsica. The situation was only saved thanks to Pflimlin keeping his cool and, having won a vote of confidence on 13 May, waiting for de Gaulle to form his new government (in which Pflimlin remained until 1962)—an act which constituted in effect a *coup d'état*.[70] The generals' failure did not prevent the massive loss of life in Algeria, the notorious cover up of the massacre of Algerians in Paris during the pro-FLN demonstration of 17 October 1961 (in which the chief of the Paris police, Maurice Papon, had previously been responsible, in his capacity as secretary general of the Bordeaux police, for the deportation of over 1,000 Jews), or the migration of over one million French settlers (*pieds noirs*) back to mainland France in the wake of Algerian independence a year later, not to mention the sad fate of the so-called *harkis*, those Algerians who had fought for France and ended up in isolated estates in mainland France after 1962.[71]

The dates of these dramatic events indicate that de Gaulle's return to office in 1958 and the creation of the Fifth Republic were not in themselves the cause of the end of conflict in Algeria, even though Algeria was the cause of the collapse of the Fourth.[72] There would be four more years of fighting, and only when the costs to France, financial and in terms of prestige, threatened to become overwhelming, did de Gaulle break with the Fourth Republic's policy towards Algeria. He advocated Algerian self-determination from as early as September 1959, and was backed by 75 per cent of French voters in a referendum of 8 January 1961; but it still took many more months—accompanied, ironically, by a radicalization of the violence—until the French finally pulled out. Despite the apparent resolution provided by the terms of the Evian Agreement (March 1962), the chaotic events between the signing of the accord and the declaration of Algerian independence on 3 July revealed that popular feeling amongst Muslim Algerians backed an FLN-led purge of Algerian territory: one million settlers and 130,000 *harki* families fled to France.[73] In response, the OAS almost assassinated de Gaulle in August 1962 and, over the longer term, the *pieds noirs* returnees poisoned French politics by forming the backbone of the *Front National*, thus continuing the anti-Dreyfusard and Vichyite tradition, now dressed up as a defence of the republic against Muslim 'swamping'.

These events help set Frantz Fanon's violent anti-colonial tirades into a meaningful context. When he wrote that 'In the colonial context the settler only ends his work of breaking in the native when the latter admits loudly and intelligibly the supremacy of the white man's values. In the period of decolonization, the colonized masses mock at these very values, insult them and vomit them up,' Fanon was merely echoing the reality of the decolonization struggle.[74] It remains noteworthy, though, that some anti-colonial commentators, such as Pierre Bourdieu and Mouloud Feraoun, who scoffed at the French project of 'integration' as, ultimately, chauvinist and racist, nevertheless resisted the sort of chiliasm and nationalism associated with Fanon, and hoped to salvage something from the Franco-Algerian conjunction. 'Have they', Feraoun asked of FLN 'liberators' before his murder by the OAS, 'considered for a moment that their "violence" will engender more "violence", will legitimize it, and will hasten its terrible manifestation?'[75]

More shocking is that these events barely resonated with most Europeans, who viewed them, if they thought about them at all, as somehow unrelated to their own concerns. Such people are exemplified by the protagonists of Georges Perec's novella *Les Choses* (*Things*), who move to Algeria for adventure and for a better quality of life, and who do not even notice when dramatic events unfold in front of their very eyes. But if the decolonization process was traumatic and violent for those involved, it soon became apparent that it was economically beneficial for Europeans to reap the benefits of trade and other links with former colonial countries without having the expense of maintaining a military or civil presence. The exception was Portugal; in a reversal of the experience of the other colonial powers' experiences, the military was responsible for forcing the hand of the authoritarian government in the colonial metropole, Lisbon. Their actions began the process that saw the end of dictatorship in Portugal as well as independence for the Portuguese colonies (although, for Angola especially, this would usher in several decades of vicious warfare). In the Portuguese case, the demise of empire thus needs to be accounted for in the context of the transition from dictatorship to democracy, as part of a wider trend in Southern Europe in the mid-1970s.

Southern Europe

As we have seen, the Iberian dictatorships survived the Second World War and, following a few years of isolation, became firmly, if awkwardly, tied to the European and Atlantic organizations which shaped the western half of the continent. In the first decades after 1945, both Salazar and Franco benefited from the Cold War, being permitted to repress their own populations internally whilst enjoying many of the fruits of international collaboration. Nevertheless, that same international collaboration contributed to the internal changes in Spanish and Portuguese society which helped finally to bring down the last of the Western European authoritarian regimes. There is no timetable for democracy, and if the presence of these dictatorships in the heart of the postwar liberal order seems paradoxical, one should simply bear in mind the *realpolitik* that effectively denied Spain's and Portugal's people the fruits of the defeat of fascism: in 1960, President Dwight Eisenhower said of the Salazar regime that: 'Dictatorships of this type are sometimes necessary in countries whose political institutions are not so far advanced as ours,'[76] a statement that spoke to American support for Portugal and its colonies in return for access to military bases on the Azores.

It is necessary to distinguish the two dictatorships, however. Salazar's Portugal was repressive, but the worst of the violence was displaced to Portugal's colonies, which served as a kind of safety valve, diverting the poor away from the metropole and from dangerous rejectionist politics. Franco's Spain was an altogether different beast. The end of the civil war did not see the end of repression. Far from it, in fact, as the regime effectively continued the war on the defeated. In other words, Francoism 'stands out because of the lasting toxicity of its original legitimating strategy, which actively created tens of thousands of perpetrators and maintained their ideological mobilization throughout the four decades of the regime, giving rise to an afterlife of violence that still burns the social and political landscape of twenty-first century Spain'.[77]

Change did come to Spain in the two decades before Franco's death, though it was painful and slow. The central claim of Franco's regime—embodied so brashly at the vast Valley of the Fallen mausoleum complex—was to have arrested time, to have created the 'true Spain'. In reality, the surface unanimity could not be sustained, although the regime penetrated deeply into Spaniards' consciousnesses and did change the way Spanish society functioned.[78] What this meant was that, throughout the postwar period, Spain was a 'regime that was at war with its own society'; Francoism succeeded by enjoying what we might call the 'largesse through neglect' of the west and, domestically, because those who were on the winning side in the civil war ensured the permanently downgraded status of the defeated, through discriminatory access (or not) to welfare, education, and the state's services and patrimony. Here the postwar antifascist consensus was replaced by a 'consensus' of the rulers, whereby ultra-nationalism would prop up the regime at home and anti-communism would do the same on the international stage. Franco's international backers, like Salazar's and post-civil war Greece's, were blind to the changes in civil society that were taking place just under the surface.

This set-up began to show cracks in the 1960s. The failures of Franco's policy of autarky meant that some economic reforms were necessary. The new industrialization that resulted had the consequence of tearing apart the traditional fabric of Spanish society, reshaping the working class. Despite the best efforts of the Opus Dei technocrats appointed by Franco to keep economics separate from social change, the working class, along with increasingly agitated nationalist movements in Catalonia and the Basque Country, and a tentatively more vocal student movement, soon gave rise in Spain to a very marked disparity between 'a dynamic society and a fossilized regime'.[79] When students in Paris and Rome faced down the police, they were—despite the famous fatalities—not generally endangering their lives or at risk of long-term imprisonment. The students who protested in Madrid, Oviedo, and Granada in 1968 were really sticking their necks out. As one British diplomat noted, 'With the evident intention of reminding students that Spain was different from France, the Supreme Court had earlier issued a statement drawing attention to decrees of 1938 and 1939 which outlawed Communism and imposed heavy prison sentences on those who indulged in Communist activities.'[80] Despite these dynamic forces, together with others, such as the impact of northern European tourists on Spanish mores from the 1960s onwards, perhaps the biggest force for change came from within the regime itself.

In December 1973, Admiral Luis Carrero Blanco, acting head of the government and the nearest thing to a natural successor to Franco, was assassinated by the Basque separatist organization ETA. This could not have come at a worse moment for the regime, with Franco seriously ill and the regime faltering thanks to the effects of the oil crisis, which only emphasized the gulf between the culturally and socially mobile new working and middle classes and the defenders of Francoism—still quite a large section of Spanish society, including the army—who wanted to believe that they were the bearers of the authentic face of Spain.

The possibility of bloodshed was very real in Spain after 1973. That it did not come to violence is thanks largely to the actions of Adolfo Suárez, the former Falangist who stole a march on the extreme right—the so-called 'bunker'—thanks to his apparently impeccable credentials, and on the left thanks to his insider status. King Juan Carlos's support was also invaluable; having been more or less in Franco's pocket, the 'bunker' regarded the king as proof of their security, and thus Suárez was able to introduce his reforms by stealth, so to speak. But if Suárez's machinations were key, it is also the case that he was, to some extent, pushing at an open door: Spain by the late 1960s was 'a society "in waiting", both for its urban and cultural diversity, but also because its most dynamic business sectors were already looking to Europe as a guarantee of continuing opportunities for growth'.[81] Nevertheless, although Spain is often lauded for the bloodlessness of its *ruptura pactada* ('negotiated break') with Francoism, it was also part of Suárez's legacy that the perpetrators were to remain untouchable. The left accepted the deal, most notably the Amnesty Law of October 1977, because it had little choice; 'it was the price of transition in a country where a still largely pro-Francoist military establishment risked having the last word.'[82] In other words, 'widespread social fear' was the necessary basis for the 'pact of silence' to work in Spain.[83]

Although the possibility of violence was greater in Spain, it was Portugal where the transition to democracy would be chaotic and confused. Salazar's regime was sustained not just by its cosying up to the West—it was a member of NATO—but by the outlet provided by the colonies for an otherwise very poor society—and by the fortuitous discovery of oil off the coast of Angola. But it was also a regime that was less at odds with postwar Western European norms than was Franco's, and one that came to power peacefully to boot. Domestic repression at the hands of the PIDE, the political police, was certainly part of the deal, but this was not a society on a war footing, as was the case in post-civil war Spain. Portugal could be stabilized in poverty thanks to the Angolan oil revenues, and the poor could be packed off in large numbers to the colonies or to work in the booming Western European economies. The country may have experienced a 'golden age' of growth in the 1960s like the rest of Western Europe, but institutionally, it remained quite static: 'one can say that the "industrialists" and "free-traders" had the upper hand, but the presence of "ruralist", protectionist and colonialist lobbies was very clear.'[84]

But if violence was not the norm in metropolitan Portugal, it certainly was in the Portuguese colonies of Guinea, Angola, and Mozambique, with which the mother country was at war from 1961, trying to fend off national liberation movements. For thirteen years, the army had been fighting an unwinnable war and many in the military were reluctant to carry on. Still, the army's actions were remarkable, even if Salazar's successor, Marcelo Caetano, did not exactly do much to rein the army in, with his limited reforms after 1968. Given the west's toleration of the Iberian dictatorships—not merely through Cold War *realpolitik* but out of a 'colonial' sense that these were 'backward' countries which needed firm leadership—it was therefore all the more surprising that the army, an institution not usually at the vanguard of progressive thought, was responsible for promoting a new thinking. As Colonel Vasco Gonçalves said in June 1975:

> The same forces that oppressed the peoples of the former territories under Portuguese administration also oppressed the Portuguese people. It is with great modesty and humility that we must say, without ambiguities, that the struggle of the colonial peoples against Portuguese fascism also aided our liberation from the same fascism.[85]

The *Movimento das Forças Armadas* (MFA) entered Lisbon on 25 April 1974 and brought an immediate end to the Salazar/Caetano regime.

Thus, as well as contributing to European prosperity in general, both economically and morally, decolonization in Portugal also helped to bring about the passage from dictatorship to democracy in that country—though not in Lusophone Africa—at the same time as the dictatorship in Spain was also coming to its negotiated end. Indeed, the actions of the MFA encouraged Suárez to take the initiative in Spain, lest revolutionary forces make the running, just as they influenced the course of events in Greece. Although the transition was more complex than in Spain, with a series of coups and countercoups, the radicalized junior officers of the MFA, in league with the Portuguese Communist Party, carried through some serious reforms on the land and in the banking system (which was nationalized). Eventually the claim of the right that these reforms were icebreakers for communism was exposed as absurd and, although many in the military switched their allegiances, the military supervision of the restoration of democracy in late 1975 and, not long afterwards, the smooth coming to power of a socialist government under Mario Soares, indicated that the old elites had made their peace with the moderate coalition that drove the transition process and saw no possibility of reviving the *Estado Novo*.[86] US Secretary of State Henry Kissinger's remark that 'there is a 50 per cent chance of losing it [Portugal]' was exposed as Cold War scaremongering.[87]

Greece was a somewhat different story, at least until 1967. The civil war left a deep suspicion of the left and, although the country was nominally a democracy, its conservative leaders ruled in the name of order. They were rewarded by the west with NATO membership (1952) and substantial Marshall Aid money, and by having a thoroughly pro-American and antidemocratic army heavily underpinned by NATO support. Constantine Karamanlis's National Radical Union (formerly the Greek Rally Party under Marshal Alexander Papagos) won elections in 1956, 1958, and 1961 with military support. Under Karamanlis, Greece was poor and corrupt, the left was suppressed, and the army had a huge influence over public affairs, especially in the context of Greece's long-running dispute with Turkey over Cyprus. But, from the NATO point of view, if Greece was not exactly a functioning liberal democracy, it was politically reliable.

Change came in 1963 when the right lost the general election to the left-wing Progressive Centre Union with communist support, and then in 1965 alone. The right, especially the military, was implacably opposed to any reform and condemned the new government as communist, and attacked it for allowing UN peace-keepers onto Cyprus. It was unconstitutionally dismissed by the king. New elections were set for 1967 but, fearing another, larger victory by the Centre Union, a military coup took place in April 1967. The king's failed countercoup eight months later led to his exile in Rome, in which he remained. Greece would be run by the colonels' junta for seven years. Far from being on the verge of a coup, it seems that the left was utterly surprised by the actions of the military; this didn't stop the junta from claiming to be the defenders of 'Helleno-Christian civilization'. As Pattakos put it at a ceremony in 1968:

> Young people of Greece...You have enfolded Greece in your breasts and your creed is the meaning of sacrifice, from the time of the 'Come and get them' of Leonidas, later of the 'I shall not give you the city' of Constantine Palaiologos, of the 'No' of Metaxas and, finally, of the 'Halt or I shoot' of 21 April 1967...Today's ceremony is a re-baptism in the well springs of ancestral tradition; an expression of the national belief that the race of the Greeks is the greatest and best under the sun.[88]

Unsurprisingly, Greece's NATO allies were not keen to do anything about the situation, other than to mouth the occasional condemnation of the authoritarian constitution. Despite some misgivings among certain members, notably the Scandinavian countries, the organization as a whole took the line advocated by the Americans and the British, typified by British MP Eldon Griffiths's comment in a February 1969 report on Greece: 'Anything that were to cast doubt on NATO's commitment to Greece, or that jeopardised the confidence and enthusiasm of the Greek nation for the Atlantic Alliance, could put at risk the best interest of every one of our countries. To suspend Greece in a fit of self-righteousness would be to cut off our noses to spite our faces.'[89] Dictatorship in Greece, in other words, was preferable to undermining Greece and allowing the threat of communism into Western Europe via NATO's south-eastern border.

The regime of colonels Georgios Papadopoulos, Nikolaos Makarezos, and Stylianos Pattakos was brutal. Socially very conservative—long hair, for example, was banned—the regime won support in the countryside but, with its policies of economic inwardness, lost support from the urban middle class who might otherwise have sympathized with a military government that kept communism at bay. Within a few years things got tougher for the colonels; inflation rose, students demonstrated, and Greece was becoming internationally isolated: it was expelled from the Council of Europe in December 1969 and the EC broke off talks in February 1970. Above all there was trouble with Cyprus. Fittingly, the Cyprus question ensured that a junta which espoused the virtues of social Darwinism would be tested and found wanting by its own measure.

As a result of events in Cyprus, with growing tension between the Greek and Turkish populations, the junta split, and hard-liner Brigadier Dimitris Ioannides took over in November 1973. Ioannides' plan for a union of Cyprus with Greece, instead of independence as demanded by the island's constitutional leader Archbishop Makarios III, failed and led to a Turkish invasion of the north of the island in July 1974 which partitioned Cyprus. Backing away from outright war with Turkey, and in the face of US pressure designed to prevent war between the two NATO members, the colonels lost face and popular support. The return of 'normal' politicians was not long in coming.[90]

Karamanlis returned from exile in France to become PM, at the head of his New Democracy movement. A referendum on the monarchy rejected the king's return, and Karamanlis headed the government until the PASOK victory under the populist Andreas Papandreou in 1981. Power transferred smoothly to the socialists and Greece appeared to have entered a period of stable parliamentary rule, with the influence of the military much reduced after its 1974 debacle, and the king unable to interfere. In 1981 Greece resumed the political course from which it was rudely interrupted by the colonels in 1967.

The bravery of the Spanish students who protested in 1968 reminds us that in certain countries, demonstrating against the government could be a dangerous business. That was not usually the case, however, in the most famous of all the 1968 student uprisings: the 'French May', Italy, and West Germany.

1968

The year 1968 was one of revolt across the world, from Mexico to China. In the west, discontent with prosperity came from critics of consumerism, who believed that the 'culture industry' was being cynically employed by elites to 'buy off' the masses and keep them politically quiescent. Conservatives trod a delicate balance between anti-communism (as in the Congress for Cultural Freedom) and anti-Americanization, with the latter usually losing out, but not without generating a substantial repertoire of distaste for supposed American vulgarity and brashness, as if a continent that had recently destroyed itself had a claim to greater civilization. 'The idea that after this war life will continue "normally"', wrote Adorno, 'or even that culture might be "rebuilt"—as if the rebuilding of culture were not already its negation—is idiotic.'[91] The rise of the New Left, which rejected orthodox Marxism-Leninism in favour of the Third World and drew its theoretical inspiration from Herbert Marcuse, Guy Debord, and Marshall McLuhan rather than Lenin and Stalin, was predicated on this dismissal of postwar culture, which it regarded as a continuation of fascism by other means. Student protestors in particular fought not only against poor conditions in the universities—though these provided good cause for grievance—but against what they perceived as the spiritually deadening effects of materialism. Hence student leader Rudi Dutschke could argue that:

> Our life is more than money. Our life is thinking and living. It's about us, and what we could do in this world...It is about how we could use technology

and all the other things which at the moment are used against the human being... My question in life is always how we can destroy things that are against the human being, and how we can find a way of life in which the human being is independent of a world of trouble, a world of anxiety, a world of destruction.[92]

Student rebellions in France, West Germany, Italy, and even Britain in 1968 were the revolts of a generation that had never known war and its compromises; they were attempts to overthrow the mores of their parents' generation which, they believed, had failed to prevent or, worse, collaborated with fascism. The disjunction between the conservative cultural atmosphere of Western Europe in the 1950s and 1960s and the burgeoning consumer society, with its unprecedented excess wealth and leisure time, was no longer sustainable. The 'children of Marx and Coca-Cola' were beneficiaries and critics of the postwar consensus. But despite being condemned by Raymond Aron as players in a mere 'psychodrama', the students' desire for revolutionary change was real.

Such desires did not come from nowhere. The generational cohort that formed the New Left was descended intellectually from the social movements of the 1950s, such as the Campaign for Nuclear Disarmament in Britain and international peace organizations such as the World Peace Council. These were groups that were seeking 'to build not another Military Force but a Third Camp or a Third Way', as American peace activist Abraham Muste put it.[93] This campaigning was joined with a distaste for the 'imperialist' politics of both sides in the Cold War—symbolized most clearly by the invasion of Hungary and the Suez Crisis in 1956—and an admiration for the new manifestations of rebellious youth culture, especially rock 'n' roll, proletarian street culture (Teddy Boys and *Halbstarken*), and beat poetry.[94] The rise of the Civil Rights Movement in the US, the 'Third Worldist' critiques of western imperialism, and, especially, the Vietnam War, all galvanized student activism in the years before 1968. Western European students were also in contact with their counterparts in Eastern Europe (of whom more in Chapter 4), being influenced, especially, by the 'Open Letter to the Party' penned in Poland by Jacek Kuroń and Karol Modzelewski in 1964.

Thus when the *évènements* of the 'French May' began (actually in March 1968), with the occupation of buildings at the University of Paris's Nanterre campus and then at the Sorbonne, there was a large hinterland of social change and intellectual questioning. The situation was quickly exacerbated with the arrival of the police. Their intervention ended with the closure of the Sorbonne and clashes between the students and police, which mush-roomed to the point at which there was a week of violence in Paris's Latin Quarter from 3 to 10 May, culminating in the Night of the Barricades on 10–11 May. The students demanded the release of their arrested peers, the withdrawal of the police, and the reopening of the Sorbonne. When the security forces were ordered to tear down the barricades on the morning of the 11th, the tension only escalated further; despite Pompidou acceding to the students' demands, a 24-hour general strike was called by trade unions in support of the students. The following days, which saw between 7.5 and 9 million workers go on strike across France, were, however, to be the height of the uprisings. Despite the existence of radical groups amongst the work-ers calling for self-management, or *autogestion* in the factories, the demands of the vast majority of workers were different from those of the students. Indeed, the CGT, the largest, communist-oriented trade union, was taken aback by how radical some of the spontaneous actions were and, as it had not authorized them, condemned them and even tried to prevent contact between students and workers. When the Grenelle Agreements were signed on 27 May, offering increased pay and greater union rights, it took most of the unionized labour force out of the revolutionary equation, although strikes by radical elements continued for some time thereafter.

Although popular memory of 1968 is of a genuinely revolutionary moment, as in 1848, in fact the student rebels' aspirations were inherently unattainable. As one scholar says, ' "power to the imagination" remained a vital programme that fascinated and mobilized individuals but was unsuc-cessful in gaining power because power is based on entirely different organizational and decision-making premises than is the mobilization of the imagination. The internal tension and limited effectiveness of the New Left were due to the fact that it could not assume power without destroy-ing itself.'[95] Hannah Arendt was harsher when she spoke of the 'theoretical sterility and analytical dullness' of the student movement, which for her was 'just as striking and depressing as its joy in action is welcome'.[96] Leszek Kołakowski went so far as to condemn the 'ideological fantasies' of the students as 'a nonsensical expression of the whims of spoilt middle-class children', the extremists among whom 'were virtually indistinguishable from Fascist thugs'.[97] The students knew what they were against but not what they were for, other than vague notions of autonomy and erotic liberation.

But in order to understand the failure of the student uprisings, perhaps more important than problems internal to the student movements was the rejection of the student movements by society at large—which was content with representative democracy as the basis of the postwar consensus—and the role played by the establishment. In West Germany, for example, the response to rock 'n' roll was often to condemn it—in ways that revealed significant continuities in thinking from the Nazi period—as threatening to sexual morals, especially teenage girls', and, as 'negro' music, to the racial order.[98] In France, the revolts certainly shook the Gaullist regime, but it ultimately came out strengthened. Apart from the fact that the radical actions of the extreme left split the left alliance—the Radicals could no longer cooperate with the communists, and neither could the SFIO (socialists)— de Gaulle's appeal to the people to choose between Gaullism or communism brought hundreds of thousands of pro-government demonstrators onto the streets of Paris. The subsequent cleverly timed general election in June provided an opportunity for the shocked middle classes to register their distaste for street action. One political commentator wrote that 'Each barricade, each burning car brought tens of thousands of votes to the Gaullist party; that's the truth.'[99] In the 1969 presidential election, Pompidou scored more votes (57.6 per cent) than even de Gaulle had done in 1964 (54.5 per cent). In other words, despite the feelings the students had as they lived through the events, they never really threatened the state.

Italy presented a rather different picture. Although discontent at the universities was also the trigger for protests, the Italian context was more explicitly connected with recent history. The killing of socialist student Paolo Rossi in a conflict between left-wing and fascist students in April 1966 was the catalyst for serious unrest and reminds us that the language of 'fascism', even if misused or misunderstood by the demonstrators, was neither random nor merely rhetorical. In Italy, as in West Germany, as we will see, the 1968 uprisings were in essence memory conflicts between the generations and between different constituencies within the young generation.

From the beginning of 1967 at the University of Trento, and more widely after Rossi's death, students occupied universities and set about creating an alternative syllabus, most famously encapsulated in the 'Manifesto for a Negative University' of October 1967. This included *controlezioni*, or counter-seminars, which took place alongside regular lectures and were designed to be 'more or less planned forms of open discussion that scandalize university indoctrination and which take place during or outside of official lectures and attempt to expose political content taught by the university in a pseudo-academic disguise'.[100] This highly disruptive programme of alternative student-led education more or less prevented Italy's universities from operating by the spring of 1968.

The turning point was the so-called Battle of Valle Giulia (Rome) of 1 March 1968. Students attacked the police and, for the next few weeks, street battles between the students and the police occurred regularly. But by taking their action to the streets, the radical students lost control of the universities, which returned to near-normal operations by autumn of 1968. More to the point, there was never a large enough support in Italian society at large for an extra-parliamentary opposition which could challenge the status quo, even though the tensions generated by '1968' in Italy actually lasted until the late 1970s. In frustration, a small minority of the students, believing that the state's crackdown confirmed their analysis that Italy was still, just below the surface of shiny postwar consumerism, a fascist state, turned to extreme violence. The Red Brigade, founded in Milan in 1970–1 by radicals such as Mara Cagol, Renato Curcio, and Alberto Franceschini, was to become Western Europe's largest left-wing terrorist organization of the 1970s. Ironically, radicals who believed that they were fighting fascism ended by doing the work of the fascists for them.

Paradoxically, this revolt against postwar 'fascism' was carried out by a middle-class generation which was wealthier, healthier, and more materially comfortable than any such cohort in history. And whilst a tiny minority of the rebels went on to careers as terrorists in the paranoid worlds of the Red Army Faction or the Red Brigades (whose fame should not obscure the existence of terrorism on the extreme right[101]), most successfully negotiated the perils of the recessions and economic challenges that lay only a few years ahead, adapting themselves to the 'system' they had previously condemned. Indeed, some, notably Joschka Fischer, became highly regarded elder statesmen of progressive politics.[102] Thus if the students could never overthrow the postwar order, they did catalyse a rethink of its norms, and contributed to accelerating an ongoing liberalization of attitudes and laws. This process has often been figured as one of unintended consequences, whereby those involved now disavow their intentions at the time but argue that their actions had positive outcomes. 'In short', as Jan-Werner Müller neatly puts it, 'retrospective dissociation by the participants could go hand in hand with the claim that history had worked behind the backs of the actors, so to speak.'[103] In a sense then, the 1968 movement 'developed into its opposite'.[104]

Nowhere do these observations appear more clearly than in West Germany. The intimate connection between the Second World War, the Nazi crimes, and the postwar change of generations is laid bare in the West German student movement: following the killing of student demonstrator Benno Ohnesorg in West Berlin in June 1967, one member of the Socialist German Students' League (*Sozialistischer Deutscher Studentenbund*, SDS), 26-year-old Gudrun Ensslin, angrily argued that 'This fascist state is trying to kill us all. We have to organise resistance. Violence can only be answered with violence. This is the Auschwitz generation—you can't argue with them!'[105]

The West German '68ers' struggle was different from those of their peers in Paris or Berkeley, for their aims were as much prophylactic—preventing a recurrence of Nazism—as they were attempts to build a better future. The failure of the student movement to galvanize wider support led an extremist minority to believe that they had to resort to extreme violence in order to bring down the full weight of the state, thus exposing its inherently fascist nature. Hence was born the Red Army Faction (RAF), better known after the names of its two most famous members as the Baader–Meinhof Gang. When the RAF (together with members of the Popular Front for the Liberation of Palestine) hijacked in July 1976 an Air France plane en route from Israel to France, precipitating an Israeli raid on the plane in Entebbe (Uganda), where it had been forced to land, the most extreme example of the way in which a fascist mindset overtook the West German far left became abundantly clear. In a grotesque echo of the recent past, the hijackers carried out a 'selection' of Jews, allowing passengers who they did not consider Jewish or Israeli to leave and holding the rest as hostages. What is in evidence here, then, is a 'compulsive repetition of Nazi crimes by those who had tried to distance themselves from them', as Fischer put it.[106]

The same is true of the kidnapping of industrialist Hanns-Martin Schleyer on 5 September 1977, which left his chauffeur and three policemen dead. Following the liberation of the Entebbe hostages, the leading RAF members, Baader, Ensslin, and Raspe, all committed suicide in prison; the next day, Schleyer was found dead by police. The result of these events was that the West German state 'had overcome the decisive confrontation with international as well as with domestic terrorism' and that the 'German Autumn' had finally severed the terrorists from the radical groups;[107] but it meant also that 'the post-war generation had, in fact, helped to make the Federal Republic more like the kind of "authoritarian" state they had always claimed it to be'.[108] One self-aware French commentator can look back at the period and say with stark honesty that 'Our favourite pastime in an era so devoid of significance was transforming it into war or insurrection. Nothing was going on so we fashioned the nothingness that befell us into the gaudy garb of revolution.'[109] But for the German students, for whom the stakes seemed higher, this realization did not come, even later, which is why there was no equivalent of the Baader–Meinhof gang in France.

The greatest achievement of '68 was in the social sphere, especially in the struggles for equal rights for women and minorities, for sexual freedom, for a thriving civil society, and for the right to protest.[110] If the 'West European May' did not revolutionize society, it did introduce ideas of lasting value; it also revealed some interesting dimensions of postwar European memory politics at work. Still, Gaullist France was more tolerant and less dull than the myth of '68 would have us believe, and the students' belief in *ouvrièrisme* was at odds with the demands of the workers themselves, for better pay and therefore access to consumer goods, as the Grenelle Agreements indicated.

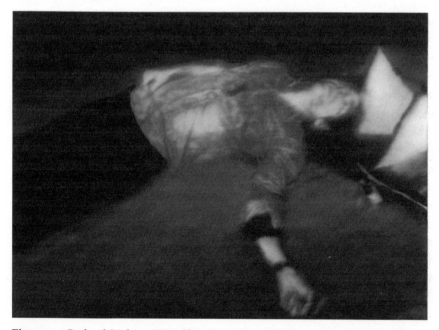

Figure 4. Gerhard Richter, 'Man Shot Down', 1988 (oil on canvas). Depicts the dead Andreas Baader.

The minority of protesters who sought to overthrow the state—which did not include the vast majority of workers—never stood a chance of doing so. And the effects of 1968 were less remarkable than is often assumed, in France at least.[111] In Italy, where society was more conservative than in France, 1968 did have lasting effects on many social attitudes, for example towards women, the family, sexuality, class, and the environment.[112]

The year 1968 shows how postwar antifascism encouraged a break with the past on the basis of formulaic slogans which led to conceptual confusion as much as to historical clarity. When the French students claimed, in response to de Gaulle's supporters' chant of 'Cohn-Bendit to Dachau!', that 'nous sommes tous juifs allemands!', they were well meaning but seemed to have little appreciation for the fact that what German Jews suffered under Nazism was rather different from their own life experiences.[113] The West German SDS's slogans were no less confused, mixing radical politics with criticism of unsavoury continuities in German political life: 'They commemorate today and exterminate tomorrow' was the slogan at one official event held at Dachau concentration camp. 'Dachau greets Hitler's successors' and 'We fight against fascism, NATO, and imperialism' read other banners. Most of the German students actually had little knowledge of the Nazi genocide, but merely employed 'Auschwitz' as a critical shorthand for the present, part of their attempt to reconcile theory and reality.[114] Nevertheless, they helped to bring about the painful discussion of Germany's past which had been only slowly developing up to that point.[115] If in 1968 'Auschwitz' was a slogan which generated 'a complex drama of imagined identities', it soon became a term that demanded a more nuanced and historically attuned ethics of memory.[116] Likewise, Italian radicals catalysed a conversation about Italy's fascist past that, until then, had been hidden beneath the official commemorative rhetoric that all Italians were antifascists.

Yet this apparently favourable change in memory politics was quickly buried under weightier concerns. One of the results of '1968' was to open up a space for discussing topics which had been suppressed, whether unconsciously or through a desire not to complicate the boom years with awkward issues that were best left alone. Ironically, many of the '68ers found that they were able to realize their ambitions of greater personal freedoms, but in a context of neo-liberalism where the solipsistic aspects of 1968 (freedom of expression sexually, sartorially, etc.) triumphed over the principles of a radical political reordering of society: transforming the self in place of transforming society: 'As radical supporters of individual

autonomy and the self-instituting society, they left a legacy of libertarian-
ism which came to be appropriated by a Right eager to dismantle bureauc-
racies and the welfare state.'[117] Despite their Third Worldism, the freedom
and prosperity of Europeans continued to be based on a capitalist system,
now writ large into a global north–south divide. Over time, the nature of
that system would challenge and subvert even the mnemonic dividends
that 1968 had won. In order to understand how that process came about,
one has to turn to the economic crises of the 1970s which brought the
great postwar boom to an end.

The end of the boom

If 1968 is remembered as the great turning point of postwar Western European history, the moment at which a monochrome society turned into
glorious technicolour, that memory comes at the expense of the far more
far-reaching mid-1970s. For as we will see in Chapters 5 and 6, the 1970s
mark the real pivot in the narrative of postwar Western Europe. In the process of turning away from the postwar consensus, the end of the thirty-year
boom and the new conditions which arose as a result were far more significant than the rebellions of 1968.

What were the economic characteristics of the boom? In Western Europe
in the years 1950–73, real per person GDP increased at an annual rate of 4.1
per cent, in contrast with a long-term increase (1870–1998) of just 1.7 per
cent. The rate of output per hour worked was even higher. By the early
1960s, there was almost full employment across Western Europe, with growth
facilitated by the fortuitous appearance of large numbers of migrants from
Eastern and Southern Europe and, from the 1950s, the overseas colonies. At
the same time, the number of hours worked dropped, leisure time increased
along with the surplus money with which to enjoy it, and welfare improved,
as indicated by measures such as life expectancy and infant mortality rates.[118]
In other words, throughout these thirty years we witness unprecedented
continuous growth at high levels; in many places a corporatist arrangement
in industry epitomized by West Germany's 'co-determinist' institutions;
trade liberalization which brought benefits to all of Europe, not just the
states in the EC; a new consumer culture that slowly expanded its reach
across all social classes; the opportunity to enjoy leisure and tourism and
thus new industries arising to meet the demand for them. The ERP and its

associated institutions—the EPU, OECD, and the ECSC—all gave an impetus to international trade and encouraged domestic cooperation with a market-led recovery, so that by the 1960s European growth was self-generating rather than being still dependent on the Americans.[119]

Nevertheless, if there is widespread agreement that the origins of the 'Golden Age' lie in the need for reconstruction after the Second World War, with a fortunate conjunction of the economic circumstances required to do the job—high investment rates, export-led growth, and a surfeit of labour—there is no unanimity over what brought the boom to an end.[120] Economically speaking, by the end of the 1960s the factors that sustained growth were all showing signs of slowing down, with decreasing productivity, high wages, and low flexibility all ever more in evidence. Corporatist labour arrangements, supported by the Marshall Plan, which encouraged wage moderation even among the communist unions in Italy (where, as in France, government controlled wages, unlike in West Germany or the Netherlands), may have been fairer and more stable than interwar labour arrangements, but they were inefficient in comparison with the US and, especially, the newly emerging economies of the Far East.

So from 1967 to 1973, high rates of growth were no longer possible. Growth that had been facilitated by the need to repair the ravages of the war had long since come to an end, and the spoils of growth itself—full employment leading to the end of the pact whereby wage moderation would help to sustain growth, declining productivity, and lower rates of investment—brought problems to the economies of Western Europe, especially those that were coordinated in the Common Market.[121] Furthermore, as these shocks to the system occurred, the Bretton Woods system of currency stability was increasingly undermined; pegging the dollar against gold became harder to justify in the light of the fall in value of sterling and the rise of the deutschmark. The destabilization of currencies followed from a political reluctance (or inability) to address issues such as wages and productivity, with the result that the devaluation of the dollar and the revaluation of key European currencies, especially the deutschmark, brought about the demise of Bretton Woods in 1973. Thus ended the 'Golden Age' period of exchange rate stability and low inflation which provided the setting for sustainable, high rates of growth. And thus was born the drive to monetary union, as a way of avoiding exchange rate fluctuations within the EC, although only after the failure of the so-called 'Snake in the Tunnel', which allowed European currencies to vary against one another within a certain prescribed band. The 'Snake' constituted a sort of regional version of Bretton Woods, and lasted haltingly for most of the 1970s, underlining in economic terms the fact that the 1970s 'was a low point for European cooperation'.[122]

It is now clear that the much-vaunted oil crisis of 1973, sometimes regarded as a turning point in postwar history, in fact only catalysed existing problems in the West European economies. 'Cost-push' explanations such as the oil shocks were indeed major contributory factors to the Western European slowdown, as OPEC sought to make up for lost revenue and punished the Western European countries for their perceived support for Israel during the Yom Kippur War by quadrupling the cost of oil. But creeping inflation before 1973 (4–6 per cent as opposed to the 2–3 per cent of the earlier period of the 'Golden Age') was also a result of the deregulation of banking and credit controls in the early 1970s as well as of governments' attempts to push growth rates higher and unions' reluctance to accept moderate wages in a context of full employment.[123] Were this not so, it would be hard to explain why the decline in productivity experienced during the 1970s continued thereafter, such that the 'annual rate of growth of GDP per worker fell by half between 1960–1975 and 1975–2000'.[124] Thus, the oil crisis brought to the fore a longstanding problem: 'the slowdown was a function not just of the OPEC shock and the collapse of Bretton Woods but also of the adjustment to a more intensive, innovation-based model of growth following the end of the catch-up process.'[125]

This focus on economic factors alone can appear harsh and inhumane: if one identifies the problem with Western European economies as being a corporatist arrangement that allowed room for negotiation into the operation of capitalism, the implication is that a race to the bottom—consisting of unfettered capitalism with no regard for labour—is the only satisfactory way to maintain competitiveness. If one thinks about 'economics as if people mattered', it is hardly surprising that the 'institutional and regulatory legacy of the Golden Age . . . turned out to be difficult to reform, as its very success had created large constituencies in favour of the status quo'.[126] That is to say, the human factor, which allowed the Western European population to identify with postwar capitalist arrangements and which delivered them a higher standard of living than any generation previously, understandably meant that when the system ran into trouble on purely economic grounds, few people advocated change. What we need, then, is to see with Barry Eichengreen that, in order to understand economic indicators, 'the historical context was key';[127] the economic analysis on its own is revealing but cannot provide the full picture unless coupled with other factors. Economic imperatives—in the limited sense of capitalist imperatives—were often at odds with political possibilities, as they have been since the mid-1970s. It was the 'achievement' of the governments of the 1980s to force through the change that few dared to envisage in the 1970s, arguing that it was the only way to salvage Western European economic strength.

The same is true of the effects of economic change: the historical context is key. It is this context that will be explored in Chapters 5 and 6. By the mid-1970s, following the shocks of 1968 and the first oil crisis, Europe's postwar settlement was beginning to unravel. The glorious years of the boom were over. As we will see, the social and economic change brought about in the mid-1970s would go hand in hand with attacks on Western Europe's version of the antifascist consensus. In economics, just as in politics, the thirty postwar years were aberrant in European history.

4
Catching Up?
Eastern Europe, 1953–1975

We have already said many times that our ideological debates with capitalism will be resolved not through war, but through economic competition.... Some comrades might object that we could cut armaments, while the enemy would not. But it is debatable if the enemy would be doing the right thing... since they would devour their budgets, reduce the economic development of these countries, thereby contributing to the increasing advantages of our system.

Nikita Khrushchev, 1959

Let those who are wont to forget the lessons of history and who would like to engage again in recarving the map of Europe know that the borders of Poland, the GDR and Czechoslovakia, as well as of any other Warsaw Pact member, are stable and inviolable.

Leonid Brezhnev, 1968

On the pedestal someone had scrawled with a piece of chalk: Workers of the world unite, or I shoot!

Ladislav Mňačko, 1968

For years Poland has been an occupied country—exactly like today's Czechoslovakia.

Witold Gombrowicz[1]

De-Stalinization and its consequences

Between 1953, when Stalin died, and 1975, with the oil crisis hitting the Soviet Bloc hard, Eastern Europe's communist countries went from appearing to be the equals of the west in terms of economic growth and political strength to being economically stagnant and politically static. This chapter will account for that trajectory, and will show that, for all Khrushchev's talk of 'catching up' and then 'overtaking' the west, if the 'golden years' were shared unevenly in Western Europe, in Eastern Europe they were largely illusory, if the term can be applied at all. The promise of 'the thaw' did not last long for the region's citizens; indeed, the regimes' response to popular de-Stalinization was a clampdown and a return to a hard-line stance; and if there was détente in the Cold War, there was little by way of entente. For ordinary people in Eastern Europe, a cooling of the 'war' only meant a stronger sense that they had been forgotten by the 'free' world, reinforcing a feeling that they had better learn to live with their lot, for the likelihood of change was remote.

In early 1956, at a closed session of the 20th Congress of the Soviet Communist Party, Nikita Khrushchev, the Party's new leader, delivered a secret report in which he condemned the crimes committed by Stalin. By the time of the speech, the USSR had already experienced a period of relative liberalization since Stalin's death, with Stalin's chosen successor Georgi Malenkov improving very low living standards, promoting agriculture, new housing projects, salary rises, and consumer goods for industrial labourers, as well as freeing some political prisoners, ending state terror, and generally edging away from the more extreme, intolerant aspects of Stalinism.[2] Khrushchev explicitly criticized 'the cult of the individual leader which was so widespread during Stalin's lifetime' and argued that the Soviet Union's 'historic victories' were not the result of Stalin's leadership, 'as was pictured during the period of the cult of the individual leader', but were 'attained thanks to the organisational work of the Party, to the many local organisations, and to the self-sacrificing work of our great people'. As a result, Khrushchev demanded that the many state enterprises, factories, farms, and the like that had been named after Stalin should be, as he put it, 'nationalised'.[3] Although the 'secret speech' was not openly available, neither was it as secret as its name suggests—there were 1,400 delegates present and the speech was published in huge numbers as a pamphlet to be read to factory or institute collectives across the country—but it was a brave one, for Khrushchev gave the speech despite opposition to it from the majority of the Politburo, hoping that his appeal over their heads to the delegates would prove successful.[4]

And so it did. Not only did the 'secret speech' crystallize Khrushchev's position as leader but, continuing Malenkov's 'new course', it set the whole communist bloc, with a few exceptions, on a new road: de-Stalinization.

Yet this was not intended as an exercise in loosening communist control; tellingly, for example, the antifascist basis of the postwar Soviet state and its rootedness in the country's sacrifice during the recent defeat of fascism was to be emphasized, not downplayed in the new, anti-Stalinist atmosphere. One of the final demands Khrushchev made as he came to the end of his long speech was for the revision of history books: 'It is especially necessary', he said, 'that in the immediate future we compile a serious textbook of the history of our party which will be edited in accordance with scientific Marxist objectivism, a textbook of the history of Soviet society, a book pertaining to the events of the Civil War and the Great Patriotic War.'[5]

It is thus worth considering what happened to the historical profession in the Soviet Union in the context of de-Stalinization, for the experience of historians can stand for Soviet society more generally. The Party's firm control over historiography since 1931, when Stalin announced that historical scholarship should be 'party scholarship', remained firmly in place until 1953, with the *History of the Communist Party of the Soviet Union (Bolsheviks): Short Course* (1938) the standard-bearer of the paradigm. With the Great Patriotic War and Stalin's and Beria's deaths, historians slowly began to take up the challenge posed by other writers to 'de-ideologize thought'. The journal *Voprosy Istorii* (*Problems of History*) announced in its editorial, following Khrushchev's lead, that it would henceforth struggle against the cult of personality and declared that the 'masses [were] the driving force of historical development'.

As soon as these aims began to stray too far from the Party's comfort zone, however, the editors (both previously loyal to the Stalinist regime), Anna Pankratova and Eduard Burdzhalov, who were pushing the new line, were brought sharply to heel. This occurred in 1956 at the time of the uprisings in Hungary and Poland, and ended with Burdzhalov's dismissal in March 1957 and Pankratova's death two months later.[6] In other words, de-Stalinization could only go so far before those who had set it in train became nervous of the process they had unleashed. As we will see below, nowhere was this sharp braking process more clearly in evidence than in Khrushchev's decision to send tanks into Budapest in order to crush an uprising which had been made possible in the first place by his criticisms of Stalin.

If in official parlance, 'de-Stalinization' referred specifically to the removal of the 'leader cult', in popular jargon and in the understanding of historians it came to mean any attempt to reform the practices of the Stalin era, for example, offering more consumer goods instead of focusing on the military and/or heavy industry; clearing away obstructive bureaucracy; permitting popular articulation of discontent; funding greater welfare such as maternity rights; or offering more spacious, comfortable housing instead of the unloved communal apartments. This conceptual mingling of condemnation of Stalin himself and criticism of the Soviet system created a dilemma for the Soviet leadership, which walked a tightrope between encouraging de-Stalinization in the sphere of the Party's internal affairs and discouraging it in the context of social policy and popular attitudes. The resulting confusion was something which the Party could not always prevent, and the implicit authorization of a move towards privatization and individualization of needs opened up difficulties for the Khrushchev regime. 'Having dismissed the cult of personality (*kul't lichnosti*)', as one historian puts it, 'the regime found it difficult to accept the new Soviet individual (*lichnost'*) which emerged from its de-Stalinizing reforms.'[7] Besides, Stalin's successors, having risen through the ranks of the CPSU during the great leader's years in office, were themselves deeply implicated in the crimes that they condemned, so limiting the speed and extent of the de-Stalinization process was in their interests from the start.

This ambivalence resulted from the fact that Stalin's 'mistakes' were condemned rather than any systemic failing that might necessitate a reconsideration of the nature of the Soviet state. The Soviet press, like the Party, found dealing with de-Stalinization quite challenging too, as it had both to encourage criticism of Stalin and his cult of personality but also, especially after the 22nd Party Congress (1961), to replicate the Party's position of discouraging de-Stalinization in the public sphere. Iconoclasts were treated harshly and by November 1956 (the first anniversary of the Bolshevik Revolution since the Secret Speech) 'there was no longer any leniency shown to those who assaulted any Soviet symbolism'.[8] When Stalin's body was removed from his mausoleum and buried in 1961, the process was undertaken thoroughly, swiftly, and without public ritual. The late stages of de-Stalinization, following the 22nd Party Congress, were actually carried out with the aim not of denigrating Stalin further, but in order to enforce 'a clearer script' about Stalin and his misdeeds, implying that the Party had now overcome the past and that the country could return to stability.[9]

Such issues were not confined to high politics. Indeed, the real force of de-Stalinization lay in the promise it held out to ordinary citizens of Eastern Europe that their lots would be bettered, and that greater progress might be made towards achieving the true ambitions of socialism instead of the valorization of the leader and the Party which passed for socialism in Stalin's last years. Economics, and the standard of living, especially, were key battlegrounds.

Whilst the western half of the continent was rebuilding in the context of American assistance and new collective settlements concerning defence and economics, the eastern half, now firmly under communist rule, was attempting to do something similar. But it faced different problems altogether. First, in terms of defence, the communists were not only concerned to shore up their region against the perceived threat from the west by creating the Warsaw Pact, but had to face down considerable internal opposition too. And in terms of economics, whilst Comecon was partly established to rival the Marshall Plan, and was not without achievements, it lacked the flexibility of the ERP system and failed to adapt.

Nevertheless, the member states did try and 'relaunch' Comecon following Stalin's death, in order to try and overcome some of its more egregious shortcomings, such as the lack of coordination between member states, duplication of production in some areas and shortages in others. But initial attempts at harmonizing production were disrupted by the events of 1956 which led to the rapid introduction of ad hoc production arrangements, with the aim of dissipating further discontent by introducing more consumer goods. Khrushchev abandoned the 1956–60 Soviet Five Year Plan in 1957 and, again hoping to hold popular discontent in check, initiated in 1959 a charter for Comecon that bore more than a passing resemblance to those newly minted by the Treaty of Rome. With a Council Session (the 'highest organ'), an Executive Committee (the 'principal executive organ'), Standing Commissions, and the Secretariat, Comecon's ostensibly supranationalist credentials were set out.[10]

Yet for all these grand-sounding institutions, Comecon remained what it had always been: an organ of Soviet domination over the Eastern European communist satellite states. When in 1962 Khrushchev pressed for a central planning body that would determine which states would produce which goods, his initiative met with strong resistance. The Romanians especially resented the Soviet attempt to treat the country as nothing more than a supplier of agricultural goods, and pressed ahead with grandiose schemes for industrialization, and János Kádár famously introduced 'goulash communism' into Hungary, permitting a carefully circumscribed free market to flourish alongside the official, planned economy, a manoeuvre which helped people to survive and served to keep dangerous levels of rejectionism seen in 1956 at bay. Thus it may be somewhat premature in this context (see Chapter 6 for more detail), but it is worth noting here that although he had been a communist all his life, Kádár supposedly came to the realization that a planned economy did not work in a modern economy.[11] Comecon was as much a political institution as an economic one, far more so than anything that the EEC dreamt up. Thus the Soviet desire for centralization was counterproductive, giving rise not to intra-bloc unity but to 'dissent and a craving for an opening to the West'.[12] Besides, after 1953 and, especially, 1956, Eastern Europeans had experienced and continued to fear the possibility of a Warsaw Pact invasion far more than any threat supposedly posed by NATO forces; this military-political paranoia was not conducive to economic cooperation.

The economic and political stagnation of the Brezhnev years could not, however, be foreseen at first; indeed, 'from the West it looked for a while as though the Warsaw Pact would bring off the combination of socialism, authoritarianism, and vigorous economic growth'.[13] 'For a time', as one economic historian reminds us, 'communist regimes commanded a sufficient degree of consensus, not so surprising in light of their early achievements and of eastern Europe's interwar history.'[14] This was not universally true—in Romania, as we have seen, with its tiny Communist Party and interwar and wartime history dominated by ethno-nationalism and fascism, communism was installed by force[15]—but across the continent, as Chapter 1 shows, there was considerable admiration for the victory of antifascism and for the economic achievements of the people's republics in the early postwar years. Social change too was rapid, with infant mortality rates and life expectancy nearly reaching western levels, education massively expanded, and poverty of the 1930s sort practically eliminated. This was recognized in the west, too, with the CCF's 1955 Milan conference, 'The Future of Freedom', for example, being premised on the assumption that Soviet economic growth was outstripping that of the west.[16] 'The idea of "catching up with the advanced Western countries" under such circumstances did not seem to us a meaningless slogan,' as Zdeněk Mlynář, one of the leading protagonists of the Prague Spring, later put it.[17]

But if communism managed to sustain economic growth comparable with the west for the first decade and a half after the war, measures such as GDP per capita hid the extent to which wealth was concentrated on military and infrastructure with ordinary people enduring endless shortages and a lack of consumer goods. Besides, no such comparison could be made in the sphere of politics. It quickly became clear, with the massive seizures of property and land, the purges of 'collaborators' that became excuses to do away with anyone 'bourgeois', and the suppression of alternative opinions, that the overthrow of the Nazi dictatorship had resulted in the ushering in of another one, albeit of a different sort. If, in Western Europe, the postwar atmosphere was fundamentally conservative, this was largely a reflection of popular will and the success of the Christian Democratic parties in translating that into votes; in Eastern Europe, the suppression of national sovereignty, especially in the Baltic States, Ukraine, and other countries incorporated directly into the Soviet Union, and the elimination of opposition, at least in the public sphere, was centrally, and violently, imposed. 'There will be a Lithuania,' one apparatchik put it, 'but there will be no Lithuanians.'[18] Post-Cold War disagreements between eastern and western memories of the Second World War and its aftermath, as we will see in Chapter 8, are direct reflections of these different circumstances.

The faltering attempts to improve the communist bloc's economic performance so that growth could be felt by ordinary citizens, coupled with the unintended consequences of de-Stalinization, precipitated the gravest challenge yet to communist rule. The 'cauldron of frustrated expectation' that already existed across the region by the time of Stalin's death now found channels through which it could be openly expressed. The response to the uprisings that rocked the communist regimes between 1953 and 1956 meant that the aspirations of communist rulers had to be recalibrated and those of the ruled filed away in the improbable hope that they might be resurrected at a later date.

From the 'thaw' to neo-Stalinism

The 'thaw' following the death of Stalin permitted people to air their grievances to an extent impossible earlier. But the series of uprisings that ensued should not be understood simply as attempts to overthrow communism, which is how it is tempting to view them from our post-1989 vantage point. Many participants, especially older proponents of workers' rights, wanted to reform communism, making it truer to its essence. They thus fought for those workers' rights which they believed communism should have upheld, and against the authoritarianism of Stalinism.[19] The revival of friendly relations with Tito and his so-called 'fascist clique' after 1953 also bespeaks a desire to create a rejuvenated socialism, as well as a recognition—on the part of Khrushchev, not his counterparts in Eastern Europe, who were embarrassed by his stance—that Tito had not broken with the practices of state socialism as much as had been claimed when Yugoslavia accepted Marshall Aid. Nevertheless, in East Germany in 1953 and in Hungary in 1956, the intervention of the USSR was decisive in saving the communist regimes. Later, during the Prague Spring of 1968, the Polish, Bulgarian, and East German regimes played a key role in precipitating the Soviet-led invasion.

The first uprisings following Stalin's death occurred at the western edge of the new Soviet empire. Plzeň, in Czechoslovakia, and Berlin were places that already had advanced industrial economies. By contrast with places further east, where workers were enjoying unprecedented levels of employment and opportunity following the destruction of the bourgeoisie, here factory workers saw their working conditions and remuneration downgraded. After price rises following the 'currency reform' in Czechoslovakia led to a fall in real wages of some 12 per cent in Plzeň, and after an unpaid increase in working hours in East Berlin, popular uprisings began in June 1953 among the very people who should have been communism's natural allies. Events in Plzeň were locally confined and soon died down, but in East Berlin 400,000 workers took to the streets on 16 June, and Red Army tanks were deployed to disperse them. The result was nearly 300 dead, thousands of arrests, and 200 executions of 'ringleaders'. Protests not just by workers but by farmers and others occurred across the country, upset not just by changing work patterns but by the sealing of the border (May 1952), forced evacuations from within the five-kilometre frontier zone with the FRG, and the actions of the pro-communist *Volkspolizei* (People's Police).[20]

The seventeenth of June confirmed Stalin's and the hard-liners' views that the trials of 'Titoists' were necessary (see Chapter 1), especially as riots occurred throughout the satellite states, even in compliant Bulgaria, during the spring of 1953. Just a few years since the Red Army had defeated fascism and liberated Eastern Europe, an apparently revanchist movement was openly defying the workers' and peasants' state. Ernst Engelberg, a leading East German historian, explained the situation as a continuation of Nazi thuggery:

> We must show that there is a method in their madness, that the parallels between *Kristallnacht* in November 1938 and the 17 June are more than superficial.... Who can forget the columns of SA thugs and murderers from the period before 1933?... The same rabid mindless infatuation, the same

violent rowdiness, the same raucous mendacity. No one shall come along and claim any connection between the 16 and 17 June and the real workers' movement.[21]

Despite such condemnations, few leading communists really believed that the demonstrators were mostly fascists or that they were being directed by a fascist coterie. As a result, post-Stalin leaderships not only clamped down on criticism, but sought to take heed of the demonstrators' complaints, with sops to consumerism and the like. Perhaps the one partial exception was Poland where, as we have seen, Stalinization never achieved the same depth as elsewhere in the first place.

In retrospect, it is clear that if 1953 marked the first sign of weakness in the Soviets' postwar empire in general, 1956 marked a turning point in the postwar history of communism in Poland in particular.[22] Cracks were already appearing in the putative unanimity of Party consensus even before Khrushchev's secret speech, but thereafter they grew rapidly. In June 1956, revolts started in Poznań, with factory workers objecting to the Polish government's refusal to consider their demands for better pay and working conditions. 'Had they not been stifled by force and the accompanying demagogy of hopes and promises', writes one historian, 'these movements could have developed into a powerful wave of social revolt, which would have threatened the foundations of the existing system, causing Soviet intervention to bring order back to Warsaw.'[23] Poland's leaders, Eduard Ochab and Józef Cyrankiewicz, ordered the troops in; over two days, they killed 53 and injured many more.

The return of Gomułka to power in October to some extent quelled this wellspring of discontent, for he represented the 'national' or 'patriotic' alternative to the Moscow-imposed communists. But the significant point is that Gomułka was first and foremost a communist and, once the social movements started to get out of hand, that is to say, once the Party felt it could no longer direct them, he crushed them—helped along in his decision by Khrushchev sending Red Army tanks in the direction of Warsaw in mid-October 1956. Gomułka did open up a very limited space for local independence from the 'Moscow Centre' (including the attempt to win popular support rather than to rely on terror), but only for those within the communist fold. 'Revisionist' communists who tended towards a 'liberalization' of communism were quashed in the 'Polish October', and outright opponents of communism did not yet have the means to get their voices heard. Still, incipient sites of such opposition existed; Jakub Berman, the Party's chief ideologist, wrote of the Catholic Church that it was 'the natural source of opposition, both ideological and philosophical'.[24] But as of October 1956, resistance in Poland, though it brought some limited change, such as private enterprise in agriculture, could not alter the three basic realities of communism: one-party rule, the command economy, and, ultimately, subordination to Moscow. Yet the Party's grip on power had been fatally weakened, as would become clear much later on.

Poznań was not the only site of revolt in 1956. But if the Hungarian case ended far more violently, that was primarily because the Hungarian leadership took their anti-Soviet stance further than Moscow could tolerate. Gomułka may have espoused a national variety of communism, and claimed to be anti-Soviet, but Khrushchev, who met with him on 19 October, would never have agreed to withdraw the tanks and to keep Gomułka in place had he not been persuaded that he would do Moscow's bidding. As Khrushchev said, Gomułka held 'a position that was most advantageous for us. Here was a man who had come to power on the crest of an anti-Soviet wave, yet who could now speak forcefully about the need to preserve Poland's friendly relations with the Soviet Union and the Soviet Communist Party.'[25] Nothing similar could be said about Imre Nagy.

In Hungary, with Rákosi in power, Stalinism was firmly enforced and 'Titoists' purged. As in Poland, with Khrushchev's secret speech, slight cracks appeared in the Stalinist façade and, following Rákosi's replacement by the more hard-line Ernő Gerő in July 1956, calls began to be heard for the reinstatement of Nagy, whose attempt to pioneer moderate reforms in 1953 had ended in his dismissal as Prime Minister. When he was reinstated with Moscow's blessing, Nagy swiftly went beyond the demands of the oppositionist Petőfi Circle and student demonstrators. Where they had been calling at mass rallies for the introduction of true soviets, i.e. workers' control in the factories, Nagy spoke of the need to 'develop toward socialism by systematically decreasing the use of force [and] utilizing democratic forms and methods in the interest of close co-operation on the widest possible scale with the masses of working people'. What this actually meant was that Hungary should withdraw from the Warsaw Pact and, as a neutral state, work towards a renewed system of democracy.[26] No wonder that other communist leaders, including Italy's Togliatti, started to refer to Nagy's 'counter-revolutionary' actions.[27] Indeed, on 30 October, Nagy, having already announced the disbanding of the ÁVO (the secret service), now took the steps necessary for creating a multiparty state, which would allow for the Smallholders' Party, the National Peasant Party, and the Social Democratic Party all to participate in government, alongside the communists. And on 1 November, Nagy made his famous radio broadcast declaring Hungary to be henceforth a neutral state and asking for UN recognition. This was bold indeed, for Nagy's opponents now had their ammunition: 'We were witnesses when the counterrevolution took off its mask', revealing its true face as a 'black carnival'—that is, as fascist—as two apologists for the hard-liners later wrote.[28] Moscow thought again about its decision to promote and support Nagy.

The result was that anti-Nagy hard-liners, led by Gerő, asked for Soviet assistance to overthrow the 'counter-revolutionary' government and, on 4 November, Moscow sent in Red Army tanks (not Warsaw Pact—Khrushchev was too nervous about the other members' loyalty to the new organization). The revolution was crushed, more than 180,000 people left the country, Kádár was installed in power (Gerő was far too unpopular, having enraged the crowds with his radio denunciations of the uprising), and Nagy, who was tricked out of the Yugoslav embassy where he had been granted asylum, was spirited away to a Romanian prison. He was returned to Budapest in April 1957 and tried in secret; on 16 June 1958, he was hanged. In a new age for the mass media, thanks to television, the invasion of Budapest demonstrated to the world at large and to the inhabitants of the communist bloc that anything that went beyond minor reform to constitute a threat to the 'people's democracies' as such would not be tolerated. Where Nagy and his advisers, such as the economist János Kornai, were planning to combine workers' control, nationalized industries, and welfare with a partially free market in agriculture and parliamentary democracy—that is, a plan for a genuine people's democracy—those who ruled in the name of the people but for the benefit of a communist oligarchy moved rapidly to snuff out the experiment.[29] Clearly, whatever Khrushchev meant by de-Stalinization did not include relinquishing communist power.

Yet the response of the ruling elite should not be understood only in terms of power politics; they also genuinely feared a supposed underground fascist threat to their accomplishments. 1956, it is easy to forget, was only a decade after the war, during which Hungary had been a key ally of the Third Reich until March 1944. Ervin Hollós wrote in 1967, justifying his role in prosecuting 'counterrevolutionaries' in 1958–9, that in 1956 a large number of 'criminal elements' were still at large:

These counterrevolutionaries, terrorists, butchers with bloodstains on their hands had escaped well-deserved conviction. Those perpetrators who should have been tried and convicted already in 1945, or latest between 1948–49, by the time the Hungarian administration had been purged of those rightist elements whose aim was nothing but to save the reactionaries and war criminals, could only be called to task after the defeat of the counterrevolution in 1958–59.[30]

The problem was that the antifascist narrative was unravelling all the faster the more the communist regimes appealed to it to cover up failings in other areas. The 200,000 people who left Hungary in the wake of the revolution, mostly young and educated, were not all 'fascists' or 'bourgeois reactionaries'.

The efforts of de-Stalinization notwithstanding, then, the officially approved reforms were insufficient to meet the needs and demands of the people. Khrushchev's response may have been driven by a need to appear to be in control, especially following his denunciation of the firmest leader of all. As he told Tito in November 1956, if they had failed to act, 'there are people in the Soviet Union who would say that as long as Stalin was in command, everyone obeyed and there were no great shocks, but now that [these new bastards] have come to power, Russia has suffered the defeat and loss of Hungary'.[31] But by acting in the way he did, communism suffered a severe loss of the status it had acquired by virtue of defeating the Third Reich in Europe. The post-1956 'compromise' between the regime and Hungarian society 'rested on complicit nontalk', in which hopes of a better future were put on hold and many people's 'more or less disturbingly guilty consciences for passive or not-so-passive collaboration before, during, or after World War II and during most of the Communist period' forced their mouths shut.[32] Outside of Hungary, the sight of tanks on the streets of Budapest shocked Western fellow-travellers, whose image of the Golden Age being realized in the here and now was shattered,[33] and provided an echo of Brecht's comment on the 1953 uprising: that the leadership should elect a new people. No further proof was needed of the real meaning of the Warsaw Pact's principle, enshrined in its charter, of 'mutual respect' for its member states' sovereignty.

Yet more was to be forthcoming, as the nervousness now instilled in the Soviet regime inclined it toward radical solutions to perceived threats to its power. According to Iurii Andropov, head of the KGB and Soviet ambassador to Budapest in 1956, events in Czechoslovakia in 1968 'are very reminiscent of what happened in Hungary'.[34] Yet the 'Prague Spring' was never such a threat to the system, which is why, as François Fejtö pointed out, this attempt by the Soviets, 'obviously short on imagination', to 'replay the Budapest scenario in Prague' only 'deteriorated into tragicomedy'.[35] Where in 1956 there was an increasingly anti-communist insurrection in train in Budapest, in 1968 there was a reformist sovereign government in power with widespread popular support.[36] Where in 1956 Moscow had the almost-legitimate excuse that it had been asked to intervene, in 1968 the Soviets claimed that an unidentified 'group of statesmen and leaders of the party, the government and the Czechoslovak National Assembly' had appealed for help.[37] We have known since 1992 that a small group of hard-liners, centred on Antonín Kapek and Vasil Bilak, did in fact ask Brezhnev, via Ukrainian party boss Petro Shelest, to intervene, but not on the scale suggested by the Soviets.[38] And where in 1956 the hard-liners' claim that the counter-revolutionaries were fascist fifth columnists at least had a ring of plausibility, in 1968 the irony of the German Ulbricht encouraging Soviet interventionism into a country that had suffered so much at the hands of the Third Reich, whilst claiming that it was Bonn which represented chauvinism, revanchism, and even fascism, was especially absurd given that Alexander Dubček and his Foreign Minister Jiří Hájek were in fact pioneers of reform communism.

Far from being an icebreaker for fascism, in reality Dubček did not generate the same degree of fear among his peers as did Nagy, because he was an idealistic reformer *within* the Party. If his concern for legality made him hard to deal with, he never sought to withdraw from the Warsaw Pact or Comecon or to declare Czech neutrality. Indeed, what shocked the Czechoslovak leadership was that the invasion took place even though they had agreed—and intended—to implement the changes that Moscow demanded; the problem, it seems, was that they did not respond quickly enough to a situation that they were finding hard to control. As Dubček told Brezhnev in a fraught telephone call on 13 August, 'I already told you what sorts of measures we are preparing and in what sequence we will carry them out. But I also told you at the time that it's impossible to do all this in a single day. We need time to take care of it.'[39] By then it was probably the case that Dubček could do nothing to stop the invasion and had resigned himself to it.[40] Perhaps the only lasting advantage that the invasion brought to Dubček and his circle was that they remained admired by the Czechoslovak people (and the west) for holding a position that was in fact some way from the one they really held: 'one now winces when reading how the crowds declared their fervent devotion to Dubček, Černik, President Svoboda and other men who in private barely resembled their public personae.'[41]

The reality was captured, ironically perhaps, by Nicolae Ceaușescu of Romania:

> Whom was this military intervention aimed at? Against the legal, leading bodies of the communist party and Czechoslovak state. Were these institutions threatening socialism in Czechoslovakia, its independence and sovereignty? But does the fact that the Czechoslovak people wishes to live free and independent, sovereign in its own home, and in ever-strengthening alliance and collaboration with other socialist countries... endanger socialism? Since when did the principles of socialist democracy, the humanism of socialist relationships become counter-revolutionary dangers?[42]

Perhaps because this sort of statement was calculated to advance Romania's independent ideological line, it has been overlooked by interpreters. However, Ceaușescu was in fact widely admired in the West for his stand against Moscow in 1968, so if people did not understand why he took that stand, it was because they wanted to believe in the reality of a liberal, reformist wing of communism, when in fact 1968 signalled the death of any such thing. Instead, one sees rule by force, or the threat of force, and the gradual emergence of dissent, a recognition that Marxism-Leninism must be overthrown rather than tinkered with, and the creation of civil societies which tried to resist the parties' attempts to 'normalize' their populations, advocating human rights instead of reformed communism. Ceaușescu in no way represented a reform communism, and defended the Czechoslovak leadership because he recognized what historians now know to be true, that Dubček was going to fall into line.

Thus the invasion accelerated what was going to happen anyway, as Dubček had already realized that there would be no alternative path to socialism. This inflexibility was the essence of what became known as the Brezhnev Doctrine, and was a result, as Fejtö noted, of the leaders of the five invading countries confusing 'their personal and group interests' with those 'of their respective states'. In other words, the Prague Spring was suppressed less because the Warsaw Pact really believed its own statements about the bloc's security being threatened than because the men in power, with their 'outdated methods', felt 'threatened, and about to be swept into the "dustbin of history"'.[43] As Gomułka told Dubček in February 1968, 'if things go badly with you [in Czechoslovakia], we in Poland, too, will find hostile

Figure 5. Tanks put an end to the Prague Spring, 1968.

elements rising against us'. Todor Zhivkov of Bulgaria was even more forth-right: 'Only by relying on the armed forces of the Warsaw Pact can we change the situation.'[44] They thus decided to strangle at birth 'the most promising Communist experiment since the war—an experiment distin-guished by competence and creativity and one that could have become a source of positive inspiration to the entire Communist movement'.[45]

The Prague Spring is often recalled as the moment when the Warsaw Pact invaded one of its own members. But although there were Bulgarian and Polish troops involved, East German troops were permitted to send non-combat troops only and the Romanians were not asked to contribute. The vast majority of the troops were Soviet and if the Warsaw Pact countries welcomed the move against Czechoslovakia it was less because they delighted in Moscow's increasing control over its client states than because they feared the implications of Czechoslovak reformism for their own regimes.[46] Once the tanks had cleared the streets, there was no opportunity for further reform. The conditions of 1956—Tito's and Khrushchev's anti-Stalinist reformism—were not present in 1968, as disenchanted Czechoslovak communist Ladislav

Mňačko explained in his memoir of the Prague Spring, written in exile in Austria: 'In Hungary the Soviet authorities allowed a certain measure of liberalization in public life, but in Czechoslovakia they will not allow the liberalization and democratization to continue, for it was precisely these tendencies that decided the question of invasion at all.'[47] The importance of 1968 lies in its adumbration of reform in the Soviet Union itself, as anticipated by the remarkable prescience of Hungarian journalist François Fejtö: 'the wavering of the Soviet leaders, even in the first eight months of 1968, before they embarked on a course of military repression, shows that in the USSR too, and in the upmost echelons, there exist forces for moderation, toleration and peaceful development.... One may hope—certainly the people of the Eastern countries hope—that the next Dubček will appear in the nerve centre of the system: Moscow.'[48] Or, as the political philosopher Hannah Arendt put it ten years earlier:

> If the dramatic events of the Hungarian Revolution demonstrate anything, it is at best the dangers which may grow out of the lawlessness and formlessness inherent in the very dynamics of this regime and so glaringly apparent in its inability to solve the succession problem. If these danger signs promise anything at all, it is much rather a sudden and dramatic collapse of the whole regime than a gradual normalization.[49]

Arendt was in advance of the facts. Rather than dramatic collapse, the process of 'normalization' seemed to bring an uneasy stability to the regimes; it was helped along by western reluctance to get involved. As Willy Brandt observed in a talk at Chatham House in 1958:

> The 17th of June 1953 and the Hungarian uprising have shown us something more, i.e. that millions in the Soviet-controlled areas believed that they could count on some form of military assistance by the West. This tragic misconception has since then been cleared up, and only one course now remains: an unflinching, stubborn, struggle for a peaceful solution by political action.[50]

In other words, neither side was willing to intervene militarily in the other's sphere; the stability of Europe depended on this unspoken acceptance of the status quo. In fact, détente depended on it.[51]

Unfortunately, not everybody was familiar with Brandt's script. Otherwise, the Prague Spring, which occurred ten years later, might not have happened. In Jáchym Topol's novel *Gargling with Tar* (2005), Ilya, the boy narrator, recounts the moment the Czechoslovaks heard of the Warsaw Pact invasion: 'everybody clapped like crazy, then Commander Žinka spoke into the loudspeaker and said that the Soviet Union was standing ready on the borders, but that this time the West wouldn't abandon us and that there would be no repetition of Munich!'[52] He was of course quite wrong.

The clearest indication that the West would not interfere in the communist bloc's affairs—apart, of course, from the fact that it was mired in its own comparable, self-created swamps, from Suez to Vietnam—and that revisionist communism was dead was the announcement of what came to be known in the west as the Brezhnev Doctrine. The concept was adumbrated by the words of the fraternal parties' leaders during the run up to the Prague Spring, for example when Ulbricht, at a meeting in Dresden in March 1968, said that it was 'self evident' that 'each Party and its Central Committee determines its own policies', but that 'on the other hand we all know that none of our parties live alone in the world. Thus developments in one socialist country and the decisions of one fraternal party can have far-reaching effects on every other party even on the situation in Europe.'[53] The theme was eagerly taken up by Brezhnev, who had succeeded Khrushchev in 1964. Addressing the Polish Central Committee in November 1968, Brezhnev reiterated the Warsaw Pact's basic watchword of 'strict respect for the sovereignty of all countries'. Then came the inevitable qualification:

> And when external and internal forces hostile to socialism try to turn the development of a given socialist country in the direction of restoration of the capitalist system, when a threat arises to the cause of socialism in that country—a threat to the security of the socialist commonwealth as a whole—this is no longer merely a problem for that country's people, but a common problem, the concern of all socialist countries.[54]

The new round of bilateral 'friendship treaties' which ensued from 1970 onwards between the USSR and the satellite states revealed that the Soviets were re-establishing the principle of communist orthodoxy under the guise of 'socialist internationalism'. The working principle is that the louder the language of working for the common good was espoused, the firmer the Soviets were asserting their control over the Eastern Europeans' 'sovereignty': 'The crime of aggression they dignify by the name of fraternal aid,' as Mňačko put it.[55] The Brezhnev Doctrine reasserted Soviet authority over a political process with which Khrushchev, many in the USSR felt, had tinkered dangerously, and it lasted throughout the 1970s, impervious to—indeed, strengthened by—the relaxations at international level brought about by Cold War détente.

The Brezhnev Doctrine was not only applicable at the level of high politics, however, where it marked a return to the Sovietization strategy of the immediate postwar years.[56] The process of 'normalization', seen most archetypically in Czechoslovakia, should be understood as the doctrine's social equivalent. Following a brief window of opportunity, when some 100,000 people left Czechoslovakia as refugees, including notable disillusioned communists such as 1960s economic reformer Ota Šik (who was on holiday in Yugoslavia at the time of the invasion, and subsequently emigrated to Switzerland), the policy of 'normalization' from 1970 onwards saw a return to more hard-line controls, including on emigration.[57] All adults who had left the country were tried *in absentia* for 'abandonment of the republic' and they were referred to subsequently as 'runaways'. Yet the regime had permitted a veritable brain drain, and began to offer inducements to return, something which several thousand did.[58] Still, the Party was purged mercilessly, especially the intelligentsia and the administration, so that Fejtö could talk of Czechoslovakia being in the grip of a 'Kafkaesque "trial", a grotesque and enormous arraignment of the whole nation'.[59] 'Normalization' meant, above all, persuading people to drop their grievances with the regime and to seek contentment in keeping up with the west in terms of consumer satisfaction. If this strategy worked at all (and it did), it was because people were now too afraid to challenge the regime and because they were too unfamiliar with the west to know quite how different from the west's their experience of consumerism really was.

As the Prague Spring showed, the Brezhnev Doctrine 'was not solely a Soviet invention and was supported by communist rulers throughout the region', with the exception of Romania, Yugoslavia, and Albania.[60] Western communists such as Togliatti had tried to insert some degree of flexibility into the system; in his 1964 'Yalta Memorandum', for example, Togliatti had argued for 'doctrinal pluralism and political diversification within the world communist movement'.[61] But Moscow was unmoving, and the invasion of Czechoslovakia kyboshed any hopes of a democratic variety of communism, leaving only rump Communist Parties in Western Europe. 'Neo-Stalinism' was the order of the day in Czechoslovakia under Gustáv Husák; elsewhere the ruling elites meekly ensured unbending loyalty to Moscow or, as in the case of Kadarism in Hungary, did not advertise (and certainly not to Moscow) the fact that they were permitting a relaxation of Stalinist principles in certain areas—something which is definitely not to be understood as an underhand attempt to reintroduce 'socialism with a human face' or, even more unthinkably, to act as a beachhead for 'bourgeois democracy'.[62]

The advent of neo-Stalinism was nowhere clearer than in the response of the communist authorities to the student uprisings of 1968. As is clear from the events of the Prague Spring, '1968' in Eastern Europe occurred in a different political context from Western Europe. Nevertheless, some of the rebels' grievances were similar, and there were important 'transnational' linkages between west and east: 1968 in both east and west was not only 'an anti-authoritarian revolt on both sides of the Iron Curtain'; it was also 'a rebellion against the grip of the war generation, founded on silences about the recent past, especially about World War II'.[63] In the same way that, in Western Europe, students' frustration grew as the contrast between their aspirations and social constraints became more marked, so in Eastern Europe frustration had been building ever since the uprisings of the 1950s had resulted in the suppression of any hint of dissent. Thus, as Prague typifies, when this frustration burst out into the open in 1968 it represented not so much an attempt to overthrow the system, as in the dreams of the romantic revolutionaries of Paris or Chicago, but an attempt to reform it, indeed to create a system in which their voices could be heard at all.

If these hopes were on the face of it less radical than those of their western counterparts, they were a graver threat to the establishment, at least as the communist establishment understood things; and taking to the streets in Eastern Europe was considerably more dangerous. Rebellions of various sorts took place across the region, including in Romania, where Ceauşescu's denunciation of the invasion of Czechoslovakia dangerously confused some intellectuals into thinking that an opportunity for domestic ideological relaxation might be opening up (although in Romania '"living in truth" was not an option for a majority of the Romanian intellectual elite'[64]), and in Yugoslavia, where the Belgrade student movement, which shared many traits with its western counterparts, appeared on the scene at the same time as revived Croatian nationalism and Kosovan separatism, thus not exactly confirming the Yugoslav script of brotherhood and unity.[65] In all cases, but perhaps especially in the GDR, the '68ers' transnational links—of clothing, music, literature, television, radio, and personal contacts—proved vital to mobilizing support.[66] Events in Czechoslovakia were to prove particularly inspiring to youngsters elsewhere, including Ukraine and other parts of the USSR, who believed in the necessity of reform and who lapped up the contents of Ludvík Vaculík's *2,000 Words*, the manifesto of 'socialism with a human face' which boldly argued that 'The incorrect line of the leadership turned the party from a political party and ideological grouping into a power organization which became very attractive to power-hungry egotists, reproachful cowards, and people with bad consciences.'[67]

As in Western Europe, 1968 did not emerge from nowhere. Typical of the background is the famous 'Open Letter to the Party' penned in 1965 by two young assistant lecturers at Warsaw University, Jacek Kuroń and Karel Modzelewski, in response to their expulsion from the Polish United Workers' Party for publishing a critique of Gomułka's Poland the year before. The Open Letter described an economically impoverished state run by a cynical bureaucracy in the interests of a narrow elite, and called for a free press and the abolition of the political police. Kuroń and Modzelewski called, in good Marxist terms, for a revolution in the name of the oppressed masses: 'Against an eventual accord between the international bureaucracy and the international imperialist bourgeoisie, which maintains systems of anti-people's dictatorship in its sphere of influence, we utter the traditional worker's slogan: "proletarians of all countries, unite!" '[68] Their letter, and especially their subsequent imprisonment, became a *cause célèbre* that radicalized the student body. Most significant, philosophy professor Leszek Kołakowski spoke in their favour, and was himself expelled from the Party, as were twenty-two of his supporters. As Judt writes, 'By the spring of 1967 the clumsy Polish leadership, enraged by criticism from its left, had succeeded in forging a genuine intellectual opposition.'[69] It also mobilized students in the west, most famously when Daniel Cohn-Bendit identified himself in court as 'Kuroń-Modzelewski'.[70]

The straw that broke the camel's back was the banning of the play *Forefather's Eve* by the Polish national poet Adam Mickiewicz, in January 1968. Two students, Adam Michnik and Henryk Szlajfer, provided an account of the situation to *Le Monde* and were expelled from Warsaw University. When Warsaw students met on 8 March to protest against Michnik and Szlajfer's expulsion, they were violently dispersed by the police. When students across the nation demonstrated in response, the Gomułka regime began to get nervous. The students were dealt with brutally and later in the year many, including a large proportion of Jewish origin, were tried and imprisoned. Once again, the language of antifascism—condemning the students as 'revisionists' and 'Zionists'—signalled, ironically, the triumph of a Stalinist wing in the Party which readily resorted to fascist language and posturing. This is perhaps unsurprising 'in view of the presence of recycled Polish fascists among the Stalinist wing of the ruling Party'.[71] But the stark fact is that the Party's exploitation of antisemitism in 1968 led to the emigration of the majority of Poland's 30,000-strong Jewish population (which had already been decimated in the Holocaust, with 3 million of the country's 3.3 million Jews killed), thus completing the Nazis' project of bringing to an end the centuries-old Jewish presence in Poland. Gomułka's 'national road to socialism' had ended in 'a variation of National Socialism plain and simple'.[72]

As in 1956, these events had a major impact outside of the Eastern Bloc. Apart from the physical and cultural effects of hundreds of thousands of refugees—and their ideological value for the west—the crushing of the Prague Spring dealt a terrible blow to West European communism. And it took a while for dissidents to brave the regime again, but the post-Helsinki emergence of human rights groups was especially important in widening the chinks in the communist regimes' armour. As one scholar famously put it, Czechoslovakia's revolution may have been 'interrupted' but it was not brought to an end.[73] The events of 1968 may have been crushed in Eastern Europe, but the demand for social change would not go away. And the ominous legacy of 1968 for the communist regimes was that they had squandered the legitimacy they had acquired through 'antifascism'; henceforth they could only survive with Soviet military backing. As Gorbachev would later admit, the Prague Spring 'represented nothing less than the beginning of the end for the totalitarian system'.[74]

The Cold War after Stalin's death

As in the domestic sphere, so in international relations the death of Stalin gave the signal for a new approach. At the same time as he tried to appease a very disgruntled, resentful population with attempts at liberalization, so Malenkov stated, in an address to the Supreme Soviet, that: 'At the present time there is no disputed or unresolved question that cannot be settled peacefully or by mutual agreement of the interested countries. This applies to our relations with all states, including the United States of America.'[75] Although the aged Churchill was interested in pursuing a summit with the aim of achieving détente, he was increasingly isolated, especially after the Soviets crushed the uprising in East Germany in 1953.[76] Moreover, the Eisenhower government had come to power on a platform of 'rollback' and

McCarthyism was still in full swing. Malenkov's reaching out fell on deaf or, rather, mistrusting ears. Were there then real chances for peace in the years 1953–5?

If there were to be such chances, they would centre on Germany. Fear of an armed West Germany was the USSR's number one priority, after Stalin's death just as before. Indeed, a measure of the importance placed on security from German aggression lies in the fact that Lavrenty Beria and Malenkov were willing to come to an agreement with the Allies involving unifying and demilitarizing Germany, as Stalin had suggested in his Note of March 1952, when he had been rebuffed by the west. After Stalin's death, the policy did not just disappear; in July 1953, the Soviet leadership approved a foreign ministers' conference on the German question and in 1954 pushed the idea of European collective security, a scenario of treaties binding all the European states together which envisaged the USSR joining NATO, the dropping of the European Defence Community, and the rearmament of West Germany coming to a halt. Unsurprisingly, the western powers rejected the proposal, on the basis that the USSR could not join NATO without the *raison d'être* of the organization being undermined.[77]

Khrushchev, however, had accused Beria (whose arrest and execution he had been involved in), Malenkov, and Foreign Minister Molotov of selling out the GDR, by offering to allow German reunification and free elections in return for the withdrawal of occupation forces. As a result, he was in no position openly to advocate the realization of socialism through parliamentary means in a unified Germany. Yet the new, bellicose stance, based on western rejections of Stalin's and Beria's proposals and thus driven by a determination to prop up the GDR, still represents a clear continuity in Soviet policy, insofar as it remained centred on the German question.

The brief opportunity for détente that Stalin's death had opened up disappeared just as quickly, as Beria and Malenkov were defeated by the constraints of the system they had done so much to create.[78] The best that was achieved at this point was the 'superficial détente' of the 1955 Geneva Summit, the first of the Cold War summits, and one which failed to overturn the established framework of policy-making on either side, as soon became apparent.[79] Once the Soviet concept of European collective security was rejected, Khrushchev turned down western proposals for a non-aggression pact whose terms allowed for a united Germany to join NATO if it so chose, the EDC met its demise in the French National Assembly, and the Federal Republic was admitted to NATO in its own right. The Soviets responded by creating the Warsaw Pact, although even at that late stage the Soviets' preferred outcome remained visible—the Warsaw Pact treaty specifically noted that the Pact could be dismantled if a pan-European treaty were to come into being. As in the early Cold War, miscomprehension and mutual distrust rather than ideologically driven aggression on the part of either side were primarily to blame for a process which began with proposals for rapprochement but which ended with the solidification of two opposing military blocs.

After the failure of the plan for European collective security in 1955–6, the notion acquired a primarily propagandistic value for the Soviets. On 27 November 1958, Khrushchev issued a six-month ultimatum calling for the Second World War Allies finally to sign a peace treaty dealing with Germany; if they did not, he would sign a pact with the GDR that would prevent western access to West Berlin. It seems that Khrushchev's actions were driven as much by Mao's attack on the Taiwan Straits in the summer of 1958—implicitly challenging Moscow to alter its post-Stalin stance towards the west and perhaps threatening to usurp Moscow as leader of world Marxism—as by Khrushchev's delight in squeezing the 'testicles of the West', as he famously put it. But such links are hard to prove, and a more compelling explanation for Khrushchev's action is Moscow's continued fear of a rearmed, specifically a nuclear-armed West Germany within NATO. As Smirnov, Soviet ambassador to Bonn, told Ulbricht on 5 October 1958: 'since April...the situation in West Germany seriously deteriorated and took an unwelcome direction.... The formation of the Bundeswehr goes on, atomic armament is now legalised.'[80] And rather than fear of Beijing, the aggressive behaviour perhaps reflects a newfound Soviet confidence in the wake of the Suez Crisis and the 'rush of adrenaline' provided by Sputnik, signalling the USSR's apparent superiority in the arms race and the space race.[81]

What is also in evidence here is the 'tyranny of the weak', that is to say, the extent to which Khrushchev was pushed by the GDR. Walter Ulbricht, the SED's leader, persuaded Khrushchev to take a stand on Berlin in order to bolster the GDR's increasingly weak economy—the country was losing thousands of its most able citizens to the Federal Republic through the 'escape hatch' of West Berlin—and to save face by protecting the USSR's most prized and strategically significant satellite. In other words, the Second Berlin Crisis reveals the extent to which the image of the Cold War as purely a bipolar affair does not stand up. Ulbricht's influence, particularly at a time of GDR weakness, dragged Khrushchev deeper into conflict than he wanted to go.[82] Still, even with Ulbricht's tendency to act unilaterally, continuity with Stalin's notion of 'security' is clear: what Khrushchev sought above all was 'Western acceptance and recognition of the post-World War II order in Europe, the fruits of the Red Army's victory over Nazism, a triumph embodied in the existence (and persistence) of a communist German state'.[83] As he asked in his speech to a Warsaw Pact conference in August 1961, 'What will it mean, if the GDR is liquidated? It will mean that the Bundeswehr will move to the Polish border... to the borders with Czechoslovakia... closer to our Soviet border.'[84] This was an intolerable scenario.

The supreme symbol of communism's need to hold its people by force, and the greatest symbol of the Cold War, was of course the Berlin Wall, or, as the East Germans called it, the 'antifascist protective rampart'.[85] Its erection signalled the end of the Berlin Crisis, and effectively an admission on the part of the GDR and its Moscow backers that the only way to stop the brain drain to the west was to wall East German citizens in. Or, as Ulbricht preferred to put it, by closing the border around East Berlin he had achieved 'the protection of the GDR against the organization of a civil war and military provocations from West Berlin' and ensured 'the cessation of economic and cultural undermining of the capital of the GDR by the West Berlin swamp'.[86] What this meant in practice was the criminalization of those *Grenzgänger* (border crossers) who had previously made their living by travelling to and from West Berlin, and a harsh regulatory regime watching over inhabitants of border zones in the GDR, not just in Berlin but across the country, especially in counties which bordered West Germany. Such measures 'were paradigmatic for the making of the SED state itself', that is to say, such untrammelled exercises of power with respect to securing the country's borders illustrate the way in which the GDR operated in general: massive regulation and policing, all in the name, as the regime understood it, of insulating the GDR's citizens from the dangerous, fascist ideology of West Germany.[87] The Wall thus represented both the regime's external strength vis-à-vis its allies and its internal weakness when it came to dealing with its population, whose 'popular scepticism' of the 1950s gave way to the 'resigned pragmatism' of the 1960s.[88]

But if Ulbricht could force Khrushchev's hand during the Berlin Crisis, his unilateralism was to be his downfall during the era of *Ostpolitik*. Khrushchev's successor, Brezhnev, saw that progress in German–German talks would be crucial to the success of the Moscow Treaty and, resentful of

Ulbricht's 'superior' attitude towards him, forced him out in favour of Erich Honecker in 1971.[89] By contrast, Nicolae Ceauşescu exploited *Ostpolitik* to resist Khrushchev's attempt to 'improve' the Warsaw Pact, which was newspeak for strengthening Soviet control over the other states. Ignoring East German, Soviet, Czechoslovak, and Polish objections, Ceauşescu in October 1966 entered into diplomatic relations with West Germany, which had now abandoned the Hallstein Doctrine. Where Ulbricht's, Gomułka's, and Novotný's 'entire credo was founded on solidarity against "revanchist West Germany" ',[90] Ceauşescu was already taking Romania down the road to 'national communism', which used the language of anti-fascism but produced something altogether different in reality.[91] With only limited success at reforming the Warsaw Pact's command structures,[92] Bucharest began to appeal more to Yugoslavia, as the events of 1967 put the brakes on Tito's liberalizing reforms. The latter 'interpreted the Israeli military victory after the military coup in Greece as the beginning of an American offensive to alter the balance of power in the Near East and the Balkans, and therefore as a threat to the security of Yugoslavia'.[93] Moving closer to Romania gave the Yugoslavs room to manoeuvre between the 'bloc of five unshakeables' (USSR, the GDR, Poland, Hungary, and Bulgaria) and a more independent-minded state (Czechoslovakia being the other in this category, until the invasion).

After the extreme dangers of the years 1958–62, after which the Hotline between the Kremlin and the White House was installed in 1963, such intra-bloc conflicts were of little interest to the west except insofar as they could be exploited for propaganda purposes or where the perception existed that such splits could be widened with suitable intervention. The return of hard-line politics within the Eastern Bloc provided the context within which Cold War rhetoric could be played down and the possibility of serious talks could begin. Although the invasion of Czechoslovakia deepened existing splits within the Eastern Bloc, it also served to entrench the status quo on the international stage. The western powers barely blinked an eyelid at what happened in 1968—just as in 1956—and thus not only was the notion of 'rollback' exposed as a sham, but the Soviets won *de facto* recognition of their sphere of interest in Eastern Europe. This stability, unpleasant though it might have been for the region's inhabitants, combined with West Germany's *Ostpolitik* and culminating in the 1975 Helsinki agreements, contributed to a period of détente which lasted until the Soviet invasion of Afghanistan in 1979. Détente was therefore a recognition of the status quo in Europe rather than an attempt to change it—which is why Brezhnev applauded the signing of the Helsinki Final Accord by saying that it was the 'summing up of the political results of the Second World War'.[94] It represented the west's recognition that 'rollback' was a pipe dream and that accommodation rather than belligerence stood a greater chance of undermining the Soviets.

The accession of Brezhnev changed the nature of the Cold War in two directions: it first of all placed more emphasis on action (military spending) than words (Khrushchev's notorious posturing), and also used the Soviets' apparent strength to improve east–west relations. On the one hand, then, Brezhnev reversed Khrushchev's decision to cut spending on conventional military forces and to rely on long-range nuclear missiles, expanding spending on both. Between 1965 and 1970, defence spending in the USSR rose by 40 per cent, from about 3 per cent of GDP to 15 per cent, as Brezhnev sought to give substance to the Soviets' claim to superpower status. 'External defence', it is worth remembering, 'was never the only—or even primary— military mission of the Warsaw Pact', unlike NATO.[95] It thus remained vital that Soviet dominance over the Warsaw Pact's structures and personnel should be guaranteed, with, for example, Soviet control over nuclear warheads deployed on Polish, East German, Hungarian, or Czechoslovak territory. Perhaps because of fears of the alliance's potential weaknesses—Albania stopped participating in 1961 and left definitively in 1968, and the Soviets feared other countries might be induced into the Chinese embrace—the satellite states 'were never given any say in the use of the alliance's "joint" nuclear arsenal'.[96] Already by the late 1950s, the Soviets' nuclear arsenal was substantial enough to give the US pause for thought before engaging in warfare, and by the time of Cuba it was plain that warfare had to be avoided because the potential for widespread destruction was clear to see. On the other hand, under Brezhnev, the superpowers signed some two dozen treaties in the 1970s, dealing with arms controls and much more besides.

Brezhnev's reputation for presiding over an increasingly grey and stagnant communist bloc is only partially justified; he was also, at least in his first decade in power, a shrewd operator. Brezhnev's vision of 'developed socialism' abandoned Khrushchev's attempts to 'keep up' with the west in favour of winning recognition for the USSR as a 'normal' country and encouraging mass participation in the administration of the state. His manoeuvring perpetuated Soviet hegemony over the deployment of Warsaw Pact weapons and ensured that the neo-Stalinist leaders of the satellite states remained loyal to him. Ironically, whilst 'developed socialism' marked a break from Khrushchev's brinkmanship, it also ended by making communism dependent on capitalism.[97] Most important, though, in the Cold War context, is that confirmation of Soviet superpower status and a drive to détente went hand in hand.

From the Soviets' point of view, the advantage of détente was not only that they were being treated as equals on the international stage—important in the face of the Chinese as well as the Americans—but that they had greater access to international trade, which would, Brezhnev believed, strengthen the Soviet economy, give Soviet citizens greater access to consumer goods, and simultaneously allow the high levels of military spending to continue.[98] In other words, détente followed logically from the deescalation of tension after Berlin and Cuba, but neither side regarded it as a way of befriending the other; rather, détente was just the latest framework in which the Cold War rivalry between east and west took place.

Still, even if détente was a form of Cold War conflict, it was a far less unpleasant one than what preceded it, and the era did see some progress on arms limitations. The Nuclear Non-Proliferation Treaty (1968), the Strategic Arms Limitation Treaties (SALT I, 1972, and SALT II, 1979), and the Anti-Ballistic Missile Treaty (1972) brought about an awareness of the need for controls, although they never stopped the acceleration in Soviet military spending (or American, for that matter). And in Europe, there was no real progress on arms limitation talks. The British and French were too wedded to their nuclear weapons, and the rest of the Western Europeans unwilling to release themselves from the US's nuclear embrace, especially in the face of Soviet strategic parity, achieved during the 1960s. For the time being, then, the citizens of the people's democracies looked destined to keep travelling down the road to 'actually existing socialism'.

Everyday life under communism

The communist countries were not inhabited by heroes and monsters. The Cold War has continued to colour our understanding of Eastern Europe for too long, and it remains too easy to slip into clichés and stereotypes. The upshot of the Prague Spring and Helsinki Accords may have been the birth of dissent in the form that became familiar in the late stage of the Cold War: *samizdat*, the 'parallel polis', underground universities and trade unions, and the like, all of which we will encounter in Chapter 6, but only a small fraction of the population were ever involved in such movements. The image of the literary underground is a western one which bears little relation to the realities of life under communism. Similarly, whilst it is true that the Helsinki accords constituted a 'legal and moral trap' for the communist regimes, very few dared to put their heads above the parapets in the manner of Solzhenitsyn or Sakharov.[99] In fact, between 1968 and the late 1970s, this sort of dissent was only just beginning to emerge, and most citizens committed themselves to getting by with their heads down, staying unnoticed by the Party and its local networks, resigned to accepting 'a conservative brand of consumer socialism' as meagre compensation for the absence of civil society.[100]

In his novel *The Iron Curtain Kid*, Oliver Fritz writes, contrary to western expectations: 'We citizens did not have to queue for absolutely everything, nor did we only communicate in hushed voices or were in constant fear of being randomly arrested.'[101] It is obviously the case that 'normality' existed under communism: people went about their daily lives, shopping, cooking, working, playing, loving, and dying. But that normality was always circumscribed, it was always fenced in to quite clearly defined borders, outside of which citizens did not step if they wanted to lead lives unmolested by the authorities. And it was a normality which developed over time, and which changed according to which political paradigm prevailed, from Stalinization to the 'thaw' to the re-imposition of hard-line rule to the period of 'normalization' after the Prague Spring.

In the early years, the regimes' social restructuring programmes created complicity among citizens, especially among those who were beneficiaries of the reallocation of private property.[102] In the period between the Great Patriotic War and the death of Stalin, for example, the Soviet Union employed a small army of informants to report 'non-political crimes', mostly the theft of state property, to the authorities. At the height of the campaign against the theft of state property, in 1947, more than 454,000 people were convicted.[103] The process of eradicating 'fascism', that is, all vestiges of private ownership of land and property, went hand in hand with the incorporation of the masses into the new system, as well as the emergence of the 'new class' of the *nomenklatura*, who grew more nepotistic, venal, and regime-dependent over time.[104]

The initial years of postwar Sovietization were devoted to bringing society into line. But after the uprisings of 1953 and 1956, the regimes focused some attention, albeit insufficiently developed, to workers' demands for goods and better living standards. In the late 1950s, under Gomułka, Moda Polska, a range of ready-to-wear clothes shops, was launched in Poland, as was Sybille in East Germany. *Lada* fashion review appeared at the same time in Bulgaria. Modern design, advertising, textiles, music, ceramics, and enamel-wares all suddenly took on western-style designs and became available in the name of a turn to consumerism.[105] Khrushchev set out his goals of creating 'communist-style consumer behaviour' in an apparent admission that the relentless pursuit of production had neglected citizens'—and especially women's—needs.[106] But how did the official turn to consumerism translate into a change in everyday life for citizens of communist states?

The pre-existence of private enterprise before collectivization meant that a thirst for consumerism was not entirely novel; what was new, in this mostly poor part of Europe, was the existence of goods other than pure essentials, as well as money to pay for them. Second, private enterprise not only survived the collectivization process—better in some regions than in others—but the strict regime that collectivization enforced on rural life meant that working to time and calculating labour and output in monetary terms was as much a part of communist life as it was of pre- and post-communism. Changes in perceptions of time wrought by communism—the need to work to timetables and to increase productivity and outputs on the one hand, and to stand in lines and endure intense boredom on the other—were different from perceptions of time under capitalism, but there were similarities nevertheless. Here one can profitably contrast 'Goulash communist' Hungary, where the strict labour and financial controls of collectivization may have helped pave the way for capitalism after 1989, with Romania, where, in contrast to 'capitalist time' which is linear and ever accelerating, under Nicolae Ceauşescu time stood still, 'the medium for producing not profits but subjection, for immobilizing persons in the Party's grip'.[107]

In general, then, consumerism in Eastern Europe meant consumerism controlled by the Party for the purpose of developing communism. In Bulgaria, for example, the Eighth Congress of the Bulgarian Communist Party (BCP) of 1963 set out its vision of creating, in the long term in Bulgaria, a 'new socialist person'. This meant a process of homogenization, the standardization of citizens in terms of their behaviour and aspirations and their reshaping into citizens. The BCP stated its goal of developing the 'citizen of the socialist and communist society toward a high cultural level and elevated spiritual and material needs', including in this process a massive expansion in the range and availability of consumer goods.[108] And Khrushchev, rather awkwardly, argued at the CPSU's Twenty-Second Party Congress in 1961 that 'Personal ownership by the toiler of a large number of things... is not at variance with the principles of communist construction as long as it keeps within reasonable bounds and does not become an end in itself.'[109]

The turn to consumerism raised a fundamental problem: how could communist daily life be conceptualized as different from capitalist daily life if it too placed more emphasis on consumption than production? The answer lay in the *content* and *context* of material goods. The placing of even as innocent an object as a vase in a room could take on unwelcome connotations of 'bourgeois viciousness' instead of 'socialist cosiness' if done wrongly. As Khrushchev went on to say, this sort of 'petty-bourgeois degeneration' means that 'the individual falls a prey to things and becomes a slave to them'.[110] Communist citizens were expected to display their possessions in a way that exemplified the correct socialist lifestyle; they therefore walked a nervous line between consumerist greed and socialist satisfaction. In Poland, residents' committees in apartment blocks (*komitety blokowe*) policed private space, and women's magazines offered a vision of the ideal home that stressed ideological conformity and the modelling of domestic life, a fact that acquired added poignancy given the communist regimes' inability to provide sufficient, not to mention decent housing.[111] The new consumerism had to conform to, indeed to help in the construction of, the ideal communist citizen: well-mannered, obliging, dedicated to the common good and to improving the public sphere, in contrast to the western consumer who was figured as individualist, inappropriate, and inauthentic.[112] At the same time, the adoption of western-style consumerism could be presented as the salvation of the 'progressive essence' of western bourgeois culture.[113] No wonder that the furniture designer Olgierd Szlekys could say that in communist Poland, 'we have changed the forms of our life. We have moved part of private life to the houses of culture, to clubs and cafes which are places to meet comrades replacing, we say, the old salons.'[114]

Throughout the Eastern Bloc, the official turn to consumerism struggled to meet people's needs and desires. Not that the regimes did not try. In January 1959 at the CPSU's Twenty-First Party Congress, Khrushchev spoke of 'catching up with and overtaking America' specifically with respect to living standards.[115] In the so-called 'kitchen debates' of 1959, when Khrushchev and Vice-President Nixon squared off over the meaning and quality of each system's kitchen appliances at the American Pavilion of the Moscow World Fair (seen by about 2.7 million visitors over six weeks), we see 'perhaps the most dramatic instance of the more general politicization of material culture'.[116] As modern socialist kitchens were being introduced, these debates marked the high point of communist claims to be able to compete with the west and, in retrospect, the beginning of the west's outstripping of communism on these economic grounds (grounds which, it should be noted, were essentially the western-defined ones of economic growth, consumer culture, and shopping as leisure. By competing on those terms, the communist countries were already acknowledging their inability to deliver much of what their citizens wanted).[117] In fact, Khrushchev's competitive claims 'contradicted the Party's concurrent goal of inventing an alternative commodity culture based on temperance', and 'locked' the Soviets into 'a double-bind, inviting a constant comparison of the two systems'.[118] The consequences of failing to live up to this promise were that people were increasingly turning to a 'make-do and mend' philosophy, as well as to the black market, smuggling, hard currency, especially the deutschmark and the dollar, and thus a correspondingly high instance of bribery and corruption in everyday business.

The new consumerism was only one way in which communism was going to be built, however. The Cold War period also 'saw pervasive efforts to permeate not only places of work and public ceremony but also the most intimate spaces of the everyday with ideological meaning'.[119] This was as true of cinema, the radio, and football as it was of union or pioneer meetings. Cinema and radio could be used to inculcate the virtues of antifascism, though radio could also be used to inspire dissent, as when the broadcasts of Radio Free Europe's Voice of Free Hungary gave (false) hope to Nagy's supporters in 1956.[120] Sport was used to promote a cult of the body and physical fitness: 'Every person, in every place, should take part in sport once a week,' declared Walter Ulbricht in 1959,[121] and the GDR devoted considerable resources to promoting sports in which competitors could win several medals, such as swimming, rowing, and athletics, though it neglected football. By contrast, the Hungarian national football team, captained by the exceptional Ferenc Puskás and led by its coach, Gusztáv Sebes, performed feats of individual sportsmanship that would have been regarded very suspiciously in any other sphere of communist life. Their exuberant displays, made on the basis of an innovative formation which was 'a hair's-breadth from 4-2-4', were forgiven on the basis that it propelled them to victory against every national team they played in 1952 and 1953, including, most famously, England at Wembley Stadium.[122]

And of course, people found that much of their 'private time' was accounted for, not only with work and obtaining life's necessities, but by the Party's attempts to inculcate socialist virtues into its citizens by engaging them in meetings and groups which pressed home the message, such as compulsory Marxism-Leninism in school, obligatory May Day parades, or communist 'invented traditions' such as Yugoslavia's Grandfather Frost. Children and youth were especially important here, with the Pioneers organizations central to the formation of a new communist consciousness, but in the process having to negotiate—in Eastern Europe, if not in the USSR—with young people's demands for spheres of autonomy and free expression. In Bulgaria, the Fatherland Front strove to construct the 'socialist way of life', with its leader (from 1974 to 1989), Pencho Kubadinski, explicitly claiming that it aimed to create the 'new man' and the 'socialist way of life'.[123] In the GDR the National Front and Cultural League, and in Hungary the socialist brigades, played similar roles. All such organizations helped to establish and maintain the 'precarious stability' of the communist regimes, as did the ambivalent relationship to communism displayed by the region's churches, most of which collaborated with the regimes in return for some religious freedom, but which could also become centres of opposition.[124] Poland had one of the highest rates of church attendance in Europe by the 1970s, and in Croatia too, Catholicism took on the role of a sort of 'opposition'.

Yet there is no getting away from the fact that by the mid-1970s, the communist regimes had become bleak—politically oppressive, economically depressed, and environmentally degraded. Czechoslovakia in the post-1968 era of 'normalization' has been aptly described as resembling 'a museum of Communism' until 1989.[125] At this point, the old men who came to power—Husák (Czechoslovakia), Honecker (GDR), Zhivkov (Bulgaria), Jaruzelski (Poland), and Kádár (Hungary)—did not quite return to the paranoia of Stalinism. But they did preside over repressive societies which attained stability and conformity through stifling dissent and by increasingly instrumentalizing the language of antifascism as a legitimization strategy.

The exceptions were considerably worse: Enver Hoxha's Albania, based on a variety of Maoism (following Albania's 1961 alignment with China), and Ceauşescu's Romania, where the possessive case is appropriate since he turned the country into a personal fiefdom by the 1980s.[126] Only Yugoslavia offered on the face of it a more liberal version of communism, but here too

Figure 6. Petrova Gora, Croatia, memorial to the communist Partisans. The memorial was largely dismantled in 2011 after being partly destroyed in the wars of the 1990s.

we should be in no doubt that the system was also ultimately backed up by the political police; furthermore, the relative liberalism also, ironically, provided the setting in which the South Slav federation could begin to be picked apart as nationalist sentiment grew.

In Albania, the country's peripheral position set the scene for 45 years of hard-line Stalinism, ironic in a country in which the communists had taken over without Soviet assistance and which set itself apart from the communist mainstream. Indeed, it was Albania's peripheral role that allowed it to take a position which contradicted the mainstream, seeing it remain Stalinist long after Stalinism had been disavowed by the rest of the Eastern Bloc. Hoxha crushed his opponents ruthlessly—most notably Xoxe who, unlike the other victims of trials elsewhere at the same period, really was a Titoist—and his break with Yugoslavia in 1949 set the scene for a long-term adherence to Stalinism. Indeed, Khrushchev's attempt to encourage Hoxha to seek a rapprochement with Tito in the mid-1950s brought about Tirana's definitive break with Moscow and its unlikely turn towards China instead. The Albanian regime's insecurity made it paranoid about any outside interference, bringing about a state which not only isolated itself from its erstwhile communist comrades elsewhere in Europe but meticulously insulated its citizens from knowledge of the outside world, with televisions and radios, not to mention foreign travel, almost entirely banned.[127]

In Romania, the leadership used the same vocabulary of reform as was emanating from Prague in 1968, but the reality was very different. Instead of 'liberalizing' communism, Romania's political leaders increasingly turned to nationalism, a trend that had begun under Dej but which reached new heights under Ceauşescu, eagerly supported by regime-friendly intellectuals. Arguing that the Czechoslovak leaders were misguided rather than ill intentioned, Ceauşescu condemned the Warsaw Pact invasion, thereby confusing western interpreters (and not a few post-communist Romanian revisionist commentators) into thinking that Ceauşescu was making a stand against orthodox Marxism-Leninism. The reverse was in fact true.[128] But by putting a spanner in the Warsaw Pact's works, and consistently breaking the bloc's unanimity—not just over West Germany, but also by not breaking diplomatic relations with Israel in 1967—Ceauşescu's prestige on the international stage reached heights that were entirely incommensurate with his domestic behaviour.

One of the few things that sustained these regimes during this period was the memory dividend that still accrued following the Great Patriotic War, with its still-meaningful and emotionally powerful traditions of 'fighters against fascism'. The tradition of antifascism did hold some sway until the very end. Indeed, the communist regimes increasingly appealed to it as of the late 1960s as other forms of legitimacy disappeared. The strength of the tradition is evident in the fact that western admirers could easily be found who were willing to defend the regimes on the grounds that they were the guardians of antifascism. Although some journalists and visitors saw through the official versions that their guides mouthed, most were impressed by the communists' declared aim of ridding the world of fascism. On the occasion of the GDR's thirtieth anniversary, campaigner Gordon Schaffer praised the state's 'antifascism and commitment to peace'. And as late as the 1980s, some British trade unionists and peace campaigners, such as Canon Kenyon Wright, believed that 'the East Germans were sincere about antifascism'.[129]

Sincere they may have been, but antifascist sincerity was insufficient compensation for the wider social deterioration. As we will see in Chapter 6, antifascism would prove unable to act as a powerful enough social glue, once the changes in the world economy started to impact on social memories of the war in both Western and Eastern Europe. Ironically, it was precisely the attempt to provide bloc unity, including subscribing to tightly choreographed antifascist ceremonies, that paved the way for Gorbachev's relative permissiveness. The attempt to straitjacket the Warsaw Pact countries by making them dependent on Moscow, meaning ultimately the threat (or promise) of military force, was appealing to the Soviets in the late 1960s and early 1970s, but was no longer viable by the early 1980s when 'it carried responsibilities that the Soviet Union simply could no longer assume'.[130] That is to say, when domestic problems forced the Soviets to revisit their policy of holding on to Eastern Europe by force rather than by popular legitimacy, the rhetoric of bloc unity was rapidly exposed as a sham and communist control swiftly melted into thin air. 'In the long run', Fejtö argued with characteristic prescience, 'the USSR will have lost, and the cause of neutrality gained.'[131]

PART III

Shock Treatment

5

Neo-Liberalism

Western Europe, 1975–1989

I am strengthened in my conviction [as a democratic socialist] when I see, here in our own country, an increase in injustice, unemployment, speculation and graft. When I look into the future that the right wing has to offer, where the workers will get less and the rich will get more, where social security will be in decline and the number of luxury yachts on the rise, where solidarity diminishes and egotism increases, where the strong can help themselves and the weak will have to beg if they are to get anything at all.

Olof Palme

It is most important not to use rash analogies to obscure the singularity of the Nazis' crimes against the Jewish people. Yet I find it morally exceedingly worrisome that the inner logic of modernity still fails to prohibit preparations for mass murder—this time not along the lines of racist ideology, but within the framework of the dispute between East and West. I do not compare this to Auschwitz; all that I am saying is that Auschwitz reminds us that we must condemn this logic whenever it appears, and fight it by political means.

Joschka Fischer[1]

The crisis of social democracy

1985 was the fortieth anniversary of the end of the war and the liberation of the Nazis' concentration and death camps. That year, Chancellor Kohl invited President Reagan to attend a ceremony and lay a wreath at Bitburg cemetery to honour German war dead. Reagan agreed in the name of reconciliation, even though he had previously turned down an offer to visit a concentration camp memorial site because, he said, he did not want to reawaken old memories. Protests quickly poured in, particularly once it became clear that included among the dead were a number of SS men. Amidst the outcry that ensued, Elie Wiesel's appeal to Reagan that 'That place is not your place' became the best known. Although Reagan hastily added a trip to Bergen-Belsen to his itinerary, he did attend the ceremony at Bitburg, thus giving the impression that all the war dead, including the SS, were equally victims of war, and equally worthy of civic (as opposed to private) commemoration.[2]

By the mid-1980s, Europe had been divided for four decades. But the apparent stability of the Cold War masked deeper shifts. Reagan and Kohl represented a turn away from the postwar settlement that helped to build Cold War societies in Western Europe and the USA. What changed in the 1970s and early 1980s to bring about a situation in which the German Chancellor could consider it appropriate to invite the American President to a ceremony at which the symbols of Nazi criminality would be on view and, worse, for the President to accept?

Historians debate the meanings of the 1970s: some see the decade as a dark period of retrenchment, terrorism, and economic decline, others point to a revival of democracy and of social democratic values, and the start of economic renewal.[3] Either way, the 1970s should be regarded as a more important turning point in Western European history than 1968. Far more so than the 1960s, in many ways, the postwar years came to an end in the 1970s and the restructuring of the economy and society which has stamped Europe since then began to take shape. Accompanying these huge changes in economy and society, which are best summed up with the German term *Tendenzwende* (the change in tendency), came a revision of the meaning of the past and hence of Europe's memory politics. Along with a new openness to breaking down the dominant silences and myths concerning the Second World War, went a new attack on the values of the postwar consensus. As the purchase of the postwar settlement ebbed away, so the antifascism that helped to build Western Europe after 1945 came increasingly under fire. Indeed, according to Judt, the consensus 'that had hitherto embraced the post-war state, together with the neo-Keynesian economics that furnished its intellectual battlements', was the 'first victim' of the 1970s' 'change of mood'.[4] 'The decade and a half from the late 1960s to the beginning of the 1980s', one historian writes, 'comprised in fact the most troubled era of postwar institutional development in the second half of the twentieth century.'[5] But where the communist regimes did not survive the turmoil, the

West European states did. The way they did so, and at what cost, will be the subject of this chapter.

With the exception of Britain's Attlee government, which itself only governed until 1951, postwar Western Europe in the two decades after the war was dominated by conservative politics. But as we have seen, these were different conservatives from before the war, and the settlement they put in place across Western Europe adhered largely to social democratic values. Ironically, by taking religion out of politics, Christian Democrats presided over a secularization of postwar society and embraced liberal democracy, the very thing they had originally been established to combat in the late nineteenth century.[6] Christian Democracy had initially replaced discredited European conservatism after 1945, but over the following decades the two merged, becoming the 'catch-all parties of the moderate right'.[7] The year 1968 had been a liberalizing moment, when the old guard across Europe came under fire from a younger generation. The question is whether the change of the 1970s represented a continuation of this liberalization or whether, to the contrary, it is better understood as a conservative backlash.

In West Germany, the SPD dominated the federal political scene in the 1970s, with Willy Brandt (1969) and Helmut Schmidt (1974) as chancellors. The difficulties they faced, from terrorism to unemployment, to *Ostpolitik*, challenged any hopes they had for further social democratic reform. Indeed, even if the FRG epitomizes 1970s social democracy, as of the 1973 oil crisis the country was subjected to the same economic and social pressures as its neighbours; 2 million West Germans were unemployed by 1981. Particularly during the 'German Autumn' of 1977, the *Tendenzwende* not only placed barriers in the way of reform but began a process which led to the CDU/CSU victory under Helmut Kohl in 1982.[8] The switch of dominant political parties disguises the fact that the *Tendenzwende* represented deeper currents of change. Kohl's victory in 1982 brought into power a set of counter-reforming tendencies and values that had been developing in West German society since the early 1970s when social philosopher Jürgen Habermas identified a West German 'legitimation crisis'; these tendencies were expressed through cultural ideas and policies as much as through more narrow political and economic legislation.[9]

In Britain, inflation was running at 20 per cent in 1975. When James Callaghan came to power the following year, following Harold Wilson's resignation, the Labour government found itself squeezed by the oil crisis. Its response was to begin the policies which would be radicalized by

Margaret Thatcher, of combating the unions. This is why the 'winter of discontent', which saw uncollected rubbish piled high in the streets and the dead left unburied, occurred in 1978–9, before Thatcher came to power. This scenario, in which social democratic ideas were steadily delegitimized, was reproduced throughout Western Europe, as we will see below. From Scandinavia to Italy, as the prosperity of the postwar boom came under threat, established political norms were severely tested.

One of the most surprising challenges to the postwar political settlement, and one of the more revealing of the changes taking place in the late 1970s, was Eurocommunism, the attempt by the leading Western European Communist Parties (especially the PCF and PCI) to initiate a reform process that would allow them to adjust to the realities of social and economic life thirty years after the end of the war. It challenged the political status quo in Western Europe as it called into question the decision made, at the start of the Cold War, to exclude communists from power at central government level— communists were well established in local politics throughout Europe and they appeared to be reconciled to the parliamentary process. And Eurocommunism challenged the Eastern European regimes because it rejected Moscow control and argued for a variety of communism that lived up to the basic rights agreed at Helsinki.

The Eurocommunist movement emerged in response to the crushing of the Prague Spring. But it did not reach full flower until after 1975, when change in Spain and Portugal, the gradual evaporation of taboos within the PCI and PCF, and the conflicts in world communism in general made new attitudes possible.[10] The Spanish communist leader Santiago Carrillo, for example, who snuck back from his French exile into Spain in disguise to try and influence the transition process, and whose PCE was legalized in 1977, made a name for himself with his book 'Eurocomunismo' y Estado, in which he highlighted the invasion of Czechoslovakia as 'the straw which broke the camel's back', revealing the need for a 'true internationalism'.[11] The importance of the Spanish example is that it showed the way for moderation after dictatorship. Eventually, this tendency towards moderation, which went further than Carrillo wanted, would destroy itself, as communist support melted away in favour of the socialists (PSOE) under Felipe González in the elections of 1982. But as well as its contribution to Spanish domestic events during the transition from Francoism, Spanish Eurocommunism contributed to developing a continent-wide critique of centralized Soviet authoritarianism that had effects in Moscow, Prague, and Budapest as well as in Madrid, Rome, and Paris.

Eurocommunism placed Moscow and the Eastern Bloc regimes in quite an awkward situation, since they did not want openly to punish the Western European parties for failing to toe the line, but nor did they want to admit that they were on the right track, especially in light of the Helsinki accords' emphasis on human rights. East Germany's SED, for example, took it for granted that the Western European CPs remained their allies; and besides, with the shift to the right in Italian politics, it was wary of condemning Enrico Berlinguer and the PCI.[12] Nevertheless, Moscow did regard Euro-communism as a threat; so too did some of the signatories of Charter 77, which underlined its seriousness. The SED 'came to its senses' when the PCI condemned the Soviet invasion of Afghanistan in 1979. At the same time, the PCF brought about the dissolution of the Eurocommunist project by returning to the fold, expressing its support for the invasion.[13]

Judt argues, quite persuasively, that Eurocommunism never seduced Western European electorates, but only 'intellectuals and academics who mistook for a political revival of Marxism what was in fact an expression of doctrinal exhaustion'.[14] Eurocommunism, in other words, was a contradic-tion in terms, since it obliged communists to abandon their links with Moscow and to work within the local liberal-parliamentary systems. That is why Enver Hoxha condemned it as 'undisguised revisionism' and 'anti-communism'.[15] Nevertheless, in another respect its legacy was important: one insightful contemporary noted that Eurocommunism 'may prove to be the most potent foreign stimulus to have affected Eastern Europe since the convulsion produced by de-Stalinization in the mid-1950s', and Mikhail Gorbachev himself admitted in 2001 that 'This project of Eurocommunism has been a very important stage and played an unquestionable role in our passing over to reforms, democracy and freedom.'[16]

When Eurocommunism died, it was not just because the PCF changed direction. Rather, by the early 1980s, Western Europe was on a new course, one which in many people's eyes rendered collectivist politics superannu-ated. For the last decade of the Cold War in Western Europe was one of neo-liberal restructuring, a euphemistic term for the triumph of the market and individualism. This sweeping economic and social change 'saved' West-ern European prosperity—at least when taken as a single figure of GDP and not in terms of how that wealth was so unevenly distributed—and at the same time made Eastern Europeans all the more keenly aware of the short-comings of the command economy. At the same time, these seismic socio-economic shifts also reordered the ways in which European memory politics functioned. At the end of this chapter, we will see how the free market in goods and services that emerged as the main characteristic of 1980s Western Europe was accompanied by a free market in European memories, when individuals and groups became able to articulate views that had been taboo for thirty years or more in the public sphere.

From Eurosclerosis to European Union

Far more influential than Eurocommunism on future developments, both within Western Europe and internationally, was the process of European integration. Referring to it as a 'process', however, makes it sound like a pre-ordained path towards 'ever closer union', when the truth could not be more different. The 1970s were years of stagnation within the EEC's institutions and not just in the member states' economies. The way out of the economic doldrums for Europe was a hard, contested one. Ambitions for intergovernmental cooperation and economic and monetary union set out at the 1969 Hague conference and in the 1970 Werner Report were placed under severe pressure. When that pressure eased, in the second half of the 1980s, Europe looked quite different.

As with the wider world economy, the oil crisis exacerbated existing difficulties within the EC. In the early 1970s, the EC was dominated by the CAP, which accounted for over 70 per cent of its budget. Of next importance was the issue of how to deal with declining industries, not least in Britain, which had finally joined the EC in 1973 following Pompidou's reversal of de Gaulle's policy in the light of Bonn's new focus on *Ostpolitik*. But any rethinking was delayed by the oil crisis and the downturn which followed. The response of the EC was one which illustrated the community's dilapidated state: instead of devising a coordinated plan, the member states retreated into protectionism (of textile industries, for example) and attempted to save their own oil stocks. When, for example, the Netherlands was subjected to an oil embargo by OPEC for its pro-Israeli stance, the other EC states did nothing to help. Instead they opted to make their own bilateral deals with oil-producing states in the Arabian Gulf and, especially the French, did everything they could to maintain good relations with Arab states. In fact the big oil companies helped the Netherlands more than did its EC 'partners', by making clandestine deliveries.

Following the collapse of Bretton Woods, the European currencies were already tied more to the deutschmark than the dollar. As a result of the oil crisis, the EMU had to be abandoned. In March 1979, it was replaced with the European Monetary System (EMS), another currency regulation tool which operated through the Exchange Rate Mechanism (ERM) on the basis of an internal currency unit, the ecu (European currency unit). After OPEC doubled the price of oil in 1979 following the Iranian Revolution, both the ERM and EMS were put in abeyance. But the shock of the second oil crisis was not as great as the first and over the next decade, the EMS did manage to bring some stability to currency convertibility within the EC— with the exception of Britain, which did not join. The late 1970s and early 1980s, then, were the EC's lowest ebb.

Yet, despite all this, the period of Eurosclerosis also gave rise to a determination, among Euro-enthusiasts, to get things moving again. Greece joined the EC in 1981, followed by Spain and Portugal in 1986. The accession of former dictatorships was itself a salutary reminder of the wider aims of integration; as Judt notes: 'For Athens, EC membership amounted to a second Marshall Plan', for it received $7.9 billion from Brussels in the years 1985–9 alone.[17] Following the failed right-wing coup attempt of February 1981 in Spain and the uncertain years after the Carnation Revolution in Portugal, accession to the EC acted to anchor the Southern European states in a stable framework, tying them to the norms and procedures of the common market. Membership of the EC 'was presented not only positively as the seal of democratic consolidation, but also negatively as an "antidote" to resurgent civil conflict'.[18]

The Single European Act (1986), which aimed to bring about a complete internal market (including reintroducing EMU) by the end of 1992, represented the 'relaunch' of Europe advocated by Commission president Jacques Delors, and was the biggest step taken by the EC since its creation at the Treaty of Rome. Its appeal lay in its business-friendliness, which persuaded Thatcher to climb aboard, although she of course baulked at some aspirations also contained in the SEA, such as a single currency—but that seemed like a pipe dream in 1986. Although Delors regarded '1992' as a social market model of capitalism that offered an alternative to the US's unfettered version, the success of the SEA rested on its ability to harmonize with—and to facilitate—the new shape that Western Europe's economies were taking in the 1990s: globalized, liberal, with 'light-touch' regulation. Where individual states were 'restructuring' their economies and rearranging the way they funded and provided their welfare states, so the EC, soon to be the EU, placed hopes of future European cooperation and prosperity less in 'social Europe' than in a free market model. This model was exemplified by the Treaty on European Union signed at Maastricht in December 1991, where a 'social charter' (condemned by Thatcher as a 'socialist charter') was tacked on separately in a clear indication of its secondary importance, and by the Schengen Agreement of 1985, which dismantled internal borders between those states which signed up but set up 'fortress Europe' at the outer edges. By the end of the process, in the 1990s and early 2000s, after a decade of real economic integration, one commentator could write that, with its promotion of free markets and its main support coming from multinational firms, 'regnant in this Union is not democracy, and not welfare, but capital'.[19] The Treaty of Amsterdam (1997) sought to make employment and social policies converge across the EU, and the Nice Summit (2000) approved the Charter of Fundamental Rights of the EU, but such rhetoric was largely devoid of meaning since any such thing as a 'European social model' remained clearly subordinate to 'economic Europe'.[20] It is not the smallest of the ironies about the EU that its chief detractor remains the UK, whose governments, since Thatcher, have had the least attachment to the postwar welfare state and the greatest devotion to free market economics of any of the member states.

One cannot understand the history of European integration just by examining each individual member state's changing attitudes to it. Rather, the complex whole has to be seen in the light of internal, transnational interactions that produced policies such as the CAP.[21] There is a whole sphere of 'hidden integration' that cannot be detected by examining the high politics of major treaties; it includes the integration of technology and infrastructure, education and culture, science and travel, energy networks and pipelines, telecommunications and road networks, as well as the very many interventions necessary to smooth the passage for trade and commerce. It involves the existence and development of transnational networks which provide guidance and clarification to local, regional, and supranational governance, and which act as intermediaries between politics and society in Europe.[22] Some believe that the 1980s is when a genuinely European public sphere also first emerged, although if it did it was at a fairly elite level.[23]

It is perhaps all the more surprising, then, that there appears to have been very little connection between European integration and the 'Second Cold War', or even between European integration and the collapse of the Cold War. With a few exceptions, the EC as such, as opposed to the member states acting individually on the international stage, had little direct involvement either in superpower relations or in trying to maintain détente in the spheres of trade or information exchange in the face of the new confrontation. This is rather surprising when one sees, from an Eastern European point of view, how attractive Western Europe was—especially fantasies of western consumerism—and how vital it would be to reform the eastern economies. This appeal was to a large extent generated by the process and success of European economic integration during the 1980s. Even more surprising, the 'big bang' of the collapse of communism 'produced merely a whimper in the European Union', whose response 'did not live up to the historical significance of this event'. The EU simply 'upgraded' some of the Eastern European states to 'developing countries'; only later did the European Association Agreement acknowledge that for these countries, their goal was full membership of the EU.[24]

That said, Western Europe did exert a pull over the east. Thus, although one cannot say that developing neo-liberal capitalism was designed to have an advantageous effect in the Cold War (along the lines of those who argue that Reaganite policies were consciously designed to cause the collapse of the USSR), nevertheless Western Europe enjoyed the benefits of being the least worst system on offer. After the war, Western Europe boomed on what one scholar calls an American-style combination of 'military and social Keynesianism'—that is, a mix of massive spending on armaments and the 'defence' industry on the one hand and pursuing full employment and high levels of consumption on the other, as well as promoting 'development' in the Third World. Following the oil-shock recession, there was a short period when communists appeared to be justified in saying that capitalism would destroy itself. Then, as Western Europe recovered and Eastern Europe slipped deeper into economic misery during the 1980s, its inability to compete was underlined as capitalism received a shot in the arm from Reaganomics: the withdrawal of the state, privatization, and a liberalization of trade and capital movements.[25] Western Europe's renewed economic strength during the 1980s was not just an agent of cohesion at home but would also prove an irresistible force in the final stage of the Cold War.

After détente

The success of Bonn's *Ostpolitik* and the treaties it signed with East Berlin, Prague, and Moscow in the early 1970s seemed to indicate that the process of change through rapprochement was working, that the 'hot peace' of liberalizing rhetoric was preferable to the 'Cold War' military stand-off. *Ostpolitik*'s and thus détente's success rested on Bonn's willingness to accept the post-Second World War territorial boundaries as well as German responsibility for the war. The relaxation of tension was the reason why the CSCE was able to take place in Helsinki. Détente brought the countries of Europe to the negotiating table and further détente emerged from it—and, as we will see, the European states sought to protect the gains of détente from the threat of the 'Second Cold War' in the 1980s.

The participation of all the European states except Albania in the CSCE talks is a reminder that, despite the dominance of the superpowers, the countries of Europe played important roles in the last phase of the Cold War. One can see this not only in the different responses to the 'Second Cold War' and then to Gorbachev that emerged in Bonn, Paris, Rome, or London, but in those and other Western European capitals' intra-European policies. It is also clear that the presence of an economically thriving, democratic Western Europe integrated into the EC and NATO acted as a magnet for many in the eastern half of the continent.[26] The EC's engagement with the CSCE indicates that the EC saw the east–west conflict through the lenses of the opportunities that international trade and cultural cooperation would provide for breaking down barriers. This effectively signalled a widespread acceptance of *Ostpolitik*'s gradualist approach amongst European leaders, although it was figured differently in the various member states. They were thus dedicated to maintaining détente; not an easy thing to do when the likes of Kissinger and Nixon, who regarded détente as a variety of containment, dismissed it as a 'dangerous affair'.[27]

At the 1–2 December 1969 meeting at The Hague, which relaunched the European integration process after the stalemate of the 1960s, one of the measures taken was the establishment of the European Political Cooperation (EPC). Its role was 'to prepare the way for a united Europe capable of assuming its responsibilities in the world of tomorrow and of making a contribution commensurate with its tradition and its mission'.[28] That rather opaque statement meant that the EPC was intended to assist with preparing for the CSCE and doing so in a way that ensured the EC states were not pressurized by NATO or, as one civil servant put it, 'squeezed by the superpowers'.[29] Its aim was to promote détente in Europe and to protect EC interests in the process. Apart from trade this meant improving living standards and advancing professional and intellectual contacts between east and west. In other words, endorsing Bonn's *Ostpolitik*, the EPC proposed a more subtle engagement with the Eastern Bloc than NATO's purely military approach could achieve, one which even had the potential for radical political change.

The achievements of Helsinki also point to the undoing of détente. Where Moscow championed Helsinki for recognizing the status quo, Washington placed more emphasis on the human rights obligations of Basket III, thereby placing the Soviets under new pressure. Yet it would be events outside of Europe, especially the Yom Kippur War of 1973 and the end of the conflict in Vietnam in 1975, that gave rise to new tensions between the superpowers and thus to the European blocs.[30] But the final straw was the Soviet invasion of Afghanistan in 1979. The Soviets maintained that they acted according to the established terms of the Brezhnev Doctrine, i.e. in order to preserve the status quo, but NATO, and the Americans in particular, regarded it as an act of aggression outside of the Soviets' sphere of interest, with the added risk that it threatened to leave the way open for the Soviets to push towards the Persian Gulf. Superpower détente swiftly became a thing of the past.[31]

Figure 7. RAF Chicksands, Bedfordshire. The antenna array was dismantled in 1996.

The West Europeans largely regretted this state of affairs, though there was relatively little they could do about it. For Western Europeans, unlike Americans, détente meant a source of trade and therefore income, especially important in 1979–80, and it also meant reducing the threat of nuclear annihilation. As Valéry Giscard d'Estaing put it in 1980, détente 'had been a basic and sound political choice' which 'never made us abandon our distrust of Soviet expansionism'.[32] It was thus not surprising that the Western Europeans did not support the US embargo of the USSR in the wake of the invasion of Afghanistan, nor that the EC states worked hard to maintain European détente in terms of trade and contacts even whilst superpower détente collapsed. Schmidt and Giscard d'Estaing both held summits with Brezhnev in 1980 and openly criticized Carter. Schmidt, Mitterrand, and even Thatcher were also highly critical of Reagan for his bellicose stance towards Poland

Figure 8. Peter Kennard, 'Protest and Survive', 1980 (photograph).

after the introduction of martial law in 1981; noting that no sanctions had been put in place in 1956 or 1968, they argued that introducing them now would hardly affect the course of the Cold War. In particular, they feared for the $10–15 billion deal that Western European firms had entered into with the Soviet Union to construct a 5,000-km natural gas pipeline from Siberia to Ireland. The benefits were largely in one direction only, as most Eastern European citizens saw few improvements to their lives as a result of détente. But by 1982, where US trade with the USSR amounted to just $2.5 billion, Western European trade with Moscow was worth $41 billion.[33]

Thus, whilst superpower détente was coming to an end after Afghanistan, and as a new Cold War was developing over the arms race (with the support of West European governments), the Western Europeans sought to stay under the radar where maintaining links with the Eastern Bloc was concerned. Both the FRG and the GDR tried 'to retreat from the deteriorating climate' of 1979–80, 'so as to safeguard against growing international tension and to pursue undisturbed intra-German relations'.[34] Like Mitterrand, Chancellor Kohl, though less sceptical about Reagan's motives, wanted to protect a policy which had brought a greater sense of normality as well as considerable economic benefit to European life. For West Germany, the policy was driven by the idea that economic diplomacy would lead to 'change through trade' (*Wandel durch Handel*), indeed, that only small steps could lead to change in East Berlin; for the GDR, despite its misgivings, it brought much-needed hard cash: from DM 599.5 million in 1975 to DM 1,556 million in 1979.[35] And, in the light of the deployment of SS-20 and cruise missiles on their territory, both sides feared German unity in destruction. By the time German–German relations cooled as Gorbachev's relationship with Kohl improved as of 1987, Bonn no longer cared very much: Moscow's pressure on East Berlin was doing the job for which *Ostpolitik* had originally been designed.

France too was primarily concerned with 'damage limitation' in the wake of the collapse of détente.[36] Nevertheless, where Giscard had continued the Gaullist policy of promoting French status by independently courting Moscow, Mitterrand—a Socialist President with four communist ministers in his government—took a more combative stance against the Soviets and a more positive one towards NATO. This 'reasoned Atlanticism' was no accident, but a recognition of the changed international and domestic atmosphere in the light of Afghanistan and Poland.[37] Still, as Mitterrand set out most famously in his speech to the Bundestag on 20 January 1983, in which he lauded Franco-German cooperation as well as loyalty to NATO, France had not switched from Gaullist independence to NATO subservience, but was trying to operate within the limits set by renewed east–west antagonism. The French still hoped, through détente, to accelerate 'the progressive opening up of [eastern] nations in their diversity' and to bring about an 'exit from Yalta'.[38] Mitterrand's watchword, indeed, was that 'all that will help leaving Yalta is good'. He thus left open the possibility that France's longstanding policy of rapprochement with Moscow could be revived. But, in the manner of de Gaulle, at the same time he also prioritized France's nuclear independence, which is why during the President's period of *cohabitation* with a Gaullist government (1986–8), Defence Minister André Giraud referred to Gorbachev's willingness to dispense with nuclear weapons in 1987 as a 'European Munich'.[39]

Once the search for cooperation between the CPI and the moderate left had come to an end in 1979, Italy too, even under the socialist government of Bettino Craxi, was an enthusiastic supporter of NATO and permitted it to deploy US cruise missiles on its territory. The Italians were especially involved with the Geneva talks of 1981–3 and, with their failure and the deployment of the 'Euromissiles', Craxi had to negotiate not just the downturn in international relations but a sharpening of domestic political antagonisms. In this, Craxi continued the policy begun by the Christian Democrats since Italy made its 'Western choice' in 1948; the notable difference was that this was a newly installed socialist prime minister acting during what was probably the most dangerous year of the Cold War since the Cuban Missile Crisis.[40]

This tension between détente, national security interests, and international obligations never seriously threatened relations between Western Europe and the US. The noise made by Danish and Norwegian rejection of nuclear weapons, for example, was out of all proportion to its importance to NATO solidarity. Most intra-NATO rifts would in any case quickly be healed once Gorbachev came to power, as the American and Western European positions started to converge once again. After the INF treaty of September 1987, east–west trade picked up, as it did again after the Soviets pulled their soldiers out of Afghanistan. Economic sanctions did less to break down communist autarchy than increased trade with and indebtedness to Western Europe.

The exception to this attempt to hold on to détente was Margaret Thatcher, as vociferously anti-communist as Ronald Reagan, and who announced shortly after coming to power that Polaris, the UK's submarine-launched missile system, would be replaced by the American Trident. Just as important, throughout the 1970s, Britain had been far less engaged with the Soviets and had thus gained less from détente than the other Western European states. The longstanding British position was summed up by one senior civil servant in 1971: 'I have never been convinced that instability within the Soviet empire would necessarily work out to the advantage of the West: and I have never thought that attempts to promote instability added up to a prudent long term policy for the West.'[41] Britain engaged in the CSCE process in order to appear to be singing from the same hymn sheet as its allies and not out of any real enthusiasm for the talks.[42] Thatcher's intensification of a British *Ostpolitik* in the 1980s, in the belief that it could contribute to the defeat of communism, was something of a departure from this traditional hands-off approach, and bore real fruit once Gorbachev came to power.[43]

As the British government vastly increased spending on civil defence measures, and created some of the most iconic structures of the Cold War, such as the FLR-9 listening facility at RAF Chicksands in Bedfordshire, its best advice to citizens was encompassed in the booklet *Protect and Survive* (1980), which 'tells you how to make your home and your family as safe as possible under nuclear attack'.[44] Few believed it, and historian E. P. Thompson countered the government with a parody, *Protest and Survive*, which led to a rapid increase in membership of the Campaign for Nuclear Disarmament (CND) and, most famously, the women's camp at RAF Greenham Common in Berkshire.

Following the nervous Soviet reaction to NATO's Able Archer 83 military exercise in 1983, Reagan calmed down his rhetoric and reached out to the Soviets to initiate talks over arms reduction, culminating in the Reykjavik summit of October 1986, at which an agreement to eliminate nuclear weapons was prevented from being reached only by Reagan's refusal to restrict SDI to the laboratory.[45] Throughout this period, the US's Western European allies negotiated a path between Cold War rhetoric and the arms race, NATO and US policies, and liberal democracy, détente, and *Ostpolitik*, all in the context of the biggest shake-up of the economy since the end of the Second World War, with all the attendant social problems that accompanied it, such as strikes, unemployment, riots, and, at the extreme, terrorism. The impact of MAD on the psyche of West Europeans in the years 1982–6, when some of the most widely watched films on nuclear war were produced—*The Day After*, *When the Wind Blows*, *Threads*—also produced severe social tension. The West German Green Party's Chair, Petra

Kelly, argued that 'we...have little time left to stop the nuclear mad-
ness...We are a country which can only be defended in the atomic age
at the price of its total destruction,' and many agreed with her, if the fact
that the anti-nuclear campaign was the largest extra-parliamentary movement in West Germany's history is anything to go by. In October 1983,
over one million people took to the streets in four West German cities to
protest against the deployment of nuclear missiles.[46] The polarized views of
those who advocated scrapping nuclear weapons and those who believed
their existence had prevented war in Europe since 1945 shared only one
thing: knowledge of certain death if ever they were used.

Even more than European relations with the US or with NATO, or
intra-European relations, the biggest European contribution to the Cold
War in the 1980s was one that can best be described as inadvertent or, at
best, 'structural'. For whilst there were some thinkers and politicians who
produced schemes for bringing about the end of the Cold War, the biggest
influence that Western Europe had on its eastern neighbours was through
the image it conveyed—especially after the start of the slow economic
recovery after 1985—of affluence, stability, and democracy. On the back of
its neo-liberal 'counter-revolution', Western Europe won the 'soft' war of
material goods and cultural influence.[47]

Its affluent image aside, perhaps the one area of Western Europe's direct
impact on the Cold War lies in the influence exercised by western socialists
over Mikhail Gorbachev's 'new thinking'. This was decidedly a way of
thinking with indigenous Russian roots, stretching back decades. Still, Gorbachev and his key aides gained in confidence in their own opinions by
hearing the views of Eurocommunists like Enrico Berlinguer and Alessandro
Natta and, in an important break with traditional Soviet hostility towards
them, socialists in power such as Felipe González, Olof Palme, and François
Mitterrand, as well as former West German Chancellor Willy Brandt, now
President of the Socialist International. González and Gorbachev got on
especially well and the latter heeded the former's advice, which, apart from
criticizing the negative influence of the USSR on world affairs, included
arguing that socialist ideals could only be attained by permitting real democracy and a free market which would bring in foreign investment.[48]

It was one thing for a handful of Western European leftist politicians and
intellectuals to exert an influence over Gorbachev's ideas, another for the
mainstream of Western European opinion to change its views of Gorbachev.
For this to occur, it was more important that conservative leaders enjoyed

warm personal relationships with Gorbachev. Most insightful was Thatcher's comment of December 1984, before Gorbachev came to power, that 'I like Mr Gorbachev. We can do business together.' Thatcher's attitude was very important in persuading Reagan that Gorbachev was serious in his pronouncements.[49]

In general, changes in Western Europeans' perceptions of Gorbachev followed the course of Gorbachev's 'new thinking'. At first, they were quite cautious, suggesting that where Churchill had once said that 'Russia fears our friendship more than our enmity', now the reverse was equally true.[50] Gorbachev's key adviser Anatoly Chernyaev notes that 'Western leaders, especially the Americans, did not trust Gorbachev for a long time; at first they believed that his "new policy" was nothing more than another Kremlin trick and the ambitions of a young leader. Later, when they came to trust his sincerity, they did not believe he would be able to do what he wanted, the way he wanted.'[51] Mitterrand noted hopefully in a letter to Thatcher of July 1986 that 'It is precisely because he wants to see a powerful and respected USSR that he will try to modernise his country'; but Thatcher, for all that she 'liked' Gorbachev, replied that he was 'no less committed to the Soviet system nor less nationalistic' than his predecessors.[52] Kohl enraged Gorbachev

Figure 9. Gorbachev and Thatcher.

in October 1986 by quipping that the latter was a propagandist from the same mould as Joseph Goebbels. But as Gorbachev and his advisers reiterated their views, and especially as they acted on them, Western Europeans decided that the latest General Secretary of the CPSU was cut from different cloth from his predecessors.

Mitterrand was the trailblazer. After 1985, for all his Atlanticism, Mitterrand soon returned France to a more traditional policy of encouraging east–west talks. When Gorbachev visited Paris in October 1985, Mitterrand told him that 'There is a situation in Europe inherited from the war' which they now had the chance to 'correct'. Later he announced, in rather stirring terms, his grand vision. 'We are living in the era of Yalta', he began, and then set out how this might change: 'the gradual affirmation of Western Europe's autonomous personality, the promotion of its complementarities with Eastern Europe, the obligation of the USSR to re-establish a more trusting climate with Community countries in order to stimulate its exchanges and to foster its development,' he went on, 'all this will slowly displace the immobile horizon of the last forty years', leading instead to 'awareness after a half century of ignorance of [our] belonging to the same continent, expressing the same civilization'. This recognition would bring about 'the hour of Europe, the true Europe, that of history and of geography'.[53] This was not the sort of thing that could have been said to Brezhnev or Khrushchev. In fact, Mitterrand and Gorbachev came to quite similar conclusions about where the Cold War conflict in Europe ought to be steered: in Mitterrand's vision, towards a pan-European confederation, in Gorbachev's, towards a 'common European home'.

Only after 1987 did Western European leaders generally have the sense that this Soviet leader was different. Perhaps the most eye-opening moment that helped to drop suspicion towards Gorbachev's motives was Deputy Foreign Minister Anatoli Kovalev's report to the Politburo in March. Kovalev noted that the Western Europeans could operate independently of the Americans, to whom they were not entirely beholden, and stressed that they were more receptive to *glasnost* and *perestroika* than their American allies. In light of Kovalev's report, Gorbachev stated that 'you have to understand that Western Europe is our essential partner'.[54] In that year, Thatcher, in another letter to Mitterrand, wrote that 'it is in our interests to favourably welcome his efforts and to encourage him in the direction in which he has engaged himself'. In October 1988, Kohl explicitly used Gorbachev's concept of a 'common European home' during his first trip to Moscow.[55]

Thereafter, Gorbachev consistently argued that the USSR and Western Europe shared common interests and values, a position which he most famously articulated in his speech to the Council of Europe in 1989. He explained that the 'common European home' would require 'a restructuring of the international order existing in Europe that would put the European common values in the forefront and make it possible to replace the traditional balance of forces with a balance of interests'.[56] Even though Gorbachev's and Mitterrand's dreams were not realized, the idea injected confidence into intra-European relations and helped to remove long-running suspicions.[57]

None of this should lead us to exaggerate the role played by Western Europeans in the Cold War of the 1980s. However vital their breaking down of suspicion towards Gorbachev was, it was the superpowers' INF treaty which gave European leaders the confidence to press ahead with their tentative support for Gorbachev; and it was perhaps President Bush's self-imposed 'pause' in superpower relations when he took office in 1989 that inadvertently gave the Eastern European people the space they needed to carry out their revolutions.[58] The end of the Cold War brought neither dreams of European federation, nor hopes of a revival of the CSCE (reborn as the OSCE) to fruition; instead the institutions which survived and expanded were the two which had endured the Cold War most successfully: NATO and the EU—in other words, the major representatives of the west.[59]

Ultimately, the European role in the last stage of the Cold War was most influential in the mid-1970s (at the CSCE) and, as we will see in Chapter 7, in 1989–91 (with German unification, enlargement of NATO and EU). The 1980s saw European involvement in trying to delimit the negative effects of the 'Second Cold War' on trade and cultural links, but the bigger picture of superpower rivalry indicates the limits of European influence. If Europe was the setting for the end of the Cold War, it was so because of events in Eastern Europe. Still, the impact of European politicians' developing ideas on Gorbachev's 'new thinking' amply justifies the historians' argument that the Cold War had more than two actors.

The turn

Somewhat ironically, the greatest impact of the liberalizing process set off by '1968' would be felt in the sphere of economics. The major theme of the

period after the first oil crisis was how to deal with the unprecedented challenges that had brought about and sustained economic recession. It only
ended with the neo-liberal 'restructuring' of the economies of Western
Europe, and then applying the same treatment, in even more concentrated
form, to the eastern half of Europe following the collapse of communism,
now in the very different circumstances of a global economy.

The postwar economic boom could not be sustained indefinitely, and
not just because of the inevitable loss of market share brought about by the
rise to prominence of new capitalist economies, especially Japan and South
Korea. In fact, by the time the oil crisis—brought about by OPEC raising
the price of a barrel of oil from $2 in mid-1973 to $12 in 1975—took effect,
the Western European economies were already suffering from low rates of
productivity, outdated industrial plant, and lack of investment. Paradoxically,
then, 'postwar prosperity in Europe undermined itself, and paved the way
for a deep economic crisis'. Inflation, partly fuelled by the ensuing wage
spiral, rose to 10 per cent in Western Europe and to almost 20 per cent in
Southern Europe. Unemployment, virtually unknown during the boom,
was between 5 per cent and 12 per cent in West Germany during the 1980s,
and in Spain was nearly 20 per cent.[60] From an average in OECD countries
of 4.8 per cent per year in the 1960s, the growth rate slowed to 3.4 per cent
and then, between 1974 and 1976, almost to zero. OPEC's decision to make
up lost income as a result of this slowdown (helped by its decision to punish
countries it deemed to have supported Israel during the Yom Kippur War)
simply exacerbated a trend that was already under way.

With the economy overheated, production declined, demand for goods
and services fell, and economic growth slowed and then stopped altogether.
The response of governments was, understandably given the success of the
New Deal, to turn to Keynesian theory, which stated that economic growth
could be encouraged by stimulating demand, primarily by government
spending on large state-led infrastructure projects and job creation. This
time, however, such efforts were stymied by the decidedly non-Keynesian
deregulation of the banking sector, which expanded the money supply and
left the financial sector unrestrained. The result was the paradoxical situation of 'stagflation', which saw both inflation and unemployment rise in a
way that contradicted the laws of classical economics. Previously, the law of
the 'Phillips curve', which placed inflation and unemployment in an inverse
relationship, had been a sure guide, but now governments had to contend
with battling inflation and unemployment without understanding why the

policies they were introducing to combat the slowdown were actually making it worse.[61] Industrial output fell dramatically and some industries were producing less in the 1980s than they had done in the 1960s. Unemployment in the primary and secondary sectors rocketed.

The response to the oil crisis and to the problem of stagflation (a term which had in fact been coined in 1965 by Conservative MP Iain Macleod) was, over a fairly short time frame and with dramatic social consequences, drastically to cut back or to shut down altogether the industries on which postwar prosperity had been built and to turn the Western European economy into a high-tech service sector.[62] The process was carried through most radically in Britain under Margaret Thatcher, but applied also to West Germany, Belgium, France, Spain, Italy, and even the Scandinavian countries, where the long-dominant Social Democrats first shifted rightwards in 1982 (following the Germans in seeing control of inflation as the key priority) and then saw their grip on power weaken (and where, in a rare moment of excitement in Swedish politics, Prime Minister Olof Palme was assassinated in 1986). Growth had returned to an average across Western Europe of 3.9 per cent by 1979, when the second oil crisis struck; after the recession of the early 1980s, it returned to 3.7 per cent by 1988. The bare figures, however, disguise a vast change in how that growth was produced.

Whatever social democratic values were originally built into the EEC were struggling to get a hearing by the mid-1980s. The most obvious economic consequence of stagflation was the rise to prominence of monetarism, an economic theory strongly at odds with Keynesianism. Derived from the Austrian school of Ludwig von Mises, Friedrich Hayek, and Joseph Schumpeter, the economic counterparts to political theorist Karl Popper and early management guru Peter Drucker, and propounded in the 1970s by its most celebrated theorist Milton Friedman, not to mention the IMF or OECD, monetarism advocated focusing not (or not only) on demand management, à la Keynes, but primarily on supply-side economics. Rather than arguing for government-induced spending, in the hope of a multiplier effect to pay back the extra borrowing, monetarism advocated focusing on controlling the money supply in the economy as a way of stimulating growth, with a drive to 'freeing' dependence on the state (i.e. cutting welfare), promoting entrepreneurship, accepting a certain level of unemployment, and slashing government spending. This was not only an intellectual break with the postwar consensus but, when Thatcher came to power, a political one too.

Under Thatcher's slogan, 'There Is No Alternative', the attempt to introduce a full-scale monetarist agenda to Britain in 1979–80 ended by adding over 1 million people to the dole queue, bringing unemployment to an unprecedented 3 million by 1983. With a 5 per cent drop in GDP between 1979 and mid-1981, and riots breaking out in London, Birmingham, Liverpool, and other cities, often sparked by accusations of police racism, the policy was soon shelved. As one historian says, although '"control of the money supply" remained central to the stated objectives of policy, the idea of straightforward, quantifiable links between something called money and the rate of inflation proved a snare and a delusion'.[63] But Thatcher pressed ahead with restructuring in a way that focused on the supply side of the economy, placing control of inflation above interest rates, privatizing supposedly inefficient state-run industries such as British Gas and British Telecom, closing declining industries such as coalmining and shipbuilding, and deregulating the City, making it one of the world's main financial centres.

Thatcher's dwindling popularity—a popularity rating of 25 per cent in autumn 1981—was rescued by the Falklands War of 1982, which, in the opinion of at least one historian, 'transformed her from an embattled rightwing ideologue to a national leader with the qualities so many of her predecessors appeared to lack: decisiveness, confidence, and the ability to unite the country'.[64] The miners who went on strike in 1984–5 to resist Thatcher's most determined effort to break the power of trade unions would probably have disagreed with the assessment, but there is no doubt that in the country at large, Thatcher's position was more widely appreciated than NUM leader Arthur Scargill's. Probably her most popular moves were to increase share ownership, giving 'ordinary' people a taste of playing the money markets, and, especially, to allow council tenants to buy their houses from the state. But the crest of this patriotic wave was short-lived; if Thatcher held on to power for so long—until November 1990, and then with the underwhelming John Major in power until 1997—this was as much to do with the parlous state of the Labour Party as with approval for Thatcher, which, thanks to measures such as the infamous Poll Tax, was never as high as it had been for Attlee, Churchill, Eden, Macmillan, or Wilson.[65]

Only Britain experienced a full-blooded monetarist experiment, although even here Thatcher only partly achieved her goal of cutting taxes (the socially regressive VAT was increased even if there were tax cuts for the rich) and reducing government spending (despite privatization, welfare spending remained high, as did NHS funding and government subsidies to big business). But nowhere in Western Europe remained unaffected by the post-oil crisis recession and all felt the necessity of change. Even countries with socialist governments, such as Spain, France, and Italy under Craxi, bought into the new free-market credo. The fact that ostensibly left-wing parties shifted their position so radically during the decade indicates clearly enough that the prevailing winds of the 1980s were rightwards. The liberalization of trade and the withdrawal of the state generated large profits and increased the money in the economy, but this was not the context of the postwar boom, and the money was by no means widely shared.

The programme of 'liberalization' meant the opposite for labour; that is, workers' rights were eroded (by state intervention) and their working and living conditions worsened. As Thatcher's adviser Alan Budd later acknowledged, 'What was engineered in Marxist terms was a crisis of capitalism which recreated a reserve army of labour, and has allowed the capitalists to make high profits ever since.'[66] In America, more important for the climb out of recession than the tight control over money supply was what economic historian Giovanni Arrighi calls 'socially regressive Keynesianism', in other words, tax breaks for the rich and massive government spending on arms.[67] In Western Europe, this process was tempered somewhat by continued spending on welfare states (especially in Scandinavia and Spain) and on large subsidies for declining industries in the first half of the 1980s, but the script of 'liberalization' was followed everywhere. Only in those countries where the social democratic corporatist arrangements were quite strong, i.e. Scandinavia, West Germany, and Austria, could liberalization be to some extent contained, thus restricting the damage to the working class 'whether in jobs, incomes, benefits, political representation, union organization, the socially organized capacities of working-class communities, or the social value accorded to labour and its culture and traditions'.[68] But even where workers suffered, by the end of the 1980s between two-thirds and three-quarters of West European employees were white collar. That figure includes those employed by the state, which actually expanded everywhere in Western Europe.[69]

In France, Mitterrand at first tried to resist the neo-liberal tide, initiating together with his communist partners a programme of nationalization and wage rises. But by March 1983 he had to abandon this attempt to stimulate demand as unemployment and inflation continued to rise. He performed a total policy about-face, and set in motion a programme of privatization and economic liberalization designed to make France, within the EC framework, ready for the realities of a globalized economy. By 1987, a year after the Socialist Party lost control of parliament to the centre right, all the nationalized industries were in private hands. And although Mitterrand won a second term as President in 1988, his political pragmatism was not matched by social reform, as the liberalization of the economy brought in its wake higher instances of social injustice, meaning not just unemployment but a rising problem of racism and the exclusion of ethnic minority communities, especially in the *banlieues*. During Mitterrand's second term in office, the extreme-right National Front made its first meaningful appearance in French politics.

Throughout the 1970s, politics in Italy blundered its way through a series of unstable governments, as a wave of right- and left-wing terrorism reached frightening proportions, making some fear that state stability was genuinely under threat. The crisis culminated in 1978 with the Red Brigades' murder of Aldo Moro, the president of the Christian Democrats, at which point the political class managed to pull together. At the same time, the PCI reached its electoral peak in 1979 with 30 per cent of the vote, but it never entered government other than as a prop to the DC before that year, and it became increasingly isolated from both international communism and the Italian electorate. The demise of the PCI, even at local level, illustrated perfectly the limits of Europeans' influence on the international architecture of the Cold War.[70] It meant too that the socialists under Bettino Craxi (1983–7) needed to toe the free market line if they were to succeed. They were emboldened to do so by the promise of taking on the cronyism and corruption of the DC's patronage networks, larger than the socialists' own. The privatization of major companies such as Alitalia and Banca di Roma followed a path already established in the UK and France. By the time of the crisis of the Italian Republic in the early 1990s, when the DC admitted to secret links with the mafia and Andreotti acknowledged in parliament the existence of NATO's secret postwar anti-communist Operation Gladio, the country had shifted firmly to the right, paving the way for Silvio Berlusconi, not to mention the Northern League and the 'post-fascist' MSI.[71]

As in Italy, the West German state faced a severe test from the sustained terrorist attacks of the 1970s. Its survival proved that despite Habermas's prognosis, the FRG, and for that matter West European states in general, enjoyed popular legitimacy to an extent that was impossible in the east. Indeed, the post-Cold War problem of democratic forms without popular participation and a centralization of power in increasingly static societies at a time of economic uncertainty is a greater threat to European values than were the crises of the 1970s.

West German stability was proven with Kohl's election victory in March 1983, following his being thrust into power by the collapse of the SPD's coalition with the liberal FDP in the autumn of 1982. Although the CDU/CSU's landslide also saw the emergence of the Green Party as a significant force in German politics, with 2.2 million votes and 27 seats in the Bundestag, Kohl was able to press ahead with the *Wende*. His Finance Minister Gerhard Stoltenburg introduced cuts to unemployment benefit and other components of the welfare state. Further, Thatcher-style cuts were fended off by the success of the West German economy after 1982, when growth returned on the back of the decline in oil prices. The survival of German industry, and its export-led growth, would prove crucial in the coming decades, as the Federal Republic first paid to incorporate East Germany—something no other European state could possibly have afforded—and then reluctantly became funder in chief of the EU bail-out money after 2008.

The Iberian peninsula in the 1980s was the same but different from the rest of Western Europe. The politics of the transition to democracy provided for a different context, but the pressure to engage in economic liberalization was just as strong, especially after 1986, when Spain and Portugal joined the EC. In Spain, González's approach was to maintain some stability in the post-dictatorship transition. The impetus for reform, however, came from two, irresistible directions: the continent-wide neo-liberal trend and the fact that under Franco, Spain's public sector had ballooned and become corrupt. Caution was required, however. Thus, on the one hand, Spain saw less of an assault on the mixed economy than other countries did; indeed, spending on welfare increased. On the other hand, as of 1984, González set about cutting inflation and oversaw a privatization programme which took 350 industrial firms and 92 banks into private hands in two years. They were followed by the privatization of the Instituto Nacional de Industria, a massive holding company which controlled 700 firms.[72] Despite this process, unemployment in Spain continued to rise, to more than 21 per cent in 1985 and not much less by the 1990s. In Portugal, the process was delayed by constitutional wrangling. Soares's government initiated the process of deregulating many protected sectors, such as banking or steel, but only with the accession to power of Anibal Cavaco Silva did the government really set about tackling the country's chaotic economy.

This process of neo-liberal restructuring was only partly driven by national imperatives, even though it sparked major social change and sometimes led to violent eruptions. The real difference between the Western European economies in 1975 and in 1989 was that they could no longer be understood in just national or regional terms. The 1980s was the first decade of globalization, when Western Europe's economy was tied into a world system. The EC, especially with the 'completion of the internal market' that the SEA represented, carried through the regional version of this worldwide process. Where countries tried to resist, as did Greece under Papandreou, the need for austerity was simply delayed until later. Whether conservative or social democratic, what most of Western Europe's governments were doing during the 1980s was eliminating the mixed economy in order to try and maintain Western European competitiveness. They did so, but at a high price.[73]

The culture of the turn

Thatcher's achievement, according to Tony Judt, consists in the fact that 'Not only did she destroy the post-war consensus but she forged a new one.'[74] His judgement is primarily an economic and social one—that economic growth returned at the cost of social equilibrium and solidarity dwindling in Britain. The claim is also true, however, for the cultural sphere. This is no mere add-on; if we are to understand the post-Cold War zeitgeist in Europe, then the relationship between economic restructuring and a re-alignment in mentalities must also be considered. Liberalization of the economy went hand in hand with tighter social control.

First of all, this meant de-emphasizing the social contract which had been accepted in 1945 as a necessary component of reconstruction: guaranteeing health and education, and benefits to those unable to support themselves. But it owed little to traditional conservative values of prudence, social order, and economic caution. The extraordinary changes that took place in the European economy in the 1980s, which largely did away with heavy industry (exceptions include the industrial belt of the Ruhr and car manufacturing in Germany and France) came at a very high price in terms of the values that provided the mood music to the postwar Western European consensus.

With respect to the welfare state, it is ironic that 'welfare state regress', which constitutes 'a reworking of the implicit social contract established in

Western Europe after World War II', has historically taken place at moments when the welfare state has been most needed.[75] The welfare state was a victim of its own success. When the baby-boomer generation reached middle age and then started retiring, Europeans lived far longer than they had done in the 1940s; this meant a vastly increased pension bill as well as huge strains on health services. At the same time, the cost of unemployment, disability, housing, and other benefits looked likely to outstrip the ability of the state to pay for them, and the decline in the birth rate meant that the population was ageing so that there would be fewer people of working age left to pay for the armies of retirees and welfare claimants. As of the late 1970s, the OECD recommended cutting welfare expenditure rather than targeting demand as the surest way of promoting growth, and the IMF told the Scandinavian countries to cut their expenditure on welfare. The result was that the 1980s saw the gradual disappearance of the idea of the state as an active agent of economic growth, social improvement, and equitable distribution of resources, to be replaced by a cynical view of the state as nepotistic, wasteful, and inefficient. 'The very term "reform" now means, virtually always,' writes historian Perry Anderson, 'the opposite of what it denoted fifty years ago: not the creation, but a contraction, of welfare arrangements once prized by their recipients.'[76] Indeed, perhaps the very arrangements which had facilitated the postwar boom and welfare state had led to a demobilization of the working classes, 'so that they acquiesced in welfare decline'.[77]

It is not hard to see what the cultural counterparts to this post-recession restructuring might be. They included an exaggerated value on individualism, scorn for 'scroungers' who take state benefits, and prioritization of wealth above all other values, including the public good. All of these emerging phenomena, fed by the popular press, highlighted real social problems but could only be expressed by failing to grasp the context for their occurrence, which was the structural changes in the economy outlined above which meant the demise of full employment. Above all, what we see in the 1980s is the start of demise of the antifascist settlement, just in time to synchronize with the 'anti-antifascist' explosion in Eastern Europe that followed the revolutions of 1989.

These processes were not all bad. First of all, deindustrialization had some positive effects, not least environmental. 'Moreover,' one historian writes, 'if labour displaced from manufacturing as a result of productivity growth is being absorbed in the service sector, this may be consistent with increased leisure time and a higher quality of life.'[78] With the exception of Britain, where overall levels of unemployment rose outside of London and the south-east, this may well have been true of most of Western Europe in the 1980s.

Continuing the century-long trend of the 'Americanization' of Europe, the advent of Reaganomics meant that, for those who benefited from it, disposable incomes rose in the 1980s as did leisure time and the culture of consumption. Television was largely deregulated, seeing big national networks split up and commercial channels introduced. In the case of Italy, the break-up of state control of radio and TV in 1975 removed a structure that had been in place more or less unchanged since Mussolini's day. Tourism boomed thanks to a new mobility, especially provided by cheap air travel. Sport became a mainstay of popular entertainment and big business.[79] Although official attempts to promote American values suffered a setback after Vietnam, a process usefully thought of as 'voluntary Americanization from below' boomed during the 1980s, as Europeans enthusiastically swallowed fast food, rap music, MTV, and, later, the internet. The whole process of conspicuous consumption and economic deregulation was considered a facet of 'Americanization', and merely designating it this way gave it a cachet—associated with the flashiness and success of Wall Street—which it might otherwise have lacked.[80] There was often a strange love–hate relationship with American culture; European bands such as Einstürzende Neubauten and Die Toten Hosen used musical forms derived from the US but wrote lyrics which were critical of America, as did later hip hop bands with music derived from African-American street culture.[81] But at a more popular level, Americanisms, from clothes to films to language, became ubiquitous.

There were of course local variants. In terms of music, the punk explosion of 1976–7 in Britain was a violent riposte to the self-indulgence of hippies and glam rock, and represented an authentically rejectionist, intelligent youth culture. More creatively, the mixed-race musical melange of Ska (with its Two-Tone record label), which to some extent overlapped with punk, reggae, and post-punk, provided an intelligent critique of British society under Thatcher. No Western European group faced the sorts of challenges of Czechoslovak band Plastic People of the Universe, who were subjected to continual police harassment and imprisonment, but at its best, the punk–reggae crossover in the music of The Clash dissected the age with serious social comment and powerful energy. The irony of the 1980s, when, as the Pet Shop Boys sang, 'we're all on the make', meant, however, that only the most determined to escape the strictures of the market (such as anarchist collective Crass, whose boldly iconoclastic 1983 single *Sheep Farming in the Falklands* provided unforgiving lyrics and an accompanying, stomach-churning poster, all for 80p) could resist their records and their style being turned into the next money-making opportunity. By the 1990s, this was a dilemma that few worried about any more.

The rise and fall of punk can act as a metaphor for 'the turn' in general. In retrospect, 1976, when the Sex Pistols shocked people with their swastika t-shirts and swearing on TV, has a postwar feel of innocence and grainy austerity about it.[82] The end of punk in the 1980s coincided with the rise of Thatcherite consumerism, deregulation, and individualism, and the emergence, not for the first time in the history of pop music, but in an unprecedented way, of manufactured bands. The 1980s mark a clearer break with the postwar world than the 1960s in that the 1980s are still immediately recognizable as contemporary. In terms of technology (VCRs, personal computers and computer games, telephony and the digital revolution, biotechnologies), economics (globalization, stock market liberalization, consumerism), and cultural politics (multiculturalism, identity politics, gender politics, celebrity culture, heritage tourism), the 1980s are when Western Europe became a part of—and helped to create—the complex, globalized world.

The complexity of globalization helps to explain the rise of movements which tried to simplify the world for people with messages of blame. There is no surer sign of the breaking down of the postwar consensus in Western Europe than the emergence as a serious social and electoral force of racist far-right parties in the 1980s. This phenomenon tends to be explained as a response to mass immigration, especially from former European colonies (Jamaica, India, Pakistan, Suriname, Indonesia, Algeria, Zaire, and so on) or, in the West German case, from Turkey, but there is no necessary reason why immigration must lead to racism. The largest immigrant groups in Western Europe during the 1950s and 1960s, the Irish in Britain and Southern Europeans (Italians and Portuguese) in West Germany, though no doubt regarded with some suspicion in certain quarters, were not hounded by the popular press or populist politicians in the way that became common in the 1980s. Cold War migrants, such as Hungarians decamping to Austria and West Germany after 1956, were warmly greeted. Nor was the 1980s the first decade when large numbers of non-whites appeared in Western Europe. There

were 12 million immigrants in Western Europe by 1970, but it took economic decline to turn this bare fact into a political issue.[83]

Racism, like any ideology, is not just 'there'; it waxes and wanes and
requires spokesmen and changes in circumstances to make it effective. Such
changes occurred in the 1980s, when 'migrant labourers' were refigured as
'ethnic minorities'. Not only did Mitterrand cynically change the law so
that a lower hurdle was required to enter parliament, in an attempt to save
the socialist government by persuading some voters to switch from the
Gaullists to the FN, thus propelling it into the mainstream; not only did
the economic policies of the 1980s create whole communities of welfare
dependants in places reliant on now-defunct industries, in a context where
the welfare safety net was being cut away, giving the impression of a competition for resources among different groups; but established political parties of all persuasions attempted to steal the arguments of the far right, thus
bringing such ideas firmly into the mainstream. The gulf between reality
and rhetoric was articulated by the CDU, which stubbornly maintained
until 1998 that 'Germany is not a country of immigration'. The racist attack
on people with different skin colour was a new expression of an old European idea and 'made sense' in the 1980s as it does to people now when we
are again experiencing hard times. Mainstream political parties must therefore take a large share of the responsibility for dismantling the postwar settlement which they had introduced and from which they and their societies
had benefited.

For the first time since the war, then, the 1980s witnessed parties such as
the FN in France, the Republikaner in West Germany, the Vlaams Blok in
Belgium, the MSI in Italy, and the FPÖ in Austria becoming political forces
that could not be ignored. However, it is insufficient to explain this process
as a sign of *ressentiment* and the political articulation of 'losers' in the globalization process, when amongst the leadership of such parties were often
found the same people who had fought for the Nazis during the war (such
as the Republikaner's Franz Schönhuber, a former SS man), or who had
fought in Algeria (most notably, Jean-Marie Le Pen, suspected of involvement in torturing Algerians). In other words, it is striking that those who
led such movements might have played on the issues of the day, but their
own entrance into far-right politics dated back to the war, suggesting that
ideological positions derived from wartime still simmered under the surface
of Western European political and cultural life. The rise of the New Right
(which first appeared as the *nouvelle droite* in France) sometimes made it

hard to recognize the old roots of such thinking, since it came dressed up as postmodern cosmopolitanism. Le Pen, for example, wrote that 'I love North Africans, but their place is in the Maghreb.... For a nation to be harmonious, it must have a certain ethnic and spiritual homogeneity.'[84] But the argument that difference should be celebrated by keeping different cultures apart was only a short step away from outright cultural triumphalism, as we have all too often heard in the post-9/11 period—for example, Berlusconi's aside about the merits of western civilization and the demerits of Islam.

Aside from the unfortunate episode of Kurt Waldheim's appointment as President of Austria, which proceeded—amidst considerable international objections, especially from the US—despite revelations about his wartime service in the Wehrmacht in Yugoslavia, the far right's growth, though disturbing, did not constitute a threat to parliamentary democracy in the 1980s. That would change after the end of the Cold War, as we will see. What did change in the 1980s, helping to ease the far right's re-emergence in the 1990s in the process, was Western European memory politics, especially the ways in which memories of the war and fascism were steadily challenged and reconfigured.

This breakdown of the antifascist consensus was a double-edged sword. In many ways, it had positive consequences, such as giving the lie to the Austrians' claim that the country had been the 'first victim of National Socialism', or recognizing that not everyone in France had been a member of the Resistance—a fact that had become steadily less easily ignored ever since Marcel Ophüls's 1969 film *Le Chagrin et la pitié* (*The Sorrow and the Pity*), which dissected Clermont-Ferrand under the occupation, and Louis Malle's *Lacombe Lucien* (1974), a portrait of an ordinary collaborator. Claude Lanzmann's masterpiece *Shoah* was released in 1985, following years of research and production. His interviews with former (or not so former) Nazis and his somewhat one-sided portrayal of antisemitic Polish peasants indicated that the darker European traditions that fascism had tapped into still lay just under the surface. However, this unveiling made it clear that among those who had not been members of the Resistance, a not inconsiderable number of them had been Vichy supporters and even Nazi sympathizers, and that they and their intellectual heirs were still around. The rise of the *nouvelle droite* grew directly out of this milieu, in which older far-right traditions were reframed around new social issues such as immigration. In a few rare cases, intellectuals who had started life on the far left shifted through 180 degrees of the political spectrum. Jules Monnerot, for example, a surrealist and communist sociologist in the 1930s, ended his career standing for the FN in 1979 and penning essays for *nouvelle droite* collections.[85]

The clearest examples of the *Tendenzwende* come, unsurprisingly, from West Germany (East Germany is a separate case, simply denying that, as an antifascist workers' state, it had any historic connection with Nazism[86]). On the one hand, as of the 1960s, with the Eichmann trial and the Frankfurt Auschwitz trials, the FRG made considerable effort to 'come to terms with the past'. This was especially so after 1969, with Brandt's attempts to normalize relations with Eastern Europe and Schmidt's plain talking on the Nazi persecution of the Jews. In contrast to Adenauer, whose talk of victimhood always meant primarily German suffering at the hands of the Soviets, Brandt insisted that the Third Reich had committed 'criminal activities for which there is no parallel in modern history', crimes which had 'disgraced the German name in all of the world'.[87]

This process of grappling with the Nazi crimes made great strides in the 1970s and 1980s, notably after the American TV four-part series *Holocaust* was shown on West German TV in 1979, attracting some 20 million viewers per episode.[88] In July of that year, the Bundestag abolished the statute of limitations for murder and genocide (although most of the CDU/CSU, including Kohl, voted against the motion).[89] On 8 May 1985, three days after the ceremony at Bitburg, President Richard von Weizsäcker spoke before the Bundestag. In one of postwar Germany's most important speeches, Weizsäcker argued that it was impossible for Germans to come to terms with the past, that the genocide of the Jews was 'unparalleled in history', and that 8 May 1945 represented a liberation 'of us all from the inhumanity and tyranny of the National Socialist regime'.[90] Although he was criticized from one side for claiming that Nazism was 'an aberration in German history' and that the Holocaust was perpetrated by 'a few people', and attacked from another for asserting that Germany's postwar division was a result of Nazi Germany's actions, Weizsäcker's speech, coming immediately after Bitburg, was widely welcomed at home and abroad.

On the other hand, Chancellor Kohl made some famously cumbersome remarks about Nazism, including voicing (in Israel!) his relief at the 'grace of late birth', his belief in the need to affirm 'the continuity of history', and his assertion that young Germans would 'refuse to acknowledge a collective guilt for the deeds of their fathers', as if anyone was expecting such a thing.[91] Seeing such gaffes alongside Bitburg and his decision to create a Museum of German History in West Berlin, critics suspected Kohl of trying to bury Nazism and to reaffirm a positive national identity for Germany. They summed up his position as the demand no longer to speak of the noose in the hangman's house.[92]

The same search for 'continuity', which sought to break away from what conservatives considered an obsession with the Nazi past, was evident in some major cultural events from the 1970s onwards. Edgar Reitz's monumental TV series *Heimat* (1984) integrated the disruptive Nazi years into a much longer time span of German history, suggesting the survival of supposedly more stable and healthy traditions instead. Films such as Hans-Jürgen Syberberg's *Hitler: A Film from Germany* and historian Joachim Fest's *Hitler: A Career* (both 1977) were simultaneously serious inquiries and harbingers of subtle revisionism, in that they both explained Hitler's seductive qualities and seduced their audiences again with the same techniques, as if the whole history of Nazi Germany could be summed up in Hitler's charisma.[93] The problem of 'fascinating fascism' was a profound one—scholars and educators wanted the topic to be discussed, but it lent itself all too easily to a sensationalizing and mythologizing treatment.[94] As we see in Joschka Fischer's epigraph to this chapter, this danger applied to the left as well as the right. Deploying the Auschwitz analogy when discussing the threat of nuclear annihilation was rhetorically powerful but owed little to a real understanding of Auschwitz.

This dilemma was voiced most articulately in the context of the *Historikerstreit* (Historians' Debate) of the mid-1980s. This debate, conducted in the pages of the national press, especially the conservative *Frankfurter Allgemeine Zeitung* and the liberal weekly *Die Zeit*, ranged historians Michael Stürmer (also Kohl's speechwriter), Ernst Nolte, and a few others against philosopher Jürgen Habermas and liberal-minded historians such as Eberhard Jäckel.[95] The former stood accused, not least by Weizsäcker, of downplaying the role played by Nazism and the Holocaust in understanding German history, while opponents of the latter argued that they were holding the German nation to ransom with their 'obsession with guilt'. The debate turned on the interpretation of the Holocaust, the liberals asserting its 'uniqueness', the conservatives arguing that it could and should be compared with other atrocities, especially Stalin's crimes. Nolte (a widely respected historian of fascism, it should be noted) offended many when he referred to the Gulag as 'an Asiatic deed' and argued that 'the so-called annihilation of the Jews by the Third Reich was a reaction or distorted copy [of the Gulag] and not a first act or an original'. Stürmer added an Orwellian feel to the debate by asserting that 'In a land without history, the future is controlled by those who determine the content of memory, who coin concepts and interpret the past.'[96] Habermas responded by arguing for what he called 'constitutional patriotism' in place of nationalism: 'The unconditional opening of the Federal Republic to the political culture of the West', he wrote, 'is the greatest intellectual achievement of our postwar period... This event cannot and should not be stabilized by a kind of NATO philosophy coloured with German nationalism.'[97] Most importantly, he pleaded for Germans not to brush aside the memory of those murdered at German hands, for otherwise 'our Jewish fellow citizens, the sons, the daughters, the grandchildren of the murdered could no longer breathe in our country'.[98]

Cumulatively, these memory debates in West Germany made the Nazi past a topic that could be openly discussed more easily than had been the case during the Adenauer years. The debates themselves reveal a contest over memory, between those who wanted to ensure that Germany's brown past was not forgotten and that it would motivate Germans to construct a better future and those who wanted to 'draw a line' over the Nazi past, to 'move on' and reaffirm a positive German identity. The latter did not 'win' the arguments in the 1980s, and the events of the years 1989–91 would change the terms of the debate. But the fact that such opinions—which had previously been widespread, but not easily articulated in the public sphere—could now be openly voiced signalled a willingness to challenge those whose vision was of West Germany as a genuinely denazified liberal republic.

West Germany was not the only place to experience 'Bitburg history', confusing victim and perpetrator and failing to pin down responsibility for past crimes.[99] The result was success for re-energized far-right movements across Western Europe. In Belgium, Italy, and Austria, the leaders of far-right parties all emulated Le Pen in appealing to anti-immigrant sentiment. The Vlaams Blok made a breakthrough in 1988, when it took 17.7 per cent of the vote in Antwerp; the city subsequently became its stronghold. In Austria, where resentment at the international reaction to Waldheim's appointment pointed to the existence of strong undercurrents of Nazi sympathies, Jörg Haider reshaped the Freedom Party after 1986 from a small liberal party to a far-right movement. Initially unsuccessful, by 1990 it was taking 16.6 per cent of the national vote. In Italy, the young, smartly dressed Gianfranco Fini exemplified the new phenomenon of 'designer fascism' when he took over the leadership of the MSI in 1987. Seeking to make the party more at home with the parliamentary process, without doing away with its key ideological positions, Fini was relatively successful.[100] It would not be until the 1990s, however, that any of these parties entered into power. The changes that the end of the Cold War wrought in Eastern Europe had a striking counterpart in the western half of the continent too, as we will see.

6

Gerontocracy

Eastern Europe, 1975–1989

The courage with which we have entered the year 1984 will one day amaze future generations. From all sides we are bombarded with evil presentiments, ominous horoscopes, bad news from the fronts, failed Soviet peace initiatives—what lies in store?

Ludvík Vaculík

The *private* convictions of party members differ in no way, however, from the opinions of those who never join the party. The leaders are perfectly well aware of this and that is why they are increasingly interested only in the *public* performances of party members. It is why, moreover, they no longer seek to use the party as a whole as a legitimating entity.

Agnes Heller

If it is possible to accomplish everything we have taken on, this will mean the final end of the Cold War era and the start of a period of real peace in the history of Europe. The Soviet Union is genuinely concerned that this unique chance for the European peoples and all of humankind not be lost. I believe that we have proven our sincerity in deed, i.e., through domestic reorganization and a new foreign policy.

Mikhail Gorbachev[1]

The end of the Brezhnev Doctrine

If it is stretching the imagination a little to say that when he kissed the ground at Warsaw airport on 2 June 1979, Pope John Paul II (formerly Cardinal Karol Wojtyła) 'began the process by which communism in Poland—and ultimately everywhere else in Europe—would come to an end', the departure of the first Polish pope was certainly greeted by the Polish government with a sigh of relief.[2] This is why Brezhnev advised Polish Party leader Edward Gierek to keep him out. When Gierek replied that domestic pressure was forcing his hand, Brezhnev grudgingly went along with the visit, saying, 'Well, do as you wish. But be careful you don't regret it later.'[3] What had happened in just a few years to reverse what Brezhnev and his colleagues in the Politburo believed was a major policy success at Helsinki? Why, only a few years after many western commentators were condemning Helsinki for ceding too much ground to the Soviets, were the latter so fearful of the potential consequences of the Pope—admittedly, a Pole—entering Poland? Where, after the signing of the accord, Helmut Schmidt stated that Europe had 'taken a new step towards the stabilization of peace', and the British ambassador to Moscow noted that 'the practice of détente may foster developments in Soviet policies which ultimately make the USSR a less intractable, even a more reliable, partner', now the whole process seemed to be unravelling.[4] With remarkable speed, unforeseen post-Helsinki complications would bring about not only the demise of détente in a 'clear-cut confirmation of the centrality of ideology in the international system of these years' but, ultimately, the end of the Brezhnev Doctrine.[5]

Such complications were most visible in the sphere of international politics, which is why détente was destroyed far more by superpower than by intra-European relations. The latter, mainly thanks to *Ostpolitik*, were in quite good shape, especially between Bonn and Moscow, where economic diplomacy and trade—for example in natural gas from the USSR—were thriving.[6] Tensions outside of Europe—in Chile, Egypt, Israel, Angola, and Ethiopia among others—led to disagreements within the Politburo about the relative weight of détente versus military preparedness. More important still were disappointments at the stalling of Soviet economic improvement as a result of the US–Soviet Trade Agreement of 1972. The Soviets' need for economic improvement was one of the key drivers of détente, as Moscow sought to obtain western technology and financial assistance. By refusing to permit 60,000 Jews to emigrate annually from the USSR (the Soviets signed up to the right to emigrate by signing the UN Covenant on Human Rights in 1973), a factor that was tied to the trade agreement, the Soviets found their trade rights with the US restricted and they failed to obtain Most Favored Nation status.[7] After trying to sustain the agreement in the wake of the Watergate scandal—which the Soviets, following Nixon's successful summits with Brezhnev in 1972–4, misunderstood as an American right-wing attempt to undermine détente—and in the face of opposition from sections of the Politburo, Brezhnev finally abrogated the trade agreement treaty in December 1974.[8]

Doing so probably helped Brezhnev fight off pressure to stand down. Whilst he successfully reasserted his pre-eminence at the CPSU Congress of February–March 1976, it is possible that he was forced to accept a new harder line on détente as the price of staying in office.[9] Certainly Brezhnev appeared to be more forceful in his statements, though this might indicate an attempt to 'placate domestic critics' more than a real change in policy.[10] Either way, after 1975, Brezhnev's leadership grew increasingly weak as did the man himself. Détente was always a way of playing out Cold War rivalries, not a means to eradicate them. But events in Angola, the Horn of Africa, Indonesia, and elsewhere in the Third World where the Soviets were lending support to national liberation movements provoked the Americans in ways that the Soviets did not expect, for they had not appreciated the change in domestic US politics that had occurred after Nixon's fall from office. Once again, a mixture of competing domestic matters and mutual mistrust and misunderstanding rather than outright aggression or provocation brought about complications on the international stage. But it was primarily Washington, first under Carter (who replaced Ford, Nixon's successor, in 1977) and then under Reagan, rather than Moscow which rejected détente.[11]

As mentioned in the previous chapter, one factor more than any other led to the abandonment of détente: the Soviet invasion of Afghanistan in 1979. As in 1956 and 1968, the Soviets claimed to be responding to a request for help from the communist government in Kabul, but this time it was in a country that was outside the Soviet sphere of interest. In an already-strained atmosphere, the invasion 'catalyzed a major revision of US policy towards the Soviet Union'.[12] The result was the return to prominence in Washington of hard-line Cold War attitudes associated with Zbigniew Brzezinski, in particular the rediscovery of containment, this time in the Persian Gulf rather than in Europe. Brezhnev, reconfirming the existence of his eponymous Doctrine, asserted that the Soviets would not allow another Chile on its southern borders; the Americans, despite Soviet assurances to the contrary, feared a Soviet push through to the Indian Ocean. The American response to the Soviet invasion, then, 'revealed the continued relevance of the same kind of security dilemmas which had played a major part in the development of the cold war in the late 1940s'.[13] What the Soviets saw as an attempt to hold on to the status quo, the Americans regarded as Soviet expansionism. It was thus Carter rather than Reagan who brought about the 'new cold war', even if Reagan was more enthusiastic about pursuing it.[14]

The process was repeated in the sphere of arms controls. The successful Nixon–Brezhnev summits had resulted in the signing of SALT I, but in the late 1970s SALT II, signed in Vienna in June 1979, came to seem surplus to requirements. Tension increased after 1977 when the Soviets deployed Pioneer (SS-20) medium-range nuclear missiles in Eastern Europe. NATO countered in late 1979 by taking the decision to install cruise and Pershing missiles in West Germany (which happened in 1983). Combined with the US Senate's throwing out of the SALT II agreement in December 1979 (even if the US more or less adhered to its terms for several years thereafter), these moves resulted in the Soviets walking out of arms control talks in Geneva; the Soviet Union, following Brezhnev's death (1982), 'had finally abandoned détente'.[15]

Détente, one scholar argues, 'had a long-term impact: that is, it accelerated the process of exchanges between East and West, a process that, it seems safe to argue, bore fruit in the late 1980s as the communist order in Eastern Europe and the Soviet Union collapsed peacefully'.[16] There is no direct line from détente to the collapse of communism, nor should the latter be understood as a necessary consequence of the former. Still, détente helped to break down barriers between the two camps politically, economically, and culturally and, most important, it provided the domestic opposition with a language of rights and an international framework in which they were supposedly supported, including by the regimes against which they protested. So if détente collapsed, the changes it had already wrought by that point were to prove irreversible, especially in the European context. Although many countries, led by West Germany, tried—unsuccessfully, for the most part—to resist Washington's tough political stance on Moscow, the economic ties they had established not only survived the demise of détente and re-emerged with new vigour after 1985 but also contributed to communism's collapse by highlighting Western Europe's affluence and tightening the Eastern Bloc's ties of financial dependence.[17] There is, however, an even clearer connection between the Helsinki process and the collapse of communism, showing that ideas are sometimes the most powerful of weapons.

The Helsinki Final Act was the result of détente and the start of its unravelling. It was also a source of danger for the communist regimes from within, although the Final Act's signatories had not appreciated this at the time. This new challenge to the authorities arose everywhere across the region, with the first Helsinki group appearing in Moscow very soon after the signing of the Final Act, and assisted by the 'Helsinki process' of the subsequent meetings held in Belgrade (1977–8), Madrid (1980–3), and Vienna (1986–9) at which compliance with the Final Act was scrutinized. Using the language of human rights was meant not to kick-start a conversation with the governments—this was impossible—but, by illustrating the gulf between rhetoric and reality, to embarrass them.[18] Monitoring and cataloguing human rights abuses were far more effective tools of international pressure than obtaining compliance with the Final Act.[19] This is why Soviet Foreign Minister Andrei Gromyko repeatedly argued that 'It would be good to cut out the bottom from under this Third Basket.'[20] It is also why the head of the KGB, Iurii Andropov, noted the following: 'The principle of inviolability of borders—this is of course good, very good. But I am concerned about something else: the borders will be inviolable in the military sense, but in all other respects, as a result of the expansion of contacts, of the flow of information, they will become transparent.' By the end of 1975, Andropov believed that his predictions had already been proven correct, claiming at a Politburo meeting that 'in the Soviet Union, there are hundreds of thousands of people who are either currently acting, or are ready to act (under certain circumstances) against the Soviet regime'.[21] In 1977–8, at the same time as détente was dying, the Soviet authorities began to crack down on these Helsinki groups, the most famous victim being Anatoly Shcharansky. It is no coincidence that the high point of this clampdown was 1980–2, following criticisms of the invasion of Afghanistan and in the run up to the Moscow Summer Olympics of 1980. In 1982, Moscow's Helsinki Watch Group was officially shut down. But the most threatening adoption of Helsinki principles occurred not in the Soviet Union but in the satellite states, whose leaders feared what Albert Norden, the GDR's leading expert on the west, termed a 'counter-revolutionary "social democratization of Eastern Europe"'.[22]

The first and most important actual post-Helsinki challenge to communist authority arose, as so often, in Poland. It turned out to be the ultimate test of 'normalization' and the Brezhnev Doctrine, and ended by signalling a new reality in the Soviet Union's relationships with the Eastern European communist states. In 1976, the price of food rose very sharply in Poland and workers went on strike. The authorities responded with force, with many workers beaten and arrested—a kind of reprise of December 1970, when troops had fired on striking workers in Gdańsk, events which brought about Gomułka's ouster in favour of Gierek. This time, however, workers and intellectuals found common cause. The Workers' Defence Committee

(KOR) was set up precisely to foster this relationship, which it successfully achieved. In its 10 October 1978 Appeal to Society, KOR spoke openly and boldly. 'The system based on arbitrary and irrevocable decisions by state and party authorities who see themselves as infallible', KOR claimed, 'has caused immeasurable damage to the social consciousness of the nation.'[23] Although its leading spokesman, Adam Michnik, was repeatedly imprisoned, KOR's policy of 'militant decency', including a refusal to use violence and willingness to compromise, brought it considerable public support.[24] In 1980, following the 'psychological earthquake' of the Pope's visit to Poland, the Solidarity trade union emerged, led by dock worker Lech Wałęsa. With a series of strikes centred on the shipyards of Gdańsk, but eventually bringing out over one million workers across Poland, the government was forced to negotiate. By signing the Gdańsk Agreement on 31 August 1980, the Polish government did more than merely legalize Solidarity; it turned the movement into a legitimate political force that could threaten communist rule.[25] Indeed, Solidarity later published a programme that spoke of the trade union being at the forefront of 'national renewal', as leading 'a protest against the existing form of power', and as being 'a movement for the moral rebirth of our people'. Most ominous for the one-party state, it put forward the desirability of a 'self-governed republic'.[26] The impact of the Pope was plain to see, and Gierek was no doubt wishing he had heeded Brezhnev's warning.

Fearing that the Polish communists would not crack down on Solidarity, Moscow intervened and in October 1981 replaced Stanisław Kania (who had himself only just replaced Gierek) with the military man, Minister of Defence, Prime Minister, and fanatical communist Wojciech Jaruzelski. Declaring that he wanted to form a 'Front for National Unity', which would presumably include Solidarity and the Church under Archbishop Józef Glemp, Jaruzelski sounded conciliatory in public. But he had no intention of giving way to the demands of men like Wałęsa, whom he considered 'social fascists'. Using forged tapes to provide 'proof' of a Solidarity plot to overthrow the government, Jaruzelski, claiming that 'national catastrophe is no longer days but only hours away', introduced martial law in Poland on 13 December 1981.[27] Wałęsa and most of the Solidarity leadership were arrested.

Jaruzelski claimed that the introduction of martial law forestalled a grimmer possibility—Soviet military intervention. He was believed at home and historians since have thought the same, arguing that the Soviets preferred martial law as a way of keeping the problem confined to Poland, preventing the USSR or the other Warsaw Pact allies from being 'infected', as happened in 1956. In fact, although the Warsaw Pact initially prepared for an invasion, Soviet policy changed and ultimately Moscow explicitly rejected sending in troops, even in the face of Jaruzelski's request to do so. Jaruzelski's real fear 'was not that of Moscow's intervention but of its non-intervention'.[28] From the Soviets' point of view, the turn to national communism and what one historian called 'enlightened tolerance', even at the expense of bloc unity, was preferable to invading Poland, simply because the USSR in the early 1980s needed to focus on domestic affairs.[29] In the end, Andropov was unequivocally clear: 'We do not intend to introduce troops into Poland. That is the right position and we must stick with it to the end....I don't know how things will turn out in Poland, but even if it falls under the control of Solidarity, so be it.... If the capitalist countries pounce on the Soviet Union...with economic and political sanctions, that would be burdensome for us. We must be concerned above all about our country and strengthening the Soviet Union.'[30] This decision was communicated to Jaruzelski on 11 December. The Soviet position was obviously borne of necessity and self-interest, and a correct assumption that Solidarity would not enjoy region-wide appeal. But it also suggested a relative openness to diversity within the Eastern Bloc which anticipated later developments.

In retrospect, the significance of the events in Poland in 1980–1 was that they formed a 'pivotal moment in the Soviet domination of Eastern Europe, when all the limitations of Soviet power came to light, and when the Kremlin began to explore the possibilities of retrenchment and retreat'.[31] Solidarity signalled the start of real change in Poland. One of the finest analysts of the late Soviet Union argues that 'In good measure Solidarity was responsible for Gorbachev and perestroika', because it made Soviet elites realize that they could not co-opt and incorporate social forces into their political control. 'Soviet leaders concluded that the Party's political leadership and organizational rectitude required them to risk "losing its life to save it".'[32] One could even say that Jaruzelski's decision to impose martial law 'unwittingly provided the Soviet Union with the time it needed to decay sufficiently from within, thus making its leaders more amenable to a peaceful East–West settlement'.[33]

It might not have felt that way to Poles living under the grim conditions of martial law, which were compared by philosopher Leszek Kołakowski to a declaration of war on the people by the government. Yet Kołakowski, in several important essays, also indicated that when dictatorships moved to concentrate power they were also hiding weakness, and he suggested ways in which opponents could operate in relative freedom in the interstices of the system.[34] These ideas inspired Adam Michnik, Jacek Kuroń, and those who ran the flying universities and underground presses to talk of 'Poland's self-limiting revolution', a way of proceeding cautiously without provoking a backlash.[35] They of course could not know that the whole edifice would come crashing down just a few years later.

The rise of Solidarity and the Helsinki monitoring groups was a sign that a new civil society was emerging in Poland. Under the grey surface unanimity, new life was bubbling up. It might have continued being stifled were it not for the fact that the Soviet elites who suppressed such groups in the early 1980s soon became infected with the same way of thinking. Some of Gorbachev's key advisers, such as Alexander Yakovlev, Anatoly Chernyaev, and Georgy Shakhnazarov, shared some of the dissidents' views and aspirations. And the exchange of ideas worked in the other direction too, as the change in mood enabled some dissidents to enter into the political process in ways that would have been impossible before 1985. 'The ideas developed by the Helsinki network and the international coalition for reform', writes one historian, 'prepared the ground for the transformation of the Soviet Union and for the eventual collapse of communism.'[36] If this sounds overly optimistic about the role of utopian ideas, at least one can note that just a few years after abandoning détente, the parlous condition of the Soviet state and economy led the Soviets to abandon the Brezhnev Doctrine itself in favour of what Gennady Gerasimov later famously called the 'Sinatra Doctrine', whereby each of the Eastern European states was free to choose their 'own way'.

The setting for this radical change of policy was the so-called 'Second Cold War' of the 1980s. Although both Moscow and Washington had decided that détente had died by 1980, it was the latter that set the pace in bringing about a return to the older antagonism.[37] The Americans initiated a renewed arms race which took advantage of the mismatch between Soviet ambition and their shambolic finances, whilst the Soviets faced numerous complications, from infighting over who would succeed the aged Brezhnev, international condemnation of the invasion of Afghanistan, and the rise of Solidarity in Poland. Thus the newfound vigour in US foreign policy towards Moscow rapidly revealed that the Soviets' acquisition of parity with the US in nuclear weapons was irrelevant. Neither side wished to use them, especially since Warsaw Pact war planning assumed that in the event of war, several thousand nuclear strikes would take place in what has aptly been called 'a recipe for paralyzing devastation'.[38] And for the USSR, maintaining them swallowed a far higher proportion of GDP than it did for the US, the UK, or France.[39] Indeed, in the 1980s it became increasingly obvious that the Soviets' earlier claims to be catching up and overtaking the US had always been fantasy and that the Soviet Union 'was never *the other* superpower' because 'the gap which separated the communist regime from the United States in economic achievement, technological innovation, and overall military capability was so great that it is impossible to place the two in the same category'.[40] Reagan's 1983 announcement that the Soviet Union was an 'evil empire' and his initiation of the Strategic Defense Initiative (SDI) known as 'Star Wars', i.e. satellite-based ballistic missile defence against Soviet nuclear attack, not only confirmed the death of détente but placed the Soviets on the back foot. Andropov's accusation that the Americans were war-mongering—'If anyone had any illusions about the possibility of an evolution for the better in the policy of the present American administration, recent events have dispelled them once and for all'—was a sure sign of Soviet weakness.[41]

Soviet nervousness was quite marked in 1982–3. On 1 September 1983 a Korean airliner, KE007, flew off course into Soviet air space where it was shot down, amid Soviet claims that the plane was on a spying mission for the US. This was improbable given the 269 people on board who lost their lives. In the wake of the incident, Reagan again increased military spending and Andropov's advisers told him that the Americans might launch a nuclear strike against the USSR, using as cover a NATO exercise called Able Archer 83 due to start on 2 November. The confusion arose because, unusually, senior US and NATO officers who controlled decisions to utilize nuclear weapons were involved, including Margaret Thatcher and Helmut Kohl. In these already-tense days, the Soviets mistook the exercise for reality. As in 1962, though this time without the knowledge of the public, the possibility of nuclear war suddenly became real again. No wonder that Andropov, issuing sabre-rattling statements from his deathbed, could describe the situation to the CPSU as 'marked by confrontation, unprecedented in the entire postwar period by its intensity and sharpness, of the two diametrically opposite world outlooks, the two political courses, socialism and imperialism'.[42] One of the few historians to take note of Able Archer 83 argues that inadvertent blundering towards nuclear war, 'and not the decline and fall of the

Soviet Union, was the return on the neoconservatives' long, cynical, and radically partisan investment in threat inflation and arms-race escalation'.[43] Still, events such as Able Archer 83 contributed to Reagan's policy 'reversal', whereby he wanted 'a shield rather than a sword', leading eventually to his offer at Reykjavik in October 1986 to slash American nuclear arms in return for a Soviet acceptance of SDI.[44] And although American military spending heightened the sense of crisis within the Soviet Union, it was not the cause of the collapse of communism.[45]

By the time Andropov died in March 1984, to be succeeded by another living fossil, Konstantin Chernenko, Soviet foreign policy more accurately resembled the society it was defending: outdated and battered. Although opponents of the USSR warned against Soviet expansionism and aggression, in fact overstretch and over-expenditure meant that by 1985, 'the Soviet empire was more vulnerable than at any other time in its history'.[46] Chernenko's short reign has been described as one of 'overwhelming conservatism' in which the country 'was paralysed in many of its actions because of the infirm and ageing nature of the leadership'.[47] The description applies to communist society of the 1980s just as well.

Late communism

In retrospect, life in these regimes can have its funny side, as in the 2001 film *Slogans* (dir. Gjergj Xhuvani), in which a young teacher from Tirana is posted to a remote village school, and reluctantly gets his pupils to create huge slogans on the hillsides that they do not understand ('American imperialism is a paper tiger') and that no one will see anyway.[48] In Romanian examples such as the 2009 film *Tales from the Golden Age* (dir. Cristian Mungiu), which captured especially well the nature of life in 1980s Romania, showing its absurdities and loopholes as well as its hardships, or György Dragomán's *The White King* (2008), whose stories deal with the life of a young boy whose father has been taken away by the secret police to work in a labour camp, the laughter is always tinged with a manic edge. In a country in which the Piteşti 're-education camp', run by a former Iron Guard (interwar Romanian fascist) activist, could exist—where people were forced to torture and sexually abuse their family members—the worst excesses of Stalin were by no means over, even if (or rather, because) Romania took an independent line from Moscow. In the USSR too, the camp system did not disappear with de-Stalinization, as Avraham Shifrin's 1980 remarkable publication *The First Guidebook to Prisons and Concentration Camps of the Soviet Union* testifies.[49] Written in the style of a travel guide, it offered maps, line drawings, and clandestine photographs of different varieties of prison camp or psychiatric institution, advising 'tourists' on how to find them, even in the remotest areas of the Soviet Union. The vast extent of the late Soviet camp system, from Moldavia to Kamchatka, is represented in the book's pull-out map by a dot for each site. It is an image which still takes one's breath away.

Outside of the independent, hard-line regimes of Albania and Romania or the harsh universe of Soviet incarceration, the 'regular' citizens of the USSR and its Eastern European satellites inhabited a rather strange world in the late 1970s and 1980s. The western image of the communist east as one of repression, economic depression, environmental catastrophe, and brave dissidents is only a partial truth, and one that was very much a Cold War construct. Each of those elements was real, but they affected different people in different ways. No matter how brave the signatories of Charter 77, for example, they only ever made up a tiny minority of Czechoslovak society. Most people's lives were focused on how to get by, how to find the basics necessary for day-to-day living and, bizarre as it now seems, on making the most of the Eastern European version of the 'consumer society'. It runs counter to the image of the Cold Warriors, but no less a commentator than Václav Havel noted of late 1970s Czechoslovakia that 'what we have here is simply another form of the consumer and industrial society, with all its concomitant social, intellectual, and psychological consequences'. For Havel, this was not frivolous or meant to downplay or otherwise beautify the regime. To the contrary; 'It is impossible', he argued, 'to understand the nature of power in our system properly without taking this into account.'[50] Consumerism was part of the 'normalization' deal whereby the Party bought off citizens, offering them some compensation for the lack of political freedoms, and the people, for their part, 'agreed' to put up with—and compromised themselves with—the regimes in return for an increase in goods.

What Havel was suggesting, of course, was not that the communist regimes were comparable to those of the West. This was a perverted form of consumerism. But it played its role nevertheless in stabilizing the regimes and in shaping everyday life. In fact, from an economic point of view, these were very inefficient states. Despite Brezhnev's programme of 'Developed Socialism', an attempt to use science and technology to recognize and rectify shortcomings in the system of planning and production, what the Soviets themselves contemptuously called *zastoi* (stagnation) could not be overcome, even though 'the ideological framework provided by Developed Socialism continued to promote, or perhaps did not hinder, the emergence of reforms in selective areas right up until the death of Brezhnev'.[51] The workings of the economics of stagnation were famously explained by Hungarian reform economist János Kornai, who demonstrated that the characteristics of the command economy meant that it would 'permanently reproduce shortage'.[52]

Kornai was right because, at least officially, there was to be little deviance or room for expression that had not been approved by the Party, as the Brezhnev Doctrine of defending the status quo ensured that room for manoeuvre in the sphere of daily life became increasingly restricted. The flow of consumer goods was rarely able to keep up with demand, and those who designed them saw their aspirations fail as shortages became the norm and the Brezhnevian focus on materialism and glossy consumer items replaced the notion of a rational society in which functional and aesthetically pleasing goods met people's needs. The much-vaunted Khrushchev kitchen did not become a reality for most Russian women, and throughout the Eastern Bloc women spent more time in queues hoping that they would find something to buy than engaging in western-style selective consumerism. So although there was no shortage of grounds for tension between regime and society, for 'a mother searching for fresh fruit and vegetables for her children, small, everyday problems were of more immediate importance than the fundamental ones such as the undemocratic election process'.[53] Technology too ended up in the doldrums, even though—at least in the case of Czechoslovakia and the GDR—there was a pre-existing industrial base and traditions of technological innovation. Thanks to central control and the fear of upsetting the status quo, new product development was stifled in favour of the continued manufacture of existing ones, and 'shortcomings in the system of planning and innovation' meant that, despite some notable successes in laser technologies or space optics, and despite the existence of what historians of technology call a 'consumption junction' (when consumers are able to make choices between competing technologies), the GDR suffered from a conflict between political decision-making and technological innovation.[54] And the focus on heavy industry and 'socialist labour' meant that pollution was endemic, the environment was dangerously degraded (even before the Chernobyl accident of 1986, which further damaged the Soviet regime's reputation), and agriculture was seriously neglected, with the result that severe food shortages were common. Many people relied on their allotments and on their family links to the countryside for a supply of fresh food.[55]

The more the turn to consumerism failed, the more the regimes emphasized antifascism, which was deliberately fostered as a social glue. In the USSR, the cult of the Great Patriotic War really took off only in the mid-1960s. Brezhnev reintroduced Victory Day celebrations in 1965, and they gradually became more important than commemorating the Bolshevik Revolution itself. 'The immortal feat of the Soviet people and their Armed Forces in achieving their historic victory in the Great Patriotic War' ran the formulation written into the new Soviet constitution of 1977. Twelve cities had been named 'Hero Cities' by the 1985 Victory Day.[56] And the collective memory being constructed by the communist regimes was highly selective, with its emphasis on the communist resistance and the people's overthrow of fascism, and a marked inability specifically to name the many victims of Nazism who were killed because they were Jewish. Indeed, 'the empathy aroused by the concentration camp memorials in the GDR was abused, instrumentalized, distorted. It was deployed, not to open the way for an illumination of the past in all its fullness and contradiction, but rather to legitimise the present, to instil a sense of political commitment that was to be beyond valid questioning'.[57] This 'enforced consensus', if one can use this paradoxical term, meant that the official line was propagated all the harder as the conditions which helped this ideology to function increasingly disappeared: 'From a genuine fear of "fascists", "class enemies", and the like in the early years there developed a ritualised rhetoric or demonology, in which very few can have really believed any more.'[58] No wonder that dark humour, especially at the expense of the *nomenklatura* and the police, became rife.[59] Still, antifascism continued to hold a powerful place in the minds of the regimes' citizens, especially those who were involved with the victory against Hitler. Vasily Grossman, for example, author of the great novel *Life and Fate* and some of the most important Soviet war journalism, remained proud of the Red Army soldiers' sacrifices to save the world from fascism long after he had become disillusioned with the Soviet Union, always standing when he sang Red Army songs such as 'Arise, the Huge Country' to his daughter.[60]

At the same time, the communist regimes increasingly turned to nationalism. It is often assumed that nationalism emerged after 1989 to fill the political vacuum opened up by the demise of communism. In fact, the opposite is the case: nationalism did not cause the collapse of communism, but it was one contributory factor. The fact that it already existed allowed nationalism rapidly to become the chief beneficiary of communism's collapse. The wars of Yugoslav succession are the clearest case of nationalism's successful rise, which took place despite the Party's official reproach, but secessionist movements in Chechnya and other areas of Russia and the CIS are direct heirs to the dangerous policy of using nationalism on a 'regional' basis whilst condemning it at the federal level of the Soviet Union.[61] At this policy's most extreme, in Romania, where the Communist Party had a tiny indigenous base until after the Second World War, nationalism, and, by the 1970s and 1980s, national socialism in the strict sense (novelist and Romanian exile Norman Manea calls it 'camouflaged fascism'[62]), was cynically employed by a regime that had nothing else up its sleeve to appeal to the population in the region least attracted to the lessons of 'antifascism' and communist internationalism. That it was backed up by intellectuals—many of whom went on to post-communist careers as radical right populists—is unsurprising in a country where the interwar intellectual elite was characterized by strikingly high and widely accepted levels of antisemitism and violent ultra-nationalism.[63]

Thus, in the late period of the Cold War, we see a growing sense of inertia, or rather a grudging acceptance of one's inability to change the situation, following the crushing of the Prague Spring. This sense of accommodation was famously embodied in Havel's image of a greengrocer displaying the slogan 'Workers of the world, unite!' in his shop: Havel argued that the man had never given the meaning of the slogan a second thought, but displayed it because he had been given it by the enterprise headquarters, because that was how things had always been, and because he could be in trouble for not displaying it. 'It is', wrote Havel, 'one of the thousands of details that guarantee him a relatively tranquil life "in harmony with society", as they say.'[64] This then was the period of 'normalization'.

Following the 1968 Warsaw Pact invasion of Prague, *normalizace* became the watchword in Czechoslovakia, even among ordinary citizens. Yet the fact that ordinary people used the term suggests that everything and yet nothing was normal after the Prague Spring. Still, the irony with which the word was initially used itself became normalized, as people increasingly used it 'to describe the society in which they now found themselves living and working'.[65] Groups such as Charter 77 in Czechoslovakia, the Prenzlauer Berg writers' groups in East Berlin, or Solidarity in Poland—which was far more widely known and politically effective—have attracted the lion's share of our attention. But this means overlooking most people's experience of daily reality under communism. Havel was right to say in 1975 that 'today's regime rests solely on the ruling minority's instinct of self-preservation and on the fear of the ruled majority', but that does not account for how people coped in this period of 'order without life'.[66]

Most people may not have been actively involved in dissident movements, but citizens became adept at 'playing the system', finding ways not only of adapting themselves to it that did not mean relinquishing all autonomy, but also getting the regime to respond to their demands. In the GDR, whilst the state reached deeply into every sphere of life, it could not control everything. In fact, the very attempt to control totally necessarily failed, inadvertently creating new zones of autonomy.[67] It seems unlikely, but one of the places where people felt most free from surveillance was in the cafés and bowling alley of the Palace of the Republic, the building which also housed the East German parliament.[68] Besides, until the end, the regime retained significant levels of support, precisely for those things the loss of which Ossis lamented after 1989: welfare, childcare, education, cheaply available culture (the Lumpenproletariat, or underclass, was far smaller in communist Eastern Europe than in, say, the UK), all the things summed up in the concept of a 'welfare dictatorship'.[69] It is salutary to be reminded that in struggling to walk a tightrope between buying people off with a reasonable standard of living but managing consumers' expectations, Brezhnev's policies contributed in no small measure to the survival of the USSR for another twenty-five years.[70] This ambivalence between the structures of power and people's emotional and personal encounters with them is nicely summed up by anthropologist Alexei Yurchak, who writes that: 'For great numbers of Soviet citizens, many of the fundamental values, ideals, and realities of socialism were of genuine importance, despite the fact that many of their everyday practices routinely reinterpreted the announced norms and rules of the socialist state.'[71]

The last Soviet generation—and those who grew up in the last years of communism in Eastern Europe as a whole—existed both within and without the mental and physical spaces created by communism. Formal participation in the regime often went hand in hand with its rejection and mental self-exclusion, paradoxical as that may seem. As with Yurchak's description of Soviet citizens acting 'as if' they accepted the regime, its rituals, and its expectations—attending Komsomol meetings, for example, but acting out the rituals on a 'pro forma' basis in order then to be able better to conduct other, meaningful work[72]—so citizens across the Eastern Bloc seem to have done likewise. Sitting through one of Khrushchev's speeches, composer Dmitry Shostakovich was busy writing in his notebook whilst all around him were applauding. He then whispered to his neighbour, poet Yevgeny Yevtushenko: 'I have my own method of avoiding applause. I try to produce an impression that I'm writing down all these great thoughts. Thank God, everyone can see that my hands are busy.'[73] Even more striking, the East German regime as a whole has been described as acting 'as if' its citizens' formal assertions of loyalty were truthful, a claim which suggests some tension between the cynical clinging on to power and the aspiration, which none of the communist states ever abandoned, of creating new socialist human beings.[74] Rather than enjoying legitimate authority, late-era communist regimes, better designated as 'late paternalism', existed on the basis of what might be called 'conditional tolerance', which operated according to the unspoken rule: 'we pretend to conform and you pretend to believe us.'[75]

For those who were children during the last decade or so of communist rule, looking back confirms many of these observations. The historian Anton Weiss-Wendt, for example, who grew up in the small town of Valdai, between Moscow and Leningrad, writes of the food shortages, the ingenuity his parents displayed in obtaining food and the rarely available shoddy goods, the dreariness of Soviet TV, the dull uniformity of Soviet apartments and of people's aspirations. But he also writes of children's play and youngsters' pranks, of collecting stamps, coins, and toy soldiers, and of friendships, in a universalizing manner. Still, as a young teenager Weiss-Wendt quickly became aware of the limits of such mischievousness. When he daubed anarchy signs around the school, Weiss-Wendt was lucky not to be denounced by his classmates to the School Director, who 'was beside herself with rage', and he concludes that schoolchildren only challenged authority 'insofar as the extremity of youth goes. In all other respects, the Soviet youth was a mere replica of the larger socialist society.' In the Pioneers, the children 'breathed ideology, without realizing', even if this did not preclude a fascination with heavy metal.[76]

In a way that a child could only have been dimly aware, if at all, this period of late communism is when we also witness the rise to prominence of new opposition movements, which gradually re-emerged following the ruthless suppressions of the 1950s and 1960s. The most famous is Charter 77, whose founding document began by noting with approval the

Czechoslovak government's signature of the Helsinki Accords but observing, however, that their publication 'serves as an urgent reminder of the
extent to which basic human rights in our country exist, regrettably, on
paper only'.[77] Apart from the growing number of such groups and networks, dissident ideas spread through *samizdat*, or underground publications which, despite the use of the term 'underground', in fact worked
openly within Soviet society to amplify the regime's discourse, making all
the more improbable its claims for unity and progress.[78] Opposition intellectuals such as Adam Michnik, Václav Havel, János Kis, György Konrád,
and Andrei Sakharov 'were consciously participants in a transnational
"republic of letters" that both traversed the East–West divide and was strategically calculated to address multiple publics.'[79] Critics went so far as to
talk of the emergence of a 'parallel polis', an alternative civil society to that
officially sanctioned by the regime, and by the late 1980s it had become a
reality, at least in Poland.[80] In Slovakia, the Catholic 'secret church', operating since 1943, became a real source of anti-regime strength during the
1980s; in Poland, a thriving rock music scene had a complex relationship
with the regime; and in Russia there was a thriving trade in 'magnetizdat',
or private cassette recordings of popular singers.[81] And if there were limits
to dissent, the alternative was not necessarily despair or cynical accommodation with the regime. 'While heroism frightens people, giving them the
truthful excuse that they are not made for it', Ludvík Vaculík wrote, 'everyone can bravely adhere to the norm of good behaviour at the price of
acceptable sacrifice, and everyone knows it.'[82]

But up until the last minute, with the exception of Poland, one can
hardly talk of a meaningful civil society outside of communist oversight, nor
could even self-styled dissidents really imagine either the demise of the
system they fought against or the Cold War itself. They were for the most
part focused on the local context. Hungarian dissident Miklós Haraszti, for
example, went so far as to suggest that in the 'textbook model of a pacified
post-Stalinist neocolony' that was Hungary, dissidents had become useful to
the state: 'if dissidents have a place at all, that place is outside official culture,
even if they are not in prison', he wrote. 'But in their isolation they have
become predictable, and their numbers can be planned for systematically.'[83]
Although Haraszti meant his book 'to be a denial of its own deliberate
exaggerations', its pessimism was quite understandable.[84] It certainly had the
merit of reminding people that a heroic model of dissidents bringing down
the regimes can only ever be part of the story.

Besides, this image of 'inner emigration' or, in Havel's terms, a split between public compliance and 'living in truth', has been challenged. Ordinary people did not have two clearly separated spheres of life, 'a compliant public mask at work and a liberated self at home'. Rather, the reality was far more complex than this neat binary division would have us believe.[85] For example, when the Czechoslovak regime promoted the vision of 'self-realization' (*seberealizace*) and 'self-actualization' (*sebeaktualizace*) in the 1980s, many ordinary people chose to counter the 'the drabness of normalization' by choosing 'to self-realize as consumers'.[86] In other words, many acts of everyday life could be both 'system-critical and system-sustaining'.[87]

Finally, if dissidents and their *samizdat* were important, both within communist society and for what they offered western Cold Warriors, the adoption of *perestroika* and *glasnost* killed them off.[88] Andrei Siniavsky, the Russian writer and dissident, noted, only half in jest, in 1996 that 'Gorbachev simply read his fill of samizdat and was fulfilling the dream of Soviet dissidents by becoming the first dissident in his own Politburo.'[89] Yet if Gorbachev went on to fulfil another of the dissidents' dreams by dismantling the one-party state and bringing about the end of communist rule, this was far from his intention in 1985.

From reform to collapse

At the start of 1989, the communist authorities in Czechoslovakia refused to grant Rita Klimová permission to go on holiday abroad; at the end of the year, she was post-communist Czechoslovakia's first ambassador to the US.[90] Yet the collapse of communism, although swift and unexpected, did not come from nowhere. In retrospect, one can see that the conditions within the communist bloc which precipitated the end were in evidence throughout the last decade of the Cold War. Despite the rhetoric of a 'Second Cold War' in the 1980s, we can see that numerous threats to communist rule were building up a head of steam.

The first threat was economic. The Eastern Bloc was falling rapidly behind in technological terms, the price of raw materials was falling, China under Deng Xiaoping appeared to be reneging on Maoist principles and turning capitalist, and the cost of the arms race from the late 1970s onwards had crippled consumerism in the USSR. Although, as we have seen, the 'normalized'

Eastern European states did 'enjoy' some sort of consumer activity in the 1970s and 1980s, the gulf between east and west in that regard grew ever larger. At the start of 1989, only 11 per cent of consumer goods that were supposed to be available in Soviet shops could actually be found.[91] Still, although living standards behind the iron curtain had fallen way behind those of Western Europe by the 1980s, vanishingly few commentators believed that that meant the end of the regime. Daniel Chirot elegantly notes:

> By the 1970s the USSR had the world's most advanced late nineteenth-century economy, the world's biggest and best, most inflexible rustbelt. It is as if Andrew Carnegie had taken over the entire United States, forced it into becoming a giant copy of U.S. Steel, and the executives of the same U.S. Steel had continued to run the country into the 1970s and 1980s.

Or, as historian Ken Jowitt succinctly put it, 'After 70 years of murderous effort, the Soviet Union had created a "German industry of the 1880s" in the 1980s.'[92] The Brezhnev Doctrine institutionalized ossification, 'as if', philosopher Karl Jaspers had written some years before, 'a principle were, so to speak, alive and as if everyone, including the dictator of the moment, had become mere functionaries of it'.[93] The 'hegemony of form' meant that even if people were only paying lip-service to the reigning ideology, they nevertheless expected the 'tyrannies of certitude' to continue to hold on to power.[94]

So when Mikhail Gorbachev was appointed General Secretary of the CPSU in 1985, few expected that empty shops and dreadful pollution would by themselves bring about change. Ironically, the communist countries' acceptance of capitalist definitions of the world meant that they remained at pains to service their $90 billion western loans, forcing their citizens into bleak austerity, when defaulting 'might well have brought down the world financial system and realized Khrushchev's threatening prophecy overnight'[95]— which just goes to show that not economic factors in the narrow sense, appalling though all the indicators were, but the political decisions which flowed from the economic facts hold the key to the collapse.[96] As we saw above, the abandonment of the Brezhnev Doctrine did not result simply from a sudden outburst of humanitarianism amongst the Soviet leadership; if the Helsinki groups influenced the *apparat*, it was because their arguments in favour of reform made sense at a time when the USSR was at its lowest ebb financially, ideologically, and politically. Gorbachev was not alone in recognizing that conditions in the USSR and Europe—including, among other things, 'the re-establishment of West German foreign policy, the transformation of west European communism, the emergence of political Islam, the decline in the Soviet will to intervene, and the domestic political successes of the United States' neo-conservative movement'—demanded an end to the status quo.[97] But he was remarkable for a Soviet leader in being bold enough to say so. Thus in order to understand the 'Gorbachev phenomenon', one has to start by grasping that he introduced his famous reforms of *glasnost* (openness) and *perestroika* (restructuring) not in order to break up the Soviet Union and to bury communism, but to save and revive both.

Much has been written, in the wake of the twentieth anniversary of the fall of communism, to try and explain a sequence of events that almost no one had been able to foresee. To a large extent, the collapse is over-determined, and it is impossible to provide a definitive explanation of such large-scale, continent-wide events. From economic stagnation to the daring of Solidarity in Poland to the bravery of the crowds in taking to the streets in 1989 in Leipzig, Prague, Sofia, and Timişoara, there are many factors that contributed to communism's demise, not least the role played by easily overlooked phenomena such as political commemorations in mobilizing protest.[98] In the US, the end of the Cold War is popularly and erroneously ascribed to Ronald Reagan 'defeating' the 'evil empire'. Outside of Europe, the cost of Third World interventions increased as the US's own interventionist counter-attack grew stronger, and the rise of Islamism in Iran and Afghanistan added a complicating factor to Cold War rivalries.

All of these factors did have some bearing on communism's collapse. But none of them would have been decisive were it not for Gorbachev's actions, first to initiate reform in the USSR and, second, not to order military intervention when the reform process took on a life of its own.[99] What therefore needs explaining, as historian Jacques Lévesque argues, is Soviet *permissiveness*.[100] The Soviets did not abandon Eastern Europe only because they believed it had become a burden that they could no longer afford to maintain; rather, they (or rather, Gorbachev and his circle) thought that reforming communism would have the result of tying the Eastern European countries to the Soviet Union all the more strongly.

In a sense, Gorbachev's position is simple to explain. As he told Soviet citizens in his last address to them on 25 December 1991, the reason why their living standards were so much worse than other large countries with huge natural resources 'was apparent even then', that is, five years previously:

our society was stifled in the grip of a bureaucratic command system. Doomed to serve ideology and bear the heavy burden of the arms race, it was strained to the utmost. All attempts at implementing half-hearted reforms—and there have been many—failed, one after the other. The country was losing hope. We could not go on living like this. We had to change everything radically.[101]

If one takes Gorbachev seriously, it becomes easier to understand why he felt able to let the Eastern Europeans abandon communism and to allow the peaceful break-up of the Warsaw Pact. One has therefore to understand Gorbachev's ideas about Europe and to see that foreign policy with respect to Europe was diminishing in importance whilst concerns at the state of the USSR domestically were growing.

Gorbachev's ideas were not fully formed when he assumed his new post in 1985. It would be nice to think that the lessons of the Prague Spring provided some sort of epiphany for Gorbachev, but in fact he came to the realization that the Soviet Union was not 'identical with socialism' only gradually, with the signing of the CSCE accords contributing to this realization.[102] As of 1983, Gorbachev claims, 'I made one more attempt at reforming the system, betting on the idea that by combining socialism with the scientific and technological revolution, using the advantages we believed were inherent in the planned economy, and making use of the concentration of governmental power, and so forth, things could be changed—that was the original plan.' As he laconically adds: 'Our calculations were not confirmed in practice.'[103]

It is not so hard to see why Gorbachev retained his optimism in reform socialism's prospects in the early 1980s. Although the USSR's own prospects were not exactly rosy in 1984, the economic crises of the late 1970s had hit the western world hard, placing considerable strains on the Western Allies as well as between the Cold War blocs. As a result, Gorbachev announced more than once after his accession to power that the 'postwar era' had come to an end and socialism's star was once again in the ascendant.[104] He failed to understand that whereas the Western European economies were restructuring, albeit painfully, the Eastern Europeans' inability and unwillingness to do likewise was forcing them deeper into indebtedness and the severe austerity which would only foment discontent in the grim years of the 1980s. Yet despite opposition from what came to be known (rather counter-intuitively) as the 'conservatives' among the Soviet *apparat*, Gorbachev had sufficient support for his vision of reform and restructuring for it to be fully ratified at the 27th Party Congress of February–March 1986. As one adviser,

Nikolai Kolikov, confirms: 'There was always among the apparat, at least at the level where I worked as a consultant, a notion that of course policy toward the East European countries had to change.... It had to change in order to afford them more freedom to act, to give them more space and more independence. Only then could we keep them in our orbit.... If not by force, then give them the ability to formulate their own policies.'[105]

Gorbachev's decision not to use troops either domestically or in foreign policy in the manner of 1953, 1956, or 1968, despite the readiness of some of his 'fraternal allies' to do so in 1989, had a solid basis in Soviet internal affairs, at least among Gorbachev's small circle of intellectual advisers, with many of them speaking of breaking up the two blocs with the aim of building an integrated Europe under the guidance of the CSCE. Key advisers and politicians such as Shakhnazarov and Eduard Shevardnadze talked of creating a 'common European home' which would see the end of NATO as well as the Warsaw Pact, and the economic integration of the EC and the CMEA. For example, in a top secret memorandum assessing the likely outcome of events in the satellite states in 1989, Marina Sylvanskaya of the reform-minded Bogomolov Institute argued that permitting a 'Finlandization' (i.e. neutrality with a pro-Soviet foreign policy) of those countries would seize the initiative from the west, make the Soviets look relatively benevolent, and leave the Eastern European countries in an intermediary position between the USSR and the west. This outcome would result in 'the growth in significance of the European factor in world politics and economics, which will favour Soviet efforts aimed at containing an anti-Soviet consolidation of the Western world and at developing a "common European home"'.[106] This latter notion would become Gorbachev's key foreign policy aim after 1987.

Gorbachev and his advisers resisted pressures from more traditionally minded Soviet figures to reinstate the Brezhnev Doctrine, because doing so, as Shevardnadze wrote, would have meant sacrificing 'freedom of choice, non-interference, and a common European home.... The very thought of it or of keeping a tight leash on the countries that some call "buffer states" was insulting to us as well as to the people of those countries.' He believed, and Gorbachev did too, that the Soviet Union would be stronger if freed from its position as regional tyrant and allowed to develop towards democracy with a set of neighbouring, independent states; this process would permit the USSR to join 'the common European process and form together with Europe a unified, legal, humanitarian, cultural and ecological space'.[107] At the same time, Gorbachev gradually came to realize the contradiction

between maintaining huge numbers of troops in Afghanistan and reinvigor-
ating détente with NATO and the US, not to mention between troops and
domestic reform. 'If we introduce 200,000 more troops', he said in early
1987, 'then our entire policy [i.e. *perestroika*] will collapse.'[108] Domestic and
foreign reform went hand in hand: 'perestroika began simultaneously in
domestic and foreign policies, successes in one area encouraging progress in
the other, set-backs slowing down progress in both.'[109]

Yet few of these politicians and policy-drafters envisaged the really radical
consequences of their proposals. Even the Bogomolov Commission did not
foresee the breaking up of the Warsaw Pact or the demise of communism.
Apart from a few disenchanted communists such as Zdeněk Mlynář, perhaps
the only people who intuited such possibilities were the hard-liners, who
feared any threat to the status quo, especially one which acknowledged Soviet
vulnerabilities and past mistakes. As Gorbachev himself noted, with more
prescience than he knew, shortly after initiating the programmes of *perestroika*
and *glasnost* that were to spiral irretrievably out of his control: 'To threaten
the socialist order, try to undermine it from outside, and tear one country or
another from the socialist community means encroachment not only on the
will of the people but also on the entire post-war order and, in the final
analysis, on peace.'[110] This threat to communism had been recognized by
Hannah Arendt, when she wrote years before Gorbachev's accession that 'a
new model' of socialism meant 'to the Russians, not only a more humane
handling of the economic or intellectual questions but also the threat of the
decomposition of the Russian empire'.[111] Gorbachev's experiment was,
therefore, a bold one from the point of view of Soviet orthodoxy, in whose
terms Gorbachev, despite trying to justify *perestroika* as a continuation of the
Leninist theory of revolution, appears as a class traitor.[112] His real achievement consisted in accepting the right of the Eastern Europeans to self-
determination even after he realized that the outcome would not be the one
for which he had hoped. We should, in other words, 'probably be grateful
that Gorbachev did not understand the consequences of his policies'.[113]

The hard-line communists were unconvinced. The Albanians feared on
the one hand that Gorbachev's 'New Thinking' was a ruse designed to trick
the Eastern Europeans into tighter dependence on Moscow, and on the
other that opening the communist countries' economies to western capital
would undermine them.[114] Romania's Nicolae Ceaușescu, the region's
staunchest defender of 'national Stalinism', condemned Gorbachev as a
'right-wing deviationist':

We must bear in mind that there are a number of theoretical and practical deviations, both on the right and on the left. Of course, both of them are equally dangerous.... However, it is my opinion that the main danger today comes from the rightist deviations, which can seriously harm socialist construction and the struggle for disarmament, peace, and mankind's overall progress.[115]

No wonder that Gorbachev described him as suffering from 'delusions of grandeur' and 'psychological instability'.[116]

Following the introduction of *perestroika*, Vasil Bilak, Gustav Husák's hard-line lieutenant in charge of ideological affairs in Czechoslovakia, sought to offer reassurance to those who needed it of the clear difference between Gorbachev's aims and those of the 'right-wing opportunists' of the 1968 Prague Spring:

> Nothing is identical. The CPSU leadership is striving to strengthen socialism and the unity of the socialist community, whereas our 'fighters for socialism with a human face' strove in 1968 to dismantle socialism and to break up the socialist community... Certain posthumous children of right wing opportunists, who are striving to 'rehabilitate' those who were politically shipwrecked... are pursuing the same goal as in 1968—to return Czechoslovakia to the lap of capitalism.[117]

The absurd insinuations of fascism aside, it must be said, however, that Ceauşescu had a point—he was never taken in by naive reformers who believed that communism could be made more acceptable, and would never have tolerated a loss of nerve or confidence among the leadership. Since the Polish crisis of the early 1980s, Ceauşescu had worked hard to ensure that Romania would be unaffected by similar threats.[118] The result was that where the Hungarian communist leadership was amenable to *perestroika*, Romania, even more so than Bulgaria, Czechoslovakia, and East Germany, was at odds with Gorbachev. This is why Ceauşescu had to be violently ejected from power.[119]

In 1956, 1968, and 1989, the aspirations of the reformers ended in the attainment of the exact opposite of what was intended: renewed Stalinism in post-1956 Hungary and post-1968 Czechoslovakia, and the demise of the communist system in Eastern Europe in 1989. Ironically, the drive to free countries from communist rule (1953, 1956, 1968) ended by tightening it, whilst the desire to reform and improve communist rule (the USSR after 1985) ended in its collapse. In fact, one could go so far as to say that it was precisely because the signals emanating from Moscow were for limited and gradual reform rather than for a complete overhaul of the system that major change could take place. Most important, only because the impetus for reform came from the heart of the system itself could the dreams of the 1956 and 1968 reformers finally be realized, even if that was the opposite of what Gorbachev set out to achieve.

Recognizing the irony of unintended consequences, however, does not account for the speed with which the end result came about. Once again, extant policies intensified the process: the 'unexpected Soviet permissiveness contributed a great deal to the rapidity with which the collapse occurred'.[120] *Perestroika* in the USSR brought instability to Eastern Europe, encouraging domestic reform in those countries where 'normalization' was still the order of the day (East Germany, Czechoslovakia, and Bulgaria) and intensifying the pressure for change in those countries where reform was already in the air (Poland, Hungary). The Albanian and Romanian leadership attempted to prevent their populations from knowing about *perestroika* at all.

In the last few years of the 1980s, Gorbachev made it plain to the Eastern European leaders that their regimes would no longer be backed up by the threat of force.[121] In wider forums after 1987, especially famous occasions at the European Parliament or the United Nations, Gorbachev argued that 'Any interference in internal affairs, any attempts to limit the sovereignty of states—whether of friends and allies or anyone else—are inadmissible.'[122] Such statements justify the historian's claim that Gorbachev's renunciation of force 'was remarkable and unique in world history'.[123] Closer to home, he feared the so-called 'Khrushchev dilemma', whereby limited reform would lead to anti-communist violence and hence suppression, thus undermining attempts at reform. In fact, this scenario did not materialize and, in the second half of 1989, events on the ground in Eastern Europe outstripped the momentum coming from Moscow. The revolutions of 1989 were sparked by Soviet policies, but ended by destroying Soviet influence in the region.

In each case, however, the possibility of the local authorities turning to force remained real and the role of Gorbachev and his aides in insisting that this would not occur should not be underestimated. He told the European Parliament, shortly after Solidarity won the elections in Poland, that the Soviets would 'maintain ties with any Polish government that emerges after the recent elections', a statement that smoothed the passage from communist to Solidarity rule under Tadeusz Mazowiecki. Gorbachev thus 'actively facilitated the demise of communist rule in Poland'. He did so despite his hope that reform would bring about democratic socialism being dashed, because he valued political stability above all, and certainly above military intervention.[124] Yet if Gorbachev provided the template for change, the details were supplied by the Eastern European people, who forced their governments into change. 'Whether it was coal miners striking in Silesia, citizens reburying a national hero, young workers fleeing to the West or protestors gathering in Wenceslas Square, people mobilized en masse to shape their own futures.'[125] Indeed, it was precisely in those countries (i.e. all except Poland and, to a lesser extent, Hungary) where there was no real opposition before 1989 that, in that year, massive crowds took to the street to force out regimes determined to cling on to power.[126]

As well as being the first, Poland was the clearest case of change through reform, a textbook example of Gorbachevian policies being followed to their logical conclusions.[127] It would be naive to think that the communist government entered into the process willingly, but the unfolding of reform was inspired by Gorbachev as was the regime's inability to stop it, thanks to force being ruled out. Hungary had already introduced some elements of market reform, and Jaruzelski followed suit, appointing Mieczysław Rakowski, a liberal-minded communist, as Prime Minister in 1982. Yet thanks partly to the western boycott of Jaruzelski's regime and partly to Solidarity's 'self-limiting revolution', Poland slipped deeper into decline. In 1984 Jaruzelski partially, and then in 1986 fully, amnestied Solidarity and, in a sign of how desperate he had become, sought to save the communist regime by sharing power with Solidarity. The 'round-table talks' Jaruzelski had mendaciously offered in 1980 were forced on him by 1988, and they actually began on 6 February 1989, with Minister of the Interior General Czesław Kiszczak announcing that 'socialism would remain the system of government' but also that 'The time of political and social monopoly of one party over the people was coming to an end.'[128] Solidarity was re-legalized in April 1989 and the elections set for June, in which the whole of the new second chamber, the Senate, would be contested, and 35 per cent of the seats in the *Sejm*, or lower house. The posts of Prime Minister, Minister of Defence, and Minister of the Interior would be reserved for the PZPR.

This compromise was blown out of the water when Solidarity won every contestable seat except one. Kiszczak could not form a government. Jaruzelski was forced to turn to Solidarity and Mazowiecki became the Warsaw Pact's first non-communist Prime Minister, followed shortly afterwards by Wałęsa becoming President. In Poland, dissent or a non-communist civil society had never been entirely suppressed; *Krytyka* was the epitome of the underground journal and in the 1980s activists from across the region travelled to Poland for 'Polish lessons' in organizing dissent.[129] In the late 1980s, Gorbachev's renunciation of force gave the opposition the leverage over the regime it had previously lacked.

The same is true for Hungary, where the regime had long included reformist elements. Over the course of the 1980s, under the new dispensation, these ideas grew in prominence, as did the articulation of popular discontent. As in the GDR, Bulgaria, and Czechoslovakia, the approach in Hungary was to stave off disaster by trying to meet the opposition half way. In each case, it would prove too little, too late. Kádár, still in power since the end of the 1956 uprising, was replaced, despite his resistance, in May 1988 with a younger group of reform-minded ministers, most notably Károly Grósz and Imre Pozsgay, the latter of whom told journalists in 1988 that Hungary, in a few years, would be 'like Austria—or perhaps Sweden'.[130] This was a little optimistic, but under the leadership of the radical reformer Miklós Németh, Hungary did move swiftly to multiparty elections and, in October 1989, the self-dissolution of the Hungarian Communist Party. Mass support for reform convinced most of the MKP that they could not resort to a 'Chinese solution' of the sort that had dispersed protestors in Tiananmen Square at the start of June, when more people were killed than in all of the European revolutions in 1989.[131] Among the most significant indications of change was Pozsgay's announcement, in January 1989, that the 1956 revolution had been a 'popular uprising' and not a 'counter-revolution'. At a meeting of the newly created Federation of Young Democrats (FIDESZ), one speaker approvingly noted: 'We've started to come out of a 30-year-long coma.'[132] The official reburial of Imre Nagy on 16 June 1989, a move which followed the authorities' re-designation of 1956, was simultaneously the symbolic burial of the Kádár era.

The wider significance of what happened in Hungary would soon become apparent. Even more so than in Poland, it set in train a series of events which transcended the domestic scene and contributed to ending the Cold War. Most significant of all were events in the GDR, for they 'demonstrated outright that this wasn't just the end of "a whole stage in the history of socialism", as we liked to think then, but the end of Yalta and Stalin's legacy in Europe'. And, Chernyaev added, 'The fact that such a sharp turn, which culminated in the unification of Germany, was relatively peaceful is the achievement of Germans themselves—as well as Czechs, Hungarians, and Poles—but above all that of Gorbachev and Bush.'[133]

The irony of history is nowhere more in evidence than in the GDR, where events took on a life of their own. From the point of view of Soviet postwar security, the GDR was the USSR's most important ally. Most of the USSR's European forces were based there. It also enjoyed the best standard of living in the Eastern Bloc and, in the Stasi, one of the best-developed domestic security apparatuses in the region. As late as January 1989, Honecker claimed that the wall would still be standing in '50 or 100 years time', although jokes had long been circulating in the GDR that a new wall would have to be built, to keep out the new thinking from the east.[134] As in Poland and Hungary, however, and with the added pressure of the West German media, East Germany also felt the lure of *perestroika*. Honecker's hard-line regime did its utmost to resist this pressure, but the combination of Gorbachev's insistence on not using force, mass protest, and, above all, the role of the unexpected, spelled the end for the SED's one-party state.

The unexpected was that, in May 1989, the Hungarians began removing the barbed wire along their border with Austria and shortly afterwards agreed to abide by the UN Convention on Refugees. In September, placing international standards (and the promise of hard currency from the FRG) above fraternity with the GDR, they opened the border with Austria. This permitted East Germans, holidaying in Hungary, to pass unhindered into Austria, and thence into West Germany, just as those escaping from Hungary in 1956 had done. Within weeks, 130,000 East Germans were in Hungary, and Erich Mielke, the Minister for State Security (and thus head of the Stasi), and one of the Eastern Bloc's most dedicated and long-serving officials, was accusing the Hungarians of 'betraying socialism' and saying: 'Because of developments in the Soviet Union, Poland and Hungary... more and more people are asking how is socialism going to survive at all?'[135] Mielke's own answer is implied in his comparison of the GDR protests to Tiananmen Square and in the question he reportedly asked his subordinates in the face of a mass rally in Leipzig on 31 August, whether things had 'gone so far that tomorrow there could be a 17th of June'.[136] Some senior figures in the SED, in other words, were willing to contemplate using force to suppress the opposition, as if the same conditions pertained as in 1953.

It is not surprising to learn that on his visit to the GDR in October 1989 to attend the state's fortieth anniversary celebrations, Gorbachev was cheered by marchers shouting 'Gorby help us! Gorby stay here!' A shell-shocked Honecker was warned by Gorbachev, rather pompously, that 'One cannot be late, otherwise one will be punished by life.'[137] The mass exodus, and the fillip given to open dissent by the chanting at Gorbachev, provided the impetus for further protest. Thereafter, increasingly huge rallies took place, primarily in Leipzig, but also in Dresden, Jena, Magdeburg, and elsewhere, spreading finally to East Berlin. The SED's authority was withering away. As in Hungary, the Politbüro tried to salvage the situation by replacing Honecker on 18 October with Egon Krenz. But it was too late, especially since Krenz was Honecker's chosen successor, and he had ruled out using force. At the same time, new opposition groups emerged, notably New Democracy and Democratic Awakening, forming an incipient multiparty political system in which the SED was forced to participate.

One senses that the end was nigh; yet, in one of the clearest illustrations of the fact that nothing in history is pre-determined, the actual end came when the Berlin Wall was breached in an unplanned and shambolic way. Germany was the heart of the Cold War conflict; from 1944 onwards, it was the Soviet Union's first concern and it provided the key mental image of superpower stalemate. The contrast between the symbolic significance of the act and its consequences, and the mundane, confused way in which it happened, is the stuff of farce.

Given the numbers of people leaving the GDR through Hungary and, after October, Czechoslovakia, the GDR authorities were under severe pressure to liberalize foreign travel and/or emigration. On the morning of 9 November, the SED authorized a decree relaxing travel restrictions for passport holders (who numbered only 4 million at this point). The decree was passed to Günter Schabowski, a Politbüro member who had not been present at the meeting, to explain to the media. Not knowing any detail, he replied to journalists' questions by saying that the decree took immediate effect.[138] Crowds quickly gathered at crossing points in East Berlin and, in order to cope with the crush at the Bornholmer Strasse crossing, the guards, lacking clear instructions, opened the gate. If the regime hoped that a glimpse of the west would convince their citizens to stay and rebuild socialism rather than throw their lot in with capitalism, they were sorely mistaken. Despite the best efforts of some of the new citizens' groups to warn against diving headlong into a society 'in which profiteers and sharpies elbow ahead', as one put it, the majority of the population thought otherwise.[139] The GDR was a corpse; it remained only to bury it.

With remarkable insight, Gorbachev's adviser Chernyaev wrote in his diary on 9 November: 'The Berlin Wall has collapsed. This entire era in the history of the socialist system is over.... This is the end of Yalta... the Stalinist legacy and "the defeat of Hitlerite Germany".[140] Such momentous events could hardly be kept secret. They infected even the most hard-line and loyal of the fraternal allies, whose end also came rapidly in late 1989. In Czechoslovakia, *normalizace* was still the watchword by the late 1980s, despite the replacement of Husák by Miloš Jakeš as head of the KSČ in December 1987. Only after the fall of the Berlin Wall did opponents feel emboldened to take to the streets. The growth of protests in Prague, Ostrava, Brno, and Bratislava led to the formalization of the opposition, which coalesced around Václav Havel and the Civic Forum, and, in Slovakia, Public Against Violence. The real collapse of the regime occurred in the ten days or so after the violent dispersal of student protests in Prague on 17 November.[141] The authorities had no legitimate response to a general strike on 27 November, and the regime swiftly disintegrated, to be replaced, after a short period of negotiation, by President Havel. In his remarkable New Year's Day speech, Havel set out his vision of an 'independent, free, and democratic' republic, 'with a prospering economy and also socially just', a noble aspiration but one difficult to achieve.[142] The poignant appointment of Alexander Dubček as Speaker of Parliament followed the Civic Forum's demand for 'respect for the right of historical truth, that is, a reevaluation of the crisis years 1968/1969, the rehabilitation of the protagonists of the "Prague Spring", and the condemnation of international aid'.[143]

In Bulgaria, where a strong variant of national communism prevailed, there was little open dissent until Todor Zhivkov was deposed very late in the day, on 10 November 1989. The act surprised everyone, including the US embassy in Sofia, which cabled Washington on 9 November—the day the Berlin Wall fell—to say that 'there probably will not be major personnel changes'.[144] It was too late for the new President, former Foreign Minister Petar Mladenov, to rescue the situation, despite the regime's attempt to exploit xenophobic measures against the Turkish minority, and opposition groups sprang up at a rapid rate. Led by the umbrella organization the Union of Democratic Forces, they forced the communists, newly renamed as the Bulgarian Socialist Party, to initiate round-table talks in the new year of 1990. Although the BSP won 47 per cent of the vote in June 1990, Mladenov was soon forced out of office.[145]

The only places where the government resisted change with violence were, unsurprisingly, Romania and Albania. In the former, Ceauşescu was so isolated from reality that he proposed a Warsaw Pact invasion of Poland following the creation of the Solidarity-led government in 1989.[146] He utterly rejected any reforms on the Gorbachev model as a betrayal of communism and sought to isolate Romania from events elsewhere in the region, mainly by diminishing Romanians' standard of living even further and unleashing the much-feared Securitate. Open dissent, such as in Braşov in November 1987, was met with immediate repression.

The revolution—and here the term can be used unequivocally—began in Timişoara in December 1989, centred on the defence of Reverend Lászlo Tökés, whose efforts to protect the rights of religious minorities (in his case, Calvinists) brought about his persecution by the authorities. Initially supported by the Banat's Hungarian minority, Tökés's cause was soon taken up more widely. When it developed into full-scale protest, the police and army fired on the crowd on 17 December. In this act, Ceauşescu immediately marked himself out from the other Warsaw Pact leaders as the only one unable or unwilling to understand the meaning of Gorbachev's words.

Believing himself untouchable, Ceauşescu ordered a mass rally to take place in his support in Bucharest on 21 December. The plan backfired, and one of the most viscerally powerful moments of the end of communist rule in Eastern Europe was captured on video as Ceauşescu suddenly realized the crowd were booing him, as he, seemingly unaware of the passage of time, delivered his fatal final speech from the same balcony where he had won popular (and western) support in 1968 for denouncing the invasion of Prague.[147] Whisked off by helicopter, Ceauşescu and his wife were arrested and, following a rapidly convened trial, executed on Christmas Day, but only after nearly 1,000 people had been killed in street fighting.[148] The shadowy National Salvation Front, headed by Ion Iliescu, took over in a situation which remained tense and in which no one was really sure whether the regime had been genuinely overthrown by popular consent or whether a *coup d'état* had taken place.

The last of the regimes to fall was Albania.[149] Under Hoxha's long rule, the country followed a rigidly Stalinist line, with Tirana directing all spheres of life. The Ministry of Justice and the legal profession were abolished in 1966, for example, and the practice of religion banned in 1967. The secret police, the Sigurimi, was much feared. Nevertheless, despite prohibitions on travel and contacts with foreigners, the estimated 200,000 television sets in Albania by 1985 meant that its citizens could watch programmes from neighbouring countries, such as Italy, Greece, and Yugoslavia. At the same time, a comprehensive education system changed a peasant country to one with wider cultural aspirations where, by 1989, the average age of the population was 27. After Hoxha's death in 1985, his successor Ramiz Alia faced these social changes and, in common with the other communist states, an economy in meltdown, thanks to the break with China and Hoxha's pursuit of 'self-reliance'. His attempts at reform failed thanks mainly to the enormity of the task, the lack of a clear plan, and the apathy of the population. Still, there was no organized opposition movement in Albania, and Alia maintained, as late as 28 December 1989:

> The Eastern European crisis has nothing to do with us; it is not a crisis of socialism. For the past three decades our party has been denouncing revisionist treachery...but it had separated itself from the revisionists some time ago.... Our party has not merely confined itself to criticizing revisionism, but has taken measures in our country to ensure that it is free of deviations of a revisionist character, and to be certain that its leadership role is not weakened... and that the position of socialism is continually strengthened.[150]

The reality, however, was that the overthrow of Ceauşescu had a powerful impact in Albania. Alia increased the pace of reform throughout 1990, opening up the economy and reversing decades' worth of debilitating social controls. But he refused to surrender the communists' monopoly of power, rejecting demands of intellectuals such as novelist Ismail Kadare and cardiologist Sali Berisha to move to a multiparty system. Yet Alia's attempt to fix the reform in favour of the communists backfired, creating the framework for democratic elections. As elections, scheduled for February 1991, approached, Alia found himself unable to resist popular pressure and approved a new constitution. Elections, delayed until March, were won by the APL (Albanian Labour Party, i.e. the communists), but with a marked rural–urban split and eventually, in June, following several months of strikes, an interim multiparty government was formed intended to smooth the transition to democracy, with new elections set for 1992.

The exception to this process was the non-aligned Yugoslavia. In Chapter 7, we will see in more detail the consequences of the collapse of communism in Yugoslavia, but it suffices here to note that the same economic and political pressures that applied elsewhere in communist Europe applied here too. Yugoslavia had the additional burden of being a federal state with a long history of tension between its two largest constituent states, Serbia and Croatia. The rise of nationalism that accompanied and hastened the collapse of communism occurred in a context which was outside of the international framework responsible for overseeing the transitions of the Warsaw Pact states. The result would be the worst violence in Europe in the second half of the twentieth century.

Each of these cases shows how domestic, local concerns drove the revolutions. At the same time, they were interconnected over the longer term thanks to a common experience of communist rule and the transnational links that had been developed to oppose it. And, with the exception of Yugoslavia and Albania, they were all able to occur thanks to Gorbachev's non-intervention policy, which left the authorities in a precarious position when faced with mass protest. Hence the Eastern European revolutions brought down communist governments locally, but only Gorbachev and the USSR in concert with other international players could end the Cold War.

Gorbachev's hopes were dashed. There would be no new European federation to replace NATO and the Warsaw Pact—only NATO and the EU, expanded eastwards, would survive; democratic socialism remained a fantasy as anything that smacked of communism was rapidly abandoned; Comecon was wound down in mid-1991; Germany was unified on the basis of the colonization of the GDR rather than the creation of a new state. The pull of the west and the rejection of the Soviet east were, taken together, too great to save anything meaningful of the notion of a 'common European home'. 'The Hollywood film, rock 'n' roll music, television soap operas, Coca Cola, Blue Jeans and McDonald's hamburgers had much greater influence in undermining communism in the Soviet Union and eastern Europe, it might be suggested, than the deterrent power of SDI or Pershing missiles.'[151] Gorbachev's belief that permitting the satellite countries to choose for themselves would secure a future for democratic socialism and strengthen the USSR's influence was naive in the extreme, given the region's experience of communist rule. As Lévesque says, a cathartic moment was needed.[152]

But if the regimes died quietly, the immediate aftermath was fraught with danger. Here we see the link with the 'antifascist consensus': the collapse of communist legitimacy was accompanied by a rejection of everything that communism stood for. The efforts of reform communists notwithstanding to show that advocating antifascism did not mean slavish subordination to the CPSU, the end of the Cold War meant not just the collapse of communism in power but the rejection of the values which it fraudulently claimed to represent. As a result, the years after the Cold War not only witnessed violence in Europe on a scale unseen since the Second World War, but an ideological reorientation across the continent whose effects we are still living through. These effects will be traced in the last section of this book.

PART
IV

The Fall of the
Postwar Consensus

7

Consensus Shattered

The GDR, Germany, is the country in which it must be decided whether Marxism-Leninism is right, that communism is the higher, better form of social organization for industrial states as well...If socialism does not triumph in the GDR, if communism does not prove itself superior and viable here, then *we* have not triumphed.

Anastas Mikoyan (1961)

When somebody asks, what was Gorbachev's main mistake, I have a standard answer: I say that he made two mistakes, or that he can be blamed for two things. First of all, that he brought political freedom to our country. And second, that he did not abandon that freedom when they began to use it to destroy the state.

Georgy Shakhnazarov

In 1989 all governments and especially all foreign ministers in the world would have benefited from a seminar on the peace settlements after the two world wars, which most of them had apparently forgotten.

Eric Hobsbawm[1]

From Eastern Europe to the Soviet Union

Twenty-five years is insufficient time for a meaningful historicization process to have occurred, if only because many of the sources that historians will need remain inaccessible. Nevertheless, the post-1989 years are becoming history; for example, the twentieth anniversary of the revolutions in 2009 saw a slew of academic and popular studies devoted to rethinking the meaning of '1989' or 'telling the unknown story' of what happened to bring about the collapse of communism.[2] Much of what has happened in Eastern Europe since then has been the preserve of political scientists (discussing issues of democratic legitimization, elections, party structures, transitional justice, lustration, and so on), economists (discussing the varieties of capitalism being developed in Eastern Europe), and 'transitologists' of all sorts, who are starting to learn that there is no pre-ordained path towards western-style democratic, predictable stability. Rather, 'post-totalitarian blues', as Jacques Rupnik names it, is not just a theoretical possibility.[3] Indeed, since postwar stability has been threatened by the rise of populism in the western half of the continent, there should be no surprise that it exists—and is growing— in the eastern half.[4] But many properly historical questions, especially con- cerning what transpired after 1989 and why the course of events played out in the way it did, are being asked. What is abundantly clear is that the post- war consensus is, if not dead, semi-comatose. Both west and east failed to live up to the fundamental premisses that underpinned them: 'Thus: the Communist Party, the self-proclaimed vanguard of history, attempted to sustain power within an economic system that by its own definition repeat- edly fell behind industrial development in the West. Thus: the nation-state system attempted to maintain its hegemony within a capitalist global economy that increasingly threatened to escape the control of nation-state political units.'[5]

One can argue that the real meaning of 1989 lies less in the end of the Cold War than in the end of the postwar consensus. One historian argues, for example, that to say that the Cold War ended in 1989 is immediately to support the Reaganite notion of the 'Second Cold War'. In fact, the Cold War had effectively passed its most dangerous phase at the conclusion of the Cuban Missile Crisis, and the Soviet Union did not break apart until two years after the fall of the Berlin Wall.[6] There is some merit to this view, which does not make the postwar period *tout court* synonymous with the Cold War. On the other hand, the 1980s really did see renewed international tension; besides, without its Eastern European satellites, the Soviet Union was, contrary to Gorbachev's expectations, fatally weakened; despite the feeble attempts of some hard-liners to regain control of the Kremlin and to restate Soviet power, one can plausibly argue that the Cold War was to all intents and purposes over by the end of 1989. It is therefore worth consider- ing what the former American ambassador to Moscow, Jack Matlock, means when he says that 'The Soviet Union collapsed as a state *despite* the end of the Cold War, not because of it.'[7]

The Soviet Union collapsed even after relinquishing Eastern Europe. Gorbachev's goal of being free to focus on domestic issues largely drove his decision to disengage from the satellite states. But this newfound freedom did not help him to realize his ambitions. Once again, Gorbachev's decision not to use force would be severely tested, this time with respect to the internal politics of the Soviet Union itself. Many Soviet officials, especially in the military, felt betrayed by the pace of change. On Gorbachev's decision to pull troops out of Eastern Europe, Marshal Viktor Kulikov, who had been Commander-in-Chief of the Warsaw Pact until February 1989, said that 'To call it a give-away is putting it far too mildly. I would say it bordered on criminality.'[8] Dmitrii Volkogonov, another of the USSR's leading generals, said that it was 'agonising' for him 'to shed his illusions' about Marxist-Leninist orthodoxy, and revealed that 'when I saw what happened in Eastern Europe in 1989, how could I not realize that so much of what we had been told, so much of what we had believed in, was just a lie?' In other words, 'the scope and the intensity of the ideological disillusionment increased drastically as a result of the events in Eastern Europe'.[9]

As Chapter 6 shows, as Gorbachev grew bolder in propounding his reforms, so the ideas of *glasnost* and *perestroika*, and the condemnation of the Brezhnev Doctrine, increasingly emboldened the other Warsaw Pact countries to take the General Secretary at his word, thus fuelling 'the ongoing political spillover'.[10] The same is true in reverse: once the East European satellites had broken free of the Soviet Union and, more to Gorbachev's surprise, had rejected his dream of a 'socialist commonwealth' or 'pan-European security', the threat to the Soviet Union's own unity, integrity, and viability swiftly followed. What made the process so rapid was 'the circumstance that the Soviet Union was organized as a conglomerate of national states'.[11]

This threat was most apparent in the Baltic States. Discussing a January 1990 visit to Vilnius in his memoirs, Gorbachev wrote: 'I must confess that, while admitting the possibility of secession in principle, I had hoped that the development of economic and political reform would outpace the secession process.'[12] Indeed, in August of the previous year, the Politburo of the CPSU had published a statement, 'On the Political Situation in the Baltic States', which condemned those who were trying to 'foment discord' and 'cast aspersions on the legitimacy of Soviet rule'. A few days after this statement, when Gorbachev's adviser Evgenii Primakov was asked whether the example of Solidarity in Poland would be a model for other Eastern European countries to follow, he said that it was up to individual countries to form their own governments without interference. But this non-interference principle, he stressed, did not apply to the Baltic States: 'Poland is a sovereign state, whereas Lithuania, Latvia, and Estonia are federative republics of the USSR.'[13] Just as with his naive belief that permitting Eastern Europeans to choose their 'own way' would strengthen the ties of the socialist 'fraternal allies', Gorbachev appears still to have been harbouring delusions about the desire of suppressed people to continue to identify with their oppressors once they had been offered the freedom to manoeuvre. This was why he, like Shevardnadze and his other advisers, was deaf to James Baker's suggestions that, as the Baltic States were the biggest irritants, it made sense for Moscow to let them become 'three little Finlands' and then to be in a stronger position to reform the union.[14]

The twenty-third of August 1989 was the fiftieth anniversary of the Hitler–Stalin Pact which carved up Eastern Europe. Under that deal the Baltic States, which won their independence after the First World War, lost it to the Soviet Union, which occupied them in 1940. They were then occupied by Nazi Germany in June 1941, when it invaded the USSR, and finally recaptured by the Soviets in 1944. Fifty years later, nearly 2 million people—fully a quarter of the population—joined hands across the three Baltic republics to form what they called the 'Baltic Way'. But the Kremlin was deaf to the three republics' aspirations, for it was still focused on reforming the USSR as a single entity.

According to Chernyaev, Gorbachev:

> was calling for realism, for a rational approach, appealing to common sense. But separatism was something apart from rational thinking, even beyond common sense. It seemed that what they stood to lose by cutting ties with the Russian 'mainland' was obvious. But national feelings were stronger than such considerations. And this was exactly what we had forgotten, burdened by Marxism-Leninism. Something unmanageable still keeps history in motion, taking precedence over both human rights and, as we see now, over the value of human life.
>
> My opinion is that we should have 'released' the Baltic countries two years earlier. Then, taking into consideration their national character, most problems could have been solved (both internal ones, and those they had with us) and in a peaceful way. We would have had loyal, conscientious neighbours.[15]

Even if Gorbachev and his advisers are right that the Baltic States were not kept in quite the state of servile fearfulness that their nationalists claimed, the Baltic States' histories under Soviet control were hardly conducive to persuading them to enter voluntarily into a new union. Certainly by failing to allow them to go their own way when they wanted, Gorbachev gave an added impetus to the independence movements in Ukraine, the Caucasus, and Central Asia. In a sign of the interconnectedness of those movements, when the Soviet leadership rejected Lithuania's declaration of independence in March 1990, Lech Wałęsa intervened with an Open Letter to Gorbachev in which he argued that Lithuania should have the same right to choose its future as the other countries of Eastern Europe had had the previous year: 'To violate Lithuania's sovereignty is a step directed against the process of constructing a new democratic order in Europe. The history of the USSR and Eastern Europe proves that force and threats used with a view to solving political problems are invalid. They have been condemned by the international community on numerous occasions.'[16] Radical Russian reformers, led by Boris Yeltsin, also condemned the Kremlin's intransigence, appealing to the army not to use force: 'Before attacking civilian sites on Baltic soil, remember your native land and think about your own republic and the present and future of your own nation. Violence against justice and against the Baltic nations will cause new and severe crises in Russia itself and will worsen the plight of Russians living in other republics.'[17] Perhaps these words gave Gorbachev pause for thought; whatever the case—and here one sees the 'doctrine' of non-intervention percolating down from the satellite states to the USSR itself—the Soviet response to the Baltic States' declarations was by no means as severe as it could have been.

Lithuania's democratically elected Supreme Soviet, led by Vytautas Landsbergis and the Sajudis independence movement, declared its independence in March 1990 (the name 'Sajudis' recalled the postwar resistance movement and was thus of symbolic importance). The Kremlin responded by calling the proclamation illegal and imposing an economic blockade. In May the Latvians followed suit, declaring their independence after a half-hearted storming of Riga's interior ministry. More dramatically, at the start of 1991 the Soviets sent troops into Vilnius; the confusing events there saw the only real bloodshed that accompanied the break-up of the western Soviet Union. On 11 January, Soviet paratroopers (OMON) stormed the Press House in Vilnius and on the night of 12–13 January they took the TV station and tower, killing 13 people and injuring several hundred. Then they mysteriously pulled back, when far more damage could easily have been done. In fact, the fierce response of Solidarity and other East European governments and people to the crackdown in Lithuania strongly indicated the inability of the USSR's leaders to salvage some sort of political union or commonwealth based on socialist solidarity. Wałęsa, for example, mused that he could 'no longer rule out the possibility that Russian generals are thinking about reclaiming Eastern Europe'.[18] Gorbachev took note and, as of April 1991, recalibrated his policy towards the Baltic States. Once again, he had pulled back from violence—just in time to avert really serious brutality.

Estonia, the richest and most western oriented of the Baltic republics, followed a slightly different path from Latvia and Lithuania. Under *glasnost* Estonia pressed for independence. This was declared on 30 March 1990 and finally recognized (by Boris Yeltsin) on 28 August 1991. But the process occurred more slowly than had been the case in Lithuania, a fact which no doubt helped its success. As Professor Endel Lippmaa, chief Estonian negotiator with Moscow, put it:

> We have in fact done what Lithuania did, but by a long series of such small steps that it was difficult for Moscow to tell when exactly we got really nasty. What Lithuania did was take a big step, as if Moscow didn't exist.[19]

This was the same 'as if' attitude which had so successfully characterized KOR's and Solidarity's rise in Poland, and it achieved the same results. By acting 'as if' the communist power were not there, it was shown to be, in the communists' own words, a 'paper tiger'.

But the tiger did not expire without a death rattle. When Gorbachev was held hostage in his Crimean dacha by a group of hard-liners in August 1991, many feared that the bloody events of January would be just the taste of things to come. In Riga on 21 August, the OMON special police force killed five Latvians before their tanks inexplicably turned and retreated from the crowds. Unknown to them, the coup against Gorbachev had failed, and the hard-line response was over. What accounted for its occurrence and what were its consequences?

The coup was the last gasp of those who were astonished at and felt betrayed by the precipitous collapse of the Soviet Union's empire in Eastern Europe and the swift disintegration of the Warsaw Pact and Comecon that followed. Many feared the consequences of Gorbachev's German policy above all, not just for leaving officers unemployed but for 'sacrificing gains achieved in the Great Patriotic War' to German revanchism and irredentism—after all, this had been the Kremlin's greatest fear since the end of the war. General Burlakov, Commander-in-Chief of Soviet forces in the former GDR, argued that Gorbachev's agreement to pull forces out of Germany in return 'for a paltry sum of money' had 'betrayed our nation's interests and left tens of thousands of officers' families homeless'.[20] By the summer of 1991, the hard-liners in the Kremlin, including Dmitri Yazov, KGB head Vladimir Kryuchkov, and others, could take no more. On 19 August they carried out their coup. But they botched it: Gorbachev was arrested, but Yeltsin was not; the republics all responded by declaring their independence—including Russia; demonstrations took place across the western Soviet Union, from Chişinau to Minsk, and in Latvia and Lithuania the demonstrators were supported by the local police; the Eastern European governments all protested vigorously and warned of the danger of the Soviets planning to retake the newly independent states. By the 21st, the danger had passed and the coup fizzled out. More to the point, the putschists ultimately strengthened the very forces they had set out to contain—nationalism and democracy—and they thus hastened the Communist Party's and the Soviet Union's demise.[21]

The US had tried at the highest levels to warn Gorbachev of the impending coup, but Gorbachev placed more store in the process of reforming the union, failing to see that Yazov and his colleagues wanted to put a halt to the whole process. Ironically, although the coup attempt put paid to reform in Gorbachev's sense, it achieved the opposite of what the putschists intended because it emboldened the republics: 'Right after the coup', says Chernyaev persuasively, 'the republics used that occasion to really start running away from the center.' As a result of the coup, then, Gorbachev 'had no leverage that he could use in order to stop that process, because there was no morale in the army, in the state security, in the interior ministry, in the party, and Gorbachev did not have any kind of social movement or social force to try to remanage the situation'.[22]

Chernyaev argues that after the attempted coup a reformed Soviet Union could not come about and, more to the point, that it should not, 'because in that form it was not just a symbol but it was a form of existence of a totalitarian and totally unitary state even though it was called a federation, a union'.[23] That is of course a retrospective view, but it shows how the hard-liners galvanized Gorbachev and his advisers into thinking they were following the right course, even at the price of their own hold on power. The Baltic States formally achieved independence as a result of the coup, Solidarity further inflamed independence movements in Ukraine, Belarus, Moldova, and the Caucasian and Central Asian Soviet Republics, and Gorbachev further dug his own political grave.

The person who benefited most from Gorbachev's willingness to let events push him from power was Boris Yeltsin, formerly a candidate for the CPSU Politburo and member of the Congress of People's Deputies. Yeltsin had made a name for himself by condemning Soviet orthodoxy throughout 1989 and, in July 1990, ostentatiously walking out of the 28th Party Congress, renouncing his membership of the Communist Party. The role played by Yeltsin (now in the newly minted role of President of the Russian Federation) in foiling the August 1991 coup was key to the success of 'reform' and to undermining Gorbachev's authority. As he had done in January, Yeltsin, atop a tank outside the Russian parliament, appealed to the army and to the Russian people not to allow the coup to succeed. His successful appeal to a mix of radical *perestroika* and Russian nationalism permitted Gorbachev's return to Moscow; it also facilitated his own rise to prominence, as the centre of power gravitated from the Kremlin to the White House, seat of the Supreme Soviet and, now, the Russian parliament.

Yeltsin's achievement was to finish the process which Gorbachev had begun but could not bear to follow to its logical conclusion, and to act as executioner for the Soviet Union. On 8 December 1991, two years after the unplanned collapse of the Berlin Wall, the leaders of Russia (Yeltsin), Ukraine (Leonid Kravchuk), and Belarus (Stanislaus Shushkevich) conspired against Gorbachev's wishes and signed the Belovezha Accord. This abolished the USSR and replaced it with the CIS. The Supreme Soviet was powerless to prevent the break-up of the Soviet Union and recognized that fact by dissolving itself on 26 December.[24] Despite the feeble attempts to hold on to the Baltic States in 1991, the end was remarkably free of violence. There is nothing mysterious about this, however; the 'reform' process took long enough for those communist apparatchiks who were sufficiently savvy to take advantage of the situation; most of the ultra-wealthy individuals in post-communist Russia (like everywhere else in the former Eastern Bloc apart from the GDR) were former communist functionaries who transferred the wealth of state-owned enterprise into private hands—their own.[25] There is even a compelling argument that the Communist Party itself gave the impetus for this transformation, since its praise for the virtues of individuality (especially the leadership cult), self-expression, and pleasure-seeking in work and consumption all paved the way for a turn to capitalism.[26] Still, given the possibilities that existed for bloodshed, which led all who dreamed of the end of the Cold War to envisage a gradualist approach, it is hardly surprising that almost no one predicted that communism would die not with a bang but with a whimper.[27]

Post-communism

If, with the exception of Romania, the demise of European communism was bloodless, that does not mean that post-communism would be plain sailing. In fact, it proved to be messy and difficult, proving Rupnik's point about post-totalitarian blues. In Albania, probably the most obvious example of Rupnik's phenomenon, Sali Berisha's government rapidly found itself engulfed in scandals: violations of democratic rights such as eliminating press opposition became commonplace and, most damaging to Albania's recovery from its harsh communist winter, the country was overwhelmed by a pyramid scheme which played on people's fantasies about the west and the possibilities of obtaining unheard-of wealth under capitalism. Berisha was only ousted with the collapse of these schemes in 1997 when the US and EU finally ran out of patience with his regime. One commentator reports that 'the whole process of getting to know the West has represented a transition from worship and mythologization to bitterness and disappointment'.[28] The ambivalence of yearning for an idealized west versus a more realistic understanding of Albania's post-communist situation, including a newfound confidence in local abilities, will continue to shape the country for some time.

Outside Albania, things were generally less explosive, at least in the former Warsaw Pact countries.[29] But they were still messy: environmental degradation which had done so much to empower the opposition movements, especially in the Baltic States and Ukraine (both victims of the Chernobyl disaster—Lithuanians were drafted to help the clean-up and many contaminated Ukrainians were re-housed in Lithuania), did not right itself overnight. And with the certainty of one-party rule gone, there was a sudden cacophony of competing voices; many were seduced by the promises of financial schemes and the appeal of alternative religions, especially evangelical varieties of Christianity, previously more or less unknown. Most of the Warsaw Pact countries went through a sharp shock of cold exposure to capitalism and only after a few years did more stable forms of regulation and social welfare bed down and bring some calm to the region.

In Eastern Europe, 'round-table talks' were generally the method used to smooth the passage of the 'velvet revolution', to prevent bloodshed, and to allow the communist apparatchiks to disappear into obscurity as parliamentary democracy gradually took control.[30] The same was true to some extent in the Soviet Union, for the signatories of the Belovezha Accord consciously compared their negotiations to those that had avoided violence in the collapse of East European communism.[31] More vigorous attacks on communism, including threats of legal action, only came in the first decade of the twenty-first century, when they became a useful instrument of social and moral control, as in Hungary, Czechoslovakia, the Baltic States, or the Kaczyński brothers' Poland, when the issue of lustration became bound up with a kind of moral panic involving 'unmasking' communists and their collaborators, especially those who had reported for the secret police. Often such feeding frenzies did indeed make shocking revelations, but equally often they failed to appreciate the compromising positions in which people who ended up spying on or denouncing their neighbours or colleagues found themselves, including threats of violence to them or their families— not to mention the fact that those who demanded lustration most vigorously gave the impression that they had something to hide themselves. In Czechoslovakia in the early 1990s, as Jan Urban noted, 'all the current noise surrounding lustration is simply a way to keep silent about that silence' after 1968—when, as we've seen, opposition to the regime was extremely limited.[32]

Post-communism certainly brought many problems: economic liberalization was a terrible shock to people who had had their economically unviable jobs protected by the state (albeit at the cost of low productivity, waste, shortages, and environmental damage) and who now faced a future of unemployment coupled with a loss of services such as free childcare. In the communist countries, such services were provided by the state less out of solidarity with the working class than as a stick with which to force people (especially women) into work. But still, exposure to the harsh realities of western capitalism, especially in its short-lived robber-capitalist variant, sent many running to the illusory warmth of *Ostalgie* (nostalgia for the east). And politically, the vacuum opened up by the collapse of the Party and its dominant narrative left plenty of room for populists with 'fantasies of salvation'.[33] In Poland, Wałęsa quickly adopted an unwelcome authoritarian stance in his attempt to become President (in which he succeeded) in 1990, and was condemned for his opportunist use of antisemitic and divisive rhetoric by his friend and colleague Adam Michnik.[34] In 1996, Solidarity aligned itself with right-wing parties against the governing Democratic Left Alliance (the former communists) and its president, Marian Krzaklewski, told voters that their financial woes were explained not by economics but by the immoral actions of 'communists' and 'atheists'.[35] Czechoslovakia split in 1992 in the so-called 'velvet divorce', as the longstanding Slovak perception of Czech domination of the state gathered strength under the strains of the transition from communism and the pace of pro-market reforms.[36] NationalistVladimir Meciar won the Slovakian elections of 1994 because he 'attracted significant working-class support by channelling economic fear and frustration into nationalist resentment directed against "anti-Slovak" influences: pro-federalists, the country's ethnic Hungarian minority, and liberal reformers portrayed as "selling out" the nation's interests and assets to foreigners'.[37] In Romania, it was not even clear whether a genuine sweeping away of the old order had taken place at all.[38] Romania's immediate post-communist phase only ended in 2004, with the ejection from power of Ion Iliescu, the man who had emerged at the forefront of the NDF at the end of 1989. Iliescu's shadowy and anachronistic rule was now being challenged by a cadre of young, pro-European democrats.[39] The first post-communist elections had been 'exciting referenda on democracy, clearly breaking with the past'. But the hope of 'regrounding politics in an ethical revival, vanquishing the "lies" of totalitarianism with civil society's "truth", failed'.[40] The expectation was too great, the hope that unity might emerge from shared joy in the demise of one-party rule too optimistic, the shock of the market too bracing.

To compensate for these socio-economic problems, states engaged in a kind of 'memory-grab' in order to try and re-enchant the public sphere and, especially, to energize the renewed sense of nationhood and national unity. Streets were renamed, monuments pulled down and new ones erected, museum displays were reworked, histories rewritten.[41] The removal of statues, especially, such as that of Enver Hoxha in Tirana or Lenin in Bucharest, is a form of iconoclasm which constitutes a 'desacralization' whereby the 'person it symbolized dissolves into an ordinary, time-bound person'[42]—a corrective to the distortions of the communist leadership cults, but also considered to be provocative in places with large ethnic Russian minorities. All such 'memory games' are clear indications of the post-communist regimes' attempts to consolidate and root their rule in what one historian calls a 'culture of historical reinvention'.[43]

Most striking in this regard were the numerous reburials of important figures from the national anti-communist pantheon. These were major public events, when huge numbers of people turned out to take part in what was in effect a performative rededication of the nation. The events combined rejection of the communist past, restoration of national identity, and a kind of pageantry that symbolically united participants. For example, in 1993 the bodies of two Polish generals, Tadeusz Bór-Komorowski (head of the Home Army during the Warsaw Uprising of 1944) and Władisław Sikorski (Prime Minister of the Polish government-in-exile and Commander-in-Chief of the Polish armed forces), were sent from Britain back to Poland for reburial. In Hungary, show trial victim László Rajk was reburied for the second time in 1989 (the first was in 1956); Admiral Horthy, Hungary's wartime leader, was disinterred and placed in a new grave in the same year. Easily the most important of Hungary's reburials, though, was that of Imre Nagy, which took place in 1989 on the same day as his execution in 1957, 16 June. Although he was a reform communist, Nagy's memory was now being mobilized as a forerunner of the post-communist transition. In 1996 the conservative government took the process even further, arguing that 'the real aim of the uprising was to resume the authentic history of the nation from the moment when it had been stopped in 1944', thus improbably positioning Nagy as an heir of interwar Hungarian nationalism.[44] Control over the national symbolism of the 1956 uprising had become central to post-communist political reorientation. After Croatia seceded from Yugoslavia, monuments began appearing to Ustasha minister Mile Budak. And across Yugoslavia, the mobilization of corpses from the Second World War, often anonymous soldiers and massacre victims, in striking contrast to the reburials of national heroes, helped in the process of polarizing the combatants, articulating their grievances, and preparing them for battle and for the mass graves that would be the consequence of war. Debates over the numbers killed by each side in the Second World War ramped up fear of 'genocide' and encouraged the deadly logic of 'kill or be killed'.[45] 'Entire battalions' of the anonymous dead 'served as "shock troops" in the Yugoslav breakup'.[46]

All of these manifestations of national memory were understandable responses to the collapse of communism, and reveal the euphoria felt by citizens who had just been freed from authoritarian rule. But if one exclusive interpretation did not exactly replace another—the post-communist states except Belarus became, at least in form if not always in function, parliamentary democracies—it certainly became unfashionable to continue to espouse anything like 'antifascism'. Instead, where communists acquired some electoral support, as in Russia, this was largely an oppositionist vote based on nostalgia for national 'greatness' rather than an ethically based political position—this is why fascists such as Pamyat, Soyuz or Vladimir Zhirinovsky's nicely named Liberal Democratic Party began to attract some attention. Thus, even where liberals or conservatives of a sort familiar in Western Europe were in power, the political scene and the public sphere were soon infused with the values of 'anti-antifascism', with consequences that we will examine in the final chapter.

But if there has been a 'general deterioration of memory discourses after 2000', the remarkable nature of what happened in 1989 should not be forgotten.[47] Adam Michnik says that for him and his colleagues at *Gazeta Wyborcza*, 'manna did fall from heaven...the democratic opposition won everything there was to gain at the bargaining table'.[48] Given the lack of democratic traditions in much of Eastern Europe—with the exception of Czechoslovakia between the wars—and given the underhand strategies that ordinary people had to develop to outwit the authorities in order to survive, especially in the most authoritarian cases of Albania and Romania, not to mention the impact of the credit crisis of the last few years, which has hit Hungary, Latvia, and Ukraine especially hard, we do not need to wonder at the existence of challenges to liberal democracy. And if in some instances— Russia, most obviously—we see democratic structures without democratic practice, it is still stability, albeit wobbly, rather than disintegration or rising radicalism that is the most striking characteristic of 1989's aftermath. 'Neo- populism' within democratic structures is not quite the same thing as (though also not wholly distinct from) anti-systemic political movements.[49] The 'ethnic rivalries, unsavoury political bickering, rampant political and economic corruption, and the rise of illiberal parties and movements' are all deplorable, but should not lead one to diminish the revolutions' 'generous message and colossal impact' or to question the validity of change per se.[50]

The GDR minus communism = The Federal Republic

The most pressing geopolitical concern stemming from the end of the Cold War was the question of German unification. It rapidly found its way onto the agendas of the US–Soviet summit in Malta on 1–2 December 1989, the NATO meeting in Brussels the next day, Gorbachev and Mitterrand's meeting in Kiev on the 6th, the European Council meeting in Strasbourg on the 8th, and so on. The rapidity with which unification occurred is its most notable characteristic since although, at least in theory, the idea that Germany should be unified one way or another was subscribed to by all actors in the Cold War, few anticipated that it could happen so easily. Willy Brandt, for example, wrote in 1989 that 'To achieve unity through self-determination was the task handed on to us by the fathers of the Constitution', but at that point he could not articulate clearly what that might mean in practice.[51] Only later that year when he spoke in the Bundestag, saying cautiously that 'a time comes to an end when our relations with the other German state were primarily helping to preserve—by many kinds of small steps—the cohesion of separated families and thereby that of the nation', did Brandt signal that he was ready to abandon the gradualism of *Ostpolitik*.[52] According to Jack Matlock, unification 'happened so quickly that many people in the West, once their initial surprise and disbelief passed, began to think of it as an inevitable, almost automatic process'. But, the former ambassador to Moscow went on, 'there was nothing inevitable about the timing, shape, and form of the settlements that reunited Germany and ended the artificial division of the European continent. I am confident that history will regard the negotiations that occurred between March and July 1990 as a model of diplomacy and their outcome as one of the most notable achievements of statesmen—ever.'[53]

The process was driven by Chancellor Kohl, who promised the East Germans 'flourishing landscapes'; their enthusiasm for the project is encapsulated in the switch in their rally slogan from the universalistic 'Wir sind das Volk' ('we are the people') to the particularistic 'Wir sind ein Volk' ('we are one people'). By early 1990, the number of Germans who agreed with Günter Grass that the Germanies should be left as 'two states, one nation' was vanishingly small.[54] Like Grass, and for similar reasons, western leaders were less sure that unification, making Germany the most populous country and the largest economy in Europe, was in their interest. Later Kohl would rail against them for speaking with forked tongues: speaking in public in favour of self-determination for the Germans, hiding behind Gorbachev's concerns about eastern expansion of NATO and voicing fears of geopolitical instability in private, and doing all they could to hinder the possibility of unification. By contrast, Kohl lauded George H. W. Bush as Germany's most important partner on the road to unification.[55]

Giulio Andreotti, Italy's long-serving Christian Democrat Prime Minister, had as early as 1984 let slip a remark about the coming '*pan-Germanismus*' and, after the fall of the Berlin Wall, reputedly remarked: 'I love Germany so much that I prefer there to be two of them.'[56] But no European leader was as set against unification as Margaret Thatcher. Fearing that a German 'super-state' would be a de-stabilizing factor in Europe, she argued in Paris, at a meeting hastily called by Mitterrand in mid-November, that there should be no border changes and certainly no talk of unification, for this would undermine Gorbachev and 'open up a Pandora's box of border claims right through central Europe'.[57] Jaruzelski even claimed to his East German colleagues that Thatcher had expressed views to him that she could not say in public: 'that unification was absolutely unacceptable. One could not allow this "Anschluss", otherwise West Germany would swallow up Austria too, and then there would be a real danger of war.'[58] At a seminar at Chequers in March 1990 it became clear that no one apart from Thatcher believed that German unification could be stopped; she could not be prevailed upon by her advisers 'to turn the necessity of acceptance of the principle of reunification into a virtue'.[59] In her intransigence Thatcher found herself the curious bedfellow of Soviet hard-line generals like Colonel A. A. Danilevich, who believed that 'revanchist and even fascist forces [have] become active in the Federal Republic of Germany and the GDR, against the backdrop of "reunification euphoria"' and that a unified Germany would request the return of territories lost after the Second World War.[60]

Mitterrand later claimed that Britain had been the prime mover in attempts to resist unification, and that he had never acted to foreclose that outcome.[61] But the reality was that he too was twitchy about the idea, and tried to fend it off with proposals for German 'confederation' or arguments that EC and CSCE institutions needed strengthening before they could accommodate a unified Germany. He even proposed a meeting in late 1989 with Gorbachev in the GDR, to offer public support for newly installed Prime Minister Hans Modrow and East German sovereignty—Gorbachev was not interested, and Mitterrand had to go alone on 20 December, in an ill-timed gesture which Kohl would later recall as 'destructive of the process of radical change in the GDR'.[62] Still, Mitterrand was more pliable than Thatcher (who complained that he refused to follow 'his and French instincts and challenge German interests'[63]), and allowed himself to be dragged along by Kohl's influence over Bush and the latter's desire for a US–German axis in foreign policy with less resistance than the British Prime Minister.

Gorbachev was also nervous, although ironically, having set in motion the process which could bring about the realization of Kohl's *Deutschland-politik* (i.e. 'the long-term hope for national unity in freedom'[64]), he was now in no position really to influence the course of events. Nor, after his visit to Germany in the summer of 1989 did he want to. Chernyaev recounts how after that visit Gorbachev saw a different country and changed his views about what a unified Germany might mean for Russia. But, according to Chernyaev, his was very much an avant-garde view: Gorbachev 'understood very well that whereas this change of mind had happened to him, it may not necessarily have happened in the party and among the people, where there were still memories of what happened during World War II'.[65] Whatever the reason for his change of heart, by the time of Kohl's visit to Moscow in February 1990 Gorbachev made it clear that the Soviet Union should not and would not stand in the way of the German people's wishes. Kohl thinks the fact that Gorbachev trusted him and knew that 'the German Chancellor Helmut Kohl keeps his word' was important, and no doubt it was; but Gorbachev was above all a realist, able to adapt when his own policies took him in unexpected and undesired directions.[66] Most important, he 'correctly saw that Germany within a transformed Europe did not represent a serious threat to Soviet security'—the biggest fear of all Soviet leaders since Stalin had disappeared.[67] Chernyaev might be exaggerating Gorbachev's far-sightedness: in 1987 Gorbachev wrote of the two Germanies that 'what there will be in a hundred years is for history to decide', and as late as early November 1989 he still envisaged two German states incorporated into his vision of a 'common European home'.[68] At that time, Kohl was himself still speaking of reforming the East German state. What changed this caution, at least from Kohl's perspective, was the fall of the Berlin Wall.[69]

The fall of the Wall and the subsequent few weeks of uncertainty regarding the Germanies propelled Kohl into a decisive intervention. The key moment in the unification process was Kohl's announcement in the Bundestag on 28 November 1989 of his Ten-Point Plan for achieving German unity. This sudden junking of *Ostpolitik* surprised the other European leaders and fatally undermined schemes such as Mitterrand's planned joint visit to the GDR with Gorbachev as well as the tacit agreement reached in Paris not to force the pace of unification. Yet fears of revanchism or irredentism even then should have been quelled; Kohl argued for bringing unification about in a way that would neither disturb east–west relations nor interrupt the process of European integration, and he explicitly appealed to Gorbachev's 'common European home', to the Helsinki process, and to the need for disarmament and arms control. What Kohl called for were free elections in the GDR and the dismantling of the command economy, the creation of more common institutions, and thereafter the creation of a federal structure to bring the two states closer together. Ultimately what this meant was that, in the words of point ten, 'we are working for a state of peace in Europe in which the German nation can recover its unity in free self-determination'.[70]

The Ten-Point Plan upset Gorbachev; he saw it, according to Chernyaev, as 'an attempt to force the pace of events and thereby upset his super-cautious approach to "the German question."The FRG's NATO allies—the English, French, and Italians—didn't want a fast reunification either.'[71] But he realized that the USSR could not stop the process; as with Eastern Europe, to his credit he did not try to do so. Thus, German unification in NATO was evidence of *perestroika*'s 'success' and the failure of Gorbachev's plans for a 'common European home' including the long-held Soviet dream of a disarmed, neutral, unified Germany. Kohl's achievement was indeed, as Chernyaev recognized, to force the pace of events and quickly to engineer a situation in which unification could not be halted and in which only the technicalities of the arrangement remained to be worked out. The East German elections of March 1990 confirmed Kohl's view that unification was now inevitable, and he pressed ahead as quickly as he could. In what followed, his European counterparts were dilatory, but Kohl enjoyed the crucial support of President Bush.

Following so-called '2 + 4 talks' (the two German states and the four Allied states—Berlin was still officially under Allied control at this point), the 2 + 4 Treaty of 12 September 1990 formally ended the division of Germany and restored full German sovereignty, including ending the special status of Berlin. Although international authorization was formally required for this process, Bonn set the pace, backed by overwhelming popular support in both Germanies. After the CDU's Alliance for Germany won 48.1 per cent in the East German election of 18 March 1990—a victory for Kohl's promise of money—monetary union at 1:1 took place on 1 July, and unification officially followed on 3 October. The CDU victory on 2 December, the date of the first all-German election, was massive, saving Kohl's chancellorship after dwindling support in West Germany. The two countries were unified according to Article 23 of the Federal Republic's constitution, which did not require a new constitution to be written, unlike Article 46—in other words, East Germany would essentially be 'colonized' and Germany would be anchored in the EC and NATO. At the time, few Germans cared. The Cold War in Germany had always been about the national question—which is why 'the "German question" was always too important to leave to the Germans'[72]—and the end of the Cold War saw the national question reassert its primacy. As Willy Brandt famously put it, 'What is growing together is what belongs together.' Or, as sociologist Ulrich Beck put it, 'Poland minus communism is still Poland; but the German Democratic Republic minus communism is—the Federal Republic.'[73]

Not everyone was delighted with this course of events and a minority of politicians and intellectuals, both inside and outside Germany, registered their objections. Jürgen Habermas feared that unification would 'threaten to undermine this nascent culture of contrition' that the left had developed in the FRG.[74] Other intellectuals feared that although antifascism had been an honourable response to the Third Reich, 'its SED instrumentalization kept it from fostering a democratic morality and an incisive scholarship'.[75] In a more geopolitical register, Thatcher wrote that although her policy had failed in the face of the irresistible desire of the Germans 'on both sides of the Elbe' for unity, she was less sure that her policy had been wrong. She claimed that the cost of absorbing East Germany had been 'economically disastrous' for the whole of Europe, not just for the Federal Republic; she argued that the subsequent rise in unemployment and recession, as well as neo-Nazism, were all forces of de-stabilization; finally, she believed that unification 'has created a German state so large and dominant that it cannot be easily fitted into the new architecture of Europe'.[76] Both Thatcher and Habermas were wrong, or at least the new Germany proved to be less disruptive than they feared. The post-unification Federal Republic, although it saw a reassertion of national identity, is closer in spirit to Habermas's 'constitutional patriotism' than one would have thought possible, given what an emotionally stultifying concept that is; and although it is clearly the dominant economic force in Europe, Germany, to continue Thatcher's architectural metaphor, has so far been much more keen on scaffolding than on the wrecking ball. If Merkel's insistence on austerity ends up by breaking the eurozone, if not the EU as a whole, it will not be the willed result of the sort of revived Prussianism that Thatcher feared. Where Thatcher was right was in her claim that Germany would press ahead with plans for a federal Europe—a view that sits uncomfortably with the notion of German dominance unless one sees the German promotion of federalism as a Teutonic plot for a more subtle takeover of Europe. This was what Nicholas Ridley, one of Thatcher's closest colleagues, thought; when he blurted out in an interview that the EC was 'a German racket designed to take over Europe' and said of British national sovereignty that 'you might just as well give it to Adolf Hitler, frankly', his days in office swiftly came to an end.[77] But we have Ridley to thank for a good example of how memories of the war continued to shape geopolitical perceptions even when they were long past their sell-by date. The East Europeans were far quicker off the mark than their western counterparts to recognize the importance of resolving the German question for European stability and development.

What was wrong with the GDR that so many of its citizens, many of whom had never known anything different, voted to kill it off and to become part of the FRG? The answer was provided by the Stasi, in one of its reports. Complaints included:

> dissatisfaction with the supply of goods, anger over insufficient services, impatience with deficiencies in medical services, limited travel possibilities within the GDR and abroad, unsatisfactory working conditions and discontinuity of the production process, insufficiency or inconsistency in applying or carrying out meritocratic principles, as well as dissatisfaction about the development of wages and salaries; anger about the bureaucratic attitude of directors and members of state organs, enterprises, and institutions as well as heartlessness in their interaction with citizens, impatience with mass media policies of the GDR.[78]

And this was clearly not a complete list, as the absence of politically related grievances indicates. In terms of ordinary people's experiences of everyday life, the appeal of West Germany, famously explored in the film *Goodbye Lenin!* (dir. Wolfgang Becker, 2002), lay largely in the seduction of consumption and a high standard of living. Only later did many East Germans find that what began as euphoria could lead to feelings of dissonance as their predictable life routines were disrupted; often they experienced 'confusion, disorientation, and anger' as the events of 1989 began to recede into the past.[79] In terms of politics, the one thing that provided the communists with some degree of legitimacy was antifascism. Crucially, antifascism really did have deep roots in East German society, and many subscribed to it in a visceral or emotional way, even if they had grown to hate their rulers. So although many East Germans hesitated to condemn communism when so many of its leaders had spent time in Nazi concentration camps, the overthrow of Honecker and the generation that had founded the 'antifascist state' signified the end of the 'antifascist covenant'.[80] But if bringing about unification proved easy, making it work turned out to be much harder.

Chancellor Kohl soon discovered that unification in practice was more complex than he had anticipated. 'In forcing the issue of unification', writes one scholar, 'Helmut Kohl gave many hostages to fortune.' Kohl had expected the incorporation of the new East German *Länder* (federal states) into the federal system to be swift and smooth, but the opposite was the case: 'By the late 1990s, the harmonious, optimistic vision of German unification appeared forlorn... Promises made to the German electorate in 1990 seemed unsustainable shortly afterwards.'[81] This was especially true of tax. 'No one would be worse off because of unification', Kohl had pledged in his 1990 election campaign, but the Solidarity Pact of March 1993 brought together all the parliamentary parties and the minister presidents of the *Länder* to agree a so-called 'Solidarity Surcharge' of 7.5 per cent of income tax on taxpayers, in order to pay for the integration of the new states (in its second incarnation, this surcharge is scheduled to last until 2019). But if unification brought unexpected hardships, few now wanted to turn back the clock.

Besides, at the same time as the Germanies grew together, so did Europe: the unification of Germany was one of those key moments in the history of the EC/EU when further integration—in this case, the Maastricht Treaty on European Union—was precipitated by the 'German question'. Indeed, following the remarkable incorporation of the 'new *Länder*' into the Federal Republic, an economic feat that would have brought any other European economy to its knees, Germany lost none of its enthusiasm for the European project, something it experienced only more recently when faced with the cost of bailing out Greece and, potentially, other indebted EU nations.

The Yugoslav exception

It is easy, when thinking about the more or less bloodless collapse of communism and the relatively smooth processes of German unification and the Czech–Slovak 'velvet divorce', to slip into a 'soothing syrup' view of history, in which the Cold War was 'won' and Europe's wrongs were righted. We have already seen that there was no easy transition to post-communism in Eastern Europe, and below we will see how the end of the Cold War reshaped Western Europe in unpredictable ways too. But the real stumbling-block in the path of the post-Cold War story of progress is, of course, the break-up of Yugoslavia and the series of wars that engulfed it. Yet what happened in Yugoslavia should be seen as the exception that proves the rule, since it represented the logical extreme of events elsewhere, showing what could have easily happened in Eastern Europe more broadly if the international framework of Warsaw Pact–NATO negotiations, 2 + 4 talks, and the like had not been in place—as it was not in Yugoslavia. It is often forgotten that Slobodan Milošević emerged out of a communist context, gradually developing his ultra-nationalist message in the period of Yugoslavia's fragmentation following Tito's death in 1980, and especially after late 1987. Yugoslavia is the prime example of 'memory' being mobilized in the name of violent ideologies, with Milošević's 1989 speech commemorating the 600th anniversary of the Battle of Kosovo Polje regularly cited as a key moment in the radicalization of nationalist fear and hatred. Recalling too the vicious history of the Second World War, in which Serbs had been victims of Croat-perpetrated genocide, Milošević and his allies set out to impose Serb domination on the Yugoslav republics that were seceding from the state.[82]

Yugoslavia was an unlikely creation, in both its monarchical and republic forms. During the 1960s and 1970s, with its independence from Moscow, its ideology of 'self-managing socialism' which supposedly offered an alternative to both western capitalism and Sovietization, its relative openness to the west, and a standard of living higher than most of the Warsaw Pact countries, Yugoslavia appeared to have brought an impressive degree of harmony to the various South Slav nations that made up the federation. By the 1980s, increasing numbers of its citizens self-identified as 'Yugoslav' in preference to one of the constituent national groups. The extraordinary 'success' of Serb and Croat ultra-nationalism in the late 1980s and early 1990s was that they convinced people that the past would always invade the present, and forced people to drop their multiple identities and to identify wholly as one thing or another.[83]

In this gloomy way of thinking, the only difference between Central Europe and the Balkans is fifty years. That's to say, where Hitler and Stalin had rendered the centuries-old ethnic melange of Central and Eastern Europe a thing of the past, Tito's Yugoslavia still conformed to the model: 'the major difference between Central and Southeast Europeans is not that the former are more tolerant and pluralistic, but that their "ethnic cleansing" was completed half a century ago, whereas in the Balkans the process of "homogeneous" nation-state building is still underway.'[84] Even if this sort of claim is true, it still does not explain why nationalism became the dominant way of thinking in Serbia, even though, as elsewhere in the region, there were reform Marxist currents around. Thus one has to delve a little deeper.

Serb nationalism emerged in the late 1960s, largely in response to the authorities' heavy-handed answer to the 1968 student movement at Belgrade University and to local nationalisms elsewhere in Yugoslavia—the Serbs were the most geographically dispersed of all the national groups and had the most to lose from local nationalisms. It gradually grew in strength to become far more powerful than these local variants of nationalism that had originally called it into being.[85] The key reason for the rise to prominence of nationalism among what was initially a fairly broad church of Serbian dissidents—like Charter 77 or Solidarity—was Kosovo. When a staunchly nationalist petition supporting Kosovo's Serbian population was published in 1986, it was signed by many Serbian intellectuals, not only reliably nationalist figures such as Dobrica Ćosić, but some (such as Ljubomir Tadić and Mihailo Marković) who had been until then associated more with reform communism. This petition, the infamous Memorandum of the Serbian Academy, 'marked the turn of Belgrade's otherwise Havelian discourse into one that was fundamentally parochial'.[86] Where the opposition movements in Czechoslovakia or Poland demanded the end of the regimes, Serbia's intellectuals joined with Milošević in appealing solely to Serbs, instead of seeking to reject all of the nationalisms, especially Tudjman's, then sweeping Yugoslavia.[87] In the context of economic decline and regime collapse, reform communism got swallowed up by ethno-nationalism.

In terms of events, the facts are both complex and straightforward. They are complex because the disintegration of Yugoslavia took place over a decade and because in reality the 'war' was made up of several discrete but related conflicts. But they are straightforward too because the driving force was the same throughout: a Serb ultra-nationalist drive first to dominate the Yugoslav federation and, once that became impossible, to create a Greater Serbia which would include parts of Croatia and Bosnia.[88] Certainly Croatian Serbs were being mistreated in Croatia, and there is no room either for trying to make Franjo Tudjman, the head of independent Croatia, look like a respectable politician (he was a Holocaust denying admirer of the Nazi-backed wartime Independent State of Croatia). The mistreatment of Serbs and Romanies by ethnic Albanian Kosovars following the Serbian withdrawal from Kosovo in 1999 was a shabby reminder that victimhood does not make people nicer. Nor does the western demonization of Serbia—which many Serbs and their friends in the region (in Romania and Greece,

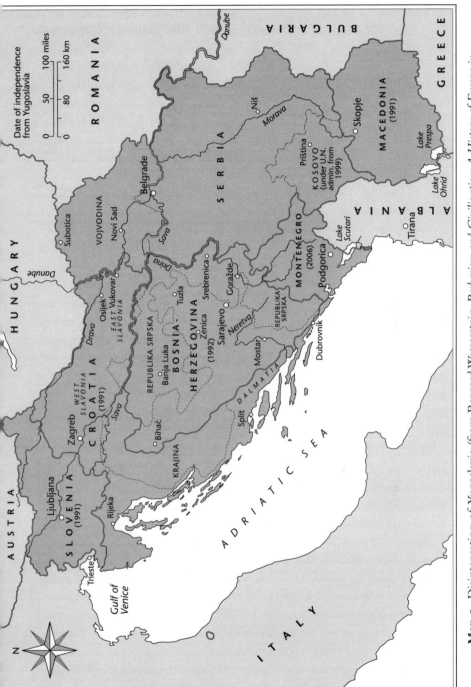

Map 2. Disintegration of Yugoslavia (from Bernard Wasserstein, *Barbarism and Civilization: A History of Europe in Our Time* (Oxford University Press, 2007), p. 752).

for example) found inexplicable—necessitate the condemnation of an entire people, for this would be to think in the same ethnic pigeonholing terms as a Milošević, Karadzić, or Mladić and to overlook the fact that during the war in Bosnia Muslims living in Serbia were mostly unmolested; the same is true during the war in Kosovo in 1999, when the 100,000 Kosovars living in Belgrade were left alone.[89] But the evidence suggests that under the guise of defending Yugoslav territorial integrity (a claim that bamboozled the US and the EU with their memories of German-sponsored Croatian fascism), Milošević set out not to reassert the legitimacy of Yugoslav federalism but to impose Serbian hegemony over the region.[90]

Following Tudjman's victory in Croatia's first post-communist election in April 1990 and Croatia's declaration of independence from Yugoslavia on 25 June 1991, the JNA (Yugoslav National Army), which was largely in Serb hands, was used to step up the level of violence in Croatia. The JNA, although it saw its role as preserving Yugoslavia, aligned itself with Milošević not only out of ethnic allegiance but also because of its ideological and institutional weaknesses, which increased the army's reliance on Serbia, especially after Slovenia's secession.[91] Air raids on Zagreb suggested that the Serbs were engaged in more than merely protecting ethnic Serbs in Croatia, but it was only once Vukovar, Eastern Slavonia, and the Krajina had been taken, and the UNESCO world heritage site of Dubrovnik was besieged, that the west realized that Serbia was overrunning Croatia. By the time of the deal brokered by Lord Carrington, Milošević was in control of more than a quarter of Croatian territory.

But it was Bosnia where the real conflict would take place, and where the term 'ethnic cleansing' took on a relevance that it had not had in Europe since the Second World War. Following Muslim President Izetbegović's declaration of Bosnian independence on 3 March 1992, the Bosnian Serbs, under Radovan Karadzić, announced the establishment of the Serbian Republic of Bosnia-Herzegovina, later renamed the Republika Srpska, based in Banja Luka. Within weeks of fighting, the Bosnian Serbs controlled 70 per cent of Bosnian territory. Of Bosnia's 4.4 million inhabitants, almost all were dislocated: 3 million were internally displaced, and 1.3 million fled as refugees abroad. Sarajevo was subjected to a brutal siege, which lasted over three and a half years and caused the deaths of more than 10,000 people. The massacre at Srebrenica in July 1995, after the UN had declared it a 'safe area', was the single worst incident of the war, and has prompted many, including the ICTY, to talk of genocide in Bosnia.[92] The Muslim-Croat Federation's fight-back in April 1995 therefore took the Serbs and the international community by surprise, and succeeded in pushing the Serbs out of most of the Krajina. The Dayton Agreement, it has been argued, froze events before they could take their natural course; it would have been preferable, so this version of events goes, to allow the Muslim-Croat Federation to defeat the Serbs completely. But no doubt Dayton also saved further large-scale bloodshed.[93]

The Serbs' last stab at victory was in Kosovo, in some ways the most significant of all the wars of Yugoslav succession, for Kosovo was part of Serbia (albeit autonomous until 1981) and the 'heartland' of Serb national identity. The movement of Bosnian Serb refugees into Kosovo was a deliberate strategy to counter the ethnic balance, which was heavily in favour of the Albanians. But Kosovo, and unofficial president Ibrahim Rugova, were ignored by Dayton, and this gave Serbia its chance to impose its will on the territory. The ensuing massacres, particularly at Račak on 15 January 1999, gave rise to large-scale refugee movements into Macedonia and Montenegro, and feverish international talks aimed at solving the crisis, at Rambouillet, near Paris. When the talks broke down, NATO bombed Serbia from 24 March for 78 days, until the country's infrastructure was ruined, and the state was turned into an international pariah. Although the bombing seemed at first to harden nationalist resolve, Milošević was deposed late in 2000. His death during his trial at The Hague was, despite the many problems with the court process, the only thing that saved him from a long jail sentence.[94] But if, fifteen years later, noises are being made that will gradually rehabilitate Serbia, and eventually permit it to join the EU, many across Europe think that NATO and the EU lost prestige by using their military might to smash a small country.

The wars of Yugoslav succession revived the frightening Second World War memories of Chetniks and Ustashe, and showed how rapidly alternatives could be eliminated if circumstances permitted. Europe still lives with the consequences of the wars, with stability in Kosovo and Bosnia now extremely fragile, and guaranteed only by large international peacekeeping forces.[95] They also confirm the continued importance of Second World War memory in postwar Europe. Reinforcing the claim that the initial postwar years hold the key to much of what subsequently occurred, Tony Judt argues that the years 1945–8 'were the moment not only of the division of Europe and the first stage of its postwar reconstruction but also, and in an intimately related manner, the period during which Europe's postwar memory was

molded'.[96] Even if, following the end of the Cold War, the politics of memory does not always follow predictable paths, Judt's point still holds.[97] After
all, the analogy of Milošević and Hitler was one of the key arguments that
persuaded liberal Europeans, such as Bernard Kouchner, founder of *Médecins
sans frontières* and later French Foreign Minister, to take up the idea of humanitarian intervention. The former '68er Joschka Fischer, in 1999 Germany's
Foreign Minister, angered those on the left of his Green Party when he
argued in favour of NATO's bombing of Serbia, but justified his stance by
saying that after Srebrenica he had no choice: 'I didn't just learn "never again
war"', he pointed out, 'I also learned "never again Auschwitz."'[98] By contrast,
radicals such as Tariq Ali, one of Britain's best-known '68ers, argued that
equating Milošević and Hitler was a purely ideological gesture: 'The only
function of the Hitler analogy is to obfuscate political discourse and to incite
a stampede to reckless military action,' he claimed.[99] Whether one supported
the analogy or not, the power of the Second World War, and especially Holocaust memory, to continue to shape the interpretation of the present could
not have been clearer, even at the end of the twentieth century.

A sterile promontory

This intrusion of memory into post-Cold War politics reminds us that even
if historians like to break time up into neatly packaged periods, to ease the
process of analysis and comprehension, reality is not so accommodating. It
is of course still possible to provide overarching narratives for the postwar
period, as has most commonly been done in a triumphalist mode, by the
likes of Francis Fukuyama, who saw the end of the Cold War as a victory for
liberal reason in the shape of the parliamentary democratic state, or in an
optimistic mood, such as Václav Havel's belief that 'the era of ideology is
over'.[100] In the years since 1989, Fukuyama's pleasing telos has been somewhat shaken, not just with the wars in Yugoslavia, but with the so-called
'war on terror' and the infantilization of politics that has taken over much
of the current European scene, with sexual antics (Italy and France), MPs'
expenses (Britain), 'reality' TV, nostalgia for pasts that never existed, and
scaremongering over Islam (Switzerland and everywhere else) taking up
more time in parliaments and the press than global warming, growing social
divisions, and economic crisis. In other words, the end of the postwar consensus was as apparent in Western as in Eastern Europe.

Italy presents the clearest example. With the demise of *partitocrazia* in the wake of the *tangentopolis* ('bribetown') scandal of the early 1990s and Berlusconi's first government in 1994, Italy's 'Second Republic' was ruled by a coalition of three parties that owed little or no allegiance to the postwar antifascist constitution.[101] Italy was the first European country since the war where neo-fascists in the shape of the MSI entered power, alongside Berlusconi's Forza Italia and Umberto Bossi's xenophobic and separatist Northern League. What did this change mean in practice? First of all, those who had been silenced under the hegemony of antifascism felt emboldened to speak; to the surprise of many Italians, what had previously been a popular but disorganized anti-antifascist sentiment became a mainstream view, as the 'losers' of 1945 now sensed that they were the victors.[102] This simultaneous identity as losers and winners manifested itself in resentment at antifascist memory politics, which was soon countered by a 'retroactive defascistization of fascism'.[103] For example, in March 1944, 335 Italians were murdered by the SS in a reprisal massacre at the Ardeatine Caves near Rome.[104] The memorial to it exemplified Italy's antifascist culture. But in the 1990s, and especially after the first trial of SS-captain Erich Priebke in Rome in 1996, the memorial, built in 1949, became steadily identified less with the antifascist Resistance and more with the Holocaust, as 'Holocaust consciousness' seeped rapidly into Western European awareness following the fiftieth anniversary of the end of the war and the phenomenal success of Steven Spielberg's *Schindler's List* (1993).[105] Increased awareness of the Holocaust was not in itself cause for concern, but the way in which Italians of all political stripes so swiftly acceded to the abandonment of the most influential narrative of the postwar period was curious, to say the least. Many people believed that the postwar emphasis on antifascism as 'the moral basis of the republic' had been excessive, 'yet the ease and rapidity with which the theory of mass consensus [under Fascism] has moved from the level of historical debate to that of the new common sense invites suspicion', as one historian put it at the start of the new millennium.[106] The Second Republic's attack on the antifascist consensus of the First—what Sergio Luzzatto called 'post-antifascism'—was one of the key components of the Italian scene in the 1990s.[107]

Yet the Italian case did not give rise to the same international outrage as did events in Austria. Following hard on the Waldheim scandal, in 1994–5, Jörg Haider's Austrian Freedom Party won around 22 per cent of the vote in parliamentary elections and then, in the October 1996 European parliament election, nearly 28 per cent. This occurred despite, or maybe because of, the release of a videotape of Haider's infamous speech at a 1995 rally of former Waffen-SS members, whom he praised as 'decent people' (recalling Himmler's Posen speech of October 1943, one of the occasions at which he spoke openly of the murder of the Jews, saying that despite the gruesomeness of the task, the SS had remained 'decent'). This brazen revisionism followed an equally bold assertion, at the outset of the post-Cold War period (1990), when Haider told another veterans' group that: 'Your sacrifices will only be seen in the correct light in the years to come because the overall development of Europe will show clearly that the basis was laid by you for peace and freedom.'[108] Such open attacks on the postwar settlement were well received in an Austria which had yet really to address its Nazi past in the way that West Germany had done, and Haider entered government in a coalition with Wolfgang Schüssel's Austrian People's Party (*Österreichische Volkspartei*, the Christian Democrats) in 2000; the EU responded by briefly imposing democratic sanctions on the new regime. Also in the 1990s, Filip Dewinter's Vlaams Blok (Flemish Block) took control of Antwerp town hall; the FN became a key player in French politics, most notably in 2002, when Le Pen forced a run-off with Lionel Jospin for French President; and in Denmark, Norway, Switzerland, and the Netherlands populist anti-immigrant parties emerged to disrupt the political scene. 'It is as if in one day', wrote *Le Monde* following Dewinter's and Haider's simultaneous electoral successes in 1994, 'the mythic gateways of the Ancient Continent—its North Sea port and the capital of Central Europe—had been swept away by a wave of extremism moving across Europe.'[109]

This revaluation of the place of antifascism in the 1990s did not occur in a vacuum; rather, it was part of a wider reshaping of Western European values, including some of the most fundamental pillars of the postwar settlement. What is most noteworthy about these changes is that they were not only instituted by right-wing revanchists (in fact, these were a minority) but predominantly by parties of the 'centre left'. In the 1980s some social democratic parties, such as in Belgium, Denmark, and Austria, had tried to resist the neo-liberal tide, continuing to argue for Keynesian reflationary measures, as had the Labour Party in Britain. But the restructuring programme first promoted by Christian Democrat or conservative parties in the 1980s was eventually accepted in the 1990s even by the centre left, exemplified by Tony Blair, Lionel Jospin, and Gerhard Schröder, whose 'third way' or *neue Mitte* between social democracy and Thatcherite neo-liberalism was their great innovation. The Italian *Uliva* (olive tree) government (1995–2001), dominated by the DS, illustrates just how far the left had shifted to the new centre ground and the extent to which the social democratic values that had oriented politics since 1945 had dissipated.[110] Given that this was a process largely driven by the centre left, one historian is right to note the 'paradoxical situation' whereby during that decade 'Social democrats held government positions in almost all European countries, while taking the lead in the most drastic reforms the welfare state had ever seen.' These reforms varied from place to place, but included the privatization of key services, such as railways and telecommunications services, cutting back on certain kinds of benefits, and state withdrawal from many other areas of public policy, under the watchwords that the market is more efficient than the state, that the state's role should be limited so as not to disrupt the workings of the market, and that market mechanisms should be introduced into areas where the state still operates, such as health services, in order to facilitate the most efficient distribution of resources.[111] Some historians go further, seeing these reforms as root and branch reconfigurations of West European society: 'Under the impact of Reaganomics and Thatcherism', writes Geoff Eley, the 'postwar settlement was dismantled'.[112]

Yet, in retrospect the OECD's 1981 report, *The Welfare State in Crisis*, seems too apocalyptic. In fact, social spending as a percentage of GDP continued to remain significant; across the OECD it is estimated that public social expenditure as a percentage of GDP increased from 15.6 per cent in 1980 to 19.2 per cent in 2007. Spending on pensions (7 per cent of GDP) and health (5.8 per cent) remains high.[113] It seems then that the problem is as much one of values and vocabulary as it is of cuts, or, more likely, it lies in the changed ways in which welfare provision is distributed and the suspicion under which claimants are held by representatives of the state. A good example is the shift from universal to means-tested benefits and from direct to indirect taxation or favouring profit-making, private providers over the not for profit public sector.[114] If the welfare state is 'a means by which labour escapes some of the implications of capitalism', then even if expenditure has remained high, there can be little doubt that during the 1990s, labour found itself more exposed.[115] And even if Thatcher failed to roll back the state in the way she had hoped, because 'welfare state spending has a tendency to increase irrespective of many of the underlying debates concerning the benefits or otherwise of the welfare state', some commentators believe that increasingly important issues such as the cost of the banking crisis or, in the longer term, climate change and its effects, especially on the poor of the global south, may shift political attention away from traditional social policy.[116] Be that as it may, welfare systems, for all that they have been denigrated, have proved remarkably durable, not least because so many depend on or are employed by them.

Welfare states have endured in Eastern Europe too, albeit in difficult circumstances. The dismantling of social democracy began long before the collapse of communism in 1989; the latter did not bring about the former.[117] But the neo-liberal reforms of the 1980s in Western Europe did make it easier to slip directly into unfettered capitalism east of the iron curtain after 1989; if social democracy had failed in the west, those warning caution and arguing for reformism were unlikely to get heard when making the case for its viability in the east. The result was a serious challenge for welfare in post-communist Eastern Europe as people suddenly found that their jobs for life and their free (if derisory) welfare provisions disappeared. In Eastern Europe, the revolutions of 1989 brought not only political changes but radical social ones too. The communist welfare state model disappeared, adding to the woes brought about by the economic difficulties of the 1980s. This brought the former communist countries up to date with developments in the west, 'under the influence of imported ideas and reform concepts in the years after 1989'[118]—not, as János Kornai points out, that this provides a terribly auspicious model to follow.[119] Since the early post-communist years, welfare states have matured in Eastern Europe, with some, particularly the Baltic States, relying more on private provision than others. In some cases, such as energy provision in Russia, one encounters 'a new patterning of social welfare mechanisms with techniques of commercialization and calculative choice', that is to say, a retention of universal provision but with delivery having to be based on the sort of microeconomic interventions that became common in Western Europe in the 1980s: targeted subsidies, price competition, and so on.[120] Nevertheless, largely for lack of interest, there has been no really radical reform since the early 1990s, and many of the changes that have taken place have occurred in response to EU regulatory demands.[121]

We thus need to turn our attention to the frameworks within which welfare states operated in the 1990s. Here, alongside the attempts by governments to outsource welfare provision to the private sector, we see changes taking place in family structures as well as social policy more broadly. With respect to families, the last third of the twentieth century witnessed sufficient change in the make-up of families for government to try and intervene. First of all, postwar West European states' family laws were slow to

catch up with the individual freedom which was the basis of their democracy; only in the 1970s were vast gender inequalities in family law dispensed
with, such as Italy's 1975 family code which established equality between
husband and wife and between children born in and outside marriage.[122]
Shortly thereafter the crisis of the welfare state began, and, in 1989, with a
marked decline in marriage, a sharp rise in divorce rates, and an increase in
the number of single-parent families, the European Commission established
an Observatory on National Family Policies. But this institution achieved
little and the development of positive relationships between families and the
state was, as one commentator notes, threatened by the challenges faced by
the welfare state: 'Just at the moment when family questions are more
clearly on the agenda of European governments than ever before, their
capacity to respond with an inclusive, rather than exclusive vision, of
family–state relations seems to be diminished.'[123]

Most significant of all, the 1990s witnessed a decline in participatory
democracy across Europe, as electors increasingly lost trust in politicians and
became resigned to a more 'managerial' style of politics in which governments, abandoning their postwar role, came to perceive their duty as doing
as little as possible other than permitting the smooth operation of the market.[124] In other words, the early years of the twenty-first century saw a
change in the meaning of 'democracy' for the worse. In Western Europe,
'Whereas in the mid-twentieth century "democracy" was tied to notions of
"social solidarity and economic equity", by the 1990s it had come to mean
"personal economic freedom within free markets".'[125] Liberal democracy, as
David Ost points out with reference to Eastern Europe, should mean more
than holding elections every four years: 'When parliaments pass radical lustration or privilege one religion or nationality over another, they are being
illiberal by creating whole groups of citizens subject to persecution by the
state. They'll still have elections and parliaments and laws and privatization,
but they'll be backsliding on the universalist promises of democracy that
1989 was all about.'[126] There is much evidence that the decline in electoral
democracy has been countered by a growth in 'civil democracy', i.e. associa-
tions, voluntary, community, and advocacy groups, thus countering the
belief in a 'new civic passivity'. Yet although it is true that 'distrust is a con-
stitutive rather than a recent feature of democratic life', the problem of
'democracy's discontent' is a serious one for early twenty-first-century
Europe, when faced with the phenomenon of 'constrained' or 'managerial
democracy'.[127]

Nothing has contributed more to this problem than the euro crisis since 2007–8. As is now clear, though as very few analysts noted at the time, the problem is less with the 'bad behaviour' of certain states (Greece, especially) in spending too much or not meeting inflation targets, and more with the design flaws of the EMU itself.[128] But since correcting these flaws would have required member states to surrender more of their economic decision-making autonomy than would have been politically feasible, it is hardly surprising that this sensitive task got overlooked. For example, the EU cannot engage in the sort of counter-cyclical policies necessary to sustain growth on an even keel because this remains largely the preserve of individual member states, and a federal currency presupposes the sort of flexible labour market and supply-side reforms which are exactly what the eurozone (unlike the US, for example) lacks.[129] Even some Europhiles are now arguing that there should be an orderly retreat from the euro before the eurozone as a whole implodes.[130]

Thanks to this tendency towards 'managerial democracy' (rather like the Keynesian technocracy of the postwar boom), the financial crisis of 2008 shocked the workings of government as much as the banking sector. Questions of the relationship between national governments and globalization, and the need to balance the workings of 'the markets' against the needs of ordinary people facing ever-tougher austerity measures, have brought the issue of the EU's 'democratic deficit' very much to the fore. Unsurprisingly, then, far-right extremism is once again a feature of European politics. This can be seen first and foremost as a response to the economic crisis and the consensus amongst the mainstream parties that there is no alternative to austerity—they lack any vision of a meaningful transition to something better. But the particular manifestation of this response, i.e., the turn specifically to Nazism, indicates that memories of the Second World War are yet again playing a powerful role in European consciousness. Nazism seems to be the 'deep unconscious' of Europe, something that people call on in desperation—not realizing, perhaps, that this desperate cry will cause more problems than it can resolve. How else to explain the appeal of Nazism in countries such as Greece, which suffered so much at the hands of German occupation during the Second World War? The vicious rhetoric between Golden Dawn and Syriza in Greece—and, if reports are correct, of beatings of leftists at the hands of Nazi thugs while the police turn a blind eye—indicates too that memories of the Civil War and the colonels' junta are all part of a dangerous mix in which traumatic pasts are being put to work as

Figure 10. Golden Dawn MPs.

fuel in a highly combustible present. We have been warned: the disintegration of the EU is a real possibility; the financial crisis 'has sharply reduced the life expectancy of governments, regardless of their political colour, and has opened the way for the rise of populist and protest parties'.[131] The current mess that Europe is in, which results from the actions of a largely unregulated financial and banking sector, allowing economic integration to outpace political cooperation, and a failure to intervene decisively, 'threatens to cut short the most peaceful, prosperous, and stable period in all of European history'.[132]

Tony Judt recently argued that we should be far angrier than we are that the achievements of a century of social democracy have been so substantially dismantled in the last three decades. Europe may have become a rich and privileged corner of the world, but the manner of its survival of the 1970s recession and its transformation into a service-sector paradise has come at a high cost—of social cohesion, respect for the worth of individuals, and deepening economic divisions, with all the attendant ills of poverty, crime, and violence that highly unequal societies suffer. Even a hardnosed economic approach ought to take some cognizance of this problem; as two leading economic historians note, 'Globalization was successful over the last half century in no small measure thanks to the existence of welfare states which, at least in the OECD countries, protected those that were threatened by freer trade. The present widespread crusade against such social intervention (quite apart from its other costs) may well turn out to be very short-sighted if it raises domestic opposition to further opening.'[133] Today's problem, according to Judt, is how to return to social democratic values in an age that still uses a social democratic vocabulary (of fairness, liberalism, tolerance) but which acts in ways that scorn those values.[134] Whatever one thinks of this argument, the challenge that faces contemporary Europe is that in the supposedly post-ideological age in which we now live, the legacies of the Second World War are acquiring meanings that fundamentally shake what are usually supposed to be 'European values'.

8

Memory Wars

Deaths don't compensate for each other; they don't cancel each other out; they simply add up.

André Sibomana

The West needs a kind of perestroika of its own.

Mikhail Gorbachev

An acceleration of history, like the one we are living through at the present, is not just a very quick passage from yesterday to tomorrow; it is also the abrupt reappearance in the present of the day before yesterday.

Régis Debray[1]

Seventy-five years since the start of the Second World War, revisionists across Europe are arguing that Stalin was as much to blame for starting the war as Hitler.[2] No historical fact, it seems, not even the one that every school pupil knows, that Hitler was responsible for the war, is any longer secure. At the same time, the British Conservative Party, the party of Churchill, has aligned itself in the European Parliament with a far-right grouping, the ECR (European Conservatives and Reformists Group), which includes the Latvian For Fatherland and Freedom Party and the Polish Law and Justice Party, whose former spokesman and MEP, Michał Kamiński, appealing to the old canard of Judaeo-Bolshevism (*Żydokomuna*), explained the murder of Jews in Jedwabne in 1941 by their Polish neighbours with reference to the 'crimes' supposedly committed by Jews during the period of Bolshevik rule in eastern Poland. As Adam Krzemiński rightly says, the Second World War is still being fought.[3] And, we might add, more intensively today than at any point in the last seven decades.

In this concluding chapter, I will show how in order to understand today's debates about the future of Europe one needs an understanding of postwar

European history and, in particular, a sense of how competing memories of the Second World War have operated in Europe since 1945. Since the end of the Cold War, the dismantling of the postwar consensus has taken shape politically and socially, with the demise of the welfare-capitalist state in Western Europe and the collapse of 'actually existing socialism' in Eastern Europe. But it has also taken place culturally including, most clearly, in the realm of collective memory. The key to grasping the historical conscious-ness of the present is less 'how it really was' than the way the past is articu-lated and remembered in the ever-changing present. Power struggles over representations of the past—including in political debate, in theatre, art, the press, museums, public spectacles and ceremonies, school textbooks, and historiography—turn on what gets selected and what left out. What is important is not just what gets 'remembered', but what gets omitted, dis-torted, falsified, or 'forgotten' in the service of present-day agendas, and thus we need to focus on the process by which certain narratives and images of the past prevail over others. Even where 'the facts' are undisputed (Hitler invaded Poland on 1 September 1939—no revisionist disputes this!), there is immense contestation over what they mean. That contestation is consider-ably less constrained and circumscribed today than was the case in the immediate postwar years and throughout the Cold War.

Out of the Cold War freezer

Until 1989, Silviu Brucan was a senior Romanian communist, including ambassador to the US in 1955 and, later, head of Romanian TV. In 1989, he was one of the signatories of the famous 'letter of the six', one of the few open challenges from within the RCP to Ceauşescu's rule, which was broadcast on Radio Free Europe and the BBC. Later that year he was one of the coordinators of the National Salvation Front, along with Ion Iliescu. But if the NSF was little more than the child of 'unrepentant but lucid Leninists' who formed 'a successor party pretending to break with all totali-tarian conditions', Brucan's and his colleagues' actions in Bucharest helped to crystallize events in Timişoara, giving the popular uprising a strong headwind.[4] After resigning from the NSF mere weeks later, in February 1990, and publicly criticizing Iliescu, in the following years Brucan became a TV-show host and one of Romania's most respected political commenta-tors. He was widely vilified for stating that Romania would need twenty

years to grow accustomed to democracy, a claim that now looks quite optimistic. In his memoirs, Brucan wrote:

> Old grudges and conflicts from as far back as the Hapsburg and tsarist empires,
> marvelously preserved in the communist freezer, are floating to surface with
> the thawing of the Cold War and the lifting of the Stalinist coercion and
> repression. Territorial, religious, and ethnic claims long suppressed are striking
> back with a vengeance, while national liberation, secessions, and declarations
> of independence are coming first on the political agenda.[5]

This is for the most part a fairly unremarkable description of the immediate
post-communist scene—one would expect a former communist to alight
on the eruption of 'old grudges' as implicitly suggesting that the communist
regimes had done well to hold them in check. The notion of the 'communist freezer', however, suggests that the years after 1989 are the 'real' postwar
years, not chronologically (obviously) but conceptually. For only with the
demise of the Cold War could a real debate over the meanings of the Second World War take place in which all sides could be heard. The end of the
'postwar parenthesis' meant a liberation from tyranny in the east and a
chance to debunk longstanding myths but also, more darkly, a chance to
express views that were long regarded as dead or, at best, marginal, in both
east and west. As we saw earlier, the end of *les trentes glorieuses* began the slow
process of taking apart the West European postwar settlement from a social
and economic point of view; the end of the Cold War accelerated the process whereby the collective memories on which the postwar world was built
were just as decisively dismantled, this time across the whole continent. The
thirty 'social democratic' years were, we have seen, aberrant in European
history; so might their antifascist counterpart in collective memory also
prove to be. Is Europe now reverting to type?

There were of course discussions of Europe's wartime past before 1989—
that fact has been key to this book's analysis of the postwar period. In Yugoslavia, for example, a certain rendering of wartime atrocity was central to
the Titoist slogan of 'brotherhood and unity'. The point is that what had
gone before was reformulated to fit new ideological realities, in this instance
the deaths of some 300,000 Bosnians at the hands of Croatian fascist Ustashe
and Serbian royalist Chetniks, which were subsumed into the narrative of
the antifascist partisan struggle.[6] Similarly, indigenous fascism and support
for Hitler's New Order were brushed under the carpet right across Eastern
Europe, as the Soviet narrative of working-class antifascism was imposed

from above, a process which facilitated the Soviets carrying out massive social restructuring through land and property 'redistribution'.

In Western Europe, the suffering caused by the liberation process, through bombing, looting, and sexual violence, was brushed aside by the Allies in favour of 'triumphalist narratives' that could compete with the Soviets'. Topics such as widespread collaboration with Nazism or the weakness of Resistance movements were too uncomfortable to mention in liberated countries. Instead, mythic narratives of resistance, Allied solidarity, and democratic renewal quickly took hold, in the interests of relatively frictionless reconstruction.[7] In the western zones of Germany, an 'exculpatory identity of victimhood', which was blind to the relationship between cause (Nazi Germany's war of aggression) and effect (the devastation of Germany), coupled with a useful anti-communist stance, quickly replaced the rare statements of guilt that had appeared at war's end.[8] There were many commemorations of the war in the Cold War years, but they did not represent all Europeans' opinions or correspond to their experiences during the war. Those whose views did not conform to the antifascist consensus expressed them in private or not at all in the east or in more or less fringe venues in the west.

The end of the Cold War permitted the articulation of sentiments that had hitherto been suppressed. Before then, something 'resembling a tacit conspiracy to tiptoe quietly around the past developed between major forces on the right and left'.[9] As we've seen in this book, revisions of the past began before the fall of the Berlin Wall, and grew in strength and influence during the 1980s, but they could only be freely voiced on a large scale after 1989. These revisions moved in two interrelated directions: on the one hand, dismantling the sort of postwar myths that had contributed to smoothing the path of social reconstruction, such as that 'everyone' had been in the Resistance in France or Italy; on the other hand, the loosening grip of such myths also enabled the return of arguments that characterized the 'other side' of the consensus. Positions—fascist, ultra-nationalist, antisemitic, and xenophobic—that it had been impossible (in the east) or difficult (in the west) openly to articulate gained strength and confidence.

Such views burst out into the open after communism's collapse, especially in the eastern half of the continent. In the search for a national heritage untainted by association with communism, they often directly reprised local interwar and wartime fascist movements. Unfortunately, in a region in which few countries had a tradition of liberalism, anti-communism before and during the Second World War often meant ultra-nationalism or fascism, so not a few war criminals, such as Ion Antonescu (Romania's wartime leader), Jozef Tiso (Slovakia's 'clero-fascist' ruler), Miklós Horthy (Hungary's wartime leader), or Ferenc Szálasi (leader of Hungary's Arrow Cross), were rehabilitated as national heroes in the immediate post-Cold War years, with statues erected and streets named in their honour. For the first post-Cold War decade, it was common for commentators to remark on the fact that although 'historical memory is incessantly invoked in public debates, narratives of self-pity and self-glorification prevail over lucid scrutiny of the past'.[10]

Yet with the exception of Yugoslavia in the 1990s, when memories of the Second World War were mobilized to fuel ethno-nationalist war on a scale not seen on the continent since 1945, the direst predictions of a return to local traditions of nationalism, fascism, or 'peasantism' have not materialized. This is thanks partly to the incorporation of East-Central Europe into the EU and partly to a widespread acceptance of the forms of liberal democracy, whether espoused by centre-right or revamped communist parties. But anti-liberal political traditions—which are by no means unknown in the EU's longer-standing members—remain potent as possible sources of alternative ideologies, and populist politicians are now close to or in government.[11] Indeed, although stability is the most noteworthy fact about the post-communist years, some commentators argue that the region is backsliding, with populism now 'the new condition of the political in Europe', especially in countries where 'long-maintained forms of amnesia' concerning fascist and communist crimes are 'bound to fuel discontent, outrage, and frustration and to encourage the rise of demagogues'.[12]

In Western Europe, the demise of the antifascist postwar settlement gave rise to confusion over the meaning of 'left' and 'right'. The ensuing vacuum in political theory was exacerbated by such phenomena as globalization and the rise of the unregulated global market and, after 11 September 2001, the 'war on terror'. Throughout contemporary Europe, far-right politicians clearly share a heritage with 'classic fascism', but mostly advance their populist agenda on the basis of more topical fears: of Muslims, financial crisis, immigration, and the threat posed to local, 'indigenous' populations by these ideological, economic, and population movements.[13] While racism in the sense of biological determinism still exists, it has been largely replaced by an older form of race understood through culture, in which somatic characteristics are understood as markers of cultural and religious difference rather than of 'a biological heredity'.[14] Still, the rise of unashamedly neo-Nazi movements in the last few years is a sign that an older ideological tradition still retains its power to attract, despite (because of?) the destruction that it wrought to Europe during the war—as one scholar writes: 'People start to make history not despite the fact that it is at odds with—yes, destroys—the stories they live by, but because it destroys the stories they live by.'[15]

The 'memory boom' that has taken place since the end of the Cold War thus reflects and brings about new challenges to European identity and politics. The common theme is the demise of the postwar consensus and the revival of previously marginalized ways of thinking. The reshaping of familiar postwar narratives has taken two forms: an unprecedented assault on the values of the postwar consensus on the one hand and an exaggerated version of them on the other.

West European populism

Nothing illustrates the first effect—the collapse of the postwar consensus—better than the creation of the so-called 'second republic' in Italy after 1994.[16] After 1944, postwar Italy, following the general trend in Western Europe, was stabilized with the aid of the founding myth of the country as a nation of antifascists. The result, according to Renzo De Felice, was 'to obscure the actual history of fascism and the war, and to allow many decidedly undemocratic political elements (Fascists and Communists) to hide behind the mask of Italy's so-called antifascist republic'.[17] Although historians had debated the role played by fascism and antifascism before the end of the Cold War, the collapse of communism and the birth of the 'second republic' sundered Italy's postwar mythic narrative and opened up an uneasy space for multiple, competing versions of the past. Within a very short space of time, 'neo-fascists', led by Gianfranco Fini, found their way into Berlusconi's government, as we saw in Chapter 7. Although the party changed its name from the fascist-connoted *Movimento Sociale Italiano* to the Alleanza Nazionale, its message was the revisionist one that all sides had been victims in the war, that Italy had overcome the divisions of the past, and that the Italian people were all 'post-fascists' now.[18] The attack on Italy's postwar antifascist consensus that began in earnest in the 1990s has continued apace since then.

In the early twenty-first century, the newly inaugurated Holocaust Memorial Day on 27 January was matched with the commemoration of the *foibe*, the murder of Italians by Yugoslav partisans in 1943 and 1945, on 10 February; revisionist claims are thus advanced by instrumentalizing Holocaust victims' fates, bringing them into competition with other Italians' wartime experiences.[19] In fact, this drive to moral equivalence actually perpetuates 'black holes' in memory, with very little discussion taking place about Italian atrocities in the Balkans or colonial territories, Italian concentration camps, or Jewish forced labour in Italian cities and countryside.[20] In general, the importance of communist identity and memory in Italy was rapidly suppressed; and a new and remarkably smooth reintegration of fascist figures occurred. As recently as August 2012, a mausoleum was unveiled in Affile, south of Rome, to Rodolfo Graziani, one of Mussolini's leading generals, Defence Minister in the Salò Republic, a man responsible for mass murder in Ethiopia and Libya and a convicted war criminal. Such occurrences signify not merely the breaking down of the postwar consensus, but revenge against its very existence.

In Austria too something similar has occurred; the Waldheim affair brought about the end of official antifascism, by breaking asunder the line that Austria had been the 'first victim of National Socialism'. As in Italy, what this exposé also revealed was that anti-antifascism had always been a strong force in postwar Austrian society, especially outside Vienna. By doing away with the official antifascist version of the past, the widespread alternative—common but less obvious to outsiders—that commemorated Austria's participation in the Third Reich was provided with the opportunity to acquire a mainstream voice. The 'impact of the victim thesis', writes one historian, 'was restricted to a small segment of the culture of memory'. In other words, 'It was not the narrative of Austrian victimhood, but rather a vibrant culture of commemoration for the fallen soldiers of the *Wehrmacht*, that shaped Austrian memory' in the postwar period. And although the victim thesis was a historical lie, it was at least 'clearly directed against National Socialism'.[21] In the late 1980s, it was no longer clear that antifascism could sustain Austrian public culture and official memory; even the West German press pilloried Austria for failing to address its Nazi past—*Der Spiegel* began 1988 with an image of Hitler in Vienna's main square, *Heldenplatz* (Heroes Square), and, underneath it, separated by a red and white banner with the words *Österreich 1938–1988* in gothic script, a grinning Waldheim at his desk, with the caption 'Trauma Anschluss, Trauma Waldheim'.[22] Both trends can be seen at work in post-Cold War (or better, post-Waldheim) Austria: on the one hand a growing appreciation and commemoration of the real victims of National Socialism, i.e. local Jews and political opponents, and a reluctance to perpetuate the commemoration of the Wehrmacht. In 1997, a Day of Remembrance for the Victims of National Socialism was announced (5 May) and in 2000 Rachel Whiteread's Holocaust memorial in Vienna was unveiled; in 2010 the veterans' ceremony at the Ulrichsberg in Carinthia where Jörg Haider had made his infamous comments twenty years earlier was cancelled. On the other hand, many memorials that cele-brated the military defence of the *Heimat* still exist and are defended by veterans' groups. More broadly, Austria, though now a much more open, cosmopolitan country than it was in the 1980s, has a powerful populist movement which feeds off resentment at the challenge to postwar folk memories of Nazism and the war just as much as immigration and the poli-tics of welfare state cuts and privatizations, implemented after 2002 by the very same populist, Karl-Heinz Grasser (who defected from the FPÖ to the ÖVP), who won the protest vote in the first place. In Austria, the oft-heard counterpart to Italy's 'post-fascist' agenda is the claim that the country should look to the future, not dwell on the past.[23]

The same phenomenon, in a slightly less extreme manifestation, is observ-able in states which were victims of Nazi aggression but in which collabora-tion played a significant role. In the Netherlands, the 1940s and 1950s saw a kind of 'truce'—Ido de Haan calls it 'a shifting political compromise between silence and speaking out'—over the question of who had suffered more, those deported to Germany as forced labourers, Jews deported to concen-tration and death camps, and those who had endured the 'Hunger Winter' of 1944–5.[24] Although Jewish victims made up about half of all Dutch war-time deaths,[25] their experiences were subsumed into a narrative of national heroism that animated the postwar reconstruction. That narrative began to break down long before 1989, but since the end of the Cold War, greater openness about Dutch–German collaboration and the role of the Dutch police and state bureaucracy in deporting Jews to the death camps as well as greater public awareness of Dutch colonial violence has been accompanied by a revival of right-wing populism, most often manifest as a 'defence' of Dutch liberty from 'radical Islam'.

In France, a similar picture has emerged, although complicated here by the more extensive and politically toxic history of French decolonization. Here the combination of the memory of Vichy and the recent reawakening of interest in the Algerian War (1954–62) has been a potent brew for mem-ory wars, which have seen laws passed and retracted on the teaching of

colonialism's 'positive' side, and unseemly debates, sparked by the publication of *The Black Book of Communism* (1997), about whether communism
was 'worse' than Nazism.[26] Mitterrand's consistent stance on the issue of
Vichy and the Holocaust—that it was nothing to do with the Republic—
prevented official recognition and dissemination of the facts. It took a run
of trials in the 1980s and 1990s to open the public debate. The trials of
former Vichy officials Paul Touvier (1994), René Bousquet (1993, murdered
before his trial could begin), and, especially, Maurice Papon (1997), a wartime administrator in Bordeaux who had signed off on the deportations of
Jews to Paris and thence to 'the East', forced the French to confront the
truth that the deportations of French Jews had been carried out by Frenchmen who subsequently enjoyed exemplary postwar careers.

This confrontation with Vichy recently culminated in July 2012 at the
ceremony marking the 70th anniversary of the Vel d'Hiv round-ups, when
President François Hollande went further than any representative of the
Republic had done before with respect to the murder of the Jews of France.
Praising Jacques Chirac for forcing France to face its role in the Holocaust in
1995, Hollande noted bluntly that: 'The truth is hard, cruel. The truth is that
the French police arrested thousands of children and families. Not one German soldier was mobilised for this operation. The truth is this was a crime
committed in France, by France.'[27] Some myths die hard—that all the *chemi-
nots*, the French railwaymen, were resistors, for example[28]—but if France still
suffers from a 'Vichy syndrome' it is at a late stage of its 'talking cure'.

At the same time, however, this greater openness with respect to Vichy
and the French role in the Holocaust is countered by increasing *ressentiment*
on the part of those who benefited from the postwar myths or whose views
were conveniently hidden by Mitterrand's veil of silence. The growth of
populism in the shape of the FN is presented in terms of the defence of the
republic (from immigration and radical Islam, primarily) and happily exploits
traditional symbols such as Marianne and Joan of Arc, but there is no doubt
that the FN's supporters are descendants of the anti-Dreyfusards whose
view of the republic is one somewhat at odds with the fundamental values
of secularism, ethnic blindness, and defence of the Rights of Man which
underpin the Revolutionary tradition.[29]

A particularly interesting case of West European memory wars is Spain,
where Franco's regime survived the war by playing up its alleged neutrality,
talking the language of anti-communism, and providing a useful base for
the US air force. Helen Graham writes that the western establishment

never put pressure on Spain to confront its Francoist past, either before or after 1989, because doing so 'would have made it rapidly apparent how the Spanish regime had replicated exactly the structural violence and coercion/repression of the cold war enemy, thus undermining notions of the West's political and ethical superiority and begging questions about what exactly it was that had "won" that war.'[30] Thus the public engagement with that past in the last decade exemplifies the ethical and political stakes of Europe's memory wars.

The literal exhumation of the past in the form of mass graves of victims of Francoist repression, combined with an assault on the dictatorship's 'repressive distortion of memory' (removing monuments of Franco, for example), has engendered a substantial public movement towards recovering 'lost' memories and investigating the extent of what really happened after the civil war.[31] The transition to democracy after 1975 was negotiated by reformist Francoists and the democratic opposition on the basis of a consensus that the civil war was a 'tragedy' over which a veil of silence should be drawn, a strategy aided by the 1977 Amnesty Law.[32] This consensus broke down in the 1990s 'history wars', when groups representing victims of Franco began to demand not just accurate historical facts but official condemnation of the dictatorship, because, they argued, the 'model transition' had allowed perpetrators to evade justice and had created a democratic deficit. A strong government-backed expression of support for the victims of Francoist violence came in 2007, with the passing of the Law of Historical Memory. 'The revision of official memory to include the individual memories of those previously silenced', Carolyn Boyd writes, 'was understood to be a necessary first step toward reconciliation and democratic consolidation.'[33] Whether it was appropriate to use legislation to mandate the control of memory (for example, banning Francoist symbols at the Valley of the Fallen) is hotly contested, but Spain's example is perhaps no different from laws banning Nazi symbols in Germany or Holocaust denial in France. Indeed, it is striking that the 2007 law was passed at the same time as there was a rapid development of 'Holocaust consciousness' in Spain—with Holocaust-related plays, monuments, and novels all appearing at a rapid rate since 2000—and whilst Holocaust commemoration was becoming a defining aspect of European identity. Memory contests over the Franco dictatorship thus typify a pan-European memory phenomenon.

This phenomenon is observable across the continent, even in places that seem on the face of it to have experienced calmer postwar and post-Cold

War periods, such as Scandinavia and Switzerland. The very title of a book such as *Even in Sweden* indicates that countries that seem, on the face of it, to have been exempt from the major upheavals of the twentieth century have not escaped them altogether.[34] Indeed, the Swedish example is enlightening and not untypical of the general European phenomenon of post-Cold War memory revisions: the postwar myth of Swedish 'neutrality' during the Second World War has gradually been unpicked by careful historical work which has uncovered that Sweden provided considerable material and organizational assistance to the Third Reich.[35] The apparently paradoxical phenomenon of neo-Nazi groups on the streets in Stockholm and elsewhere in one of the most prosperous countries in the world during the 1990s was a wake-up call to the Swedish establishment. It was Sweden, with British backing, which pushed for a European Holocaust Memorial Day and initiated contemporary Holocaust commemoration at the Stockholm Forum in 2000.

Unsurprisingly, Denmark and Norway, both occupied by Nazi Germany, offer a slightly different picture. Both countries, regarded as racially exemplary Nordic 'kin' by the Nazis, had a substantial minority of Nazi sympathizers and, especially in the case of Norway, an organized Nazi regime under Vidkun Quisling. Yet their postwar narratives, which emphasized domestic resistance (the Heroes of Telemark and the like), have also been subjected to revision. The famous rescue of the Jews of Denmark in the so-called 'Bridge over the Øresund' (when most of Denmark's Jews were rowed to safety in Sweden across the narrow sound) is still rightly honoured as a remarkable achievement, but the knowledge that the Jews were endangered is ascribed to infighting among the Nazi occupation authorities leading to a deliberate leak of information.[36] In both countries, the recent resurgence of populist parties in the form of the People's Party (Denmark) and the Progress Party (Norway) builds on a link with the suppressed memories of those who collaborated with or were sympathetic to the Nazi cause, even as they continue to appeal to the 'resistance narrative' and regard with distaste recent attempts by historians to revise it.[37] In Denmark, one commentator argues that 'the entire Danish value system is tilting to the radical right, even as many Danes trivialize, naturalize, and normalize this development'.[38]

A case that has similarities with neutral Sweden and the other two Scandinavian countries in terms of the recent rise of populism is Switzerland. Long regarded, especially in Swiss folk culture and popular memory, as a haven for the oppressed and as a potential victim of Nazism, historians—

particularly in the wake of the Swiss banks affair of the 1990s, when investigations revealed that Holocaust-era assets, both legitimate and stolen, had been hidden away for decades and that during the war the country had provided financial aid to Nazi Germany—have undone many cosy Swiss myths. 'Recent debates', one historian writes, 'suggest that Switzerland is the paradigmatic case of a neutral playing an ambiguous role in a global conflict now increasingly seen as a struggle to preserve civilization, a struggle in which economic resources were mobilized on an unprecedented scale.'[39] The revision of the Swiss past provided by these myth-busting studies went hand in hand with international class action law suits directed against the banks. These suits and the findings of the government-appointed Volcker Committee led to the Swiss authorities' decision temporarily to lift banking secrecy laws in order to provide details of some 50,000 dormant bank accounts; the Swiss banks published the details and also paid out $1.25 billion in a Settlement Fund in return for a halt on any further legal action.[40] This sort of outcome was simply not possible during the Cold War period, when postwar myths prevailed. But as well as overturning unsatisfactory, rose-tinted stories about the Swiss past, it is perhaps not surprising that a rise in populist antisemitism (Jews as venal and so on) and anti-immigration sentiment occurred at the same time. The 'sensational advance' of the Swiss People's Party (*Schweizerischen Volkspartei*, SVP) in the 1990s 'not only altered the political balance between the four government parties but also resulted in Swiss politics becoming less consensual and more polarised'.[41] The SVP's Christoph Blocher's election to the Federal Council in December 2003 gave the far right a foothold in federal politics for the first time since the war. On 29 November 2009, 57.5 per cent of the voters in a nationwide referendum approved the banning of new minarets in Switzerland, and the SVP became the poster-boy for Europe's right-wing populists.[42]

These populists are now widespread from Belgium to Finland. The Lijst Dedecker in the former country took advantage of the gap between the mainstream parties and the far-right Vlaams Belang to grow quite rapidly after 2007.[43] Timo Soini's True Finns (*Perussuomalaiset*) appeared seemingly out of nowhere to become a serious political force in the Finnish elections of 2011.[44] This 'populist zeitgeist' across Western Europe is usually understood as a response to the establishment's supposed corruption in post-industrial conditions; even where populists are not part of the government, their success has pushed the mainstream to the right and thus lent credibility to their claims that the EU and national governments are working against the interests of the 'silent majority' of the people.[45] Whatever the precise reasons for right-wing populism's growth, it could only have happened in the context of the breakdown of the postwar settlement. At the same time, the rise of populism confirms that settlement's end.

Anti-antifascism in Eastern Europe

This breaking down of the postwar consensus can also be seen at work in the rhetoric of the 'double genocide' that informs a wave of new museums in post-communist Eastern Europe. In Budapest's Terror House, in Tallinn's and Riga's Occupation Museums, and in Vilnius's Museum of the Victims of Genocide (housed in the former KGB building), the memories of Nazism and communism are placed in competition with each other and antifascism is only employed insofar as it does not impinge on the anti-communist narrative. In Budapest, the Terror House sets great store by the fact that the communist regime lasted decades as opposed to the mere months of the Nazi occupation, forgetting, as István Rév notes, that 'there was a sort of connection between the coming in of the Soviets and the end of the Arrow-Cross rule'. Indeed, Rév goes so far as to argue that the Terror House, with its overwhelming focus on the communist period, is not meant as a space of memory at all, but is 'a total propaganda space, where death and victims are used as rhetorical devices'.[46] In Tallinn, images of local support for the Nazi invasion are willingly shown, since they imply the horror of the first Soviet occupation (June 1940–June 1941) and thus 'confirm the anti-communist script'.[47]

The exaggerated nature of this 'equality of suffering' argument, with its suggestion that the Nazi invasion constituted a 'national liberation' from Soviet terror, and with its antisemitic subtext which 'justifies' Jewish persecution in terms of Jews' alleged support for communism, is explicable as an over-compensation for or a counter-memory to the rejection of communism after 1989 (1991 in the case of the Baltic States), in an attempt to remind West Europeans of Eastern Europe's continued suffering after the end of the Second World War.[48] As Rév notes:

> The collapse of Communism and the revelation of its crimes caught large groups in Eastern Europe unprepared: if the essence of Fascism was its anti-Communist nature as taught by Communist historiography, then how should the post-Communist public evaluate the most determined adversary of the

criminal Communist regime? After 1989 it was not only (the official history of) World War II that was lost but certainty about the true nature of Fascism as well. The return of anti-Semitic rhetoric and politics in the public sphere filled with anxiety those who had been taught that the iron curtain built by the Communist guards would prevent Fascism and anti-Semitism from returning. With the fall of the iron curtain and the Berlin Wall, these false promises were gone as well.[49]

And gone they have; on a domestic level, the rapid emergence of right-wing populist and radical-right groups confirms Rév's claims. In November 2012, for example, Marton Gyongyosi, one of the leaders of Jobbik in Hungary, called for a 'list' of Jews in Hungary who might pose a 'national security risk'; in doing so, he recalled Hungary's enactment in 1920 of a 'numerus clausus' restricting the number of Jews who could study at Hungarian universities, the first major piece of twentieth-century European antisemitic legislation.[50] One commentator claims that 'the new Hungarian democracy is a direct heir of the 1956 Revolution, a fact that later more recent disputes cannot alter'.[51] It would be ironic if the populism now so prominent in Hungary were to become the dominant political force, for it would suggest that the communists' claim in 1956—which some of them clearly genuinely believed—that they were fighting against 'fascists' might turn out to have some basis in fact.

If it were the case that 1956 was being exploited to advance right-wing populist or even fascist views, then this would confirm the experiences of many in Hungary who supported antifascism because of what they had seen during the Second World War. Such people 'emphasised that no matter how perverted this ideology had become, it once had an authentic core which predated the growth of the Communist party or the communist takeover, and lay in the real experience of either suffering under, or the struggle against, the forces of Fascism'.[52] As one interviewee said, the arrival of the Red Army in Hungary 'was a liberation for everyone, who had really suffered under Hitler, or hated it, or did not agree with it. It meant the end of Hitlerism, it was a liberation from Hitler.'[53] Thus, although many Hungarians abandoned the language of antifascism, some on the left have continued to use it and have consciously contested the appropriation of 1956 as a forerunner of post-communist right-wing politics. Many 'wanted to make it clear that their experience of Fascism led to communism, and that their antifascist stories were not later inventions of the communist period', and that stories of 'resistance and, in particular, involvement in the 1956 uprising, were crucial in the construction of an authentic antifascism for the post-communist period', i.e. one that 'might be used to express opposition to communist practice'.[54] This narrative serves the purpose of countering the right's subversion of 1956, its attempt to belittle all who were not outright opponents of communism, and its exploitation of the powerful symbolic value of Imre Nagy, who has been turned by the right from a reform communist 'to a politically decontextualized symbol of the violence of communist dictatorship'.[55] Both left and right then sought to appropriate the 1956 revolution as validations of their post-communist positions. The socialist left needed to explain that their antifascist views had been silenced under Kádár, and now had relevance; the right needed to lump them all together as communists and portrayed 1956 as a popular uprising against communism. The demise of the communist variant of antifascism leaves the term (not to mention its content) open to exploitation by whoever chooses to do so.

In Lithuania, the notion that Lithuanians were victims of genocide under communism, building on claims made by Lithuanians in exile during the Cold War, became common currency during the collapse of the USSR, and from the early 1990s onwards a commemorative ceremony was held on 14 June to mark the Soviet mass deportations of 1941. But the narrative of national liberation quickly became entangled with antisemitic claims that communism had been imposed by 'the Jews', and sections of the Lithuanian press began arguing that Lithuanian Jews had been active collaborators with the Soviets.[56] The logic of anti-antifascism came to a head with the attempted prosecution of former partisan and survivor of the Vilna Ghetto Rachel Margolis in 2008. As recently as May 2012, the Lithuanian government reburied wartime fascist collaborator and puppet Prime Minister Juozas Ambrazevičius-Brazaitis at a ceremony in Kaunas's Church of the Resurrection attended by Landsbergis and other officials.[57]

What is true of museums, memorials, and commemorative ceremonies is also the case for textbooks. With respect to Romanian textbooks, for example, one commentator argues that 'the de-communization of the Romanian cultural and political discourse has to be equally accompanied by its de-fascization. . . . Ample paragraphs are dedicated to the history of communism, while the fascist one is almost lacking.'[58] Elsewhere in Romanian culture, the same phenomenon is easily observed, as the Memorial of the Victims of Communism and Anticommunist Resistance in Sighet attests.[59] Endless rooms are devoted to suffering under communism, with very little to explain why and how communism came to power in Romania. Still, if the communist version of antifascism, which distorted the past in Romania so that Romanians became victims of history and the Holocaust was an event carried out by Germans and their Hungarian accomplices, has been buried, the outburst of ultranationalist sentiment that followed has itself been tempered in recent years. In October 2009 President Traian Băsescu unveiled Bucharest's Holocaust memorial, built on the recommendation of the 2004 Wiesel commission. The official recognition of Romania's involvement in the murder of Jews and Romanies constitutes an abrupt about-face; how long it will take to filter down to the level of popular consciousness, for so long fed a diet of ultra-nationalism and national Stalinism, is not yet possible to say.

Still, if the Polish case is anything to go by, there is reason for hope. In Poland, the recent flowering of historical research on the Holocaust has given rise to a slew of often hard-hitting studies dealing with the details of the experiences of Poland's large Jewish community and the involvement of Catholic Poles in their murder. On the 'periphery of the Holocaust', as Jan Tomasz Gross notes, Catholic Poles—the religious adjective is relevant, as the Church did not object—in large numbers looted and exploited their Jewish neighbours.[60] Of course, there is a predictable backlash from commentators who fear that Poland's good name is being defamed. But as is slowly happening in the Baltic States, there is a recognition that acknowledging the suffering of one group, even at the expense of 'one's own' community's self-image, need not mean the denial or denigration of another group's suffering. For example, the publication of the English-language volume *Inferno of Choices*, which includes Barbara Engelking's 'Dear Mr Gestapo', a study of denunciation letters sent by Poles to the German occupying forces, gave rise to a storm of protest by those who fear that focusing on the darker sides of Polish history negates altogether the more familiar, positive narrative, especially when such dirty laundry is being aired in international skies.[61] But such works, beginning in the early 1990s with examples such as the film *Birthplace* (dir. Paweł Łoziński, 1992), which follows author Henryk Grynberg to the village of his birth where his brother was killed by gentile Poles, are contributing to a reshaping of the public sphere in Poland, in which the anti-antifascist resentments and distortions which appeared after 1989 are being forcefully challenged. The fact that Poles were victims of the Second World War does not disappear because one can also show that some Catholic Poles were perpetrators in the Nazi genocide against their Jewish neighbours.

Internationally, these developments reveal how what has aptly been called 'geopolitical vertigo'[62] informs the ambivalent relationship of Eastern European states with Western European narratives of the 'good war': the memory of the Second World War is employed both to challenge 'smug' Western European accounts and to assure 'core Europe' of Eastern European commitment to a shared definition of 'Europe'.[63] So in 2008 more than half of all MEPs urged the adoption of the 'Prague Declaration', which demanded EU recognition of the 'equality' of the crimes committed by 'Nazi and communism totalitarian regimes' and the establishment of a common day of remembrance for those regimes' victims (23 August—the day of the Hitler–Stalin Pact). Most historians recognize that investigating and commemorating the crimes of communism is entirely legitimate; indeed, there is a Reconciliation of European Histories Group within the European Parliament which attempts to give meaning to the declaration's demands. And there have indeed been historical commissions of inquiry in Poland and the Baltic States which have to varying degrees addressed some of the most difficult questions, especially concerning collaboration in the Holocaust.

Some, however, regard the Prague Declaration as a sinister attempt to minimize the Holocaust. As a result, in 2012, the Seventy Years Declaration, signed by 71 MEPs and national politicians, was announced, denouncing the equating of Nazi and Soviet crimes, 'as this blurs the uniqueness of each and threatens to undermine the important historical lessons drawn from each of these distinct experiences'. It also rejected the 'glorification' of war criminals and collaborators, such as the Waffen-SS in Latvia and Estonia or the Lithuanian Activist Front, and condemned the increasing acceptance of the swastika being displayed at public events.[64] Indeed, whilst war criminals and former fascists are still being reburied and otherwise commemorated and musealized in the name of anti-communism, one can see why suspicions of the 'double genocide' rhetoric coming from Eastern Europe arise— the claim that communism and Nazism are equivalent is undermined by the lion's share of the attention being paid to the former, and by the negative sentiments directed towards those who fought against the latter. The hope must be that the mercantilist theory of memory in Europe—which regards memory as a fixed resource so that time devoted to the Gulag necessarily detracts from the Holocaust and vice versa—will be overcome in a reconciled history which does not need to reduce past crimes to 'the same' in order to get them publicly recognized and acknowledged.

It may well already be true that 'Collective memories in Eastern Europe no longer form new emerging islands of nationalism which appear again under the melting ice of the Cold War. What may be described as a common feature is the projection of history as a departure from a place to which no one ever wants to return.'[65] But in order for that to remain true, more work needs to be done to ensure that a transnational European collective memory that recalls the difficult facts of the Second World War such as local collaboration in the Holocaust, but that also does not flinch from recollecting the dark side of communism—and that does so without downplaying or beautifying either—prevails over the growing trend towards a transnational populist narrative which equates antifascism with communism and offers *ressentiment* as acceptable historical narrative. The example of Poland shows that it is worth working for such an outcome, but it is by no means guaranteed, especially if the politics of austerity continues without respite.[66]

Russia: the antifascist caricature

All of the above examples illustrate how the postwar consensus has been broken down since the end of the Cold War. The opposite side of the coin is when that consensus is maintained, even at the cost of caricaturing it. This is the case in Russia. Since the Russian master narrative of the war has been subjected to tendentious revisionism in the Baltic States and other former parts of the Soviet Union, it should come as no surprise that in Russia itself under Putin and his successors the cult of the Great Patriotic War has been revived. Indeed, as Martin Evans writes, 'the more Russia's loss of superpower status became apparent, the more the defeat of fascism has been held up as a source of national pride that transcends the end of the USSR'.[67] The same is true in Belarus, routinely (and rather lazily) described as 'the last dictatorship in Europe', where Alexander Lukashenko's regime has increasingly publicized Belarus's role in the Great Patriotic War, in which the death rate of Belarusian citizens and the amount of antifascist resistance were among Europe's highest. But in trying to suppress alternative views, Lukashenko runs the risk that when his regime falls the backlash against antifascism will more than match anything that has been seen in the Baltic States and Ukraine.[68]

It is noteworthy that the Central Museum of the Great Patriotic War in Moscow's Victory Park was not opened until after the collapse of the Soviet

Union, in 1995, even though the decision to build a museum on the site had been taken as early as 1942,[69] and that a museum to commemorate the siege of Leningrad was built in 1989 on the same site as the original museum, constructed during the siege itself (and which closed in 1953).[70] Post-communist Russian governments want to bask in the glow that the memory of the war emits, for it is one of the few sources of continuity and popular legitimacy in a country that had always been synonymous with its empire and is therefore still grappling with its national identity. Thus, dissenters such as the Belarusian writer Ales Adamovich believe that the overburdened term 'Great Patriotic War' should be dropped in favour of 'the war with Hitler', and Viktor Suvorov scurrilously though understandably in the context of the break-up of the USSR argued that Stalin had supported Nazi Germany from the outset because he believed that Hitler would unleash a destructive war that would act as the 'icebreaker' for revolution in Europe.[71] If it is something of an exaggeration to argue, as some do, that debates about the past contributed to the collapse of the Soviet Union,[72] it is nevertheless correct to state that contemporary Russia 'has not yet arrived at a consensus about its past, and thus is forced to contend with conflicting and contradictory visions of its future'.[73] This claim is confirmed, for example, in continued denials of the existence of the secret clauses in the Molotov–Ribbentrop Pact.[74]

Studies of Russia's precipitous post-communist population decline have shown, quite startlingly, that areas that suffered especially high casualty rates during the Great Patriotic War, such as Smolensk, continue to be disproportionately affected by low life expectancy (55 in Smolensk *oblast'* for a baby boy born in 2009, compared to a rural average of 61). 'One could even say', as one commentator puts it, 'that, in demographic terms, the country's past is still unfolding, long after the dead of Stalin's era and the Great Patriotic War have been buried.'[75] Yet the insistence on maintaining a certain (Russian nationalist) version of the antifascist narrative is not just a result of post-communist Russia's search for a world role in an age of shrinking population, capital flight, and energy conflict. It is also a response to the fact that 'More than half a century after their death [i.e. of Soviet military casualties], the winners of WWII have become the losers of the Cold War.'[76] In other words, because Red Army veterans and war casualties represented the communist regime, it is hard to embrace them in the new, post-communist memorial universe. Ukrainians can envelop them into the memory of the Holodomor (famine of 1932–3) or nationalist resistance, Belarusians into a tale of national suffering. Estonia symbolically threw off communist memory when in 2007 the statue of the Soviet soldier in Tallinn was removed, sparking off a diplomatic spat with Moscow. The non-Russian nationalities of the former Soviet Union can all 'externalize' communism, blaming its presence on the Russians. That leaves the Russians facing the difficulty of trying to nationalize memory on the basis of memorials and narratives that were creations of the Brezhnev era. Thus in Russia populist nationalism is based on retaining the antifascist narrative, albeit in an almost unrecognizable and unappealing form, whereas in the former satellite countries and Soviet republics, that narrative can be rejected as a 'foreign' imposition.[77]

Antifascism was fundamental in justifying the installation of communist regimes and in legitimizing the Soviet regime; it was utilized to condemn the reformers of 1956 and, to some extent, 1968. But by the time of Gorbachev's reforms, which saw a kind of institutionalization of the reformist critique, only the hard-liners such as Ceaușescu continued to appeal to antifascism as a reason for rejecting reform. This partly explains the severity with which antifascism along with social democracy has been rejected in post-communist Eastern Europe—antifascism smacks of cover for communist nostalgia. Yet the mention of Ceaușescu also reveals resentment at work, that is to say a rejection of antifascism not because of its instrumentalization by the communists but for a more fundamental reason: that many in the region, especially in the countries that became Soviet satellites, never subscribed to the idea in the first place. This is a victory for nationalist *ressentiment*, and the current Eastern European anti-Russianism, though it is of course justified in terms of the history of Soviet hegemony and the unappealing nature of Putin's rule, is also a rewriting of history, 'forgetting' that 'Russia, not the United States or the UK, beat Germany, saving the world from a fate far worse than Soviet communism.' Forgetting, too, that the Eastern Europeans did not 'liberate' themselves from Soviet rule but that Russia is responsible for that process.[78]

These examples could easily be multiplied, including more countries, more case studies of museums, monuments, or other foci of 'memory wars'. What is striking, because it seems to be the source of so much strife, is that across the continent 'Holocaust consciousness' has become so important. The Holocaust, which, in Judt's felicitous phrase, has been made the 'entry ticket' to contemporary Europe, has been the subject of historical commissions across Europe and, since the Stockholm Forum of 2000, has been enshrined in official European collective memory.[79] Questions of compensation for slave labour and the restitution of stolen property and land—topics which were impossible to discuss under communism—have become burning issues.[80] At the same time, most Eastern European countries have conducted commissions into the experience of communism. These two sets of commissions have been conducted with remarkable scholarly dispassion and expertise, and even in the most difficult cases, such as Romania with its history of ethno-nationalism and a communist regime akin to a form of 'totalitarianism-cum-Sultanism',[81] they have provided judicious and impartial models for examining difficult pasts.[82] Yet, these 'EU-friendly' measures are simultaneously being challenged (in all parts of the continent) both at the official level, by government-sponsored revisionist museums or populist state-controlled media, for example, and at the grassroots, by the resurgence of populism, which breeds on resentment towards Eurocrats and anger at 'exorbitant' Holocaust memory, itself a recapitulation of resentment towards pre-war minorities treaties.[83] Indeed, the extent of the anger at Holocaust memory is itself indicative of the ways in which postwar values have been subverted, to the extent that Holocaust memory is in some quarters shouted down in favour of emphasizing the evils of communism, as if the two memories were incompatible or cannot both be held. The balance of the commissions needs to be brought into mainstream discussions, where many have yet to discover that a recovery of Holocaust memory need not come at the expense of the memory of communism: between transnational commemoration of the Holocaust and recognition of specific national and regional suffering under communism there can be coexistence. Memory need not be a zero-sum game. The deaths don't cancel each other out, they simply add up.

The international context

Although this book is about Europe, it is worth very briefly situating these European memory wars into a broader context, since they occur worldwide, especially in societies scarred by civil war, genocide, and authoritarianism, such as post-apartheid South Africa, Rwanda, Guatemala, and Argentina. Besides, many of the European memory wars have a far wider resonance than their national or intra-European contexts might suggest; after all, many of the debates over memory concern colonial legacies, and therefore debates over Belgium's role in the Congo, or France's in Algeria or Indochina, for example, are obviously not merely European issues.[84] However, the impact of these memories varies considerably depending on local context. The recent revelations of British atrocities in Kenya during the Mau Mau Emergency revealed that there is more appetite for revising histories of colonialism in some countries than others: in the UK, there is no need to pass laws teaching the benefits of imperial rule, not because Britain's imperial past constitutes an unblemished record, but because for most people it has vanished without trace.[85] Memories of Britain 'standing alone' in 1940 have facilitated 'a fifty year inflation of the national ego' and still inform British attitudes towards the EU, with a popular suspicion that it constitutes 'simply a peaceful form of German domination'.[86] Perhaps the different emphases that colonial histories have had in French and Belgian memory debates in comparison with Britain have something to do with the former countries' experience of the Second World War, and the rise of English as a world language—certainly as the language of European diplomacy—and are not solely a reflection of the violence that characterized their decolonization processes?[87]

Once again, it is obvious that the Second World War is central to these debates. Since it really was a *world* war (in a way that even the First World War was not), its effects are being debated more than ever across the world, now that the Cold War lenses have been removed.[88] Issues of race, for example, or American awareness of the Soviet war effort, have recently come to the fore.[89] However, memory wars taking place outside of the European public sphere have tended to be focused less on the Second World War than on postwar phenomena, such as apartheid, the putting down of anti-colonial resistance movements, and national traumas such as the 'disappeared' in Argentina or the 'stolen children' in Australia. 'Truth and reconciliation committees' have been a notable characteristic of the post-Cold War years, as have related phenomena such as states apologizing for former crimes or the search for forms of justice other than retribution.[90] Like memory, restitution and compensation processes need not be zero-sum games: compensating one formerly abused group can be in the best interests of society as a whole.[91] The reality, however, is that such bodies as Guatemala's Commission for Historical Clarification or Rwanda's *gacaca* system of local trials for relatively minor *génocidaires* create new divisions even as they help to heal old wounds.[92]

Just as important as these phenomena has been the rise to prominence of a human rights agenda, since 1945 (and inspired by it—most obviously in the 1948 United Nations Genocide Convention and Universal Declaration of Human Rights and 1951 Refugees Convention), but especially since 1989. The development of a human rights culture has gone hand in hand with the globalization of Holocaust memory, although the precise relationship between the two is blurred.[93] After the Second World War, the League of Nations' dedication to group rights, which had failed miserably, was partially replaced with the weaker but politically expedient United Nations' commitment to individual rights.[94] The emphasis in twentieth-century diplomacy on 'state sovereignty rooted in national homogeneity' meant that humanitarian intentions went hand in hand with forced deportations and territorial partition along ethnic lines.[95] Although the history of human rights pre-dates the Second World War, its advocates employ the memory of the war to justify the concept and to provide a linear, progressive history of its unfolding towards global prominence. This history is both complicated/disrupted and reinvigorated by recent catastrophes, such as the wars in the former Yugoslavia and genocide in Rwanda or Darfur. Competing versions of the origins and necessity to protect human rights are bound up with debates over humanitarian intervention, pre-emptive wars, and the rights and wrongs of 'regime change', and are thus prime examples of how memory informs contemporary international relations and political action.

Memory 'peace'?

Memory, we have been usefully reminded, is 'multidirectional'. That is to say, sometimes a process takes place 'in which transfers occur between events that have come to seem separate from each other'.[96] Rothberg gives the examples of the Holocaust and decolonization, but there are others, such as slavery, the use of the atom bomb, and genocides of indigenous peoples. One cannot easily predict how the contested memories of one event will help or hinder the 'discovery' of memories of other events, which may then become equally contentious. Besides, as recent arguments about the Second World War show, one can hardly suggest that memory animates public and academic concerns less now than it did twenty years ago. Germany may present an exemplary face of a nation that has confronted its dark past (if one brackets off for the moment the critical voices which regard this self-satisfaction as a kind of *Sündenstolz*, or pride in one's own sins); but Russia has yet to do so, and most of the countries of the former Eastern Bloc have barely begun the process (not to mention other areas of the world in Latin America or Africa where such processes are also relevant). Spain is another major European example where memory politics are fundamental to contemporary life. One cannot look to Germany and argue that because the job has been done there, the trajectory to be followed by other states is mapped out and thus, for scholars, predictable and boring. Indeed, the reverse seems to be the case: the more that the myth of the Holocaust as an act committed by an impersonal evil force called Nazism that has nothing to do with 'us' is challenged, the more resistance in European countries to official commemoration seems to grow. In other words, the more uncertain the present and the future look, the more memory—precisely because it is future-oriented—will continue to be an arena of contestation, giving rise in some cases to conflict, in others to reconciliation.[97] In the case of the former, it might turn out that the 'negation of nationalism as the central force in politics was a short interlude that lasted less than an intellectual generation'.[98] In the case of the latter, we might argue that with the extension of the EU, the upsurge of populism will be contained within democratic structures and thus that Europe 'has not had such a good opportunity to establish lasting peace since the Congress of Vienna'.[99] Postwar Europe, especially post-Cold War Europe, has been a period of intense memory scrutiny, primarily of the Second World War. Now that postwar Europe is itself fast on the road to becoming history its very pastness means it too is ripe for inclusion in ongoing struggles to control memory and thus to shape the 'new Europe'.

From their study of revolution, anti-communist intellectuals such as Adam Michnik learned to be concerned that 'by using force to storm the existing Bastilles we shall unwittingly build new ones'.[100] Much of recent European history is about what shape the new Bastille in the guise of Fortress Europe will take. When one examines the 'return of memories' that could not be articulated in the public sphere during the Cold War—when the antifascist narrative was imposed in the east and prevailed in the west, albeit in a conservative, anti-communist form—one can see that the years since 1989 are intimately connected to the Second World War and its aftermath. In many ways, we are only now living through the postwar period.

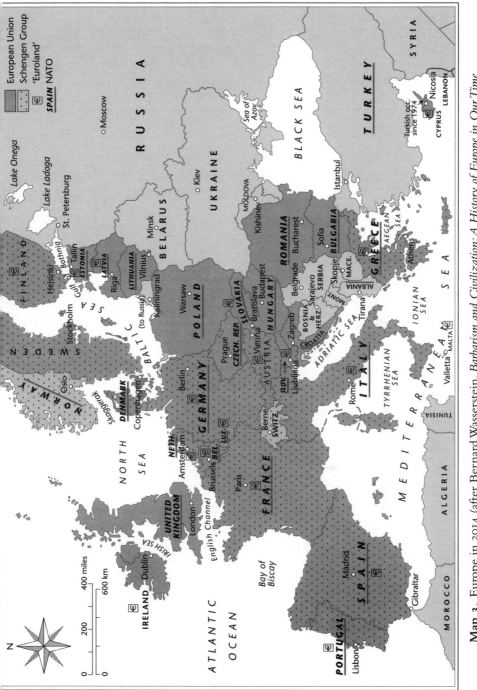

Map 3. Europe in 2014 (after Bernard Wasserstein, *Barbarism and Civilization: A History of Europe in Our Time* (Oxford University Press, 2007), p. 735).

Conclusion

The Dead Season of Our Fortunes

This sin will haunt humanity to the end of time.
It does haunt me. And I want it to be so.

Jan Karski, 1981

There may, therefore, be ahead of us a long, silent process of semi-starvation, and of a gradual, steady lowering of the standards of life and comfort. The bankruptcy and decay of Europe, if we allow it to proceed, will affect every one in the long run, but perhaps not in a way that is striking or immediate.... in this autumn of 1919 in which I write, we are at the dead season of our fortunes.

John Maynard Keynes[1]

In the wake of the oil crises and the recessions of the 1970s, neo-liberal economists, whose views had been silenced during the Keynesian boom of the 1950s and 1960s, found their voices again. They attacked the role of government, arguing that taxation, state-led planning, and nationalized industries and services were hampering revival by squandering energy and blocking the sort of entrepreneurship and efficiency that was required to return to economic growth and make Europe competitive against American and Far Eastern economies. 'In many places', writes Judt, 'this rhetorical strategy was quite seductive to younger voters with no first-hand experience of the baneful consequences of such views the last time they had gained intellectual ascendancy, half a century before.'[2] We are again in the same situation, except this time following thirty years during which the economic growth and accompanying 'feel-good factor' of the *trentes glorieuses* has been considerably attenuated.

Even after the great dismantling of the last thirty years, the cry is being heard that government stymies creativity, productivity, and efficiency. In Britain, there are few industries left to denationalize, with the tote and air-traffic control among the last few dregs that the government can finger (perhaps the only big prize is the Post Office). But a broader change is afoot that will have Hayek laughing in his grave. This broader change seeks to restrict citizens' pension rights, cut welfare benefits to the bare bones, and force people into work irrespective of whether they have chosen the job for themselves. Funding for schools and, above all, universities is being cut mercilessly, with governments arguing this will lead to a 'professionalization' of teachers and lecturers (when in fact, Lucky Jim is no longer in post, and universities are already at the forefront of R&D and the hi-tech and creative industries). At the same time, 'professionalization' increasingly means the rise of audit culture, whereby bureaucratization replaces real creativity and the vast paperwork involved serves little purpose other than to satisfy the audit itself—this is what has been aptly called 'Stalinist capitalism'.[3] At the same time as welfare-dependent families are being moved from their communities in London to cheaper housing in other parts of the country, the British government, along with other European governments, has managed to find vast sums of money to wage neo-colonial wars in Afghanistan and Libya.

The scale of the economic crisis of 2008 onwards was and still is real. As a share of GDP, many countries' national debt was at levels never before encountered in the postwar world. Some changes were necessary, and it is hardly a neo-liberal point to note that the cost of welfare states was far more expensive in an age when far more people lived longer than ever before, when at the same time the working population had proportionately shrunk. The neo-liberal input was to claim that national debt operates like house-hold debt, and that austerity measures imposed on ordinary citizens were the only way to restore confidence. Centre-right governments across Europe—and the few remaining social democratic ones—all signed up to this position, or were 'forced' to do so by 'the markets', which protected the banks and the transnational structures of finance from having to admit that their venality and short-sighted profit-making had exacerbated the situation, if not caused it. The situation is of course more complex: across Europe, with the exception of the poorest sections of society (which, defined as a relational concept, i.e. those who had the proportionately smallest share of the cake, had grown noticeably since the 1980s), most people had thrown in their lot with the nostrums of economic growth and consumerism. But the shameless abandonment of those same people by governments whose interests lay in protecting banks more than their citizens has had some startling consequences.

This book has argued that from the 1970s onwards, the demise of antifascism went hand in hand with the dismantling of social democracy in Western Europe and the rise of alternative anti-Enlightenment ideologies in Eastern Europe. Since the end of the Cold War, the triumph of a supposedly 'liberal' narrative has legitimized the final stage of the attack on the concept of social welfare in the west and state control (or direction) over the supply of goods and services in the east. The result is the rise of right-wing populism, as people's justifiable anger over the loss of most of the certainties that enabled postwar stability is directed not against those who are dismantling those structures, but 'others' who can be blamed for the 'loss' of European 'values'. That means Muslims above all, but also the millions of Romanies in Central Europe whose lives are still mired in poverty and prejudice, and other minority groups. For the time being, we are witnessing the apparently paradoxical phenomenon of a privatization or liberalization of morals going hand in hand with increasingly illiberal socio-economic policies. The state no longer criminalizes homosexuality or other sexual practices, or abortion (up to different points in different states), and seeks too to educate its citizens that racial or religious hatred is wrong. But this is in reality no paradox. As Aldous Huxley wrote in the foreword to his dystopian novel *Brave New World*: 'as political and economic freedom diminishes, sexual freedom tends compensatingly to increase. And the dictator... will do well to encourage that freedom. In conjunction with the freedom to daydream under the influence of dope and movies and the radio, it will help to reconcile his subjects to the servitude which is their fate.'[4] How long can these positive achievements—of a mere forty years' standing—be maintained? It would be naive to think that the populists who argue against the 'Islamization' of Europe will not also seek to reverse many of the gains of the social movements of the 1960s and 1970s. There is a 'drag' or time lag here, which will be 'corrected' if populists such as the *Front National*, the True Finns, or the Dutch Freedom Party ever form majority governments. Should Jobbik or Golden Dawn ever get near power, Europe will be in for a new politics of revenge.

What we see today, then, is the coming together of two strands, not by coincidence but as enablers of each other: on the one hand, the economic argument that the social welfare state is either too expensive (Western Europe) or a form of authoritarianism (Eastern Europe) and, on the other hand, a steady revisionism of the past, which baulks at the rise of 'Holocaust consciousness' and human rights discourse, and which seeks to replace antifascism with a 'post-fascist' narrative which will succeed as a result of people's ignorance of history and by appealing to resentment and frustration at 'political correctness'. A mere thirty years after the most destructive war in world history, fuelled by Nazism, a movement whose inner dynamic leads first to the annihilation of others and then to self-destruction, Europeans faced a revision of the past, which gradually eroded the strength of the antifascist settlement. The Cold War and its demise confused the issue, making people think that the discrediting of communism necessarily led to the rejection of antifascism. If this trend is not halted, then by the hundredth anniversary of the outbreak of the Second World War, a Europe of protectionist, nationalist micro-states led by populists demanding 'national preference', but without the means to pay for it and unwilling to admit the foreign labour necessary to sustain it, will once again march the continent into the abyss.

Notes

CHCW   Melvyn P. Leffler and Odd Arne Westad (eds.), *The Cambridge History of the Cold War*, 3 vols. (Cambridge: Cambridge University Press, 2010)

CW   Jussi M. Hanhimäki and Odd Arne Westad (eds.), *The Cold War: A History in Documents and Eyewitness Accounts* (Oxford: Oxford University Press, 2003)

MF   Mary Fulbrook (ed.), *Europe since 1945* (Oxford: Oxford University Press, 2001)

OHPEH   Dan Stone (ed.), *The Oxford Handbook of Postwar European History* (Oxford: Oxford University Press, 2012)

TMEH   Rosemary Wakeman (ed.), *Themes in Modern European History since 1945* (London: Routledge, 2003)

INTRODUCTION

1. *Le Franc-tireur, Organe du Mouvement de Libération Nationale*, Édition Sud, 1 March 1944, cited in Walter Lipgens, 'European Federation in the Political Thought of Resistance Movements during World War II', *Central European History*, 1:1 (1968), 9; Anatol Girs, 'From the Publisher', in Janusz Nel Siedlecki, Krystyn Olszewski, and Tadeusz Borowski, *We Were in Auschwitz* (New York: Welcome Rain, 2000 [1946]), 2; Waldemar Gurian, 'After World War II', *Review of Politics*, 8:1 (1946), 6; Gregor von Rezzori, *Memoirs of an Anti-Semite: A Novel in Five Stories* (London: Pan Books, 1983), 251.

2. Primo Levi, 'Gladiators', in *A Tranquil Star: Unpublished Stories* (London: Penguin, 2008), 83–9.

3. Eric Hobsbawm, *The Age of Extremes: A History of the World, 1914–1991* (London: Michael Joseph, 1994).

4. Milovan Djilas, *Wartime* (London: Secker & Warburg, 1980), 447.

5. See Dan Stone, *Histories of the Holocaust* (Oxford: Oxford University Press, 2010), ch. 1 for more detail.

6. Curzio Malaparte, *The Skin* (London: Ace Books, 1959), 228–9.

7. Milovan Djilas, *Conversations with Stalin* (Harmondsworth: Penguin, 1969), 19.

8. William I. Hitchcock, *Liberation: The Bitter Road to Freedom, Europe 1944–1945* (London: Faber and Faber, 2009).

9. Philipp Ther and Ana Siljak (eds.), *Redrawing Nations: Ethnic Cleansing in East-Central Europe, 1944–1948* (Lanham, Md.: Rowman and Littlefield, 2001); Alfred-Maurice

de Zayas, *A Terrible Revenge: The Ethnic Cleansing of the East European Germans*, 2nd edn. (Houndmills: Palgrave Macmillan, 2006); Pertti Ahonen, Gustavo Corni, Jerzy Kochanowski, Rainer Schulze, Tamás Stark, and Barbara Stelzl-Marx, *People on the Move: Forced Population Movements in Europe in the Second World War and its Aftermath* (Oxford: Berg, 2008).

10. Mark Mazower, *Dark Continent: Europe's Twentieth Century* (London: Allen Lane, The Penguin Press, 1998), 224.

11. Mark Mazower, *No Enchanted Palace: The End of Empire and the Ideological Origins of the United Nations* (Princeton: Princeton University Press, 2009), 143.

12. Martin Conway and José Gotovitch (eds.), *Europe in Exile: European Exile Communities in Britain 1940–45* (New York: Berghahn Books, 2001).

13. István Deák, Jan T. Gross, and Tony Judt (eds.), *The Politics of Retribution in Europe: World War II and its Aftermath* (Princeton: Princeton University Press, 2000); Roderick Kedward and Nancy Wood (eds.), *The Liberation of France: Image and Event* (Oxford: Berg, 1995).

14. Mark Wyman, *DPs: Europe's Displaced Persons 1945–1951* (Ithaca, NY: Cornell University Press, 1998); Angelika Königseder and Juliane Wetzel, *Waiting for Hope: Jewish Displaced Persons in Post-World War II Germany* (Evanston, Ill.: Northwestern University Press, 2001); Avinoam J. Patt and Michael Berkowitz (eds.), *We Are Here: New Approaches to Jewish Displaced Persons in Postwar Germany* (Detroit: Wayne State University Press, 2009).

15. See <http://www.hpol.org/jfk/cuban> for audio transcripts.

16. Odd Arne Westad, *The Global Cold War: Third World Interventions and the Making of our Times* (Cambridge: Cambridge University Press, 2005). See also Jeremi Suri, 'The Cold War, Decolonization, and Global Social Awakenings: Historical Intersections', *Cold War History*, 6:3 (2006), 353–63 and the essays in Richard H. Immerman and Petra Goedde (eds.), *The Oxford Handbook of the Cold War* (Oxford: Oxford University Press, 2013).

17. Silvio Pons and Federico Romero, 'Introduction', in Pons and Romero (eds.), *Reinterpreting the End of the Cold War: Issues, Interpretations, Periodizations* (London: Frank Cass, 2005), 9.

18. Joel Isaac, 'The Human Sciences in Cold War America', *Historical Journal*, 50:3 (2007), 731.

19. Frank Costigliola, 'The Nuclear Family: Tropes of Gender and Pathology in the Western Alliance', *Diplomatic History*, 21:2 (1997), 163–83; Robert D. Dean, 'Masculinity as Ideology', *Diplomatic History*, 22:1 (1998), 29–62; Peter Carlson, *K Blows Top* (London: Old Street, 2009).

20. Theodor Adorno, *Minima Moralia: Reflections from Damaged Life* (London: Verso, 1989 [1951]), 55. For classic studies of the bomb, see John Hersey, *Hiroshima* (Harmondsworth: Penguin, 1946); Robert Jungk, *Brighter Than a Thousand Suns: A Personal History of the Atomic Scientists* (Harmondsworth: Penguin, 1960 [1956]); Karl Jaspers, *The Future of Mankind* (Chicago: University of Chicago Press, 1961).

21. As two famous works that book-end the period attest: Karl Popper's *The Open Society and its Enemies* (2 vols., 1944), with its famous condemnation of Hegelianism as the precursor to terror, and Francis Fukuyama's *The End of History and the Last Man* (1992), which marked the return of Hegelianism, albeit with short-lived enthusiasm.

22. On culture, see the useful essays by Patrick Major and Rana Mitter: 'Culture', in Saki R. Dockrill and Geraint Hughes (eds.), *Palgrave Advances in Cold War History* (Houndmills: Palgrave Macmillan, 2006), 240–62; 'East is East and West is West? Towards a Comparative Socio-Cultural History of the Cold War', *Cold War History*, 4:1 (2003), 1–22. As they note ('Culture', 255), 'what seems undeniable is that popular culture exploited the cold war as much as cold warriors used the culture industry'. There is not space to deal with all of these topics in this book; see the essays in *OHPEH*.

23. Max-Stephan Schulze, 'Introduction', in Schulze (ed.), *Western Europe: Economic and Social Change since 1945* (London: Longman, 1999), 1.

24. In reality, though, the GDP figures for Eastern Europe disguised the fact that the vast majority of this 'wealth' was being spent on military and industrial infrastructure, and that the population were enjoying very little benefit from it.

25. For example, Norman Manea, *On Clowns: The Dictator and the Artist* (London: Faber and Faber, 1994).

26. Richard Griffiths, 'Anti-Fascism and the Post-War British Establishment', in Nigel Copsey and Andrzej Olechnowicz (eds.), *Varieties of Anti-Fascism: Britain in the Inter-War Period* (Houndmills: Palgrave Macmillan, 2010), 247–64.

27. David Kettler, 'Antifascism as Ideology: Review and Introduction', 16. Online at <www.bard.edu/contestedlegacies/lib/kettler_articles.php?action=getfile&id=362394>.

28. Enzo Traverso, 'Intellectuals and Anti-Fascism: For a Critical Historization', *New Politics*, 9:4 (2004), online at: <http://nova.wpunj.edu/newpolitics/issue36/Traverso36.htm>.

29. See, for example, Copsey and Olechnowicz (eds.), *Varieties of Anti-Fascism*; Samuel Moyn, 'Intellectuals and Nazism', in *OHPEH*, 671–91.

CHAPTER 1

1. Stalin, cited in *The Diary of Georgi Dimitrov, 1933–1949*, ed. Ivo Banac (New Haven: Yale University Press, 2003), 358; Milan Kundera, *The Joke* (London: Faber and Faber, 1992), 71.

2. Stalin, cited in Hiroaki Kuromiya, 'World War II, Jews, and Post-Soviet Society', *Kritika: Explorations in Russian and Eurasian History*, 3:3 (2002), 521.

3. Alexander Statiev, *The Soviet Counterinsurgency in the Western Borderlands* (Cambridge: Cambridge University Press, 2010), 163. See also Alexander V. Prusin, *The Lands Between: Conflict in the East European Borderlands, 1870–1992* (Oxford: Oxford University Press, 2010), ch. 8.

4. Geoff Eley, 'Europe after 1945', *History Workshop Journal*, 65 (2008), 208. See also Eley, 'When Europe Was New: Liberation and the Making of the Post-War Era', in Monica Riera and Gavin Schaffer (eds.), *The Lasting War: Society and Identity in Britain, France and Germany after 1945* (Houndmills: Palgrave Macmillan, 2008), 17–43.

5. Mazower, *Dark Continent*, 211. Cf. James D. Wilkinson, *The Intellectual Resistance in Europe* (Cambridge, Mass.: Harvard University Press, 1981); Örjan Appelqvist, 'International Socialist Attempts at Bridge-Building in the Early Postwar Period', in Konrad H. Jarausch and Thomas Lindenberger (eds.), *Conflicted Memories: Europeanizing Contemporary Histories* (New York: Berghahn Books, 2007), 221–36.

6. Judt, *Postwar*, 71.

7. Mark Pittaway and Hans-Fredrik Dahl, 'Legitimacy and the Making of the Post-War Order', in Martin Conway and Peter Romijn (eds.), *The War for Legitimacy in Politics and Culture 1936–1946* (Oxford: Berg, 2008), 193–4.

8. Anita J. Prażmowska, 'The Kielce Pogrom 1946 and the Emergence of Communist Power in Poland', *Cold War History*, 2:2 (2002), 101–24. See also Joanna Tokarska-Bakir, 'Cries of the Mob in the Pogroms in Rzeszów (June 1945), Cracow (August 1945), and Kielce (July 1946) as a Source for the State of Mind of the Perpetrators', *East European Politics and Societies*, 25:3 (2011), 553–74.

9. Jan T. Gross, *Fear: Anti-Semitism in Poland after Auschwitz. An Essay in Historical Interpretation* (New York: Random House, 2007). Prażmowska ('The Kielce Pogrom') correctly notes that Gross's arguments oversimplify the complexity of postwar Poland, but his book is nevertheless an important study which tries to overturn many presuppositions about Jews and the rise to power of communism in Poland.

10. László Karsai, 'The People's Courts and Revolutionary Justice in Hungary, 1945–46', in Deák, Gross, and Judt (eds.), *The Politics of Retribution in Europe*, 246, citing judge Ákos Major. On the black market: Peter Kenez, *Hungary from the Nazis to the Soviets: The Establishment of the Communist Regime in Hungary, 1944–1948* (New York: Cambridge University Press, 2006), 126–7.

11. On Stalin's belief in the essentialism of national character—based on sociological conditions rather than 'race', though in practice with little to choose from between the two explanations—see Erik Van Ree, 'Heroes and Merchants: Joseph Stalin and the Nations of Europe', in Michael Wintle (ed.), *Imagining Europe: Europe and European Civilisation as Seen from its Margins and by the Rest of the World, in the Nineteenth and Twentieth Centuries* (Brussels: Peter Lang, 2008), 64–5.

12. Timothy Snyder, *The Reconstruction of Nations: Poland, Ukraine, Lithuania, Belarus, 1569–1999* (New Haven: Yale University Press, 2003).

13. See Mark Kramer, 'Introduction', in Ther and Siljak (eds.), *Redrawing Nations*; Hoover cited at 7. Kramer goes on to note (8) that the irony is that the production of homogeneous nation-states has been a source of stability in the post-Cold War era, but it is hard to know whether or not this is true as it cannot be tested (against, say, economic prosperity as an alternative explanation for stability). On Soviet wartime policies towards 'punished peoples', see Nicolas Werth,

'The Crimes of the Stalin Regime: Outline for an Inventory and Classification', in Dan Stone (ed.), *The Historiography of Genocide* (Houndmills: Palgrave Macmillan, 2008), 400–19. For broader context, see also Ahonen et al., *People on the Move*, esp. chs. 4 and 5; Donald Bloxham and A. Dirk Moses, 'Genocide and Ethnic Cleansing', in Donald Bloxham and Robert Gerwarth (eds.), *Political Violence in Twentieth-Century Europe* (Cambridge: Cambridge University Press, 2011), 87–139, esp. 123–5. On Poland, see Anita J. Prażmowska, *Civil War in Poland, 1942–48* (Houndmills: Palgrave Macmillan, 2004).

14. István Bibó, *Die Misere des osteuropäischen Kleinstaaterei*, trans. Béla Rásky (Frankfurt/M:Verlag Neue Kritik, 1992 [orig. Hungarian 1946]), 97 [*Landstraße heimatloser Massen*].

15. Judt, *Postwar*, 49.

16. Alexander V. Prusin, 'Poland's Nuremberg: The Seven Court Cases of the Supreme National Tribunal, 1946–1948', *Holocaust and Genocide Studies*, 24:1 (2010), 1–25.

17. Donald Bloxham, 'From Streicher to Sawoniuk: The Holocaust in the Courtroom', in Dan Stone (ed.), *The Historiography of the Holocaust* (Houndmills: Palgrave Macmillan, 2004), 398. See also Alexander V. Prusin, '"Fascist Criminals to the Gallows!" The Holocaust and Soviet War Crimes Trials, December 1945–February 1946', *Holocaust and Genocide Studies*, 17:1 (2003), 1–30.

18. See, for example, John Lewis Gaddis, *We Now Know: Rethinking Cold War History* (Oxford: Clarendon Press, 1997), 292.

19. Djilas, *Conversations with Stalin*, 90.

20. Albert Resis, 'The Churchill–Stalin Secret "Percentages Agreement" on the Balkans, Moscow, October 1944', *American Historical Review*, 83:2 (1978), 368–87.

21. Molotov, cited in Vojtech Mastny, 'Soviet Plans for Postwar Europe', in Antonio Varsori and Elena Calandri (eds.), *The Failure of Peace in Europe, 1943–48* (Houndmills: Palgrave, 2002), 68.

22. Marc Trachtenberg, 'The Marshall Plan as Tragedy', *Journal of Cold War Studies*, 7:1 (2005), 140.

23. Mastny, 'Soviet Plans for Postwar Europe', 61.

24. Eduard Mark, 'Revolution by Degrees: Stalin's National-Front Strategy for Europe, 1941–1947', *Cold War International History Project Working Papers*, 31 (2001), 17, 22. See also Mark, 'American Policy Toward Eastern Europe and the Origins of the Cold War, 1941–1946: An Alternative Interpretation', *Journal of American History*, 68:2 (1981), 313–36.

25. Dimitrov, diary entry for 28 January 1945, cited in Silvio Pons, 'Stalin and the European Communists after World War Two (1943–1948)', *Past and Present*, Supplement 6 (2011), 127.

26. Jeronim Perović, 'The Tito–Stalin Split: A Reassessment in the Light of New Evidence', *Journal of Cold War Studies*, 9:2 (2007), 32–63.

27. Mastny, 'Soviet Plans for Postwar Europe', 68.

28. See, for example, the comments in Geir Lundestad, 'How (Not) to Study the Origins of the Cold War', in Odd Arne Westad (ed.), *Reviewing the Cold War: Approaches, Interpretations, Theory* (London: Frank Cass, 2000), 64–80. Cf. Vladislav Zubok and Constantine Pleshakov, *Inside the Kremlin's Cold War: From Stalin to Khrushchev* (Cambridge, Mass.: Harvard University Press, 1996).

29. Vladimir Tismaneanu, *Stalinism for All Seasons: A Political History of Romanian Communism* (Berkeley and Los Angeles: University of California Press, 2003), 25.

30. See Stefano Bottoni, 'Reassessing the Communist Takeover in Romania: Violence, Institutional Continuity, and Ethnic Conflict Management', *East European Politics and Societies*, 24:1 (2010), 59–89.

31. Jeffrey Herf, *Divided Memory: The Nazi Past in the Two Germanys* (Cambridge, Mass.: Harvard University Press, 1997), 108.

32. Walter Ulbricht, 'Warum Nationale Front des demokratischen Deutschland? Aus dem Referat auf der Parteiarbeiterkonferenz der SED Groß-Berlin, 17. Mai 1949', cited in Herf, *Divided Memory*, 110.

33. Norman M. Naimark, 'Stalin and Europe in the Postwar Period, 1945–53: Issues and Problems', *Journal of Modern European History*, 2:1 (2004), 29, 33. See also Naimark, 'The Sovietization of Eastern Europe, 1944–1953', in *CHCW*, i: *Origins*, 175–97; Melvyn P. Leffler, 'The Cold War: What Do "We Now Know"?', *American Historical Review*, 104:2 (1999), 501–24; Alfred J. Rieber, 'The Origins of the Cold War in Eurasia: A Borderland Perspective', in Jarausch and Lindenberger (eds), *Conflicted Memories*, 117–29; Mark Pittaway, 'Making Postwar Communism', in *OHPEH*, 265–82.

34. Cited in Antonio Varsori, 'Reflections on the Origins of the Cold War', in Westad (ed.), *Reviewing the Cold War*, 284.

35. Rákosi and Stalin, cited in Mark Kramer, 'Stalin, Soviet Policy, and the Consolidation of a Communist Bloc in Eastern Europe, 1944–53', in Vladimir Tismaneanu (ed.), *Stalinism Revisited: The Establishment of Communist Regimes in East-Central Europe* (Budapest: Central European University Press, 2009), 79 and 79 n. 56.

36. János Rainer, 'Revisiting Hungarian Stalinism', in Tismaneanu (ed.), *Stalinism Revisited*, 247.

37. Rainer, 'Revisiting Hungarian Stalinism', 253–4.

38. Bradley Abrams, 'Hope Died Last: The Czechoslovak Road to Stalinism', in Tismaneanu (ed.), *Stalinism Revisited*, 347. The following paragraph is indebted to Abrams's valuable analysis.

39. Ludvík Vaculík, 'A Day in August' (1986), in *A Cup of Coffee with my Interrogator*, trans. George Theiner (London: Readers International, 1987), 111. For a useful survey, see Martin Myant, 'New Research on February 1948 in Czechoslovakia', *Europe-Asia Studies*, 60:10 (2008), 1697–715.

40. William Taubman, 'How Much of the Cold War was Inevitable?', in Francesca Gori and Silvio Pons (eds.), *The Soviet Union and Europe in the Cold War, 1943–53* (Basingstoke: Macmillan Press, 1996), 192. On Finland, see Jussi M. Hanhimäki,

'The Lure of Neutrality: Finland and the Cold War', in Klaus Larres and Kenneth Osgood (eds.), *The Cold War after Stalin's Death: A Missed Opportunity for Peace?* (Lanham, Md.: Rowman & Littlefield, 2006), 257–76.

41. Anna Di Biagio, 'The Marshall Plan and the Founding of the Cominform, June–September 1947', in Gori and Pons (eds.), *The Soviet Union and Europe in the Cold War*, 208–21. See also Di Biagio, 'The Cominform as the Soviet Response to the Marshall Plan', in Varsori and Calandri (eds.), *The Failure of Peace in Europe, 1943–48*, 297–305, which shows that the creation of the Cominform cannot be put down solely to the need to come up with an answer to US aid to Europe, but was also conceived as 'the pivotal point in the political structure of the Socialist camp . . . a tool to strengthen the Eastern bloc and determine the definitive Sovietization of eastern Europe' (298). See also Kramer, 'Stalin, Soviet Policy', 80–1, for the assertion that the decision to create the Cominform, which had been envisaged from at least as early as 1946, had nothing to do with the Marshall Plan but was solely a matter of Stalin's need to impose his rule on the Eastern European states.

42. Pons, 'Stalin and the European Communists', 134–8, quotation on 135.

43. Geoffrey Roberts, 'Moscow and the Marshall Plan: Politics, Ideology and the Onset of the Cold War, 1947', *Europe-Asia Studies*, 46:8 (1994), 1371–86. As Roberts points out, however, even after the boycott, Poland increased its trade with the west—the split was not as sudden and momentous as it is sometimes portrayed by historians.

44. Vojtech Mastny, 'The New History of Cold War Alliances', *Journal of Cold War Studies*, 4:2 (2002), 55–84.

45. Alfred J. Rieber, 'Popular Democracy: An Illusion?', in Tismaneanu (ed.), *Stalinism Revisited*, 103–28; Pittaway, 'Making Postwar Communism'.

46. Tarik Cyril Amar, 'Sovietization as a Civilizing Mission in the West', in Balász Apor, Péter Apor, and E. A. Rees (eds.), *The Sovietization of Eastern Europe: New Perspectives on the Postwar Period* (Washington, DC: New Academia Publishing, 2008), 29–45.

47. Stephen Kotkin, *Magnetic Mountain: Stalinism as a Civilization* (Berkeley and Los Angeles: University of California Press, 1995).

48. Sheila Fitzpatrick, *Everyday Stalinism: Ordinary Life in Extraordinary Times. Soviet Russia in the 1930s* (New York: Oxford University Press, 1999), 3–4.

49. Cited in Pittaway, 'Making Postwar Communism'. See also Malcolm Mackintosh, 'Bulgaria at the End of the Second World War 1944–1945', in Gill Bennett (ed.), *The End of the War in Europe 1945* (London: HMSO, 1996), 221–30.

50. Judt, *Postwar*, 137.

51. Norman Naimark and Leonid Gibianskii, 'Introduction', in Naimark and Gibianskii (eds.), *The Establishment of Communist Regimes in Eastern Europe, 1944–1949* (Boulder, Colo.: Westview Press, 1997), 9.

52. Jan T. Gross, 'Themes for a Social History of War Experience and Collaboration', in Deák, Gross, and Judt (eds.), *The Politics of Retribution in Europe*, 23.

53. E. A. Rees, 'Leader Cults: Varieties, Preconditions and Functions', in Balász Apor, Jan C. Behrends, Polly Jones, and E. A. Rees (eds.), *The Leader Cult in Communist Dictatorships: Stalin and the Eastern Bloc* (Houndmills: Palgrave Macmillan, 2004), 18.

54. Mark Pittaway, 'The Politics of Legitimacy and Hungary's Postwar Transition', *Contemporary European History*, 13:4 (2004), 453–75; Ulf Brunnbauer, 'Making Bulgarians Socialist: The Fatherland Front in Communist Bulgaria, 1944–1989', *East European Politics and Societies*, 22:1 (2008), 44–79.

55. Norman Naimark, 'The Persistence of "the Postwar": Germany and Poland', in Frank Biess and Robert G. Moeller (eds.), *Histories of the Aftermath: The Legacies of the Second World War in Europe* (New York: Berghahn Books, 2010), 15.

56. Dinu C. Giurescu, *Romania's Communist Takeover: The Rădescu Government* (Boulder, Colo.: East European Monographs, 1994), 12–13; Tismaneanu, *Stalinism for All Seasons*, 87.

57. Communiqué of the National Peasant Party, 15 March 1945, in Giurescu, *Romania's Communist Takeover*, 194.

58. *Graiul Nou*, 3 March 1945, cited in Sergiu Verona, *Military Occupation and Diplomacy: Soviet Troops in Romania, 1944–1958* (Durham, NC: Duke University Press, 1992), 31.

59. Alfred J. Rieber, 'The Crack in the Plaster: Crisis in Romania and the Origins of the Cold War', *Journal of Modern History*, 76:1 (2004), 104.

60. Tismaneanu, *Stalinism for All Seasons*, 90.

61. Cited in Susanne zur Nieden, 'Antifaschismus und Kalter Krieg: Vom Hauptausschuß für die Opfer des Faschismus zur Vereinigung der Verfolgten des Naziregimes', in Günter Morsch (ed.), *Von der Erinnerung zum Monument: Die Entstehungsgeschichte der Nationalen Mahn- und Gedenkstätte Sachsenhausen* (Berlin: Edition Hentrich, 1996), 78.

62. Herf, *Divided Memory*, 81–3.

63. zur Nieden, 'Antifaschismus und Kalter Krieg', 85.

64. Annette Leo, 'Das kurze Leben der VVN', in Morsch (ed.), *Von der Erinnerung zum Monument*, 100.

65. Susanne zur Nieden, 'Das Museum des antifaschistischen Freiheitskampfes der europäischen Völker', in Morsch (ed.), *Von der Erinnerung zum Monument*, 255–63.

66. Cited in Mark Pittaway, *Eastern Europe, 1939–2000* (London: Arnold, 2004), 44.

67. Valentina Fava, 'Between American Fordism and "Soviet Fordism": Czechoslovak Way towards Mass Production', in Apor, Apor, and Rees (eds.), *The Sovietization of Eastern Europe*, 47–64. See also Mark Pittaway, 'The Social Limits of State Control: Time, the Industrial Wage Relation and Social Identity in Stalinist Hungary, 1948–1953', *Journal of Historical Sociology*, 12:3 (1999), 271–301.

68. Balázs Apor, 'Spatial Aspects of the Communist Leader Cult: The Case of Mátyás Rákosi in Hungary', in Apor, Apor, and Rees (eds.), *The Sovietization of Eastern Europe*, 149–69.

69. On Pătrăşcanu, see Tismaneanu, *Stalinism for All Seasons*, 110–20.

70. Hodos, cited in Vladimir Tismaneanu, 'Diabolical Pedagogy and the (Il) logic of Stalinism in Eastern Europe', in Tismaneanu (ed.), *Stalinism Revisited*, 38.

71. *Rudé Právo* and Gottwald, cited in Judt, *Postwar*, 186.

72. John Klier, 'The Holocaust and the Soviet Union', in Stone (ed.), *The Historiography of the Holocaust*, 288. For the *Pravda* article, see *CW*, 426–7.

73. Judt, *Postwar*, 188. On the Doctors' plot and postwar Stalinist antisemitism, see Joshua Rubenstein and Vladimir Pavlovich Naumov (eds.), *Stalin's Secret Pogrom: The Postwar Inquisition of the Jewish Anti-Fascist Committee* (New Haven: Yale University Press, 2001), and Jonathan Brent and Vladimir P. Naumov, *Stalin's Last Crime: The Doctors' Plot* (London: John Murray, 2003).

74. On the distinction, see the important study by Jan Pakulski, 'Legitimacy and Mass Compliance: Reflections on Max Weber and Soviet-Type Societies', *British Journal of Political Science*, 16:1 (1986), 35–56.

75. Agnes Heller, 'Legitimation Deficit and Legitimation Crisis in East European Societies', in Tismaneanu (ed.), *Stalinism Revisited*, 154.

76. Pittaway, 'Making Postwar Communism'.

CHAPTER 2

1. Victor Gollancz, *Shall Our Children Live or Die? A Reply to Lord Vansittart on the German Problem* (London: Victor Gollancz, 1942), 150–1; Leonard Woolf, 'Introduction', in *When Hostilities Cease: Papers on Relief and Reconstruction Prepared for the Fabian Society* (London: Victor Gollancz, 1943), 11.

2. Percy Knauth, *Germany in Defeat* (New York: Alfred A. Knopf, 1946), 32.

3. Cited in Hitchcock, *Liberation*, 299.

4. Brewster Chamberlin and Marcia Feldman (eds.), *The Liberation of the Nazi Concentration Camps 1945: Eyewitness Accounts of the Liberators* (Washington, DC: United States Holocaust Memorial Council, 1987), 149–50 (Van Velsen) and 151 (Meed).

5. Cited in Antero Holmila, *Reporting the Holocaust in the British, Swedish and Finnish Press, 1945–50* (Houndmills: Palgrave Macmillan, 2011), 34.

6. Kenneth G. Brooks, 'The Re-establishment of Displaced Peoples', in *When Hostilities Cease*, 99.

7. Judt, *Postwar*, 31.

8. Jacques Vernant, *The Refugee in the Post-War World* (London: George Allen & Unwin, 1953), 62–3.

9. Johannes-Dieter Steinert, 'British Post-War Migration Policy and Displaced Persons in Europe', in Jessica Reinisch and Elizabeth White (eds.), *The Disentanglement of Populations: Migration, Expulsion and Displacement in Post-War Europe, 1944–9* (Houndmills: Palgrave Macmillan, 2011), 233.

10. Mazower, *Dark Continent*, 218.

11. Judt, *Postwar*, 29. See also Jessica Reinisch, 'Internationalism in Relief: The Birth (and Death) of UNRRA', *Past and Present*, Supplement 6 (2011), 258–89.

12. Cited in Abraham Peck, 'Liberated But Not Free: Jewish Displaced Persons in Germany after 1945', in Walter H. Pehle (ed.), *November 1938: From 'Kristallnacht' to Genocide* (Oxford: Berg, 1991), 228.

13. Judt, *Postwar*, 32.

14. David Cesarani, 'The British Security Forces and the Jews in Palestine, 1945–48', in Claus-Christian W. Szejnmann (ed.), *Rethinking History, Dictatorship and War: New Approaches and Interpretations* (London: Continuum, 2009), 191–210; Tony Kushner, 'Anti-Semitism and Austerity: The August 1947 Riots in Britain', in Panikos Panayi (ed.), *Racial Violence in Britain in the Nineteenth and Twentieth Centuries*, 2nd edn. (London: Leicester University Press, 1996), 150–70.

15. See, for example, Avinoam J. Patt, 'Stateless Citizens of Israel: Jewish Displaced Persons and Zionism in Post-War Germany', in Reinisch and White (eds.), *The Disentanglement of Populations*, 162–82.

16. Francesca M. Wilson, *Aftermath: France, Germany, Austria, Yugoslavia, 1945 and 1946* (Harmondsworth: Penguin, 1947), 133. See also Tara Zahra, ' "A Human Treasure": Europe's Displaced Children Between Nationalism and Internationalism', *Past and Present*, Supplement 6 (2011), 332–50.

17. See Judith Tydor Baumel, 'Kibbutz Buchenwald and Kibbutz Hafetz Hayyim: Two Experiments in the Rehabilitation of Jewish Survivors in Germany', *Holocaust and Genocide Studies*, 9:2 (1995), 231–49; Baumel, *Kibbutz Buchenwald: Survivors and Pioneers* (New Brunswick, NJ: Rutgers University Press, 1997); Zeev W. Mankowitz, *Life Between Memory and Hope: The Survivors of the Holocaust in Occupied Germany* (Cambridge: Cambridge University Press, 2002).

18. See Atina Grossmann, 'Victims, Villains, and Survivors: Gendered Perceptions and Self-Perceptions of Jewish Displaced Persons in Occupied Postwar Germany', in Dagmar Herzog (ed.), *Sexuality and German Fascism* (New York: Berghahn Books, 2005), 298–9.

19. See Alice Weinreb, ' "For the Hungry Have No Past nor Do They Belong to a Political Party": Debates over German Hunger after World War II', *Central European History*, 45:1 (2012), 50–78.

20. Justice Jackson's opening statement for the prosecution, 21 November 1945, in *The Trial of German Major War Criminals: Proceedings of the International Military Tribunal Sitting at Nuremberg, Germany. Part I: 20th November, 1945 to 1st December, 1945* (London: His Majesty's Stationery Office, 1946), 86.

21. Hannah Arendt to Karl Jaspers, 17 August 1946, in Lotte Kohler and Hans Saner (eds.), *Hannah Arendt/Karl Jaspers Correspondence 1926–1969* (San Diego: Harcourt Brace & Company, 1992), 54,

22. On popular support for Nazism, see Peter Fritzsche, *Life and Death in the Third Reich* (Cambridge, Mass.: The Belknap Press of Harvard University Press, 2008).

23. Donald Bloxham, *Genocide on Trial: War Crimes Trials and the Formation of Holocaust History and Memory* (Oxford: Oxford University Press, 2001), 162–72.

24. Paul Herzog, 'Cholm: Heaps of Skulls', *Partisan Review*, 13 (1946), 534.

25. See, for example, Hilary Earl, *The Nuremberg SS-Einsatzgruppen Trial, 1945–1958* (New York: Cambridge University Press, 2009); Kevin Jon Heller, *The Nuremberg Military Tribunals and the Origins of International Criminal Law* (Oxford: Oxford University Press, 2011); David Bankier and Dan Michman (eds.), *Holocaust and Justice: Representation and Historiography of the Holocaust in Post-War Trials* (New York: Berghahn Books, 2010). Kim C. Priemel and Alexa Stiller (eds.), *Reassessing the Nuremberg Military Tribunals: Transitional Justice, Trial Narratives, and Historiography* (New York: Berghahn Books, 2012).

26. See, for example, Tom Lawson, 'The Church of England and the German Past, Present and Future 1944–5: A Case Study in the International Search for a "Usable Past"', in Riera and Schaffer (eds.), *The Lasting War*, 188–206; John Kent, 'British Postwar Planning for Europe 1942–45' and Georges-Henri Soutou, 'De Gaulle's Plans for Postwar Europe', both in Varsori and Calandri (eds.), *The Failure of Peace in Europe*, 40–8 and 49–58; and for an American example: Marjorie Lamberti, 'German Antifascist Refugees in America and the Public Debate on "What Should be Done with Germany after Hitler," 1941–1945', *Central European History*, 40 (2007), 279–305.

27. Victor Gollancz, *Our Threatened Values* (London: Victor Gollancz, 1946), 114. For early Gollancz publications, see *The Brown Book of the Hitler Terror* (1933); *The Yellow Spot* (1934).

28. Gollancz, *Shall Our Children Live or Die?*, 124. Gollancz, *What Buchenwald Really Means* (London: Victor Gollancz, 1945). See also Aaron Goldman, 'Germans and Nazis: The Controversy over "Vansittartism" in Britain during the Second World War', *Journal of Contemporary History*, 14:1 (1979), 155–91; Matthew Frank, 'The New Morality—Victor Gollancz, "Save Europe Now" and the German Refugee Crisis, 1945–46', *Twentieth-Century British History*, 17:2 (2006), 230–56.

29. Heinrich Bodensieck, '*Welt im Film*: Origins and Message', in K. R. M. Short and Stephan Dolezel (eds.), *Hitler's Fall: The Newsreel Witnesses* (London: Croom Helm, 1988), 147 n. 77.

30. John Herz, 'The Fiasco of Denazification in Germany', *Political Science Quarterly*, 63 (1948), 569.

31. Herz, 'The Fiasco of Denazification in Germany', 590, 591.

32. Karl Jaspers, *The Future of Germany* (Chicago: University of Chicago Press, 1967), 67.

33. Stig Dagerman, *German Autumn*, trans. Robin Fulton (London: Quartet Books, 1988 [orig. 1947]), 24–5. On the question of whether the 'antifas' really had the potential to govern in 1945, see Gareth Pritchard, 'Schwarzenberg 1945: Antifascists and the "Third Way" in German Politics', *European History Quarterly*, 35:4 (2005), 499–522.

34. Dagerman, *German Autumn*, 57.
35. Rainer Schulze, 'Forced Migration of German Populations During and After the Second World War: History and Memory', in Reinisch and White (eds.), *The Disentanglement of Populations*, 57.
36. On revenge, see Keith Lowe, *Savage Continent: Europe in the Aftermath of World War II* (London: Penguin, 2012), part II.
37. Martin Conway, 'Legacies of Exile: The Exile Governments in London during the Second World War and the Politics of Post-War Europe', in Martin Conway and José Gotovitch (eds.), *Europe in Exile: European Exile Communities in Britain 1940–45* (New York: Berghahn Books, 2001), 256. The following paragraphs are indebted to Conway's chapter.
38. Wilfried Loth, 'Socialist Parties between East and West', in Varsori and Calandri (eds.), *The Failure of Peace in Europe*, 138–48.
39. Robert Ventresca, 'The Virgin and the Bear: Religion, Society and the Cold War in Italy', *Journal of Social History*, 37:2 (2003), 444, 441. In general, see Monique Scheer, 'Catholic Piety in the Early Cold War Years, Or How the Virgin Mary Protected the West from Communism', in Annette Vowinckel, Marcus M. Payk, and Thomas Lindenberger (eds.), *Cold War Cultures: Perspectives on Eastern and Western European Societies* (New York: Berghahn Books, 2012), 130–51.
40. Monica Black, 'Miracles in the Shadow of the Economic Miracle: The "Supernatural '50s" in West Germany', *Journal of Modern History*, 84:4 (2012), 834, 834 n. 2.
41. M. Jane Slaughter, ' "What's New" and Is It Good For You? Gender and Consumerism in Postwar Europe', in Joanna Regulska and Bonnie G. Smith (eds.), *Women and Gender in Postwar Europe: From Cold War to European Union* (London: Routledge, 2012), 116.
42. David Gilgen, 'Socialism and Democracy: The Debate about a New Social and Economic Order in West Germany after the Second World War', in Dominik Geppert (ed.), *The Postwar Challenge: Cultural, Social, and Political Change in Western Europe, 1945–58* (Oxford: Oxford University Press, 2003), 101–28.
43. Geir Lundestad, 'Empire by Invitation? The United States and Western Europe, 1945–1952', *Journal of Peace Research*, 23:3 (1986), 263–77.
44. Perry Anderson, *The New Old World* (London: Verso, 2009), 484. For the text of the Ventotene Manifesto, see Mette Eilstrup-Sangiovanni (ed.), *Debates on European Integration: A Reader* (Basingstoke: Palgrave Macmillan, 2006), 37–42; and, for discussion, see Matthew D'Auria, 'The Ventotene Manifesto: The Crisis of the Nation State and the Political Identity of Europe', in Menno Spiering and Michael Wintle (eds.), *European Identity and the Second World War* (Basingstoke: Palgrave Macmillan, 2011), 141–58.
45. Pieter Lagrou, 'Victims of Genocide and National Memory: Belgium, France and The Netherlands 1945–1965', *Past and Present*, 154 (1997), 195. This paragraph is greatly indebted to Lagrou's article and to his book *The Legacy of Nazi*

NOTES TO PAGES 61–66

Occupation: Patriotic Memory and National Recovery in Western Europe, 1945–1965 (Cambridge: Cambridge University Press, 2000).

46. Lagrou, 'Victims of Genocide and National Memory', 208. Quotation from H. W. Sandberg, secretary of the Advisory Committee of the Dutch Underground Movement.

47. Nils Arne Sørensen, 'Narrating the Second World War in Denmark since 1945', *Contemporary European History*, 14:3 (2005), 295–315.

48. Lagrou, 'Victims of Genocide and National Memory', 215. But note Lagrou's further point (*Legacy of Nazi Occupation*) that: 'There may have been an ideological hegemony assimilating various experiences to some holistic martyrdom, but this was at the same time what many of the Jewish victims who actively adhered to the anti-fascist paradigm needed at the moment. Anti-fascism as a "universalizing" device offered a generous and heroic interpretation.'

49. Luciano Segreto, 'The Importance of the Foreign Constraint: Debates about a New Social and Economic Order in Italy, 1945–1955', in Geppert (ed.), *The Postwar Challenge*, 129–50.

50. Gilgen, 'Socialism and Democracy', 106–7.

51. Cited in Jeffrey Herf, 'Multiple Restorations: German Political Traditions and the Interpretation of Nazism', *Central European History*, 26:1 (1993), 29. It should be noted here that Schumacher often criticized Adenauer and the CDU for failing to mention the extermination of the Jews and that he was one of the main driving forces behind Germany's agreement to pay compensation to the state of Israel.

52. Helen Graham and Alejandro Quiroga, 'After the Fear was Over? What Came after Dictatorships in Spain, Greece and Portugal', in *OHPEH*, 505.

53. Graham and Quiroga, 'After the Fear was Over?', 507.

54. Helen Graham, *The War and its Shadow: Spain's Civil War in Europe's Long Twentieth Century* (Brighton: Sussex Academic Press, 2012).

55. Paul Preston, *The Spanish Holocaust: Inquisition and Extermination in Twentieth-Century Spain* (London: HarperPress, 2012).

56. Cited in Juan Carlos Pereira, 'Spain's Changing Role in International Relations in the 1950s', in Antonio Varsori (ed.), *Europe 1945–1990s: The End of an Era?* (New York: St Martin's Press, 1995), 269.

57. Cited in Barbara Marshall, 'British Democratization Policy in Germany', in Ian D. Turner (ed.), *Reconstruction in Post-War Germany: British Occupation Policy and the Western Zones, 1945–1955* (Oxford: Berg, 1989), 212.

58. Frank Biess, 'Survivors of Totalitarianism: Returning POWS and the Reconstruction of Masculine Citizenship in West Germany, 1945–1955', and Robert G. Moeller, 'Remembering the War in a Nation of Victims: West German Pasts in the 1950s', both in Hanna Schissler (ed.), *The Miracle Years: A Cultural History of West Germany, 1949–1968* (Princeton: Princeton University Press, 2001), 57–82 and 83–109.

59. See especially Melvyn P. Leffler, 'The Cold War: What do "We Now Know"?', *American Historical Review*, 104:2 (1999), 501–24.

60. See Geoff Eley's comments along these lines in 'A Disorder of Peoples: The Uncertain Ground of Reconstruction in 1945', in Reinisch and White (eds.), *The Disentanglement of Populations*, 291–314; 'Corporatism and the Social Democratic Moment: The Postwar Settlement, 1945–1973', in *OHPEH*, 37–59.

61. See especially John Lewis Gaddis, *We Now Know: Rethinking Cold War History* (New York: Oxford University Press, 1997).

62. Geir Lundestad, 'The European Role at the Beginning and Particularly the End of the Cold War', in Olav Njølstad (ed.), *The Last Decade of the Cold War: From Conflict Escalation to Conflict Transformation* (London: Frank Cass, 2004), 63. For an illustration of the argument, see Fraser J. Harbutt, *Yalta 1945: Europe and America at the Crossroads* (Cambridge: Cambridge University Press, 2010).

63. David Reynolds, 'From World War to Cold War: The Wartime Alliance and Post-War Transitions, 1941–1947', *Historical Journal*, 45:1 (2002), 219.

64. Cited in Bruno Arcidiacono, 'Between War and Peace: The Western Perception of Soviet East European Policy', in Varsori (ed.), *Europe 1945–1990s*, 49.

65. Marc Trachtenberg, 'The United States and Eastern Europe in 1945: A Reassessment', *Journal of Cold War Studies*, 10:4 (2008), 94–132.

66. Annie Guénard, 'The Cultural Policy of France in Eastern Europe', in Varsori and Calandri (eds.), *The Failure of Peace in Europe*, 229–37.

67. Harry S. Truman, *Years of Trial and Hope, 1946–1953* (London: Hodder & Stoughton, 1956), 111.

68. The literature on which is vast. See, for useful introductions: Greg Behrman, *The Most Noble Adventure: The Marshall Plan and the Reconstruction of Post-War Europe* (London: Aurum, 2008), which stresses the importance of the money and the programme's success; Michael J. Hogan, *The Marshall Plan: America, Britain, and the Reconstruction of Western Europe, 1947–1952* (Cambridge: Cambridge University Press, 1989); Martin Schain (ed.), *The Marshall Plan: Fifty Years After* (New York: Palgrave, 2001).

69. Gordon Connell-Smith, *Pattern of the Post-War World* (Harmondsworth: Penguin, 1957), 69.

70. Vyshinsky, 'Speech to the United Nations General Assembly, September 1947', in *CW*, 128.

71. Catherine R. Schenk, *International Economic Relations since 1945* (London: Routledge, 2011), 26–31. GATT was only replaced by the World Trade Organization in 1995.

72. As Alan Milward famously argues in *The Reconstruction of Western Europe 1945–51*, 2nd edn. (London: Routledge, 1987).

73. Vera Zamagni, 'The Marshall Plan: An Overview of its Impact on National Economies', in Varsori (ed.), *Europe 1945–1990s*, 83–9.

74. Barry Eichengreen, *The European Economy since 1945: Coordinated Capitalism and Beyond* (Princeton: Princeton University Press, 2007), 65. See also J. Bradford De Long and Barry Eichengreen, 'The Marshall Plan: History's Most Successful

Structural Adjustment Program' (1991), online at: <http://www.j-bradford-delong.net/pdf_files/marshall_large.pdf>.

75. Eichengreen, *The European Economy since 1945*, 68.

76. Bevin, letter to Attlee, July 1948, in *CW*, 95.

77. See, for example, Carolyn Woods Eisenberg, *Drawing the Line: The American Decision to Divide Germany, 1944–1949* (New York: Cambridge University Press, 1996), which argues that the US was much more active than the USSR in making the decisions which led to Germany's division, because it was desperate to ensure that Germany's economic potential would remain at the disposal of the West.

78. Charles S. Maier, 'The Presence of the Superpowers in Europe (1947–54): An Overview', in Varsori (ed.), *Europe 1945–1990s*, 152. See also Wolfgang Krieger's comments in 'Germany', in David Reynolds (ed.), *The Origins of the Cold War in Europe: International Perspectives* (New Haven: Yale University Press, 1994), 144–65.

79. Kennan memorandum (8 March 1949), cited in Ludolf Herbst, 'Deutschland und Europa aus amerikanischer Sicht. Ein geheimes Grundsatzpapier der US-State Department aus dem Jahr 1949', in Rüdiger Hohls, Iris Schröder, and Hannes Siegrist (eds.), *Europa und die Europäer: Quellen und Essays zur modernen europäischer Geschichte* (Wiesbaden: Franz Steiner Verlag, 2005), 438.

80. 'The Economic Interdependence of Germany and Western Europe. Means for Achieving Closer Economic Association', undated 'top secret' paper from US State Department (March 1949), in Hohls, Schröder, and Siegrist (eds.), *Europa und die Europäer*, 440–1, here 440.

81. Maier, 'The Presence of the Superpowers in Europe', 147.

82. David W. Ellwood, 'The Propaganda of the Marshall Plan in Italy in a Cold War Context', in Giles Scott-Smith and Hans Krabbendam (eds.), *The Cultural Cold War in Western Europe, 1945–1960* (London: Routledge, 2003), 225–36.

83. Cited in Segreto, 'The Importance of the Foreign Constraint', 145.

84. Maier, 'The Presence of the Superpowers in Europe', 148.

85. Martina Kessel, 'The Art of Failure: British and French Policies towards Germany and the Council of Foreign Ministers, 1947', in Varsori and Calandri (eds.), *The Failure of Peace in Europe*, 255; Frédéric Bozo, 'France, "Gaullism", and the Cold War', in *CHCW*, ii. 162.

86. Scott Parrish, 'The Marshall Plan, Soviet–American Relations, and the Division of Europe', in Naimark and Gibianskii (eds.), *The Establishment of Communist Regimes*, 267–90, argues that the Marshall Plan was decisive in this regard. I would suggest, instead, that it catalysed a process already under way. See, for a more balanced account, Mikhail M. Narinskii, 'The Soviet Union and the Marshall Plan', in Varsori and Calandri (eds.), *The Failure of Peace in Europe*, 275–87. As Eichengreen argues ('The Market and the Marshall Plan', in Schain (ed.), *The Marshall Plan: Fifty Years After*, 136), the Marshall Plan could encourage European integration 'only because the appropriate predispositions were in place'.

87. Movimento Federalista Europeo, 28 August 1943, cited in Lipgens, 'European Federation in the Political Thought of Resistance Movements', 13.

88. John Pinder, *The Building of the European Union*, 3rd edn. (Oxford: Oxford University Press, 1998), 3.

89. Lipgens, 'European Federation in the Political Thought of Resistance Movements', 16.

90. Adenauer, cited in Bernard Wasserstein, *Barbarism and Civilization: A History of Europe in our Time* (Oxford: Oxford University Press, 2007), 454.

91. Robert Latham, 'Cooperation and Community in Europe: What the Marshall Plan Proposed, NATO Disposed', in Schain (ed.), *The Marshall Plan: Fifty Years After*, 61–90.

92. Antonio Varsori, 'Reflections on the Origins of the Cold War', in Westad (ed.), *Reviewing the Cold War*, 289. For a classic statement condemning the confusion of postwar Stalinism with Hitlerism, see 'X' [George Kennan], 'The Sources of Soviet Conduct', *Foreign Affairs*, 25:4 (1947), 566–82.

93. Primo Levi, *If This Is a Man/The Truce*, trans. Stuart Woolf (London: Abacus, 1987), 381.

94. Fernando Claudín, 'Stalin and the Second World War', in Tariq Ali (ed.), *The Stalinist Legacy: Its Impact on 20th-Century World Politics* (Harmondsworth: Penguin, 1984), 197. On the Soviet Union's enormous contribution to the war, and the tremendous cost of that contribution in human lives, see Richard Overy, *Russia's War* (London: Penguin, 1999).

95. Elena Zubkova, *Russia after the War: Hopes, Illusions, and Disappointments, 1945–1957*, trans. Hugh Ragsdale (Armonk, NY: M. E. Sharpe, 1998), 12.

96. Vojtech Mastny, *The Cold War and Soviet Insecurity: The Stalin Years* (New York: Oxford University Press, 1996), 23–9. See also Vladislav Zubok and Constantine Pleshakov, *Inside the Kremlin's Cold War: From Stalin to Khrushchev* (Cambridge, Mass.: Harvard University Press, 1996), for the importance of Stalin's ideology, by which they mean less the spreading of world revolution than the defence of Soviet security (as perceived by Stalin, of course).

CHAPTER 3

1. Willy Brandt, 'The East–West Problem as Seen from Berlin', *International Affairs*, 34:3 (1958), 302; John F. Kennedy, Address to UN General Assembly, 25 September 1961, online at: <http://www.jfklibrary.org/Asset-Viewer/DOPIN64xJUGRKgdHJ9NfgQ.aspx>.

2. The costs of that euphemistically named process of 'restructuring' in terms of joblessness and social and cultural change will be discussed in Chapter 5.

3. Eley, 'Corporatism and the Social Democratic Moment', 38.

4. Eley, 'Corporatism and the Social Democratic Moment', 43.

5. Theodor W. Adorno, 'The Meaning of Working Through the Past', in *Critical Models: Interventions and Catchwords* (New York: Columbia University Press,

1998), 90. For a powerful depiction of the political culture of Bonn, West Germany's unlikely capital city, see Wolfgang Koeppen's 1953 novel, *The Hothouse* (London: Granta Books, 2002).

6. Erika Weinzierl, 'The Origins of the Second Republic: A Retrospective View', in Kurt Richard Luther and Peter Pulzer (eds.), *Austria 1945–95: Fifty Years of the Second Republic* (Aldershot: Ashgate, 1998), 3–27; Andrew E. Harrod, 'Austrian Neutrality: The Early Years, 1955–1958', *Austrian History Yearbook*, 41 (2010), 216–46; Heidemarie Uhl, 'Of Heroes and Victims: World War II in Austrian Memory', *Austrian History Yearbook*, 42 (2011), 185–200.

7. Daniel E. Rogers, 'Restoring a German Career, 1945–1950: The Ambiguity of Being Hans Globke', *German Studies Review*, 31:2 (2008), 303–24, here esp. 317.

8. Susanna Schrafstetter, 'The Diplomacy of *Wiedergutmachung*: Memory, the Cold War, and the Western European Victims of Nazism, 1956–1964', *Holocaust and Genocide Studies*, 17:3 (2003), 464–5, 472 (Erhard).

9. Percy Allum, 'The Changing Face of Christian Democracy', in Christopher Duggan and Christopher Wagstaff (eds.), *Italy in the Cold War: Politics, Culture and Society 1948–58* (Oxford: Berg, 1995), 117 (Gorresio), 125 ('syndicate'—from sociologist Alessandro Pizzorno), and 125 n. 15 ('swindle law'). See also Rosario Forlenza, 'A Party for the Mezzogiorno: The Christian Democratic Party, Agrarian Reform and the Government of Italy', *Contemporary European History*, 19:4 (2010), 331–49.

10. Martin Conway, 'Democracy in Postwar Western Europe: The Triumph of a Political Model', *European History Quarterly*, 32:1 (2002), 59–84; Martin Conway, 'The Rise and Fall of Western Europe's Democratic Age, 1945–1973', *Contemporary European History*, 13:1 (2004), 67–88; Martin Conway and Volker Depkat, 'Towards a European History of the Discourse of Democracy: Discussing Democracy in Western Europe, 1945–60', in Martin Conway and Kiran Klaus Patel (eds.), *Europeanization in the Twentieth Century: Historical Approaches* (Basingstoke: Palgrave Macmillan, 2010), 132–56; Paolo Pombeni, 'The Ideology of Christian Democracy', *Journal of Political Ideologies*, 5:3 (2000), 289–300.

11. Cited in Donald Sassoon, 'The Rise and Fall of West European Communism 1939–48', *Contemporary European History*, 1:2 (1992), 161.

12. Jan-Werner Müller, 'What Did They Think They Were Doing? The Political Thought of the (West European) 1968 Revisited', in Vladimir Tismaneanu (ed.), *Promises of 1968: Crisis, Illusion, and Utopia* (Budapest: Central European University Press, 2011), 82.

13. Churchill, speech at University of Zurich, 19 September 1946, in A. G. Harryvan and J. van der Harst (eds.), *Documents on European Union* (Houndmills: Macmillan, 1996), 38–41, here 41.

14. Eichengreen, *The European Economy since 1945*, 195.

15. Jan-Werner Müller, 'On "European Memory": Some Conceptual and Normative Remarks', in Małgorzata Pakier and Bo Stråth (eds.), *A European Memory?*

Contested Histories and Politics of Remembrance (New York: Berghahn Books, 2010), 25–37, here 30.

16. On the birth of the CAP, see N. Piers Ludlow, 'The Making of the CAP: Towards a Historical Analysis of the EU's First Major Policy', *Contemporary European History*, 14:3 (2005), 347–71.

17. François Duchêne, 'French Motives for European Integration', in Robert Bideleux and Richard Taylor (eds.), *European Integration and Disintegration: East and West* (London: Routledge, 1996), 23.

18. Duchêne, 'French Motives for European Integration', 25.

19. Martin J. Dedman, *The Origins and Development of the European Union 1945–95: A History of European Integration* (London: Routledge, 1996), 64.

20. Anderson, *The New Old World*.

21. Wolfram Kaiser, *Christian Democracy and the Origins of the European Union* (Cambridge: Cambridge University Press, 2007). Kaiser argues that 'the ECSC resulted from a transnational political struggle in which the continental European Christian Democrats succeeded in imposing their core ideas sufficiently adjusted to garner enough domestic and transnational support for it' (252).

22. Egon Bahr, 'Europa 1945 und heute', in Joachim Lund and Per Øhrgaard (eds.), *Return to Normalcy or a New Beginning: Concepts and Expectations for a Postwar Europe around 1945* (Copenhagen: University Press of Southern Denmark/ Copenhagen Business School Press, 2008), 11.

23. But see Jean Leca, ' "The Empire Strikes Back!" An Uncanny View of the European Union. Part I—Do We Need a Theory of the European Union?', *Government and Opposition*, 44:3 (2009), 285–340, for a sophisticated analysis, which shows that the dichotomy between federalism and a Europe of nation-states is no longer satisfactory for understanding the way the EU works.

24. Although I wrote of the integrating effects of the ERP in Chapter 2, this was far from the unified response that the Americans wished for; rather, it established buoyant bilateral relationships between the US and each of the European recipients of Marshall Aid, although the common experience of those recipients was itself conducive to further moves towards integration.

25. Piers Ludlow, 'Introduction', in N. Piers Ludlow (ed.), *European Integration and the Cold War: Ostpolitik–Westpolitik, 1965–1973* (London: Routledge, 2007), 1–10. I am greatly indebted to Ludlow's contributions to his innovative edited volume in this paragraph and the next.

26. See also Wilfried Loth, 'The "Empty Chair" Crisis', in Michel Dumoulin (ed.), *The European Commission, 1958–72: History and Memories* (Luxembourg: Office for Official Publications of the European Communities, 2007), 91–108 and, in greater detail, N. Piers Ludlow, *The European Community and the Crisis of the 1960s: Negotiating the Gaullist Challenge* (London: Routledge, 2006).

27. De Gaulle, cited in Wilfried Loth, 'Walter Hallstein, a Committed European', in Dumoulin (ed.), *European Commission*, 85.

28. Piers Ludlow, 'An Insulated Community? The Community Institutions and the Cold War, 1965 to 1970', in Ludlow (ed.), *European Integration and the Cold War*, 144.

29. Ludlow, 'An Insulated Community?', 137–51. Also Vladislav Zubok, 'The Soviet Union and European Integration from Stalin to Gorbachev', *Journal of European Integration History*, 2:1 (1996), 85–98; Klaus Schwabe, 'The Cold War and European Integration, 1947–63', *Diplomacy and Statecraft*, 12:4 (2001), 18–34.

30. David Edgerton, *Warfare State: Britain, 1920–1970* (Cambridge: Cambridge University Press, 2006), esp. ch. 7.

31. Martin Shaw, 'The Rise and Fall of the Military-Democratic State', in Colin Creighton and Martin Shaw (eds.), *The Sociology of War and Peace* (London: Macmillan, 1987), 143–58, cited in Edgerton, *Warfare State*, 292.

32. David Holloway, 'Nuclear Weapons and the Escalation of the Cold War, 1945–1962', in *CHCW*, i. 376–97.

33. 'Exterminism' is a reference to E. P. Thompson's classic essay 'Notes on Exterminism, the Last Stage of Civilization', in New Left Review (ed.), *Exterminism and Cold War* (London: Verso, 1982), 1–33.

34. Karl Jaspers, *The Future of Mankind*, trans. E. B. Ashton (Chicago: University of Chicago Press, 1961 [orig. 1958]), vii.

35. For further details of the Berlin Crisis, see Chapter 4.

36. See Sagi Schaefer, 'Hidden Behind the Wall: West German State Building and the Emergence of the Iron Curtain', *Central European History*, 44:4 (2011), 506–35.

37. Douglas Selvage, 'The Treaty of Warsaw: The Warsaw Pact Context', in David C. Geyer and Bernd Schaefer (eds.), *American Détente and German Ostpolitik, 1969–1972, Bulletin of the German Historical Institute*, Supplement 1 (2003), 67–79. See also, in the same volume, Mary Elise Sarotte, '"Take No Risks (Chinese)": The Basic Treaty in the Context of International Relations', 109–17.

38. For the texts of the Berlin and Basic Treaties, see Konrad Jarausch and Volker Gransow (eds.), *Uniting Germany: Documents and Debates, 1944–1993* (Oxford: Berghahn Books, 1994), 20–3.

39. Gottfried Niedhart, 'Ostpolitik: Phases, Short-Term Objectives, and Grand Design', in Geyer and Schaefer (eds.), *American Détente and German Ostpolitik, 1969–1972*, 120–1.

40. Heath, cited in Niedhart, 'Ostpolitik', 131.

41. Jeremi Suri, '*Ostpolitik* as Domestic Containment: The Cultural Contradictions of the Cold War and the West German State Response', in Belinda Davis, Wilfried Mausbach, Martin Klimke, and Carla MacDougall (eds.), *Changing the World, Changing Oneself: Political Protest and Collective Identities in West Germany and the U.S. in the 1960s and 1970s* (New York: Berghahn Books, 2010), 147.

42. Rush, cited in Niedhart, 'Ostpolitik', 124. In general, on the significance of Germany's change of attitudes towards Eastern Europe as a facilitator of peace in Europe, see Jonathan Rynhold, 'The German Question in Central and Eastern

Europe and the Long Peace in Europe after 1945: An Integrated Theoretical Explanation', *Review of International Studies*, 37:1 (2010), 249–75.

43. Odd Arne Westad, 'Beginnings of the End: How the Cold War Crumbled', in Silvio Pons and Federico Romero (eds.), *Reinterpreting the End of the Cold War: Issues, Interpretations, Periodizations* (London: Frank Cass, 2005), 69.

44. Anders Stephanson, 'The United States', in Reynolds (ed.), *The Origins of the Cold War in Europe*, 25. Also Marc Trachtenberg, *A Constructed Peace: The Making of the European Settlement, 1945–1963* (Princeton: Princeton University Press, 1999), ch. 9. Trachtenberg's argument (352) is that as of 1963 the Cold War's 'focus moved away from Europe and toward areas of secondary or even tertiary importance; the basic interests of each side were no longer seriously threatened; the conflict lost its apocalyptic edge'.

45. Judt, *Postwar*, 501.

46. Daniel C. Thomas, *The Helsinki Effect: International Norms, Human Rights, and the Demise of Communism* (Princeton: Princeton University Press, 2001), 62.

47. Judt, *Postwar*, 502. For the text of the Helsinki Final Act, see: <http://www.osce.org/mc/39501?download=true>.

48. Judt, *Postwar*, 503.

49. Andreas Wenger and Vojtech Mastny, 'New Perspectives on the Origins of the CSCE Process', in Andreas Wenger, Vojtech Mastny, and Christian Nuenlist (eds.), *Origins of the European Security System: The Helsinki Process Revisited, 1965–75* (London: Routledge, 2008), 18.

50. Iurii Andropov, Report to the Central Committee, 15 November 1976, in *CW*, 532.

51. Sarah Snyder, 'The Foundation for Vienna: A Reassessment of the CSCE in the Mid-1980s', *Cold War History*, 10:4 (2010), 493–512; Daniel C. Thomas, 'Human Rights Ideas, the Demise of Communism, and the End of the Cold War', *Journal of Cold War Studies*, 7:2 (2005), 117–18; also Wenger, Mastny, and Nuenlist (eds.), *Origins of the European Security System*; Leopoldo Nuti (ed.), *The Crisis of Détente in Europe: From Helsinki to Gorbachev, 1975–85* (London: Routledge, 2008); Oliver Bange and Gottfried Niedhart (eds.), *Helsinki 1975 and the Transformation of Europe* (New York: Berghahn Books, 2008). See Chapter 6.

52. Thomas, *The Helsinki Effect*.

53. Tony Shaw, 'The Politics of Cold War Culture', *Journal of Cold War Studies*, 3:3 (2001), 59. An important study offering proof of Shaw's claims is David Caute, *The Dancer Defects: The Struggle for Cultural Supremacy during the Cold War* (Oxford: Oxford University Press, 2003).

54. Peter Coleman, *The Liberal Conspiracy: The Congress for Cultural Freedom and the Struggle for the Mind of Post-War Europe* (New York: Free Press, 1989); Giles Scott-Smith, 'The Congress for Cultural Freedom, the End of Ideology and the 1955 Milan Conference: "Defining the Parameters of Discourse"', *Journal of Contemporary History*, 37:3 (2002), 437–55; Scott-Smith, *The Politics of Apolitical Culture: The Congress for Cultural Freedom, the CIA, and Post-War American*

Hegemony (London: Routledge, 2002); Michael Hochgeschwender, 'A Battle of Ideas: The Congress for Cultural Freedom (CCF) in Britain, Italy, France, and West Germany', in Geppert (ed.), *The Postwar Challenge*, 319–38.

55. Hochgeschwender, 'A Battle of Ideas', 323.

56. Richard Crossman (ed.), *The God That Failed: Six Studies in Communism* (London: Hamish Hamilton, 1950).

57. Caute, *The Dancer Defects*, 612.

58. On Americanization as a concept, see Philipp Gassert, 'The Spectre of Americanization: Western Europe in the American Century', in *OHPEH*, 182–200; Alexander Stephan (ed.), *The Americanization of Europe: Culture, Diplomacy, and Anti-Americanism after 1945* (New York: Berghahn, 2006); Jessica C. E. Gienow-Hecht (ed.), *Decentering America* (New York: Berghahn, 2007); Dan Diner, *America in the Eyes of the Germans: An Essay on Anti-Americanism* (Princeton: Markus Wiener, 1996).

59. Cited in Leopoldo Nuti, 'A Continent Bristling with Arms? Continuity and Change in Western European Security Policies after the Second World War', in *OHPEH*, 352.

60. Martin Evans, 'Colonial Fantasies Shattered', in *OHPEH*, 490. This section owes a good deal to Evans's chapter.

61. See, for example, Benjamin Grob-Fitzgibbon, *Imperial Endgame: Britain's Dirty Wars and the End of Empire* (Basingstoke: Palgrave Macmillan, 2011). For a comparative approach, see Robert Holland (ed.), *Emergencies and Disorder in the European Empires after 1945* (London: Routledge, 1994); Martin Shipway, *Decolonization and its Impact: A Comparative Approach to the End of the Colonial Empires* (London: Wiley-Blackwell, 2008).

62. Jennifer L. Foray, *Visions of Empire in the Nazi-Occupied Netherlands* (New York: Cambridge University Press, 2012).

63. Richard Wright, *The Color Curtain* (1956). For President Sukarno's welcoming speech, see *CW*, 349–51.

64. Martin Thomas, 'French Decolonization', in Martin Thomas, Bob Moore, and L. J. Butler, *Crises of Empire: Decolonization and Europe's Imperial States, 1918–1975* (London: Bloomsbury Academic, 2008), 230–1.

65. See Matthew Connelly, *A Diplomatic Revolution: Algeria's Fight for Independence and the Origins of the Post-Cold War Era* (New York: Oxford University Press, 2002).

66. William B. Cohen, 'The Sudden Memory of Torture: The Algerian War in French Discourse, 2000–2001', *French Politics, Culture and Society*, 19:3 (2001), 82–3. Oradour refers to the village famously razed by German occupation forces in response to partisan attacks; see Sarah Farmer, *Martyred Village: Commemorating the 1944 Massacre at Oradour-sur-Glane* (Berkeley and Los Angeles: University of California Press, 1999).

67. Cohen, 'The Sudden Memory of Torture'.

68. Jean-Paul Sartre, 'Preface: A Victory', in Henri Alleg, *The Question*, trans. John Calder (Lincoln, Nebr.: University of Nebraska Press, 2006), xliv [orig. French edn. 1958].

69. William B. Cohen, 'The Algerian War and French Memory', *Contemporary European History*, 9:3 (2000), 494.

70. James D. Le Sueur calls de Gaulle's takeover a 'military coup d'état' in his introduction to Alleg's *The Question*, xiv. For an example of one of the generals' justification of torture—which he could publish because of de Gaulle's amnesty laws of the 1960s—see Paul Aussaresses, *The Battle of the Casbah: Terrorism and Counter-Terrorism in Algeria, 1955–1957* (New York: Enigma Books, 2001). Aussaresses was prosecuted in January 2002, not for admitting to kidnap, torture, and murder, but for publishing his story and for 'justifying war crimes', for which he was fined 7,500 euros.

71. Jim House and Neil MacMaster, *Paris 1961: Algerians, State Terror, and Memory* (Oxford: Oxford University Press, 2006).

72. For a narrative account, see Jean-Pierre Rioux, *The Fourth Republic 1944–1958* (Cambridge: Cambridge University Press, 1987), ch. 15. In general, see Martin Evans, *Algeria: France's Undeclared War* (Oxford: Oxford University Press, 2011).

73. On the *harkis*, see Martin Evans, 'The *Harkis*: The Experience and Memory of France's Muslim Auxiliaries', in Martin S. Alexander, Martin Evans, and J. F. V. Keiger (eds.), *The Algerian War and the French Army, 1954–62* (Basingstoke: Palgrave Macmillan, 2002), 117–33. And on the *pieds noirs* exodus, see Todd Shepard, *The Invention of Decolonization: The Algerian War and the Remaking of France* (Ithaca, NY: Cornell University Press, 2006), ch. 8.

74. Frantz Fanon, *The Wretched of the Earth*, trans. Constance Farrington (London: Penguin, 1990 [1961]), 33–4.

75. Stephen Tyre, 'From *Algérie Française* to *France Musulmane*: Jacques Soustelle and the Myths and Realities of "Integration", 1955–1962', *French History*, 20:3 (2006), 276–96; Feraoun, cited in Ned Curthoys, 'The Refractory Legacy of Algerian Decolonization: Revisiting Arendt on Violence', in Richard H. King and Dan Stone (eds.), *Hannah Arendt and the Uses of History: Imperialism, Nation, Race, and Genocide* (New York: Berghahn Books, 2007), 124.

76. Cited in Kenneth Maxwell, *The Making of Portuguese Democracy* (Cambridge: Cambridge University Press, 1995), 7.

77. Graham and Quiroga, 'After the Fear was Over?', 503.

78. See, for example, Ángela Cenarro, 'Memories of Repression and Resistance: Narratives of Children Institutionalized by Auxilio Social in Postwar Spain', *History & Memory*, 20:2 (2008), 39–59.

79. Graham and Quiroga, 'After the Fear was Over?', 512.

80. A. L. S. Coltman (British Embassy, Madrid) to A. E. Palmer (Foreign Office), 31 May 1968, cited in Kostis Kornetis, 'Spain and Greece', in Martin Klimke and Joachim Scharloth (eds.), *1968 in Europe: A History of Protest and Activism, 1956–1977* (New York: Palgrave Macmillan, 2008), 260.

81. Graham and Quiroga, 'After the Fear was Over?', 516.

82. Graham and Quiroga, 'After the Fear was Over?', 515.

83. Helen Graham, 'The Spanish Civil War, 1936–2003: The Return of Republican Memory', *Science & Society*, 68:3 (2004), 324.

84. João L. César Das Neves, 'Portuguese Postwar Growth: A Global Approach', in Nicholas Crafts and Gianni Toniolo (eds.), *Economic Growth in Europe since 1945* (Cambridge: Cambridge University Press, 1996), 339.

85. Maxwell, *The Making of Portuguese Democracy*, 96. For an interesting discussion, see Ellen W. Sapega, 'Remembering Empire/Forgetting the Colonies: Accretions of Memory and the Limits of Commemoration in a Lisbon Neighborhood', *History & Memory*, 20:2 (2008), 18–38.

86. António Costa Pinto, 'Political Purges and State Crisis in Portugal's Transition to Democracy, 1975–76', *Journal of Contemporary History*, 43:2 (2008), 305–32. See also Richard A. H. Robinson, 'The Influence of Overseas Issues in Portugal's Transition to Democracy', in Stewart Lloyd-Jones and António Costa Pinto (eds.), *The Last Empire: Thirty Years of Portuguese Decolonization* (Bristol: Intellect, 2003), 1–15.

87. Kissinger, cited in Pedro Ramos Pinto, 'Urban Social Movements and the Transition to Democracy in Portugal, 1974–1976', *Historical Journal*, 51:4 (2008), 1025 n. 1.

88. Richard Clogg, *A Concise History of Greece* (Cambridge: Cambridge University Press, 2002), 163–4.

89. Griffiths, cited in Konstantina Maragkou, 'Favouritism in NATO's Southeastern Flank: The Case of the Greek Colonels, 1967–74', *Cold War History*, 9:3 (2009), 358. See also Maragkou, 'The Wilson Government's Response to the "Rape of Greek Democracy"', *Journal of Contemporary History*, 45:1 (2010), 162–80.

90. For details of the true complexity of the situation—including secret negotiations involving US military access to Greek facilities during the Yom Kippur War—see Vassilis K. Fouskas, 'Uncomfortable Questions: Cyprus, October 1973–August 1974', *Contemporary European History*, 14:1 (2005), 45–63.

91. Adorno, *Minima Moralia*, 55.

92. Cited in Ingo Cornils, '"The Struggle Continues": Rudi Dutschke's Long March', in Gerard DeGroot (ed.), *Student Protest: The Sixties and After* (London: Longman, 1998), 114.

93. Abraham J. Muste, 'Tract for the Times', *Liberation*, 1:1 (1956), 6, cited in Michael Frey, 'The International Peace Movement', in Klimke and Scharloth (eds.), *1968 in Europe*, 36.

94. This paragraph and the next are indebted to Martin Klimke, '1968: Europe in Technicolour', in *OHPEH*, 243–61.

95. Ingrid Gilcher-Holtey, 'May 1968 in France: The Rise and Fall of a New Social Movement', in Carole Fink, Philipp Gassert, and Detlef Junker (eds.), *1968: The World Transformed* (Cambridge: Cambridge University Press, 1998), 272.

96. Hannah Arendt, *Crises of the Republic* (Harmondsworth: Penguin, 1973), 168.

97. Leszek Kołakowski, *Main Currents of Marxism* (New York: W. W. Norton, 2005 [1978]), 1179.

98. Uta G. Poiger, 'Rock 'n' Roll, Female Sexuality, and the Cold War Battle over German Identities', *Journal of Modern History*, 68:3 (1996), 577–616.

99. René Andrieu in *L'Humanité*, cited in Gilcher-Holtey, 'May 1968 in France', 269.

100. Jan Kurz and Marica Tolomelli, 'Italy', in Klimke and Scharloth (eds.), *1968 in Europe*, 90.

101. Andrea Mammone, 'The Transnational Reaction to 1968: Neo-fascist Fronts and Political Cultures in France and Italy', *Contemporary European History*, 17:2 (2008), 213–36; Guido Panvini, 'Neo-Fascism, the Extraparliamentary Left Wing, and the Birth of Italian Terrorism', in Karen Dubinsky, Catherine Krull, Susan Lord, Sean Mills, and Scott Rutherford (eds.), *New World Coming: The Sixties and the Shaping of Global Consciousness* (Toronto: Between the Lines, 2009), 87–96.

102. Paul Hockenos, *Joschka Fischer and the Making of the Berlin Republic: An Alternative History of Postwar Germany* (New York: Oxford University Press, 2007).

103. Müller, 'What Did They Think They Were Doing?', 74.

104. Giuseppe Carlo Marino, 'Italy: "We Demand the Impossible!"', in Philipp Gassert and Martin Klimke (eds.), *1968: Memories and Legacies of a Global Revolt*, *Bulletin of the German Historical Institute*, Supplement 6 (2009), 219. As Müller writes ('What Did They Think They Were Doing?', 78), 'The real move towards violence and all-out criminality was actually a sign of desperation, of the failure of what can meaningfully be called '68.'

105. Cited in Hans Kundnani, *Utopia or Auschwitz: Germany's 1968 Generation and the Holocaust* (London: C. Hurst & Co., 2009), 9. There are question marks over whether or not Ensslin actually said these words.

106. Kundnani, *Utopia or Auschwitz*, 145.

107. Sebastian Gehrig, 'Sympathizing Subcultures? The Milieus of West German Terrorism', in Martin Klimke, Jacco Pekelder, and Joachim Scharloth (eds.), *Between Prague Spring and French May: Opposition and Revolt in Europe, 1960–1980* (New York: Berghahn Books, 2011), 242.

108. Kundnani, *Utopia or Auschwitz*, 145.

109. Alain Finkielkraut, *The Imaginary Jew*, trans. Kevin O'Neill and David Suchoff (Lincoln, Nebr.: University of Nebraska Press, 1994), 18.

110. Bryn Jones and Mike O'Donnell (eds.), *Sixties Radicalism and Social Movement Activism: Retreat or Resurgence?* (London: Anthem Press, 2010).

111. Michael Seidman, *The Imaginary Revolution: Parisian Students and Workers in 1968* (New York: Berghahn Books, 2004).

112. Stuart J. Hilwig, *Italy and 1968: Youthful Unrest and Democratic Culture* (Basingstoke: Palgrave Macmillan, 2009), 140.

113. On the context, see David Caute, *Sixty-Eight: The Year of the Barricades* (London: Hamish Hamilton, 1988), 219.

114. Jan-Werner Müller, '1968 as Event, Milieu and Ideology', *Journal of Political Ideologies*, 7:1 (2002), 15–37.

115. Harold Marcuse, 'The Revival of Holocaust Awareness in West Germany, Israel, and the United States', in Fink, Gassert, and Junker (eds.), *1968: The World Transformed*, 421–38; Michael Schmidtke, 'The German New Left and National Socialism', in Philipp Gassert and Alan E. Steinweis (eds.), *Coping with the Nazi Past: West German Debates on Nazism and Generational Conflict, 1955–1975* (New York: Berghahn Books, 2006), 176–93.

116. Christoph Schmidt, 'The Israel of the Spirit: The German Student Movement of the 1960s and its Attitude to the Holocaust', *Dapim: Studies on the Shoah*, 24 (2010), 269–318.

117. Müller, '1968 as Event', 33.

118. Nicholas Crafts and Gianni Toniolo, ' "*Les trentes glorieuses*": From the Marshall Plan to the Oil Crises', in *OHPEH*, 357–60.

119. Barry Eichengreen, 'Institutions and Economic Growth: Europe after World War II', in Crafts and Toniolo (eds.), *Economic Growth in Postwar Europe*, 38–72; Barry Eichengreen and Andrea Boltho, 'The Economic Impact of European Integration', in Stephen Broadberry and Kevin H. O'Rourke (eds.), *The Cambridge Economic History of Modern Europe*, ii: *1870 to the Present* (Cambridge: Cambridge University Press, 2010), 267–95; Gianni Toniolo, 'Europe's Golden Age, 1950–1973: Speculations from a Long-run Perspective', *Economic History Review*, 51:2 (1998), 264.

120. Toniolo, 'Europe's Golden Age, 1950–1973', 254, 257; Peter Temin, 'The Golden Age of European Growth: A Review Essay', *European Review of Economic History*, 1:1 (1997), 127–49.

121. Eichengreen, *The European Economy since 1945*, 252.

122. Eichengreen, *The European Economy since 1945*, 250.

123. Andrea Boltho and Gianni Toniolo, 'The Assessment—The Twentieth Century: Achievements, Failures, Lessons', *Oxford Review of Economic Policy*, 15:4 (1999), 10.

124. Eichengreen, *The European Economy since 1945*, 254.

125. Eichengreen, *The European Economy since 1945*, 256.

126. Crafts and Toniolo, '*Les trentes glorieuses*', 376. 'Economics as if people mattered' is E. F. Schumacher's phrase.

127. Eichengreen, *The European Economy since 1945*, 194.

CHAPTER 4

1. Nikita Khrushchev, memorandum for CPSU CC Plenum, December 1959, cited in James G. Hershberg, 'The Crisis Years, 1958–1963', in Westad (ed.), *Reviewing the Cold War*, 311; Leonid Brezhnev, 'Speech to the Fifth Congress of the Polish United Workers' Party (12 November 1968)', in Gale Stokes (ed.), *From Stalinism to Pluralism: A Documentary History of Eastern Europe since 1945* (New York: Oxford University Press, 1991), 134; Ladislav Mňačko, *The Seventh Night* (London: J. M. Dent & Sons, 1969), 220; Witold Gombrowicz, *Diary* (New Haven: Yale University Press, 2012), 737 (entry for 1969).

2. Giuseppe Mammarella, 'The Soviet System from the "Thaw" to the Hungarian Crisis', in Varsori (ed.), *Europe 1945–1990s*, 249–64.

3. A short extract of the text of the 'secret speech' is in *CW*, 247–9, and the full version can be found in Ali (ed.), *The Stalinist Legacy*, 221–72.

4. Susanne Schattenberg, ' "Democracy" or "Despotism"? How the Secret Speech was Translated into Everyday Life', in Polly Jones (ed.), *The Dilemmas of De-Stalinization: Negotiating Cultural and Social Change in the Khrushchev Era* (London: Routledge, 2006), 65.

5. Nikita S. Khrushchev, 'Secret Report to the 20th Party Congress of the CPSU', in Ali (ed.), *The Stalinist Legacy*, 271.

6. These details are all taken from Roger D. Markwick, 'Thaws and Freezes in Soviet Historiography, 1953–64', in Jones (ed.), *The Dilemmas of De-Stalinization*, 73–92.

7. Polly Jones, 'Introduction: The Dilemmas of De-Stalinization', in Jones (ed.), *The Dilemmas of De-Stalinization*, 8.

8. Polly Jones, 'From the Secret Speech to the Burial of Stalin: Real and Ideal Responses to De-Stalinization', in Jones (ed.), *Dilemmas of De-Stalinization*, 50.

9. Jones, 'From the Secret Speech to the Burial of Stalin', 58–9.

10. I am indebted in this paragraph to Robert Bideleux, 'The Comecon Experiment', in Bideleux and Taylor (eds.), *European Integration and Disintegration*, 174–204.

11. This is what Kádár supposedly said at a private meeting during a Group of Thirty meeting in Budapest in 1982, cited in Boltho and Toniolo, 'The Assessment', 11 n. 9.

12. Jussi M. Hanhimäki, 'Europe's Cold War', in *OHPEH*, 291.

13. Tilly, 'Europe Transformed', 20.

14. Toniolo, 'Europe's Golden Age, 1950–1973', 265; Crafts and Toniolo, '*Les trentes glorieuses*', 356–78.

15. Kevin Adamson, 'Discourses of Violence and the Ideological Strategies of the Romanian Communist Party, 1944–1953', *East European Politics and Societies*, 21:4 (2007), 559–87.

16. See the essays in Raymond Aron et al., *The Soviet Economy: A Discussion* (London: Secker & Warburg, 1956).

17. Mikhail Gorbachev and Zdeněk Mlynář, *Conversations with Gorbachev: On Perestroika, the Prague Spring, and the Crossroads of Socialism* (New York: Columbia University Press, 2002), 60.

18. Czesław Miłosz, *The Captive Mind* (London: Penguin, 1985), 230.

19. Kevin McDermott and Matthew Stibbe, 'Revolution and Resistance in Eastern Europe: An Overview', in McDermott and Stibbe (eds.), *Revolution and Resistance in Eastern Europe: Challenges to Communist Rule* (Oxford: Berg, 2006), 6.

20. Matthew Stibbe, 'The SED, German Communism and the June 1953 Uprising: New Trends and New Research', in McDermott and Stibbe (eds.), *Revolution and Resistance in Eastern Europe*, 38. On Plzeň, see Kevin McDermott, 'Popular

Resistance in Communist Czechoslovakia: The Plzeň Uprising, June 1953', *Contemporary European History*, 19:4 (2010), 287–307.

21. Cited in Stibbe, 'The SED, German Communism and the June 1953 Uprising', 46.

22. I am indebted in this paragraph to Krystyna Kersten, '1956—The Turning Point', in Odd Arne Westad, Sven Holtsmark, and Iver B. Neumann (eds.), *The Soviet Union in Eastern Europe, 1945–89* (Basingstoke: Macmillan, 1994), 47–62, and to Mark Kramer, 'The Soviet Union and the 1956 Crises in Hungary and Poland: Reassessments and New Findings', *Journal of Contemporary History*, 33:2 (1998), 163–214. See also Tony Kemp-Welch, 'Khrushchev's "Secret Speech" and Polish Politics: The Spring of 1956', *Europe-Asia Studies*, 48:2 (1996), 181–206, esp. 201–2, which talks of the 'turning-point in Polish post-war politics'.

23. Kersten, '1956—The Turning Point', 53–4.

24. Cited in Tony Kemp-Welch, 'Dethroning Stalin: Poland 1956 and its Legacy', *Europe-Asia Studies*, 58:8 (2006), 1263.

25. Cited in Johanna Grenville, 'Poland and Hungary 1956: A Comparative Essay Based on New Archival Findings', in McDermott and Stibbe (eds.), *Revolution and Resistance*, 66.

26. Imre Nagy, 'On Communism' (1956), cited in Geoffrey Swain and Nigel Swain, *Eastern Europe since 1945* (Basingstoke: Macmillan, 1993), 85.

27. See Togliatti's note to Khrushchev of 30 October 1956, in *Cold War International History Project Bulletin*, 8–9 (1996), 357.

28. Ervin Hollós and Vera Lajtai, cited in István Rév, *Retroactive Justice: Prehistory of Post-Communism* (Stanford, Calif.: Stanford University Press, 2005), 215. Hollós was a historian and head of the Political Department of the Budapest Police Headquarters.

29. Jan-Werner Müller, *Contesting Democracy: Political Ideas in Twentieth-Century Europe* (New Haven: Yale University Press, 2011), 163–4.

30. Hollós, cited in Rév, *Retroactive Justice*, 216.

31. Cited in Kramer, 'The Soviet Union and the 1956 Crises', 213.

32. Rév, *Retroactive Justice*, 33. The resentments this silence bred burst out in post-1989 Hungary, as we will see in Chapter 8.

33. Miłosz, *The Captive Mind*, 234: 'The Western Communist needs a vision of a golden age which is *already* being realized on earth. The Stalinist of the East does everything in his power to instil this vision in the minds of others, but he never forgets that it is merely a useful lie.'

34. Mark Kramer, 'The Kremlin, the Prague Spring, and the Brezhnev Doctrine', in Tismaneanu (ed.), *Promises of 1968*, 304.

35. François Fejtö, 'Moscow and its Allies', *Problems of Communism*, 17:6 (1968), 30.

36. On the background to Czechoslovak reform communism, see Vladimir V. Kusin, *The Intellectual Origins of the Prague Spring: The Development of Reformist Ideas in Czechoslovakia, 1956–1967* (Cambridge: Cambridge University Press, 1971).

37. See Zdenek Mlynar, 'From Prague to Moscow: August 1968', *Telos*, 42 (1979–80), 21–55, esp. 25.

38. Kieran Williams, 'The Prague Spring: From Elite Liberalisation to Mass Movement', in McDermott and Stibbe (eds.), *Revolution and Resistance in Eastern Europe*, 103.

39. *CW*, 260.

40. Mark Kramer, 'The Czechoslovak Crisis and the Brezhnev Doctrine', in Fink, Gassert, and Junker (eds.), *1968: The World Transformed*, 153.

41. Williams, 'The Prague Spring', 113. For strong criticisms on the image of Dubček as political innocent, see Mary Heimann, 'The Scheming *Apparatchik* of the Prague Spring', *Europe-Asia Studies*, 60:10 (2008), 1717–34. Heimann concludes (1733) that Dubček did not begin the process of 'normalization' because it was necessary for communism to hang on to power in Czechoslovakia. 'Rather,' she says, 'like other *apparatchiks* shaped by the same political system, he began oppressing colleagues and fellow citizens because to do so offered his only hope—however slim—of being able to hang on to power.' Heimann's claims ring true given that Dubček clung on to power until April 1969 in an ultimately vain attempt to accommodate Soviet demands. Still, it is indeed remarkable—if it is true—that the Prague Spring reformers did not realize that they would be charged with attempting to break up the Warsaw Pact, Comecon, and international socialist cooperation, as Zdeněk Mlynář later claimed (Gorbachev and Mlynář, *Conversations with Gorbachev*, 63).

42. *Scînteia*, 23 August 1968, cited in Vladimir Tismaneanu and Bogdan Iacob, 'Betrayed Promises: Nicolae Ceauşescu, the Romanian Communist Party, and the Crisis of 1968', in Tismaneanu (ed.), *Promises of 1968*, 261, translation slightly modified.

43. Fejtö, 'Moscow and its Allies', 36.

44. Cited in Kramer, 'The Kremlin, the Prague Spring, and the Brezhnev Doctrine', 307 (Gomułka) and 336 (Zhivkov). See also Kramer's comments in 'Bulgaria, the "Prague Spring" and the Invasion of Czechoslovakia: A Commentary', in M. Mark Stolarik (ed.), *The Prague Spring and the Warsaw Pact Invasion of Czechoslovakia, 1968: Forty Years Later* (Mundelein, Ill.: Bolchazy-Carducci Publishers, 2010), 193–202. Kramer shows that despite Zhivkov's own attempts to claim, in 1990, that he had supported the reformers and only reluctantly agreed to support the invasion, he was in fact one of the most vociferous proponents of military intervention. Zhivkov too feared something similar happening in Bulgaria.

45. Fejtö, 'Moscow and its Allies', 36. See Galia Golan, *Reform Rule in Czechoslovakia: The Dubček Era 1968–1969* (Cambridge: Cambridge University Press, 1973), for details.

46. Vojtech Mastny, 'The Warsaw Pact: An Alliance in Search of a Purpose', in Ann Heiss and S. Victor Papacosma (eds.), *NATO and the Warsaw Pact: Intrabloc Conflicts* (Kent, Oh.: Kent State University Press, 2008), 149. See also Günter Bischof,

Stefan Karner, and Peter Ruggenthaler (eds.), *The Prague Spring and the Warsaw Pact Invasion of Czechoslovakia in 1968* (Lanham, Md.: Lexington Books, 2010), for the idea of the 'tail wagging the dog'.

47. Mňačko, *The Seventh Night*, 192.

48. François Fejtö, *A History of the People's Democracies: Eastern Europe since Stalin* (Harmondsworth: Penguin, 1977), 462–3.

49. Hannah Arendt, 'Totalitarian Imperialism: Reflections on the Hungarian Revolution', *Journal of Politics*, 20:1 (1958), 43.

50. Brandt, 'The East–West Problem as Seen from Berlin', 303.

51. See also John G. McGinn, 'The Politics of Collective Inaction: NATO's Response to the Prague Spring', *Journal of Cold War Studies*, 1:3 (1999), 111–38.

52. Jáchym Topol, *Gargling with Tar*, trans. David Short (London: Portobello Books, 2010), 133–4 [orig. Czech 2005].

53. 'Stenografische Niederschrift der Beratung der fünf "Brüderparteien" mit der KPČ in Dresden' (23 March 1968), in Stefan Karner et al. (eds.), *Prager Frühling: Das internationale Krisenjahr 1968*, ii: *Dokumente* (Cologne: Böhlau Verlag, 2008), 411.

54. Brezhnev, 'Speech to the Fifth Congress of the Polish United Workers' Party', 133. See also Brezhnev's speech in Bratislava on 3 August 1968, cited in Judt, *Postwar*, 443.

55. Mňačko, *The Seventh Night*, 207.

56. See Robert A. Jones, *The Soviet Concept of 'Limited Sovereignty' from Lenin to Gorbachev: The Brezhnev Doctrine* (Houndmills: Macmillan Press, 1990), 257: the Brezhnev Doctrine 'in no sense represented a qualitative shift in Soviet attitudes towards the concept of sovereignty'.

57. Antonín Kostlán and Soňa Štrbáňová, 'Czech Scholars in Exile, 1948–1989', in Shula Marks, Paul Weindling, and Laura Wintour (eds.), *In Defence of Learning: The Plight, Persecution, and Placement of Academic Refugees 1933–1980s* (Oxford: Oxford University Press, 2011), 247.

58. Paulina Bren, 'Mirror, Mirror, on the Wall... Is the West the Fairest of Them All? Czechoslovak Normalization and its (Dis)Contents', *Kritika*, 9:4 (2008), 838–9.

59. Fejtö, *A History of the People's Democracies*, 472.

60. McDermott and Stibbe, 'Revolution and Resistance', 7.

61. Togliatti, cited in Vladimir Tismaneanu, 'Introduction', in Tismaneanu (ed.), *Promises of 1968*, 12–13 n. 21.

62. H. Gordon Skilling, 'Stalinism and Czechoslovak Political Culture', in Robert C. Tucker (ed.), *Stalinism: Essays in Historical Interpretation* (New York: W. W. Norton, 1977), 257. But note György Péteri's point that at the Brussels Exposition in 1958, Hungary spent money it could ill afford on presenting an image of itself to the world as modern, in order to emphasize the break of Kádár's Hungary from Rákosi's. Péteri, 'Transsytemic Fantasies: Counterrevolutionary Hungary at Brussels Expo '58', *Journal of Contemporary History*, 47:1 (2012), 137–60.

63. Irena Grudzinska Gross, '1968 in Poland: Spoiled Children, Marxists, and Jews', in Tismaneanu (ed.), *Promises of 1968*, 44.

64. Vladimir Tismaneanu, *Stalinism for All Seasons*, 212.

65. Cristian Vasile, '1968 Romania: Intellectuals and the Failure of Reform', and Nick Miller, 'Yugoslavia's 1968: The Great Surrender', both in Tismaneanu (ed.), *Promises of 1968*, 241–53 and 227–39.

66. Timothy S. Brown, ' "1968" East and West: Divided Germany as a Case Study in Transnational History', *American Historical Review*, 114:1 (2009), 69–96.

67. Ludvík Vaculík, 'Two Thousand Words to Workers, Farmers, Scientists, Artists, and Everyone' (27 June 1968), in Stokes (ed.), *From Stalinism to Pluralism*, 126.

68. A. R. Johnson, 'Kuroń and Modzelewski's "Open Letter to the Party" ', *Radio Free Europe Research*, 16 November 1966, online at <http://storage.osaarchivum.org/low/67/e4/67e411f1-4d4a-482d-bca8-7a5e7b1f3001_l.pdf>. In general on Poland, see Jerzy Eisler, 'March 1968 in Poland', in Fink, Gassert, and Junker (eds.), *1968: The World Transformed*, 237–52.

69. Judt, *Postwar*, 433.

70. Klimke, '1968: Europe in Technicolour', 250.

71. Judt, *Postwar*, 435. Judt writes sensitively about the situation in Poland in 1968.

72. Gross, *Fear*, 243.

73. H. Gordon Skilling, *Czechoslovakia's Interrupted Revolution* (Princeton: Princeton University Press, 1976).

74. Gorbachev and Mlynář, *Conversations with Gorbachev*, 199.

75. Malenkov, cited in Mammarella, 'The Soviet System', 251.

76. Klaus Larres, 'Preserving Law and Order: Great Britain, the United States and the East German Uprising of 1953', *Twentieth Century British History*, 5:3 (1994), 320–50.

77. Geoffrey Roberts, 'Moscow's Campaign against the Cold War, 1948–1955', in Frédéric Bozo, Marie-Pierre Rey, N. Piers Ludlow, and Bernd Rother (eds.), *Visions of the End of the Cold War in Europe, 1945–1990* (New York: Berghahn Books, 2012), 47–60; Roberts, 'A Chance for Peace? The Soviet Campaign to End the Cold War, 1953–1955', *Cold War International History Project Working Paper*, 57 (2008).

78. Vojtech Mastny, 'The Elusive Détente: Stalin's Successors and the West', in Larres and Osgood (eds.), *The Cold War after Stalin's Death*, 20.

79. Klaus Larres, 'The Road to Geneva 1955: Churchill's Summit Diplomacy and Anglo-American Tension after Stalin's Death', in Larres and Osgood (eds.), *The Cold War after Stalin's Death*, 150. See also Antonio Varsori, 'The Western Powers and the Geneva Summit Conference (1955)', in Varsori (ed.), *Europe 1945–1990s*, 221–48; and Ernest R. May, 'The Early Cold War', in Günter Bischof and Saki Dockrill (eds.), *Cold War Respite: The Geneva Summit of 1955* (Baton Rouge, La.: Louisiana State University Press, 2000), 21–34, who talks (21) of Geneva producing a 'temporary easing of tension'.

80. Smirnov, cited in Vladislav Zubok, 'Khrushchev and the Berlin Crisis (1958–1962)', *Cold War International History Project Working Paper*, 6 (1993), 9.

81. Hershberg, 'The Crisis Years', 308. I am indebted throughout this paragraph and the next to Hershberg's chapter. On Sputnik, see Lewis Siegelbaum, 'Sputnik Goes to Brussels: The Exhibition of a Soviet Technological Wonder', *Journal of Contemporary History*, 47:1 (2012), 120–36.

82. See also here Hope M. Harrison, 'Ulbricht and the Concrete "Rose": New Archival Evidence on the Dynamics of Soviet–East German Relations and the Berlin Crisis, 1958–61', *Cold War International History Project Working Paper*, 5 (1993).

83. Hershberg, 'The Crisis Years', 310.

84. Khrushchev, speech to Warsaw Pact meeting, Moscow, 4 August 1961, in *CW*, 328.

85. Patrick Major, *Behind the Berlin Wall: East Germany and the Frontiers of Power* (Oxford: Oxford University Press, 2010); Noel D. Cary, 'Farewell Without Tears: Diplomats, Dissidents, and the Demise of East Germany', *Journal of Modern History*, 73:3 (2001), 617–51.

86. Ulbricht, letter to Khrushchev, 15 September 1961, reproduced in Harrison, 'Ulbricht and the Concrete "Rose"', 126.

87. Thomas Lindenberger, 'Divided, but Not Disconnected: Germany as a Border Region of the Cold War', in Tobias Hochscherf, Christoph Laucht, and Andrew Plowman (eds.), *Divided, but Not Disconnected: German Experiences of the Cold War* (New York: Berghahn Books, 2010), 16–17.

88. Hope M. Harrison, 'The Berlin Wall, Ostpolitik, and Détente', in David C. Geyer and Bernd Schaefer (eds.), *American Détente and German Ostpolitik, 1969–1972, Bulletin of the German Historical Institute*, Supplement 1 (2003), 5; Corey Ross, 'East Germans and the Berlin Wall: Popular Opinion and Social Change before and after the Border Closure of August 1961', *Journal of Contemporary History*, 39:1 (2004), 43.

89. Harrison, 'The Berlin Wall, Ostpolitik, and Détente', 10.

90. Fejtö, 'Moscow and its Allies', 33. As Fejtö notes, economic necessity dragged these countries into the West German orbit nonetheless in the coming years.

91. Irina Gridan, 'Du communisme national au national-communisme: Réactions à la soviétisation dans la Roumanie des années 1960', *Vingtième Siècle: Revue d'histoire*, 109:1 (2011), 113–27.

92. Dennis Deletant and Mihail Ionescu, 'Romania and the Warsaw Pact: 1955–1989', *Cold War International History Project Working Paper*, 43 (2004), 80–4.

93. Fejtö, *A History of the People's Democracies*, 207–8.

94. Mike Bowker, 'Brezhnev and Superpower Relations', in Edwin Bacon and Mike Sandle (eds.), *Brezhnev Reconsidered* (Houndmills: Palgrave Macmillan, 2002), 96–7.

95. Mark Kramer, 'Ideology and the Cold War', *Review of International Studies*, 25:4 (1999), 548.

96. Kramer, 'The Kremlin, the Prague Spring, and the Brezhnev Doctrine', 290.

97. Jeremi Suri, 'The Promise and Failure of "Developed Socialism": The Soviet "Thaw" and the Crucible of the Prague Spring, 1964–1972', *Contemporary European History*, 15:2 (2006), 133–58.

98. Bowker, 'Brezhnev and Superpower Relations', 92.

99. John Lewis Gaddis, *The Cold War* (London: Penguin, 2007), 190.

100. Ross, 'East Germans and the Berlin Wall', 43. See also Christoph Boyer, 'Stabilisation of Power through Social and Consumer Policy in the GDR', in Jerzy W. Borejsza and Klaus Ziemer (eds.), *Totalitarian and Authoritarian Regimes in Europe: Legacies and Lessons from the Twentieth Century* (New York: Berghahn Books, 2006), 209–27; Isabelle de Keghel, 'Western in Style, Socialist in Content? Visual Representations of GDR Consumer Culture in the *Neue Berliner Illustrierte* (1953–64)', in Sari Autio-Sarasmo and Brendan Humphreys (eds.), *Winter Kept Us Warm: Cold War Interactions Reconsidered* (Helsinki: Aleksanteri Institute, 2010), 76–106.

101. Oliver Fritz, *The Iron Curtain Kid* (n.p.: Lulu.com, 2009), 3.

102. Liviu Chelcea, 'Ancestors, Domestic Groups, and the Socialist State: Housing Nationalization and Restitution in Romania', *Comparative Studies in Society and History*, 45:4 (2003), 714–40.

103. James Heinzen, 'Informers and the State under Late Stalinism: Informant Networks and Crimes against "Socialist Property", 1940–53', *Kritika*, 8:4 (2007), 796.

104. Most famously examined in Milovan Djilas, *The New Class: An Analysis of the Communist System* (London: Thames and Hudson, 1957).

105. David Crowley, 'Thaw Modern: Design in Eastern Europe after 1956', in David Crowley and Jane Pavitt (eds.), *Cold War Modern: Design 1945–1970* (London: V&A Publishing, 2008), 130.

106. Milla Minerva, 'Narratives and Images of Socialist Consumption: A Study of the Visual Construction of Consumer Culture in Bulgaria in the 1960s', in Maria Todorova (ed.), *Remembering Communism: Genres of Representation* (New York: Social Science Research Council, 2010), 349; Susan E. Reid, 'Cold War in the Kitchen: Gender and the De-Stalinization of Consumer Taste in the Soviet Union under Khrushchev', *Slavic Review*, 61:2 (2002), 211–52.

107. Martha Lampland, *The Object of Labor: Commodification in Socialist Hungary* (Chicago: University of Chicago Press, 1995); Katherine Verdery, *What Was Socialism, and What Comes Next?* (Princeton: Princeton University Press, 1996), 57.

108. Minerva, 'Narratives and Images of Socialist Consumption', 350–1.

109. N. S. Khrushchev, 'Report of the Central Committee of the 22nd Congress of the Communist Party of the Soviet Union', in *Documents of the 22nd Congress of the CPSU* (New York: Crosscurrents Press, 1961), i. 131–2, online at: <www.archive.org/details/DocumentsOfThe22ndCongressOfTheCpsuVolI>.

110. Khrushchev, 'Report of the Central Committee of the 22nd Congress', 132.

111. David Crowley, 'Warsaw Interiors: The Public Life of Private Spaces, 1949–65', in David Crowley and Susan E. Reid (eds.), *Socialist Spaces: Sites of Everyday Life*

in the Eastern Bloc (Oxford: Berg, 2002), 187–8. See also, in the same volume (207–30), Katerina Gerasimova, 'Public Privacy in the Soviet Communal Apartment', for an analysis of an institution that cannot easily be characterized as either private or public, and, more broadly, Steven E. Harris, 'In Search of "Ordinary" Russia: Everyday Life in the NEP, the Thaw, and the Communal Apartment', *Kritika*, 6:3 (2005), 583–614.

112. Paul Betts, *Within Walls: Private Life in the German Democratic Republic* (Oxford: Oxford University Press, 2010), ch. 4, argues that the SED consciously sought to reorganize domestic life as part of the project to build a model socialist culture.

113. Greg Castillo, 'East as True West: Redeeming Bourgeois Culture, from Socialist Realism to *Ostalgie*', in György Péteri (ed.), *Imagining the West in Eastern Europe and the Soviet Union* (Pittsburgh: University of Pittsburgh Press, 2010), 89.

114. Cited in Crowley, 'Warsaw Interiors', 188.

115. Cited in Susan E. Reid, ' "Our Kitchen Is Just as Good": Soviet Responses to the American Kitchen', in Ruth Oldenziel and Karin Zachmann (eds.), *Cold War Kitchen: Americanization, Technology, and European Users* (Cambridge, Mass.: MIT Press, 2009), 85.

116. Betts, *Within Walls*, 266 n. 11. See also Oldenziel and Zachmann (eds.), *Cold War Kitchen*; Susan E. Reid, 'The Khrushchev Kitchen: Domesticating the Scientific-Technological Revolution', *Journal of Contemporary History*, 40:2 (2005), 289–316; Reid, 'Who Will Beat Whom? Soviet Popular Reception of the American National Exhibition in Moscow, 1959', in Péteri (ed.), *Imagining the West*, 194–236.

117. See the excellent discussion in Pittaway, *Eastern Europe*, ch. 5.

118. Greg Castillo, *Cold War on the Home Front: The Soft Power of Midcentury Design* (Minneapolis: University of Minnesota Press, 2010), 170; Reid, ' "Our Kitchen Is Just as Good" ', 94.

119. David Crowley and Susan E. Reid, 'Socialist Spaces: Sites of Everyday Life in the Eastern Bloc', in Crowley and Reid (eds.), *Socialist Spaces*, 3.

120. René Wolf, *The Undivided Sky: The Holocaust on East and West German Radio in the 1960s* (Basingstoke: Palgrave Macmillan, 2010); Mark Pittaway, 'The Education of Dissent: The Reception of the Voice of Free Hungary, 1951–56', in Patrick Major and Rana Mitter (eds.), *Across the Blocs: Exploring Comparative Cold War Cultural and Social History* (London: Frank Cass, 2004), 76–90.

121. Cited in Jutta Braun, 'The People's Sport? Popular Sport and Fans in the Later Years of the German Democratic Republic', *German History*, 27:3 (2009), 414.

122. Jonathan Wilson, *Inverting the Pyramid: The History of Football Tactics* (London: Orion, 2008), 92; see also David Goldblatt, *The Ball is Round: A Global History of Football* (London: Penguin, 2007), 341–6.

123. Ulf Brunnbauer, 'Making Bulgarians Socialist: The Fatherland Front in Communist Bulgaria, 1944–1989', *East European Politics and Societies*, 22:1 (2008), 44–79.

124. See Jeanette Z. Madarász, *Conflict and Compromise in East Germany, 1971–1989: A Precarious Stability* (Basingstoke: Palgrave Macmillan, 2003); Pittaway, *Eastern Europe*, 151.

125. Jan Pauer, 'Czechoslovakia', in Klimke and Scharloth (eds.), *1968 in Europe*, 175.

126. Miranda Vickers, *The Albanians: A Modern History* (London: I. B. Tauris, 1997), ch. 9; Tismaneanu, *Stalinism for All Seasons*, ch. 7; Dennis Deletant, *Ceauşescu and the Securitate: Coercion and Dissent in Romania, 1965–89* (London: C. Hurst & Co., 1996). See also Tismaneanu, 'National Stalinism', in *OHPEH*, 462–79.

127. I am indebted here to Robert C. Austin, 'Purge and Counter-Purge in Stalinist Albania, 1944–1956', in Kevin McDermott and Matthew Stibbe (eds.), *Stalinist Terror in Eastern Europe: Elite Purges and Mass Repression* (Manchester: Manchester University Press, 2010), 198–216.

128. Tismaneanu and Iacob, 'Betrayed Promises', 257–83.

129. Stefan Berger and Norman LaPorte, 'In Search of Antifascism: The British Left's Response to the German Democratic Republic during the Cold War', *German History*, 26:4 (2008), 550.

130. Matthew J. Ouimet, *The Rise and Fall of the Brezhnev Doctrine in Soviet Foreign Policy* (Chapel Hill, NC: University of North Carolina Press, 2003), 245.

131. Fejtö, *A History of the People's Democracies*, 331.

CHAPTER 5

1. Olof Palme, excerpt from televised Swedish election debate, 17 September 1982, in *CW*, 442; Joschka Fischer, speech to Bundestag, 23 June 1983, cited in Schmidt, 'The Israel of the Spirit', 317.

2. Geoffrey H. Hartman, 'Introduction: 1985', in Hartman (ed.), *Bitburg in Moral and Political Perspective* (Bloomington, Ind.: Indiana University Press, 1986), 1–12 and the chapters in that book.

3. Hartmut Kaelble, *The 1970s in Europe: A Period of Disillusionment or Promise?* (London: German Historical Institute, 2010); Konrad Jarausch, 'Krise oder Aufbruch? Annäherungen an die 1970er-Jahre', *Zeithistorische Forschungen*, online edition 3:3 (2006).

4. Judt, *Postwar*, 535.

5. Charles E. Maier, 'Two Sorts of Crisis: The "Long" 1970s in the West and the East', in Hans Günter Hockerts (ed.), *Koordinaten deutscher Geschichte in der Epoche der Ost–West Konflikts* (Munich: Oldenbourg, 2004), 49.

6. Stathis N. Kalyvas, *The Rise of Christian Democracy in Europe* (Ithaca, NY: Cornell University Press, 1996), 256, 264.

7. Anton Pelinka, 'European Christian Democracy in Comparison', in Michael Gehler and Wolfram Kaiser (eds.), *Christian Democracy in Europe since 1945*, ii (Abingdon: Routledge, 2004), 205–6. The description of Christian Democrats as 'catch-all parties' was German political scientist Otto Kirchheimer's; see Müller, *Contesting Democracy*, 139.

8. Bernd Faulenbach, 'Die Siebzigerjahre—ein sozialdemokratisches Jahrzehnt?', *Archiv für Sozialgeschichte*, 44 (2004), 1–37.

9. Axel Schildt, ' "Die Kräfte der Gegenreform sind auf breiter Front angetreten": Zur konservativen Tendenzwende in den Siebzigerjahren', *Archiv für Sozialgeschichte*, 44 (2004), 449–78; Jürgen Habermas, *Legitimation Crisis* (Cambridge: Polity Press, 1988 [orig. *Legitimationsprobleme im Spätkapitalismus*, 1973]).

10. Maud Bracke, *Which Socialism, Whose Détente? West European Communism and the Czechoslovak Crisis, 1968* (Budapest: CEU Press, 2007), 323–4.

11. Santiago Carrillo, *'Eurocommunism' and the State* (London: Lawrence and Wishart, 1977), 132. See also Fernando Claudín, *Eurocommunism and Socialism* (London: NLB, 1978). On Carillo, see Jorge Semprun, *Communism in Spain in the Franco Era: The Autobiography of Federico Sanchez* (Brighton: Harvester Press, 1980). Semprun referred to Eurocommunism as 'Eurocarrilloism' (213), an ironic reversal of Carillo's obedience to Moscow in the 1960s, and mocked Carillo's U-turn, noting that 'The invasion of Czechoslovakia could come as a surprise only to those who had not yet understood the true character of the "institutional system" in the USSR' (215).

12. Laura Fasanero, 'Eurocommunism: An East German Perspective', in Nuti (ed.), *The Crisis of Détente in Europe*, 248.

13. Bracke, *Which Socialism, Whose Détente?*, 352. See also Wolfgang Leonhard, *Eurocommunism: Challenge for East and West* (New York: Holt, Rinehart and Winston, 1979) and, for the best recent summary, Silvio Pons, 'The Rise and Fall of Eurocommunism', in *CHCW*, iii. 45–65.

14. Judt, *Postwar*, 496.

15. Enver Hoxha, *Eurocommunism is Anti-Communism* (Tirana: 8 Nëntori, 1980).

16. Judt, *Postwar*, 496; Charles Gati, 'The "Europeanization" of Communism?', *Foreign Affairs*, 55:3 (1977), 547; Gorbachev interview with Lilly Marcou for French TV Channel 1, June 2001, cited in Jacques Lévesque, 'The Messianic Character of "New Thinking": Why and What For?', in Njølstad (ed.), *The Last Decade of the Cold War*, 170.

17. Judt, *Postwar*, 528.

18. Graham and Quiroga, 'After the Fear Was Over?', 518.

19. Anderson, *The New Old World*, 67.

20. Josefina Cuesta Bustillo, 'A Social Europe (1970–2006)?', in Wilfried Loth (ed.), *Experiencing Europe: 50 Years of European Construction, 1957–2007* (Baden-Baden: Nomos, 2009), 193–216, esp. 207–8.

21. Gary Marks, Liesbet Hooghe, and Kermit Blank, 'European Integration from the 1980s: State-Centric v. Multi-level Governance', *Journal of Common Market Studies*, 34:3 (1996), 341–78. See also Mark Gilbert's review article 'A Polity Constructed: New Explorations in European Integration History', *Contemporary European History*, 19:2 (2010), 169–79, which shows how historians have recently focused less on member states than on the internal workings of the EC itself, and, for background, Wilfried Loth, 'Explaining European Integration:

The Contribution from Historians', *Journal of European Integration History*, 14:1 (2008), 9–26.

22. Christian Kleinschmidt, 'Infrastructure, Networks, (Large) Technical Systems: The "Hidden" Integration of Europe', *Contemporary European History*, 19:3 (2010), 275–84; Wolfram Kaiser, Brigitte Leucht, and Morten Rasmussen (eds.), *The History of the European Union: Origins of a Trans- and Supranational Polity, 1950–72* (London: Routledge, 2009); Wolfram Kaiser and Peter Starie (eds.), *Transnational European Union: Towards a Common Political Space* (London: Routledge, 2005).

23. Hartmut Kaelble, 'The Concept and Debates on the Idea', in Loth (ed.), *Experiencing Europe*, 127–33 and the subsequent chapters in the section of that book devoted to 'The Construction of a European Public Sphere' (125–67). See also the discussion in Lorenzo Mechi, 'Formation of a European Society? Exploring Social and Cultural Dimensions', in Wolfram Kaiser and Antonio Varsori (eds.), *European Union History: Themes and Debates* (Houndmills: Palgrave Macmillan, 2010), 150–68.

24. Bartolomiej Kaminski, 'The European Agreements and Transition: Unique Returns from Integrating into the European Union', in Sorin Antohi and Vladimir Tismaneanu (eds.), *Between Past and Future: The Revolutions of 1989 and their Aftermath* (Budapest: CEU Press, 2000), 310–11.

25. Giovanni Arrighi, 'The World Economy and the Cold War, 1970–1990', in *CHCW*, iii. 22–44, esp. 32.

26. John W. Young, 'Western Europe and the End of the Cold War, 1979–89', in *CHCW*, iii. 289–310.

27. Gottfried Niedhart, ' "The Transformation of the Other Side": Willy Brandt's Ostpolitik and the Liberal Peace Concept', in Bozo et al. (eds.), *Visions of the End of the Cold War*, 153.

28. Cited in Angela Romano, 'The Main Task of the European Political Cooperation: Fostering Détente in Europe', in Poul Villaume and Odd Arne Westad (eds.), *Perforating the Iron Curtain: European Détente, Transatlantic Relations, and the Cold War, 1965–1985* (Copenhagen: Museum Tusculanum, 2010), 124; see also Romano, 'The EC Nine's Vision and Attempts at Ending the Cold War', in Bozo et al. (eds.), *Visions of the End of the Cold War*, 134–46.

29. Cited in Romano, 'The Main Task', 125.

30. Mike Bowker and Phil Williams, *Superpower Détente: A Reappraisal* (London: Royal Institute of International Affairs/Sage, 1988), 94.

31. See Chapter 6 for more on superpower relations and the collapse of détente.

32. Cited in Georges-Henri Soutou, 'Valéry Giscard d'Estaing and his Vision of the End of the Cold War', in Bozo et al. (eds.), *Visions of the End of the Cold War*, 214.

33. Romano, 'The Main Task', 137.

34. Hans-Hermann Hertle, 'Germany in the Last Decade of the Cold War', in Njølstad (ed.), *The Last Decade of the Cold War*, 266.

35. Hertle, 'Germany in the Last Decade of the Cold War', 266. On 'change through trade', see Karsten Rudolph, *Wirtschaftsdiplomatie im Kalten Krieg: Die Ostpolitik der westdeutschen Großindustrie, 1945–1991* (Frankfurt am Main: Campus Verlag, 2004), chs. 10 and 11.

36. Frédéric Bozo, 'Before the Wall: French Diplomacy and the Last Decade of the Cold War, 1979–89', in Njølstad (ed.), *The Last Decade of the Cold War*, 289. This paragraph is indebted to Bozo's chapter.

37. Alistair Cole, *François Mitterrand: A Study in Political Leadership* (London: Routledge, 1994), 122.

38. Memorandum from Pierre Morel to Mitterrand, 1 June 1982, cited in Bozo, 'Before the Wall', 294. See also Philip H. Gordon, *A Certain Idea of France: French Security Policy and the Gaullist Legacy* (Princeton: Princeton University Press, 1993), 120 and, for more detail, Frédéric Bozo, *Mitterrand, the End of the Cold War, and German Unification* (New York: Berghahn Books, 2009), 1–28; Michael Sutton, *France and the Construction of Europe, 1944–2007: The Geopolitical Imperative* (New York: Berghahn Books, 2007), 198–201; Beatrice Heuser, 'Mitterrand's Gaullism: Cold War Policies for the Post-Cold War World?', in Varsori (ed.), *Europe 1945–1990s*, 346–69. Mitterrand's *Bundestag* speech is available (in French) at: <http://discours.vie-publique.fr/notices/847900500.html>.

39. Robert Gildea, 'Myth, Memory and Policy in France since 1945', in Jan-Werner Müller (ed.), *Memory and Power in Post-War Europe* (Cambridge: Cambridge University Press, 2002), 64.

40. Leopoldo Nuti, 'Italy and the Battle of the Euromissiles: The Deployment of the US BGM-109G "Gryphon", 1979–83', in Njølstad (ed.), *The Last Decade of the Cold War*, 332–59.

41. Sir T. Brimelow, minute of August 1971, cited in Sean Greenwood, 'Helping to Open the Door? Britain in the Last Decade of the Cold War', in Njølstad (ed.), *The Last Decade of the Cold War*, 323.

42. Martin D. Brown, 'A Very British Vision of Détente: The United Kingdom's Foreign Policy during the Helsinki Process, 1969–1975', in Bozo et al. (eds.), *Visions of the End of the Cold War*, 124–5.

43. Archie Brown, 'The Change to Engagement in Britain's Cold War Policy: The Origins of the Thatcher–Gorbachev Relationship', *Journal of Cold War Studies*, 10:3 (2008), 3–47.

44. Available at various online sites, including: <http://scyfilove.com/wp-content/uploads/2011/01/Nuclear-War-Survival-Guide-British-Government.pdf>. *Protect and Survive* was also made available as a series of short public information films. On the built environment, see Wayne D. Cocroft and Roger J. C. Thomas, *Cold War: Building for Nuclear Confrontation 1946–1989* (Swindon: English Heritage, 2003).

45. See Chapter 6 for more detail.

46. P. D. Smith, '"Gentlemen, You are Mad!" Mutual Assured Destruction and Cold War Culture', in *OHPEH*, 458.

47. See Arrighi, 'The World Economy and the Cold War', 31.

48. Robert English, 'Ideas and the End of the Cold War: Rethinking Intellectual and Political Change', in Pons and Romero (eds.), *Reinterpreting the End of the Cold War*, 127; English, 'The Sociology of New Thinking: Elites, Identity Change, and the End of the Cold War', *Journal of Cold War Studies*, 7:2 (2005), 60. Perhaps Gorbachev's friendship with Natta on the one hand and Mitterrand on the other had something to do with the different trajectories followed by the PCI and PCF: the latter ended up as an island of hard-line opposition to Gorbachev in the west, whereas the former adapted to post-Cold War realities, re-emerging as the PDS (Partito dei Democratici di Sinistra), later the DS, following the 1992–4 crisis in Italy.

49. James J. Sheehan, 'The Transformation of Europe and the End of the Cold War', in Jeffrey A. Engel (ed.), *The Fall of the Berlin Wall: The Revolutionary Legacy of 1989* (New York: Oxford University Press, 2009), 46. See also Greenwood, 'Helping to Open the Door?', 324; Rodric Braithwaite, 'Gorbachev and Thatcher: Witness Remarks', *Journal of European Integration History*, 16:1 (2010), 31–44.

50. Churchill, cited in Jaclyn Stanke, 'Stalin's Death and Anglo-American Visions of Ending the Cold War, 1953', in Bozo et al. (eds.), *Visions of the End of the Cold War*, 66.

51. Anatoly S. Chernyaev, 'Foreword', in Svetlana Savranskaya, Thomas Blanton, and Vladislav Zubok (eds.), *Masterpieces of History: The Peaceful End of the Cold War in Europe, 1989* (Budapest: CEU Press, 2010), xxiii.

52. Mitterrand to Thatcher, 31 July 1986; Thatcher to Mitterrand, 21 August 1986, cited in Marie-Pierre Rey, 'Gorbachev's New Thinking and Europe, 1985–1989', in Bozo et al. (eds.), *Europe and the End of the Cold War*, 26.

53. Frédéric Bozo, 'Mitterrand's Vision and the End of the Cold War', in Bozo et al. (eds.), *Visions of the End of the Cold War*, 283 (citing François Mitterrand, *Réflexions sur la politique extérieure de la France* (Paris: Fayard, 1986), although Bozo gets the title of Mitterrand's book wrong and the precise quotation appears to come from somewhere else). See also Frédéric Bozo, 'Mitterrand's France, the End of the Cold War, and German Unification: A Reappraisal', *Cold War History*, 7:4 (2007), 455–78.

54. Rey, 'Gorbachev's New Thinking and Europe', 28.

55. Rey, 'Gorbachev's New Thinking and Europe', 30.

56. Gorbachev, speech to Council of Europe, 6 July 1989, online at: <http://chnm.gmu.edu/1989/archive/files/gorbachev-speech-7-6-89_e3ccb87237.pdf>.

57. Marie-Pierre Rey, ' "Europe is our Common Home": A Study of Gorbachev's Diplomatic Concept', *Cold War History*, 4:2 (2004), 33–65. See Chapter 7. Chernyaev ('Foreword', xxiii) thinks that a western failure of imagination contributed to Gorbachev's inability to preserve the Soviet Union, which, could it have been preserved in a 'new, democratic form', would have made the dream of a 'common European home' more realistic.

58. Thomas Blanton, 'U.S. Policy and the Revolutions of 1989', in Savranskaya, Blanton, and Zubok (eds.), *Masterpieces of History*, 52–3.

59. Vojtech Mastny, 'Eastern Europe and the Early Prospects for EC/EU and NATO Membership', in Bozo et al. (eds.), *Europe and the End of the Cold War*, 235–46.

60. Ivan T. Berend, 'A Restructured Economy: From the Oil Crisis to the Financial Crisis, 1973–2009', in *OHPEH*, 407.

61. J.-P. Fitoussi and E. S. Phelps, 'Causes of the 1980s Slump in Europe', *Brookings Papers on Economic Activity*, 2 (1986), 487–520.

62. For a detailed analysis, see Maurice Kirby, 'Industrial and Structural Change', in Schulze (ed.), *Western Europe*, 81–104.

63. Jim Tomlinson, 'Britain', in Schulze (ed.), *Western Europe*, 278.

64. William I. Hitchcock, *The Struggle for Europe: The Turbulent History of a Divided Continent, 1945–2002* (London: Profile Books, 2004), 324.

65. Hitchcock, *The Struggle for Europe*, 331.

66. Budd, cited in Arrighi, 'The World Economy and the Cold War', 33.

67. Arrighi, 'The World Economy and the Cold War', 33.

68. Geoff Eley, *Forging Democracy: The History of the Left in Europe, 1850–2000* (New York: Oxford University Press, 2002), 427.

69. Ivan T. Berend, *Europe since 1980* (Cambridge: Cambridge University Press, 2010), 118.

70. Pons, 'Eurocommunism', 63.

71. See Daniele Ganser, *NATO's Secret Armies: Operation Gladio and Terrorism in Western Europe* (London: Routledge, 2004).

72. Berend, *Europe since 1980*, 175.

73. Wim Meeusen, 'European Economic Integration: From Business Cycle to Business Cycle', in *TMEH*, 247.

74. Judt, *Postwar*, 547.

75. Walter Korpi, 'Welfare State Regress in Western Europe: Politics, Institutions, Globalization, and Europeanization', *Annual Review of Sociology*, 29 (2003), 589–609. See also Manfred G. Schmidt, 'The Welfare State and the Economy in Periods of Economic Crisis: A Comparative Study of Twenty-Three OECD Nations', *European Journal of Political Research*, 11 (1983), 1–26; Herbert Kitschelt, *The Transformation of European Social Democracy* (Cambridge: Cambridge University Press, 1994), ch. 7.

76. Anderson, *The New Old World*, 66.

77. Colin Crouch, *Social Change in Western Europe* (Oxford: Oxford University Press, 1999), 398–9, citing Johannes Berger, 'Market and State in Advanced Capitalist Societies', *Current Sociology*, 38:2–3 (1990), 103–32.

78. Kirby, 'Industrial and Structural Change', 103.

79. Rosemary Wakeman, 'Veblen Redivivus: Leisure and Excess in Europe', in *OHPEH*, 423–42.

80. Philipp Gassert, 'The Spectre of Americanization: Western Europe in the American Century', in *OHPEH*, 185.

81. Jessica C. E. Gienow-Hecht, 'Culture and the Cold War in Europe', in *CHCW*, i. 414.

82. See Matthew Boswell, *Holocaust Impiety in Literature, Popular Music and Film* (Houndmills: Palgrave Macmillan, 2012), ch. 4.

83. Stephen Castles, 'Immigration and Asylum: Challenges to European Identities and Citizenship', in *OHPEH*, 206.

84. Jean-Marie Le Pen, cited in Richard Wolin, 'Designer Fascism', in Richard J. Golsan (ed.), *Fascism's Return: Scandal, Revision, and Ideology since 1980* (Lincoln, Nebr.: University of Nebraska Press, 1998), 55.

85. Dan Stone, 'The Uses and Abuses of "Secular Religion": Jules Monnerot's Path from Communism to Fascism', in Stone, *The Holocaust, Fascism and Memory: Essays in the History of Ideas* (Houndmills: Palgrave Macmillan, 2013), ch. 9.

86. Thomas C. Fox, *Stated Memory: East Germany and the Holocaust* (Rochester, NY: Camden House, 1999).

87. Willy Brandt, *Friedenspolitik in Europa* (Frankfurt am Main: Fischer Verlag, 1971), 34–5, cited in Jeffrey Herf, *Divided Memory: The Nazi Past in the Two Germanys* (Cambridge, Mass.: Harvard University Press, 1997), 345.

88. Jeffrey Herf, 'The "Holocaust" Reception in West Germany: Right, Center, and Left', in Anson Rabinbach and Jack Zipes (eds.), *Germans and Jews since the Holocaust: The Changing Situation in West Germany* (New York: Holmes & Meier, 1986), 209.

89. Herf, *Divided Memory*, 342.

90. Richard von Weizsäcker, speech to Bundestag, 8 May 1985, in Hartman (ed.), *Bitburg in Moral and Political Perspective*, 262–73.

91. See A. Dirk Moses, *German Intellectuals and the Nazi Past* (New York: Cambridge University Press, 2007), 26.

92. Detlev Claussen, 'In the House of the Hangman', in Rabinbach and Zipes (eds.), *Germans and Jews since the Holocaust*, 63. See also H. Glenn Penny III, 'The Museum für Deutsche Geschichte and German National Identity', *Central European History*, 28:3 (1995), 343–72, esp. 367–72.

93. Jean-Paul Bier, 'The Holocaust, West Germany, and Strategies of Oblivion, 1947–1979', in Rabinbach and Zipes (eds.), *Germans and Jews since the Holocaust*, 199.

94. Susan Sontag, 'Fascinating Fascism' (1974), in Elizabeth Hardwick (ed.), *The Susan Sontag Reader* (London: Penguin, 1983), 305–25; Saul Friedländer, *Reflections of Nazism: An Essay on Kitsch and Death* (New York: Discus, 1986).

95. On the *Historikerstreit*, see Charles S. Maier, *The Unmasterable Past: History, Holocaust, and German National Identity* (Cambridge, Mass.: Harvard University Press, 1988); Geoff Eley, 'Nazism, Politics and Public Memory: Thoughts on the West German *Historikerstreit*, 1986–1987', *Past and Present*, 121 (1988), 171–208; Dominick LaCapra, 'Revisiting the Historians' Debate: Mourning and Genocide', *History & Memory*, 9:1–2 (1997), 80–112.

96. Ernst Nolte, 'Between Historical Legend and Revisionism? The Third Reich in the Perspective of 1980' (24 July 1980) and Michael Stürmer, 'History in a Land without History' (25 July 1986), both in James Knowlton and Truett Cates (eds.), *Forever in the Shadow of Hitler? Original Documents of the* Historikerstreit, *the Controversy Concerning the Singularity of the Holocaust* (Atlantic Highlands, NJ: Humanities Press, 1993), 14, 16.

97. Jürgen Habermas, 'A Kind of Settlement of Damages: The Apologetic Tendencies in German History Writing' (11 July 1986), in Knowlton and Cates (eds.), *Forever in the Shadow of Hitler?*, 43.

98. Jürgen Habermas, 'On the Public Use of History: The Official Self-Understanding of the Federal Republic is Breaking Up' (7 November 1986), in Knowlton and Cates (eds.), *Forever in the Shadow of Hitler?*, 165.

99. 'Bitburg history' is Charles Maier's term; see *The Unmasterable Past*, 13–14.

100. Statistics in this paragraph come from Paul Hainsworth, *The Extreme Right in Western Europe* (London: Routledge, 2008), 32–4.

CHAPTER 6

1. Ludvík Vaculík, 'How to Survive 1984', in *A Cup of Coffee with my Interrogator*, 66; Agnes Heller, 'Phases of Legitimation in Soviet-Type Societies', in T. H. Rigby and Ferenc Fehér (eds.), *Political Legitimation in Communist States* (London: The Macmillan Press, 1982), 62; 'Mikhail Gorbachev on the 40th Anniversary of the GDR, 6 October 1989', in Jarausch and Gransow (eds.), *Uniting Germany*, 53.

2. Gaddis, *The Cold War*, 193; Adam Michnik, 'A Lesson in Dignity' (1979), in *Letters from Prison and Other Essays*, trans. Maya Latynski (Berkeley and Los Angeles: University of California Press, 1987), 160, begins: 'The pope is gone. The government has heaved a sigh of relief.' On the Pope, see Agostino Giovagnoli, 'Karol Wojtyla and the End of the Cold War', in Pons and Romero (eds.), *Reinterpreting the End of the Cold War*, 82–9, and Bernd Schäfer, 'The Catholic Church and the Cold War's End in Europe: Vatican *Ostpolitik* and Pope John Paul II, 1985–1989', in Bozo et al. (eds.), *Europe and the End of the Cold War*, 64–77.

3. Cited in Victor Sebestyen, *Revolution 1989: The Fall of the Soviet Empire* (London: Phoenix, 2010), 26.

4. Helmut Schmidt, speech to CSCE, 30 July/1 August 1975; T. Garvey to PM [Wilson], 9 September 1975, in *CW*, 342.

5. Leopoldo Nuti, 'On *recule pour mieux sauter*, or "What Needs to be Done" (To Understand the 1970s)', in Pons and Romero (eds.), *Reinterpreting the End of the Cold War*, 47.

6. Werner D. Lippert, 'Economic Diplomacy and East–West Trade during the Era of Détente: Strategy or Obstacle for the West', in Nuti (ed.), *The Crisis of Détente in Europe*, 190–201.

7. Olav Njølstad, 'The Collapse of Superpower Détente, 1975–1980', in *CHCW*, iii. 138. See also Noam Kochavi, 'Idealpolitik in Disguise: Israel, Jewish Emigration from the Soviet Union, and the Nixon Administration, 1969–1974', *International History Review*, 29:3 (2007), 550–72.

8. Bowker and Williams, *Superpower Détente*, 196–8. The next two paragraphs are indebted to Bowker and Williams's study.

9. Bowker and Williams, *Superpower Détente*, 198 are sceptical about this but note a 'change in tone' of Brezhnev's statements in the second half of the 1970s.

10. Bowker and Williams, *Superpower Détente*, 200.

11. For details of events in these regions of the world, see Odd Arne Westad, *The Global Cold War: Third World Interventions and the Making of our Times* (Cambridge: Cambridge University Press, 2005) and John Lamberton Harper, *The Cold War* (Oxford: Oxford University Press, 2011), ch. 6. As Harper notes in the context of the 1950s and early 1960s, western leaders might be forgiven for rejecting Soviet offers, since Soviet methods amounted to a 'pointed pistol' (135).

12. Njølstad, 'The Collapse of Superpower Détente', 150.

13. Bowker and Williams, *Superpower Détente*, 247.

14. Bowker and Williams, *Superpower Détente*, 250; Westad, *Global Cold War*, 331; Olav Njølstad, 'The Carter Legacy: Entering the Second Era of the Cold War', in Njølstad (ed.), *The Last Decade of the Cold War*, 196–225.

15. Mike Bowker, 'Brezhnev and Superpower Relations', in Edwin Bacon and Mike Sandle (eds.), *Brezhnev Reconsidered* (Houndmills: Palgrave Macmillan, 2002), 98. On SALT, see also Zbigniew Brzezinski, *Power and Principle: Memoirs of the National Security Advisor 1977–1981* (New York: Farrar Straus Giroux, 1983), 316–53.

16. Jussi M. Hanhimäki, 'Ironies and Turning Points: Détente in Perspective', in Westad (ed.), *Reviewing the Cold War*, 327.

17. See Poul Villaume and Odd Arne Westad, 'Introduction: The Secrets of European Détente', in Villaume and Westad (eds.), *Perforating the Iron Curtain*, 7–8, and the chapters in that book.

18. Judt, *Postwar*, 567.

19. Sarah B. Snyder, *Human Rights Activism and the End of the Cold War: A Transnational History of the Helsinki Network* (Cambridge: Cambridge University Press, 2011), 245. See the section on 'late communism' in this chapter.

20. Cited in Svetlana Savranskaya, 'Unintended Consequences: Soviet Interests, Expectations and Reactions to the Helsinki Final Act', in Bange and Niedhart (eds.), *Helsinki 1975 and the Transformation of Europe*, 181. See also Richard Davy, 'Helsinki Myths: Setting the Record Straight on the Final Act of the CSCE, 1975', *Cold War History*, 9:1 (2009), 16 for other Soviet officials' objections to the text of the Final Accord.

21. Cited in Savranskaya, 'Unintended Consequences', 181, 185.

22. Oliver Bange, 'The GDR in the Era of Détente: Conflicting Perceptions and Strategies, 1965–1975', in Villaume and Westad (eds.), *Perforating the Iron Curtain*, 64.

23. 'KOR's Appeal to Society', in Stokes (ed.), *From Stalinism to Pluralism*, 198.

24. Jonathan Schell, 'Introduction', in Michnik, *Letters from Prison*, xxix.

25. The text of the agreement is in Lyman H. Legters (ed.), *Eastern Europe: Transformation and Revolution, 1945–1991* (Lexington, Mass.: D. C. Heath and Company, 1992), 255–62.

26. 'The Solidarity Program' (16 October 1981), in Legters (ed.), *Eastern Europe*, 268–89.

27. 'Jaruzelski Declares Martial Law', in Stokes (ed.), *From Stalinism to Pluralism*, 214.

28. Sebestyen, *Revolution 1989*, 55; Vojtech Mastny, 'The Soviet Non-Invasion of Poland in 1980/81 and the End of the Cold War', *Cold War International History Project Working Papers*, 23 (1998), 31; Andrzej Paczkowski, 'Playground of Superpowers, Poland 1980–89: A View from Inside', in Njølstad (ed.), *The Last Decade of the Cold War*, 374.

29. See Hélène Carrère D'Encausse, *Big Brother: The Soviet Union and Soviet Europe* (New York: Holmes and Meier, 1987), 217.

30. Cited in Sebestyen, *Revolution 1989*, 55.

31. Vladislav M. Zubok, 'Soviet Foreign Policy from Détente to Gorbachev, 1975–1985', in *CHCW*, iii. 90.

32. Ken Jowitt, 'The Leninist Extinction', in *New World Disorder: The Leninist Extinction* (Berkeley and Los Angeles: University of California Press, 1992), 254–5.

33. Mastny, 'Soviet Non-Invasion', 34. Gorbachev too (*Memoirs*, 619) suggests, rather optimistically, that 'Martial law under Jaruzelski did not put an end to the reforms; in its own way, it facilitated them. Polish reformers took advantage of the newly instituted law and order in the country not to turn back but, on the contrary, to rally all the healthy forces of society that supported political pluralism and a market economy.'

34. Such as 'Stalin's Countries: Theses on Hope and Despair' (1971), published in Paris in *Politique Aujourd'hui* and available online from Radio Free Europe: <http://storage.osaarchivum.org/low/23/52/2352ec23-187b-40d7-972cb2806a30a2e2_l.pdf>.

35. Jadwiga Staniszkis, *Poland's Self-Limiting Revolution*, ed. Jan T. Gross (Princeton: Princeton University Press, 1984).

36. Savranskaya, 'Unintended Consequences', 188.

37. For a useful narrative of this period, see Caroline Kennedy-Pipe, *Russia and the World 1917–1991* (London: Arnold, 1998), ch. 8.

38. R. Craig Nation, 'Programming Armageddon: Warsaw Pact War Planning, 1969–1985', in Nuti (ed.), *The Crisis of Détente in Europe*, 128.

39. See Harry Gelman, *The Brezhnev Politburo and the Decline of Detente* (Ithaca, NY: Cornell University Press, 1984), 192–200.

40. Westad, 'Introduction: Reviewing the Cold War', in Westad (ed.), *Reviewing the Cold War*, 19.

41. *Pravda*, 29 September 1983, cited in Raymond L. Garthoff, *Détente and Confrontation: American–Soviet Relations from Nixon to Reagan* (Washington, DC: Brookings Institution, 1985), 1017.

42. Cited in Garthoff, *Détente and Confrontation*, 1015.
43. Richard Rhodes, *Arsenals of Folly: The Making of the Nuclear Arms Race* (London: Simon & Schuster, 2008), 166. See also Sebestyen, *Revolution 1989*, ch. 8.
44. Westad, 'Beginnings of the End', 78–9; Beth A. Fischer, 'The United States and the Transformation of the Cold War', in Njølstad (ed.), *The Last Decade of the Cold War*, 226–40; Fischer, 'Visions of Ending the Cold War: Triumphalism and U.S. Soviet Policy in the 1980s', in Bozo et al. (eds.), *Visions of the End of the Cold War*, 294–308; Fischer writes (306 n. 2): 'The notion that President Reagan had a hard-line policy towards the Soviet Union throughout his two terms in office is one of the fundamental myths of triumphalism. In fact, the President had jettisoned this approach by 1984 and adopted a more conciliatory posture.' For excerpts from the Reykjavik summit, see Hanhimäki and Westad (eds.), *CW*, 581–3.
45. Jeffrey A. Engel, '1989: An Introduction to an International History', in Engel (ed.), *The Fall of the Berlin Wall*, 29.
46. Zubok, 'Soviet Foreign Policy from Détente to Gorbachev', 90.
47. Kennedy-Pipe, *Russia and the World*, 180.
48. To understand the context of such slogans, see Timothy Less, 'Seeing Red: America and its Allies through the Eyes of Enver Hoxha', in Andrew Hammond (ed.), *The Balkans and the West: Constructing the European Other, 1945–2003* (Aldershot: Ashgate, 2004), 57–68.
49. Avraham Shifrin, *The First Guidebook to Prisons and Concentration Camps of the Soviet Union* (Toronto: Bantam Books, 1982 [1980]).
50. Václav Havel, 'The Power of the Powerless' (1978), in Havel, *Living in Truth*, ed. Jan Vladislav (London: Faber and Faber, 1987), 40.
51. Mark Sandle, 'Brezhnev and Developed Socialism: The Ideology of *Zastoi?*', in Bacon and Sandle (eds.), *Brezhnev Reconsidered*, 184. See also, for a still-valuable analysis, James R. Millar, 'The Little Deal: Brezhnev's Contribution to Acquisitive Socialism', *Slavic Review*, 44:4 (1985), 694–706.
52. János Kornai, 'Resource-Constrained Versus Demand-Constrained Systems', *Econometrica*, 47:4 (1979), 801–19.
53. Jeanette Z. Madarász, *Conflict and Compromise in East Germany, 1971–1989: A Precarious Stability* (Basingstoke: Palgrave Macmillan, 2003), 142–3.
54. Raymond G. Stokes, *Constructing Socialism: Technology and Change in East Germany 1945–1990* (Baltimore: Johns Hopkins University Press, 2000). See also Stokes, 'Plastics and the New Society: The German Democratic Republic in the 1950s and 1960s', in Susan E. Reid and David Crowley (eds.), *Style and Socialism: Modernity and Material Culture in Post-War Eastern Europe* (Oxford: Berg, 2000), 65–80 for the argument that there was a vicious circle as poor-quality goods left workers unmotivated, meaning they produced inferior consumer and producer goods. On the 'consumption junction', see Karin Zachmann, 'A Socialist Consumption Junction: Debating the Mechanization of Housework in East Germany, 1956–1957', *Technology and Culture*, 43:1 (2002), 73–99.

55. For example: Narcis Tulbure, 'Drink, Leisure, and the Second Economy in Socialist Romania', in David Crowley and Susan E. Reid (eds.), *Pleasures in Socialism: Leisure and Luxury in the Eastern Bloc* (Evanston, Ill.: Northwestern University Press, 2010), 259–81; Małgorzata Mazurek, 'Keeping It Close to Home: Resourcefulness and Scarcity in Late Socialist and Postsocialist Poland', in Paulina Bren and Mary Neuberger (eds.), *Communism Unwrapped: Consumption in Cold War Eastern Europe* (New York: Oxford University Press, 2012), 298–320.

56. Roger Markwick, 'The Great Patriotic War in Soviet and Post-Soviet Collective Memory', in *OHPEH*, 703.

57. Mary Fulbrook, *German National Identity after the Holocaust* (Cambridge: Polity Press, 1999), 33–4. See also Amir Weiner, 'When Memory Counts: War, Genocide, and Postwar Soviet Jewry', in Omer Bartov, Atina Grossmann, and Mary Nolan (eds.), *Crimes of War: Guilt and Denial in the Twentieth Century* (New York: The New Press, 2002), 191–216.

58. Mary Fulbrook, *Anatomy of a Dictatorship: Inside the GDR 1949–1989* (Oxford: Oxford University Press, 1995), 27.

59. See, for a famous example, Milan Kundera, *The Joke* (London: Faber and Faber, 1992).

60. Ann Douglas, 'War Envy and Amnesia: American Cold War Rewrites of Russia's War', in Joel Isaac and Duncan Bell (eds.), *Uncertain Empire: American History and the Idea of the Cold War* (Oxford: Oxford University Press, 2012), 121.

61. Rogers Brubaker, *Nationalism Reframed: Nationhood and the National Question in the New Europe* (Cambridge: Cambridge University Press, 1996), ch. 2; Yuri Slezkine, 'The USSR as a Communal Apartment: or How a Socialist State Promoted Ethnic Particularism', *Slavic Review*, 53:2 (1994), 414–52.

62. Norman Manea, *On Clowns: The Dictator and the Artist* (London: Faber and Faber, 1994), 121.

63. Brindusa Palade, 'The Romanian Utopia: The Role of the Intelligentsia in the Communist Implementation of a New Human Paradigm', *Southeast European and Black Sea Studies*, 2:2 (2002), 93–100; Vladimir Tismaneanu, 'Understanding National Stalinism: Reflections on Ceauşescu's Socialism', *Communist and Post-Communist Studies*, 32:2 (1999), 155–73; Katherine Verdery, 'Nationalism and National Sentiment in Post-Socialist Romania', *Slavic Review*, 52:2 (1993), 179–203. For background to Ceauşescu's ultra-nationalism, see Dragoş Petrescu, 'Community-Building and Identity Politics in Gheorghiu-Dej's Romania, 1956–64', in Tismaneanu (ed.), *Stalinism Revisited*, 401–22.

64. Havel, 'The Power of the Powerless', 41.

65. Paulina Bren, *The Greengrocer and his TV: The Culture of Communism after the 1968 Prague Spring* (Ithaca, NY: Cornell University Press, 2010), 3.

66. Havel, 'Letter to Dr Gustáv Husák', in *Living in Truth*, 33.

67. Jan Palmowski, *Inventing a Socialist Nation: Heimat and the Politics of Everyday Life in the GDR, 1945–1990* (Cambridge: Cambridge University Press, 2009), 9–10.

68. Brian Ladd, *The Ghosts of Berlin: Confronting German History in the Urban Land-scape* (Chicago: University of Chicago Press, 1997), 58–9. In the absence of a 'civil society', perhaps there were few alternative places to meet. In an act of historical vandalism, the *Palast der Republik* was finally demolished between 2006 and 2008, to be replaced by a replica of the Imperial Palace that stood on the site until after the Second World War.

69. Thomas Lindenberger, '"Asociality" and Modernity: The GDR as a Welfare Dictatorship', in Katherine Pence and Paul Betts (eds.), *Socialist Modern: East German Everyday Culture and Politics* (Ann Arbor: University of Michigan Press, 2008), 211–33.

70. Susan E. Reid, 'Cold War in the Kitchen: Gender and the De-Stalinization of Consumer Taste in the Soviet Union under Khrushchev', *Slavic Review*, 61:2 (2002), 252.

71. Alexei Yurchak, *Everything Was Forever, Until It Was No More: The Last Soviet Generation* (Princeton: Princeton University Press, 2006), 283.

72. Yurchak, *Everything Was Forever, Until It Was No More*, 93.

73. Cited in Serguei Alex. Oushakine, 'Crimes of Substitution: Detection in Late Soviet Society', *Public Culture*, 15:3 (2003), 428.

74. Palmowski, *Inventing a Socialist Nation*, 12.

75. Tony Judt, *The Memory Chalet* (London: William Heinemann, 2010), 105. 'Late paternalism' comes from Laszlo Bruszt, '"Without Us but For Us?" Political Orientation in Hungary in the Period of Late Paternalism', *Social Research*, 55:1&2 (1988), 43–76, and 'conditional tolerance' from Jan Pakulski, 'Legitimacy and Mass Compliance: Reflections on Max Weber and Soviet-Type Societies', *British Journal of Political Science*, 16:1 (1986), 35–56. On the emphasis on the *form* of normalization rather than correct ideological *content* after the mid-1970s, see also Libora Oates-Indruchová, 'The Limits of Thought? The Regulatory Framework of Social Sciences and Humanities in Czechoslovakia (1968–1989)', *Europe-Asia Studies*, 60:10 (2008), 1767–82.

76. Anton Weiss-Wendt, *Small Town Russia: Childhood Memories of the Final Soviet Decade* (Gainesville, Fla.: Florida Academic Press, 2010), 98, 103, 106, and ch. 14.

77. 'Charter 77' (1 January 1977), in Legters (ed.), *Eastern Europe*, 231. See also Christian Domnitz, 'Overcoming Bloc Division from Below: Jiří Hájek and the CSCE Appeal of Charter 77', in Bozo et al. (eds.), *Visions of the End of the Cold War*, 177–90.

78. Serguei Alex. Oushakine, 'The Terrifying Mimicry of Samizdat', *Public Culture*, 13:2 (2001), 191–214.

79. Barbara J. Falk, 'Resistance and Dissent in Central and Eastern Europe: An Emerging Historiography', *East European Politics and Societies*, 25:2 (2011), 339.

80. See the discussion in Václav Benda et al., 'Parallel Polis, or An Independent Society in Central and Eastern Europe: An Inquiry', *Social Research*, 55:1&2 (1988), 211–46.

81. David Doellinger, 'Prayers, Pilgrimages and Petitions: The Secret Church and the Growth of Civil Society in Slovakia', *Nationalities Papers*, 30:2 (2002), 215–40; Raymond Patton, 'The Communist Culture Industry: The Music Business in 1980s Poland', *Journal of Contemporary History*, 47:2 (2012), 427–49. On 'magnetizdat', see Vladislav Zubok, 'Die sowjetrussische Gesellschaft in den sechziger Jahren', in Stefan Karner et al. (eds.), *Prager Frühling: Das internationale Krisenjahr 1968*, i: *Beiträge* (Cologne: Böhlau Verlag, 2008), 837; Vladislav Zubok, *Zhivago's Children: The Last Russian Intelligentsia* (Cambridge, Mass.: Belknap Press of Harvard University Press, 2009), 268.

82. Vaculík, 'On Heroism', in *A Cup of Coffee with my Interrogator*, 51.

83. Miklós Haraszti, *The Velvet Prison: Artists under State Socialism* (London: I. B. Tauris, 1988), 158, 161. The book was published in France in 1983 and in *samizdat* in Hungary in 1986.

84. Haraszti, *The Velvet Prison*, 162. See also Barbara J. Falk, *The Dilemmas of Dissidence in East-Central Europe: Citizen Intellectuals and Philosopher Kings* (Budapest: CEU Press, 2003), 296–7.

85. Bren, *The Greengrocer and his TV*, 7. See also Annemarie Sammartino, 'We are the State We Seek: Everyday Life in Czechoslovakia and East Germany, 1945–1989', *Contemporary European History*, 21:3 (2012), 477–91.

86. Bren, *The Greengrocer and his TV*, 189. See also Paul Betts, 'The Politics of Plenty: Consumerism in Communist Societies', in S. A. Smith (ed.), *The Oxford Handbook of Communism* (Oxford: Oxford University Press, 2013).

87. Betts, *Within Walls*, 226. Betts is here talking about GDR domestic photography of the 1970s and 1980s.

88. Indeed, the historical record of *samizdat* is hazy, there is no obvious 'archive'. See Olga Zaslavskaya, 'From Dispersed to Distributed Archives: The Past and the Present of Samizdat Material', *Poetics Today*, 29:4 (2008), 669–712; Ann Komaromi, 'The Material Existence of Soviet Samizdat', *Slavic Review*, 63:3 (2004), 597–618.

89. Cited in Oushakine, 'Terrifying Mimicry', 214. On Siniavsky, see Zubok, *Zhivago's Children*.

90. Archie Brown, 'Introduction', in Gorbachev and Mlynář, *Conversations with Gorbachev*, xi.

91. William Taubman and Svetlana Savranskaya, 'If a Wall Fell in Berlin and Moscow Hardly Noticed, Would it Still Make a Noise?', in Engel (ed.), *The Fall of the Berlin Wall*, 73.

92. Daniel Chirot, 'What Happened in Eastern Europe in 1989?', in Tismaneanu (ed.), *The Revolutions of 1989*, 22; Jowitt, 'The Leninist Extinction', 256. For useful surveys of the economics of the Eastern Bloc, see Barry Eichengreen, 'Economy', in *MF*, 136–9; Eichengreen, *The European Economy since 1945: Coordinated Capitalism and Beyond* (Princeton: Princeton University Press, 2007), ch. 10.

93. Karl Jaspers to Hannah Arendt, 23 November 1957, in Lotte Kohler and Hans Saner (eds.), *Hannah Arendt/Karl Jaspers Correspondence 1926–1969* (San Diego: Harcourt Brace and Company, 1993), 334.

94. Yurchak, *Everything Was Forever, Until It Was No More*, esp. ch. 2; 'tyrannies of certitude' is Daniel Chirot's phrase.

95. Katherine Verdery, *What Was Socialism, and What Comes Next?* (Princeton: Princeton University Press, 1996), 37.

96. For a useful analysis of the various factors that contributed to the demise of communism, see Georg Schöpflin, *Politics in Eastern Europe 1945–1992* (Oxford: Blackwell, 1993), ch. 9. See also Michael Bernhard, 'The Revolutions of 1989', *Angelaki*, 15:3 (2010), 109–22, esp. 110–12 on economics.

97. Westad, 'Beginnings of the End', 79. See also Robert English, 'Ideas and the End of the Cold War: Rethinking Intellectual and Political Change', in Pons and Romero (eds.), *Reinterpreting the End of the Cold War*, 116–36.

98. Steven Pfaff and Guobin Yang, 'Double-Edged Rituals and the Symbolic Resources of Collective Action: Political Commemorations and the Mobilization of Protest in 1989', *Theory and Society*, 30:4 (2001), 539–89; Renée de Nevers, *Comrades No More: The Seeds of Change in Eastern Europe* (Cambridge, Mass.: MIT Press, 2003).

99. But, for the importance of a bottom-up approach, see Padraic Kenney, *A Carnival of Revolution: Central Europe 1989* (Princeton: Princeton University Press, 2003), and Vojtech Mastny, 'Did Gorbachev Liberate Eastern Europe?', in Njølstad (ed.), *The Last Decade of the Cold War*, 402–23. And for interviews with and analysis of ordinary people who took to the streets in 1989, see Henri Vogt, *Between Utopia and Disillusionment: A Narrative of the Political Transformation in Eastern Europe* (New York: Berghahn Books, 2005).

100. Jacques Lévesque, *The Enigma of 1989: The USSR and the Liberation of Eastern Europe* (Berkeley and Los Angeles: University of California Press, 1997).

101. Transcript of televised 'Address to the Soviet Citizens', 25 December 1991, in Gorbachev, *Memoirs*, xxxiv.

102. Snyder, *Human Rights Activism*, 247. See also Gorbachev, *Memoirs*, 517.

103. Gorbachev and Mlynář, *Conversations with Gorbachev*, 65.

104. Westad, *Global Cold War*, 365. At the same time, the CIA regularly overestimated the quality of Soviet weapons and the seriousness of the Soviet military threat.

105. Cited in Matthew J. Ouimet, *The Rise and Fall of the Brezhnev Doctrine in Soviet Foreign Policy* (Chapel Hill, NC: University of North Carolina Press, 2003), 253.

106. 'Memorandum from the Bogomolov Institute, "Changes in Eastern Europe and their Impact on the USSR", February 1989', in Savranskaya, Blanton, and Zubok (eds.), *Masterpieces of History*, 365–81, here 377.

107. Shevardnadze, cited in Svetlana Savranskaya, 'In the Name of Europe: Soviet Withdrawal from Eastern Europe', in Bozo et al (eds.), *Europe and the End of the Cold War*, 46, 47.

108. Cited in Westad, *Global Cold War*, 372.

109. Gorbachev, *Memoirs*, 517. One has of course to remember that what Gorbachev meant by 'successes' and 'set-backs' might have been different in 1987 from when he published his memoirs in 1995.

110. Gorbachev, speech to the Warsaw Congress, 30 June 1986, cited in Vladimir Tismaneanu, *The Crisis of Marxist Ideology in Eastern Europe: The Poverty of Utopia* (London: Routledge, 1988), 203. See also Vladislav M. Zubok, 'Gorbachev and the End of the Cold War: Perspectives on History and Personality', *Cold War History*, 2:2 (2002), 61–100; Archie Brown, 'Perestroika and the End of the Cold War', *Cold War History*, 7:1 (2007), 1–17; Melvyn P. Leffler, 'The Beginning and the End: Time, Context and the Cold War', in Njølstad (ed.), *The Last Decade of the Cold War*, 29–59.

111. Hannah Arendt, *Crises of the Republic* (Harmondsworth: Penguin, 1973) 179.

112. On Lenin, see Mikhail Gorbachev, *Perestroika: New Thinking for our Country and the World* (New York: Harper & Row, 1988), 11–12.

113. Jacques Lévesque, 'The Messianic Character of "New Thinking": Why and What For?', in Njølstad (ed.), *The Last Decade of the Cold War*, 159–76; William E. Odom, 'The Sources of "New Thinking" in Soviet Politics', in Njølstad (ed.), *The Last Decade of the Cold War*, 149. See also John Van Oudenaren, 'Gorbachev and his Predecessors: Two Faces of New Thinking', in Michael T. Clark and Simon Serfaty (eds.), *New Thinking and Old Realities: America, Europe, and Russia* (Washington, DC: Seven Locks Press, 1991), 3–27. By the mid-1990s, Gorbachev admitted that the mix of socialism and democracy he had envisaged had not materialized, implicitly suggesting that he had not realized where his reforms would lead, but having the good sense not to try and stop them once he did finally realize.

114. Stefanos Katsikas, 'An Overview of Albania's Foreign Policy-Making in the 1980s', *Slovo*, 16:2 (2004), 93.

115. Nicolae Ceauşescu in *Scînteia*, 4 May 1988, cited in Tismaneanu, *Stalinism for All Seasons*, 32.

116. Gorbachev, *Memoirs*, 612.

117. Cited in Tismaneanu, *The Crisis of Marxist Ideology*, 202.

118. Petre Opriş, 'The Polish Crisis and its Impact on the Romanian Economy in the Early 1980s', in Nuti (ed.), *The Crisis of Détente in Europe*, 202–13.

119. Mariana Hausleitner, 'Romania and Hungary 1985–90: The Soviet Perspective', in Westad, Holtsmark, and Neumann (eds.), *The Soviet Union in Eastern Europe*, 137–49.

120. Jacques Lévesque, 'Soviet Approaches to Eastern Europe at the Beginning of 1989', *Cold War International History Project Bulletin*, 12–13 (2001), 49. Also Lévesque, 'The East European Revolutions of 1989', in Leffler and Westad (eds.), *Cambridge History of the Cold War*, iii. 311–32.

121. Mark Kramer, 'Gorbachev and the Demise of East European Communism', in Pons and Romero (eds.), *Reinterpreting the End of the Cold War*, 179. This paragraph is indebted to Kramer's chapter.

122. Council of Europe Speech, 6 July 1989, online at: <http://chnm.gmu. edu/1989/archive/files/gorbachev-speech-7-6-89_e3ccb87237.pdf>.

123. Vladislav M. Zubok, *A Failed Empire: The Soviet Union in the Cold War from Stalin to Gorbachev* (Chapel Hill, NC: University of North Carolina Press, 2009), 320.

124. Kramer, 'Gorbachev and the Demise', 191.

125. Gregory F. Domber, 'Ending the Cold War, Unintentionally', in Bozo et al. (eds.), *Visions of the End of the Cold War*, 225.

126. Stephen Kotkin, *Uncivil Society: 1989 and the Implosion of the Communist Establishment* (New York: Modern Library, 2009), xv.

127. For these brief country-by-country narratives, I have relied, along with previously mentioned studies, on: Gale Stokes, *The Walls Came Tumbling Down: The Collapse of Communism in Eastern Europe* (New York: Oxford University Press, 1993); Ivan T. Berend, 'The Central and Eastern European Revolution, 1989–2000', in *TMEH*, 190–210; Pittaway, *Eastern Europe*, ch. 8; Robert Bideleux and Ian Jeffries, *A History of Eastern Europe: Crisis and Change*, 2nd edn. (London: Routledge, 2007), ch. 33; Tom Buchanan, *Europe's Troubled Peace, 1945–2000* (Oxford: Blackwell, 2006), ch. 10.

128. Cited in Berend, 'The Central and Eastern European Revolution', 196.

129. Michael Bernhard and Henryk Szlajfer (eds.), *From the Polish Underground: Selections from Krytyka, 1978–1993* (University Park, Pa.: Penn State University Press, 1995); Kenney, *A Carnival of Revolution*, contains much detail on Hungarians, Czechoslovaks, Slovenians, Ukrainians, and others developing their underground activities with Polish assistance.

130. Cited in Sebestyen, *Revolution 1989*, 213.

131. Nigel Swain, 'Negotiated Revolution in Poland and Hungary, 1989', in McDermott and Stibbe (eds.), *Revolution and Resistance*, 152; Gaddis, *Cold War*, 242–3.

132. William Echikson, 'Bloc Buster' (June 1989), in Legters (ed.), *Eastern Europe*, 427.

133. Anatoly S. Chernyaev, *My Six Years with Gorbachev*, trans. and ed. Robert D. English and Elizabeth Tucker (University Park, Pa.: Pennsylvania State University Press, 2000), 235.

134. Patrick Major, *Behind the Berlin Wall: East Germany and the Frontiers of Power* (Oxford: Oxford University Press, 2010), 231, 232.

135. Gaddis, *Cold War*, 243–4.

136. Charles S. Maier, *Dissolution: The Crisis of Communism and the End of East Germany* (Princeton: Princeton University Press, 1997), 153.

137. Gorbachev later claimed to Krenz that he had been speaking about himself. See the memorandum of conversation between Gorbachev and Krenz, 1 November 1989, *Cold War International History Project Bulletin*, 12–13 (2001), 141.

138. For the transcript of the interview, see *Cold War International History Project Bulletin*, 12–13 (2001), 157–8.

139. Major, *Behind the Berlin Wall*, 255–6. For a detailed narrative of events, see Hans-Hermann Hertle, 'The Fall of the Wall: The Unintended Self-Dissolu-

tion of East Germany's Ruling Regime', *Cold War International History Project Bulletin*, 12–13 (2001), 131–40.

140. 'Diary of Anatoly Chernyaev Regarding the Fall of the Berlin Wall' (10 November 1989), in Savranskaya, Blanton, and Zubok (eds.), *Masterpieces of History*, 586.

141. Oldřich Tůma, 'Czechoslovak November 1989', *Cold War International History Project Bulletin*, 12–13 (2001), 181.

142. Havel, 'New Year's Day Speech, 1990', in Stokes (ed.), *From Stalinism to Pluralism*, 260–4.

143. 'Summary of the Demands Made by Opposition Groups Represented by the Civic Forum', 23 November 1989, *Cold War International History Project Bulletin*, 12–13 (2001), 186. On Dubček's actual role in 1968, see Chapter 4.

144. 'Cable from US Embassy in Sofia to State Department' (9 November 1989), in Savranskaya, Blanton, and Zubok (eds.), *Masterpieces of History*, 576.

145. See Jordan Baev, '1989: Bulgarian Transition to Pluralist Democracy', *Cold War International History Project Bulletin*, 12–13 (2001), 165–7.

146. Tismaneanu, *Stalinism for All Seasons*, 229.

147. Mircea Munteanu, 'The Last Days of a Dictator', *Cold War International History Project Bulletin*, 12–13 (2001), 217–25, which includes the transcript of a key conversation between Gorbachev and Ceauşescu on 4 December 1989.

148. For transcript of the trial, see *CW*, 605–7. For a more detailed narrative of events, see Dennis Deletant, 'Romania 1948–1989: An Historical Overview', in Deletant and Mihail Ionescu, 'Romania and the Warsaw Pact, 1955–1989', *Cold War International History Project Working Papers*, 43 (2004), esp. 38–58; Peter Siani-Davies, *The Romanian Revolution of December 1989* (Ithaca, NY: Cornell University Press, 2005).

149. This paragraph is indebted to Nicholas Pano, 'The Process of Democratization in Albania', in Karen Dawisha and Bruce Parrott (eds.), *Politics, Power, and the Struggle for Democracy in South-East Europe* (Cambridge: Cambridge University Press, 1997), 285–352.

150. Cited in Pano, 'The Process of Democratization', 301–2. On foreign tourists, see Derek R. Hall, 'Foreign Tourism under Socialism: The Albanian "Stalinist" Model', *Annals of Tourism Research*, 11 (1984), 539–55.

151. Peter G. Boyle, 'The Cold War Revisited', *Journal of Contemporary History*, 35:3 (2000), 488.

152. Lévesque, 'East European Revolutions', 332.

CHAPTER 7

1. Mikoyan, cited by Wilfried Loth, 'The Cold War and the Social and Economic History of the Twentieth Century', in *CHCW*, ii. 517; Shakhnazarov in 'Dialogue: The Musgrove Conference, 1–3 May 1998', in Savranskaya, Blanton, and Zubok (eds.), *Masterpieces of History*, 121; Eric Hobsbawm, *The Age of Extremes* (London: Little, Brown, 1994), 3.

2. For example: Sebestyen, *Revolution 1989*; Mary Elise Sarotte, *1989: The Struggle to Create Post-Cold War Europe* (Princeton: Princeton University Press, 2009); Michael Meyer, *The Year that Changed the World: The Untold Story Behind the Fall of the Berlin Wall* (London: Simon and Schuster, 2009); Constantine Pleshakov, *There Is No Freedom Without Bread! 1989 and the Civil War that Brought Down Communism* (New York: Farrar Straus Giroux, 2009); Stephen Kotkin, *Uncivil Society: 1989 and the Implosion of the Communist Establishment* (New York: Modern Library, 2009); Engel (ed.), *The Fall of the Berlin Wall*; Padraic Kenney, *1989: Democratic Revolutions at the Cold War's End* (New York: Palgrave Macmillan, 2010).

3. Jacques Rupnik, 'The Post-Totalitarian Blues', in Tismaneanu (ed.), *The Revolutions of 1989*, 231–43.

4. Daniele Albertazzi and Duncan McDonnell (eds.), *Twenty-First Century Populism: The Spectre of Western European Democracy* (Houndmills: Palgrave Macmillan, 2008).

5. Susan Buck-Morss, *Dreamworld and Catastrophe: The Passing of Mass Utopia in East and West* (Cambridge, Mass.: MIT Press, 2000), 39.

6. Anders Stephanson, 'Cold War Degree Zero', and Odd Arne Westad, 'Exploring the Histories of the Cold War: A Pluralist Approach', both in Isaac and Bell (eds.), *Uncertain Empire*, 19–49 and 51–9.

7. Jack F. Matlock, Jr, *Reagan and Gorbachev: How the Cold War Ended* (New York: Random House, 2004), 318.

8. Interview with Kulikov in *Vremya MN* (6 September 1999), cited in Mark Kramer, 'The Demise of the Soviet Bloc', in Vladimir Tismaneanu (ed.), *The End and the Beginning: The Revolutions of 1989 and the Resurgence of History* (Budapest: CEU Press, 2012), 248.

9. Mark Kramer, 'The Collapse of East European Communism and the Repercussions within the Soviet Union (Part 2)', *Journal of Cold War Studies*, 6:4 (2004), 8. Kramer interviewed Volkogonov in Moscow in 1995.

10. Kramer, 'The Demise of the Soviet Bloc', 192.

11. Kotkin, *Uncivil Society*, 137.

12. Gorbachev, *Memoirs*, 738. It is unlikely that Gorbachev really believed in secession as an option for the Soviet republics, even in principle, at the start of 1990.

13. Cited in Mark Kramer, 'The Collapse of East European Communism and the Repercussions within the Soviet Union (Part 1)', *Journal of Cold War Studies*, 5:4 (2003), 31–2.

14. Baker in William C. Wohlforth (ed.), *Cold War Endgame: Oral History, Analysis, Debates* (University Park, Pa.: Pennsylvania State University Press, 2003), 136. The text is the transcript of a conference that took place at Princeton University on 29–30 March 1996.

15. Chernyaev, *My Six Years with Gorbachev*, 252.

16. Wałęsa in *Gazeta Wyborcza*, 28 March 1990, cited in Anthony Kemp-Welch, *Poland under Communism: A Cold War History* (Cambridge: Cambridge University Press, 2008), 427. See also Kramer, 'The Collapse (Part 1)', 211.

17. Yeltsin in *Izvestiya*, 15 January 1991, cited in Kramer, 'The Collapse (Part 2)', 48.

18. Cited in Kramer, 'The Collapse (Part 1)', 215.

19. Lippmaa, cited in Anatol Lieven, *The Baltic Revolution: Estonia, Latvia, Lithuania, and the Path to Independence* (New Haven: Yale University Press, 1993), 242.

20. Burlakov, cited in Mark Kramer, 'The Collapse of East European Communism and the Repercussions within the Soviet Union (Part 3)', *Journal of Cold War Studies*, 7:1 (2005), 62.

21. Alex Pravda, 'The Collapse of the Soviet Union, 1990–1991', in *CHCW*, iii. 360, 373.

22. Chernyaev in Wohlforth (ed.), *Cold War Endgame*, 123.

23. Chernyaev in Wohlforth (ed.), *Cold War Endgame*, 120.

24. Graeme Gill and Roger D. Markwick, *Russia's Stillborn Democracy? From Gorbachev to Yeltsin* (Oxford: Oxford University Press, 2000), 110; Jacques Lévesque, 'The Emancipation of Eastern Europe', in Richard K. Hermann and Richard Ned Lebow (eds.), *Ending the Cold War: Interpretations, Causation, and the Study of International Relations* (New York: Palgrave Macmillan, 2004), 107–29.

25. As Stephen Kotkin explains in *Armageddon Averted: The Soviet Collapse 1970–2000* (Oxford: Oxford University Press, 2001).

26. Anna Paretskaya, 'The Soviet Communist Party and the Other Spirit of Capitalism', *Sociological Theory*, 28:4 (2010), 377–401.

27. For a useful discussion, see David Rowley, 'Interpretations of the End of the Soviet Union: Three Paradigms', *Kritika*, 2:2 (2001), 395–426.

28. Fatos Lubonja, 'Albania after Isolation: The Transformation of Public Perceptions of the West', in Hammond (ed.), *The Balkans and the West*, 127–35, here 135. See also, in the same volume, Stephanie Schwandner-Sievers, 'Albanians, Albanianism and the Strategic Subversion of Stereotypes', 110–26.

29. The Caucasian and Central Asian republics are beyond the scope of this book. For useful analyses, see: Karen Dawisha and Bruce Parrott (eds.), *Conflict, Cleavage, and Change in Central Asia and the Caucasus* (Cambridge: Cambridge University Press, 1997); Amanda E. Wooden and Christoph H. Stefes (eds.), *The Politics of Transition in Central Asia and the Caucasus: Enduring Legacies and Emerging Challenges* (London: Routledge, 2009).

30. Jon Elster (ed.), *The Roundtable Talks and the Breakdown of Communism* (Chicago: University of Chicago Press, 1996).

31. Kramer, 'The Collapse (Part 2)', 56–7. Shushkevich later said that 'when I went to Belovezhskaya Puschcha in late 1991 I had in mind people like Havel and Wałęsa in Czechoslovakia and Poland who sat down in 1989 and negotiated a way out of their own internal crises. I hoped we could be as civilized in dismantling the USSR' (57).

32. Csilla Kiss, 'Transitional Justice: The (Re)Construction of Post-Communist Memory', in Ene Kõresaar, Epp Lauk, and Kristin Kuutma (eds.), *The Burden of Remembering: Recollections and Representations of the 20th Century* (Helsinki: Finnish Literature Society, 2009), 134.

33. Vladimir Tismaneanu, *Fantasies of Salvation: Democracy, Nationalism, and Myth in Post-Communist Europe* (Princeton: Princeton University Press, 1998).

34. Michnik, 'My Vote against Wałęsa', in Michnik, *Letters from Freedom: Post-Cold War Realities and Perspectives*, ed. Irena Grudzińska Gross (Berkeley and Los Angeles: University of California Press, 1998), 157–66 (orig. in *New York Review of Books*, 20 December 1990). Michnik wrote, for example (165), that 'perhaps unintentionally, Lech Wałęsa clearly promises neglect of the law and democratic procedures, revenge on his political opponents, unprofessional ideas, and rule by incompetent people'.

35. David Ost, *The Defeat of Solidarity: Anger and Politics in Postcommunist Europe* (Ithaca, NY: Cornell University Press, 2005), 2.

36. Scott Brown, 'Prelude to a Divorce? The Prague Spring as Dress Rehearsal for Czechoslovakia's "Velvet Divorce" ', *Europe-Asia Studies*, 60:10 (2008), 1783–804.

37. Jonathan Stein, cited in Ost, *Defeat of Solidarity*, 181.

38. Vladimir Tismaneanu, 'The Quasi-Revolution and its Discontents: Emerging Political Pluralism in Post-Ceauşescu Romania', *East European Politics and Societies*, 7:2 (1993), 309–48; Peter Siani-Davies, 'Romanian Revolution or Coup d'état? A Theoretical View of the Events of December 1989', *Communist and Post-Communist Studies*, 29:4 (1996), 453–65. But as Jowitt noted ('The Leninist Extinction', 259), with reference to Bulgaria and Romania in an essay of 1991, 'even regimes whose new political profiles contain elements recognizably derived from their Leninist predecessors will no longer be Leninist or part of an international regime world'.

39. Peter Gross and Vladimir Tismaneanu, 'The End of Postcommunism in Romania', *Journal of Democracy*, 16:2 (2005), 146–62.

40. Eley, *Forging Democracy*, 449.

41. See, for example, Meike Wulf and Pertti Grönholm, 'Generating Meaning Across Generations: The Role of Historians in the Codification of History in Soviet and Post-Soviet Estonia', *Journal of Baltic Studies*, 41:3 (2010), 351–82; Arnold Bartetsky, 'Changes in the Political Iconography of East Central European Capitals after 1989 (Berlin, Warsaw, Prague, Bratislava)', *International Review of Sociology*, 16:2 (2006), 451–69; Nikolai Vukov, 'Protean Memories, "Permanent" Visualizations: Monuments and History Museums in Post-Communist Eastern Europe', in Kõresaar, Lauk, and Kuutma (eds.), *The Burden of Remembering*, 139–59.

42. Katherine Verdery, *The Political Lives of Dead Bodies: Reburial and Postsocialist Change* (New York: Columbia University Press, 1999), 5.

43. James Mark, *The Unfinished Revolution: Making Sense of the Communist Past in Central-Eastern Europe* (New Haven: Yale University Press, 2010), 215. 'Memory games' is from Georges Mink and Laure Neumayer (eds.), *History, Memory and Politics in Central and Eastern Europe: Memory Games* (Houndmills: Palgrave Macmillan, 2013).

44. Rév, *Retroactive Justice*, 87.

45. Robert M. Hayden, 'Recounting the Dead: The Rediscovery and Redefinition of Wartime Massacres in Late- and Post-Communist Yugoslavia', in Ruby S. Watson (ed.), *Memory, Opposition, and History under State Socialism* (Santa Fe, N. Mex.: School of American Research Press, 1994), 167–84; Tomislav Dulić, *Utopias of Nation: Local Mass Killings in Bosnia and Herzegovina, 1941–1942* (Uppsala: Uppsala University Press, 2005); for numbers killed in the 1990s, see Ewa Tabeau and Jakub Bijak, 'War-Related Deaths in the 1992–1995 Armed Conflicts in Bosnia and Herzegovina: A Critique of Previous Estimates and Recent Results', *European Journal of Population*, 21 (2005), 187–215.

46. Verdery, *The Political Lives of Dead Bodies*, 21.

47. Eric Langenbacher, 'Ethical Cleansing? The Expulsion of Germans from Central and Eastern Europe', in Nicholas A. Robins and Adam Jones (eds.), *Genocides by the Oppressed: Subaltern Genocide in Theory and Practice* (Bloomington, Ind.: Indiana University Press, 2009), 67. Cf. Eva Hahn and Hans Henning Hahn, 'The Holocaustizing of the Transfer-Discourse: Historical Revisionism or Old Wine in New Bottles?', in Michal Kopeček (ed.), *Past in the Making: Historical Revisionism in Central Europe after 1989* (Budapest: Central European University Press, 2008), 39–58.

48. Adam Michnik, 'Independence Reborn and the Demons of the Velvet Revolution', in Antohi and Tismaneanu (eds.), *Between Past and Future*, 85.

49. Michael Shafir, 'What Comes after Communism?', in *OHPEH*, 526–45.

50. Vladimir Tismaneanu, 'The Revolutions of 1989: Causes, Meanings, Consequences', *Contemporary European History*, 18:3 (2009), 272. See also, in the same issue (253–69), Charles S. Maier, 'What Have We Learned since 1989?'

51. Willy Brandt, *My Life in Politics* (London: Hamish Hamilton, 1992 [first German edition 1989]), 477.

52. Brandt, speech in Bundestag, 1 September 1989, cited in Bernd Rother, 'Common Security as a Way to Overcome the (Second) Cold War? Willy Brandt's Strategy for Peace in the 1980s', in Bozo et al. (eds.), *Visions of the End of the Cold War*, 250.

53. Jack F. Matlock, Jr, *Autopsy on an Empire: The American Ambassador's Account of the Collapse of the Soviet Union* (New York: Random House, 1995), 386–7.

54. Günter Grass, *Two States—One Nation? The Case against German Reunification* (London: Secker & Warburg, 1990).

55. Helmut Kohl, *Vom Mauerfall bis zur Wiedervereinigung: Meine Erinnerungen* (Munich: Knaur Taschenbuch Verlag, 2009), 80–1 (Thatcher, Andreotti, Mitterrand), 82 (Bush).

56. Andreotti's actual words are disputed but are most likely to have been: 'Amo talmente tanto la Germania che ne preferivo due', and the quip comes originally from François Mauriac, who said that he loved Germany so much, he was happy that there were two of them ['J'aime tellement l'Allemagne que je suis heureux qu'il y en ait deux']. See Pavel Palazhchenko, *My Years with Gorbachev and Shevardnadze: The Memoir of a Soviet Interpreter* (University Park, Pa.: Pennsylvania

State University Press, 1997), 158–9 and Pleshakov, *There Is No Freedom Without Bread!*, 208 for different variations. For a sober account, see Leopoldo Nuti, 'Italy, German Unification and the End of the Cold War', in Bozo et al. (eds.), *Europe and the End of the Cold War*, 191–203.

57. Margaret Thatcher, *The Downing Street Years* (New York: HarperCollins, 1993), 791, 793–4.

58. Jaruzelski, cited in Sarotte, *1989*, 28.

59. Ilaria Poggiolini, 'Thatcher's Double-Track Road to the End of the Cold War: The Irreconcilability of Liberalization and Preservation', in Bozo et al. (eds.), *Visions of the End of the Cold War*, 275.

60. Danilevich, cited in Kramer, 'The Collapse (Part 3)', 40–1.

61. Mitterrand, *De l'Allemagne, de la France* (Paris: Odile Jacob, 1996), cited in Sutton, *France and the Construction of Europe*, 245.

62. Sutton, *France and the Construction of Europe*, 250, 252 (citing Kohl, *Erinnerungen, 1982–1990* (Munich: Droemer, 2005), 1033).

63. Thatcher, *Downing Street Years*, 791.

64. Karl-Rudolf Korte, 'The Art of Power: The "Kohl System", Leadership and *Deutschlandpolitik*', in Clay Clemens and William E. Paterson (eds.), *The Kohl Chancellorship* (London: Frank Cass, 1998), 67.

65. Chernyaev in Wohlforth (ed.), *Cold War Endgame*, 52.

66. Kohl, *Vom Mauerfall bis zur Wiedervereinigung*, 208.

67. Sheehan, 'The Transformation of Europe and the End of the Cold War', 62.

68. Gorbachev, *Perestroika*, 186. He went on: 'For the time being, one should proceed from the existing realities and not engage in incendiary speculations.'

69. Sheehan, 'The Transformation of Europe and the End of the Cold War', 56; see also Zubok, *A Failed Empire*, 326: 'the fall of the Wall doomed Gorbachev's grand design for gradual European reconciliation.'

70. 'Kohl's Ten-Point Plan for German Unity, 28 November 1989', in Jarausch and Gransow (eds.), *Uniting Germany*, 86–9.

71. Chernyaev, *My Six Years with Gorbachev*, 239.

72. Jost Dülffer, 'Cold War History in Germany', *Cold War History*, 8:2 (2008), 135.

73. Brandt's much more elegant German phrase was 'Es wächst zusammen, was zusammen gehört.' Beck, cited in Corey Ross, *The East German Dictatorship: Problems and Perspectives in the Interpretation of the GDR* (London: Arnold, 2002), 92.

74. Moses, *German Intellectuals and the Nazi Past*, 232.

75. Konrad Jarausch, 'The Failure of East German Antifascism: Some Ironies of History as Politics', *German Studies Review*, 14:1 (1991), 96; Eve Rosenhaft, 'The Uses of Remembrance: The Legacy of the Communist Resistance in the German Democratic Republic', in Francis R. Nicosia and Lawrence D. Stokes (eds.), *Germans against Nazism: Nonconformity, Opposition and Resistance in the Third Reich* (New York: Berg, 1990), 369–88.

76. Thatcher, *Downing Street Years*, 814.

77. Ridley, cited in Poggiolini, 'Thatcher's Double-Track Road', 275.

78. Cited in Maier, *Dissolution*, 152.

79. Elizabeth A. Ten Dyke, 'Tulips in December: Space, Time and Consumption before and after the End of German Socialism', *German History*, 19:2 (2001), 253–76.

80. Alan L. Nothnagle, *Building the East German Myth: Historical Mythology and Youth Propaganda in the German Democratic Republic, 1945–1989* (Ann Arbor: University of Michigan Press, 1999), 141–2.

81. Alistair Cole, 'Political Leadership in Western Europe: Helmut Kohl in Comparative Perspective', in Clemens and Paterson (eds.), *The Kohl Chancellorship*, 127.

82. Gino Raymond and Svetlana Bajic-Raymond, 'Memory and History: The Discourse of Nation-Building in the Former Yugoslavia', *Patterns of Prejudice*, 31:1 (1997), 21–30; Florian Bieber, 'Nationalist Mobilization and Stories of Serb Suffering: The Kosovo Myth from 600th Anniversary to the Present', *Rethinking History*, 6:1 (2002), 95–110; Milica Bakić-Hayden, 'Nesting Orientalisms: The Case of Former Yugoslavia', *Slavic Review*, 54:4 (1995), 917–31.

83. Dan Stone, 'Genocide and Memory', in Donald Bloxham and A. Dirk Moses (eds.), *The Oxford Handbook of Genocide Studies* (Oxford: Oxford University Press, 2010), 102–19; Anthony Oberschall, 'The Manipulation of Ethnicity: From Ethnic Cooperation to Violence and War in Yugoslavia', *Ethnic and Racial Studies*, 23:6 (2000), 982–1001.

84. Jacques Rupnik, 'On Two Models of Exit from Communism: Central Europe and the Balkans', in Antohi and Tismaneanu (eds.), *Between Past and Future*, 21. Rupnik is quick to point out that this is a description, not a prescription—'It would be absurd to suggest that ethnic "homogeneity" is a prerequisite for democracy'.

85. Nick Miller, 'Where Was the Serbian Havel?', in Tismaneanu (ed.), *The End and the Beginning*, 367–71.

86. Miller, 'Where Was the Serbian Havel?', 374.

87. Miller, 'Where Was the Serbian Havel?', 375.

88. Eric Gordy, 'Destruction of the Yugoslav Federation: Policy or Confluence of Tactics?', in Lenard J. Cohen and Jasna Dragović-Soso (eds.), *State Collapse in South-Eastern Europe: New Perspectives on Yugoslavia's Disintegration* (West Lafayette, Ind.: Purdue University Press, 2008), 281–99.

89. Janine Natalya Clark, 'Collective Guilt, Collective Responsibility and the Serbs', *East European Politics and Societies*, 22:3 (2008), 668–92; Cathie Carmichael, 'Brothers, Strangers and Enemies: Ethno-nationalism and the Demise of Communist Yugoslavia', in *OHPEH*, 551.

90. For good analyses of the violent collapse of Yugoslavia, see, among others: Jasminka Udovički and James Ridgeway (eds.), *Burn This House: The Making and Unmaking of Yugoslavia*, rev. edn. (Durham, NC: Duke University Press, 2000); Nebojša Popov (ed.), *The Road to War in Serbia: Trauma and Catharsis* (Budapest: Central European University Press, 2000); Susan L. Woodward, *Balkan Tragedy: Chaos and Dissolution after the Cold War* (Washington, DC: The Brookings Institution, 1995); John R. Lampe, *Yugoslavia as History: Twice There Was a Country* (Cambridge: Cambridge University Press, 1996).

91. Florian Bieber, 'The Role of the Yugoslav People's Army in the Dissolution of Yugoslavia: The Army without a State?', in Cohen and Dragović-Soso (eds.), *State Collapse in South-Eastern Europe*, 301–32.

92. Robert M. Hayden, 'Mass Killings and Images of Genocide in Bosnia, 1941–5 and 1992–5', in Stone (ed.), *The Historiography of Genocide*, 487–516.

93. Noel Malcolm, *Bosnia: A Short History*, rev. edn. (London: Macmillan, 1996), 270–1.

94. See Gideon Boas, *The Milošević Trial: Lessons for the Conduct of Complex International Criminal Proceedings* (Cambridge: Cambridge University Press, 2007).

95. Robert M. Hayden, '"Democracy" without a Demos? The Bosnian Constitutional Experiment and the Intentional Construction of Nonfunctioning States', *East European Politics and Societies*, 19 (2005), 226–59; Paul B. Miller, 'Contested Memories: The Bosnian Genocide in Serb and Muslim Minds', *Journal of Genocide Research*, 8:3 (2006), 311–24.

96. Tony Judt, 'The Past is Another Country: Myth and Memory in Postwar Europe', in Deák, Gross, and Judt (eds.), *The Politics of Retribution*, 296.

97. Cf. Padraic Kenney, 'Martyrs and Neighbors: Sources of Reconciliation in Central Europe', *Common Knowledge*, 13:1 (2007), 149–69.

98. Fischer, cited in Kundnani, *Utopia or Auschwitz*, 248.

99. Tariq Ali, 'Springtime for NATO', *New Left Review*, 234 (1999), 64, cited in Kundnani, *Utopia or Auschwitz*, 248.

100. Havel in Adam Michnik, 'The Strange Epoch of Post-Communism: A Conversation with Václav Havel', in Michnik, *Letters from Freedom*, 240 (orig. in *Gazeta Wyborcza*, 30 November 1991).

101. On *partitocrazia*—the cosy sharing of power and opposition among the established parties, including the PCI—see Joseph LaPalombara, *Democracy Italian Style* (New Haven: Yale University Press, 1989).

102. I owe this idea to Alessandro Portelli's lecture, 'Reflecting on a Life in Progress and Stories of Oral History', Royal Holloway, University of London, 6 November 2012.

103. Emilio Gentile, cited in Stéfanie Prezioso, 'Antifascism and Anti-totalitarianism: The Italian Debate', *Journal of Contemporary History*, 43:4 (2008), 555.

104. Alessandro Portelli, *The Order Has Been Carried Out: History, Memory and Meaning of a Nazi Massacre in Rome* (Houndmills: Palgrave Macmillan: 2003).

105. Rebecca Clifford, 'The Limits of National Memory: Anti-Fascism, the Holocaust and the Fosse Ardeatine Memorial in 1990s Italy', *Forum for Modern Language Studies*, 44:2 (2008), 128–39.

106. Paul Corner, 'Italian Fascism: Whatever Happened to Dictatorship?', *Journal of Modern History*, 74:2 (2002), 325–6.

107. Luzzatto, cited in Robert S. C. Gordon, *The Holocaust in Italian Culture, 1944–2010* (Stanford, Calif.: Stanford University Press, 2011), 191.

108. Richard J. Golsan, 'Introduction', in Golsan (ed.), *Fascism's Return*, 6–7.

109. Cited in Richard Wolin, 'Designer Fascism', in Golsan (ed.), *Fascism's Return*, 50.

110. Cf. René Cuperus and Johannes Kandel (eds.), *European Social Democracy: Transformation in Progress* (Amsterdam: Wiardi Beckman Stichting/Friedrich Ebert Stichting, 1998). Cuperus and Kandel's introduction (11–28) is entitled 'The Magical Return of Social Democracy'. But right-wing ideas and policies do not become left-wing ones when implemented by parties with a socialist or social democratic heritage.

111. Ido De Haan, 'The Western European Welfare State beyond Christian and Social Democratic Ideology', in *OHPEH*, 316.

112. Eley, *Forging Democracy*, 455. Cf. Paul Johnson, 'Social Policy in Europe in the Twentieth Century', *Contemporary European History*, 2:2 (1993), 197: 'The post-war "welfare consensus", which perhaps had never been quite so strong or coherent as many contemporary historians and commentators had assumed, was finally laid to rest' in the 1980s.

113. Willem Adema, Pauline Fron, and Maxime Ladaique, 'Is the European Welfare State Really More Expensive? Indicators on Social Spending 1980–2012, and a Manual to the OECD Social Expenditure Database (SOCX)', *OECD Social, Employment and Migration Working Papers*, 124 (2011), 9. See also Hartmut Kaelble, *A Social History of Europe 1945–2000: Recovery and Transformation after Two World Wars* (New York: Berghahn Books, 2013), 263–4.

114. Jack Hayward, 'From Citizen Solidarity to Self-Serving Inequality: Social Solidarity, Market Economy and Welfare Statecraft', in James Connelly and Jack Hayward (eds.), *The Withering of the Welfare State: Regression* (Houndmills: Palgrave Macmillan, 2012), 12. See also Martin Seeleib-Kaiser (ed.), *Welfare State Transformations: Comparative Perspectives* (Houndmills: Palgrave Macmillan, 2008).

115. Crouch, *Social Change in Western Europe*, 381.

116. James Connelly, 'Conclusion: Remaining the Welfare State?', in Connelly and Hayward (eds.) *The Withering of the Welfare State*, 209; Howard Glennerster, 'The Sustainability of Western Welfare States', in Francis G. Castles, Stephan Leibfried, Jane Lewis, Herbert Obinger, and Christopher Pierson (eds.), *The Oxford Handbook of the Welfare State* (Oxford: Oxford University Press, 2010), 697.

117. Cornel Ban, 'Was 1989 the End of Social Democracy?', in Tismaneanu (ed.), *The End and the Beginning*, 127–68.

118. Frank Nullmeier and Franz-Xaver Kaufmann, 'Post-War Welfare State Development', in Castles et al. (eds.), *The Oxford Handbook of the Welfare State*, 86.

119. János Kornai, *Welfare after Communism* (London: Social Market Foundation, 1999).

120. Stephen J. Collier, *Post-Soviet Social: Neoliberalism, Social Modernity, Biopolitics* (Princeton: Princeton University Press, 2011), 26. Collier argues that neo-liberalism is not a single 'thing' that one can be for or against, but a set of practices to be analysed in anthropological fashion as they are produced and realized.

121. Martin Potůček, 'Metamorphoses of Welfare States in Central and Eastern Europe', in Seeleib-Kaiser (ed.), *Welfare State Transformations*, 79–95.

122. Paul Ginsborg, 'The Politics of the Family in Twentieth-Century Europe', *Contemporary European History*, 9:3 (2000), 438.

123. Ginsborg, 'Politics of the Family', 444.

124. Colin Crouch, *Post-Democracy* (Cambridge: Polity Press, 2004).

125. Heidi Tinsman, 'Cold War Memories', *Social History*, 34:4 (2009), 477–8, citing Greg Grandin, *The Last Colonial Massacre: Latin America in the Cold War* (Chicago: University of Chicago Press, 2004).

126. Ost, *Defeat of Solidarity*, 10.

127. Pierre Rosanvallon, 'Democracy in an Age of Distrust', in Rosanvallon, *Democracy Past and Future*, ed. Samuel Moyn (Ithaca, NY: Columbia University Press, 2006), 236–7, 248.

128. Philip Arestis and Malcolm Sawyer, 'The Design Faults of the Economic and Monetary Union', *Journal of Contemporary European Studies*, 19:1 (2011), 21–32.

129. Hubert Zimmermann, 'The Euro under Scrutiny: Histories and Theories of European Monetary Integration', *Contemporary European History*, 10:2 (2001), 340.

130. Robert Bideleux, 'European Integration: The Rescue of the Nation State?', in *OHPEH*, 404. See also João Carlos Espada, 'The Sources of Extremism', *Journal of Democracy*, 23:4 (2012), 15–22.

131. Ivan Krastev, 'A Fraying Union?', *Journal of Democracy*, 23:4 (2012), 23.

132. Sheri Berman, 'Warnings from History', *Journal of Democracy*, 23:4 (2012), 8. For a similar conclusion, arrived at on the basis of a rather different argument, see Francesco M. Bongiovanni, *The Decline and Fall of Europe* (Houndmills: Palgrave Macmillan, 2012). See also David Marquand, *The End of the West: The Once and Future Europe* (Princeton: Princeton University Press, 2011).

133. Boltho and Toniolo, 'The Assessment', 15–16.

134. Tony Judt, 'What is Living and What is Dead in Social Democracy?' Lecture at New York University, 19 October 2009, online at: <http://remarque.as.nyu.edu/object/io_1256242927496.html>. See the fuller discussion in Judt, *Ill Fares the Land: A Treatise on our Present Discontents* (London: Allen Lane, 2010).

CHAPTER 8

1. André Sibomana, *Hope for Rwanda: Conversations with Laure Gilbert and Hervé Deguine*, trans. Carina Tertsakian (London: Pluto Press, 1999), 117; Gorbachev and Mlynář, *Conversations with Gorbachev*, 142; Régis Debray, *Charles de Gaulle: Futurist of the Nation* (London: Verso, 1994), 92.

2. See, for example, Viktor Suvorov's lecture at the United States Naval Academy, 'Who Started World War II?' (7 October 2009), online at: <http://www.youtube.com/watch?v=wYSy8oWlmWY> (accessed 20 November 2012).

3. Adam Krzeminski, 'As Many Wars as Nations: The Myths and Truths of World War II', *Sign and Sight*, 6 April 2005, <www.signandsight.com/features/96. html> (original in *Polityka*, 23 March 2005). Kamiński stood down from the Law and Justice Party in November 2010, saying it was becoming too right wing; he went on to co-found the Poland Comes First Party.

4. Tismaneanu, *Stalinism for All Seasons*, 29; Victor Neumann, *Between Words and Reality: Studies on the Politics of Recognition and the Changes of Regime in Contemporary Romania* (Washington, DC: Council for Research in Values and Philosophy, 2000), 68–9.

5. Silviu Brucan, *The Wasted Generation: Memoirs of the Romanian Journey from Capitalism to Communism and Back* (Boulder, Colo.: Westview Press, 1993), x.

6. Dubravka Ugrešić, 'The Confiscation of Memory', in her *The Culture of Lies: Antipolitical Essays* (London: Phoenix, 1998), 217–35. For a more recent reincarnation of antifascism in Bosnia, see the activities of the 'Antifascist Action' group, online at: <http://www.antifa-bih.org/>.

7. Hitchcock, *Liberation*, 369; Lagrou, 'Victims of Genocide and National Memory'.

8. Hitchcock, *Liberation*, 370–1.

9. Richard Ned Lebow, 'The Memory of Politics in Postwar Europe', in Richard Ned Lebow, Wulf Kansteiner, and Claudio Fogu (eds.), *The Politics of Memory in Postwar Europe* (Durham, NC: Duke University Press, 2006), 19.

10. Vladimir Tismaneanu, 'Civil Society, Pluralism, and the Future of East and Central Europe', *Social Research*, 68:4 (2001), 989.

11. Marc Morjé Howard, 'The Leninist Legacy Revisited', in Vladimir Tismaneanu, Marc Morjé Howard, and Rudra Sil (eds.), *World Disorder after Leninism: Essays in Honor of Ken Jowitt* (Seattle: University of Washington Press, 2006), 34–46; Jeffrey Kopstein, '1989 as a Lens for the Communist Past and Post-communist Future', *Contemporary European History*, 18:3 (2009), 289–302. On the role of the EU, see Milada Anna Vachudova, *Europe Undivided: Democracy, Leverage, and Integration after Communism* (Oxford: Oxford University Press, 2005).

12. Ivan Krastev, 'The Strange Death of the Liberal Consensus', *Journal of Democracy*, 18:4 (2007), 63; Vladimir Tismaneanu, 'Leninist Legacies, Pluralist Dilemmas', *Journal of Democracy*, 18:4 (2007), 38. Cf. Charles S. Maier, 'What Have We Learned since 1989?', *Contemporary European History*, 18:3 (2009), 253–69; Michael Shafir, 'From Historical to "Dialectical" Populism: The Case of Post-Communist Romania', *Canadian Slavonic Papers*, 50:3–4 (2008), 425–70.

13. Dieter Prowe, '"Classic" Fascism and the New Radical Right in Western Europe: Comparisons and Contrasts', *Contemporary European History*, 3:3 (1994), 289–314; Golsan (ed.), *Fascism's Return*; Tamir Bar-On, 'Fascism to the Nouvelle Droite: The Dream of Pan-European Empire', *Journal of Contemporary European Studies*, 16:3 (2008), 327–45.

14. Etienne Balibar, 'Is There a "Neo-Racism"?', in Etienne Balibar and Immanuel Wallerstein, *Race, Nation, Class: Ambiguous Identities* (London: Verso, 1991), 17–28;

Lisa Lampert, 'Race, Periodicity, and the (Neo-) Middle Ages', *Modern Language Quarterly*, 65:3 (2004), 391–421.

15. Eelco Runia, 'Burying the Dead, Creating the Past', *History and Theory*, 46:3 (2007), 319.

16. Claudio Fogu, '*Italiani brava gente*: The Legacy of Fascist Historical Culture on Italian Politics of Memory', in Lebow, Kansteiner, and Fogu (eds.), *The Politics of Memory in Postwar Europe*, 161–5.

17. Robert A. Ventresca, 'Mussolini's Ghost: Italy's *Duce* in History and Memory', *History & Memory*, 18:1 (2006), 96–7.

18. Ventresca, 'Mussolini's Ghost', 102–4. See also Ventresca, 'Debating the Meaning of Fascism in Contemporary Italy', *Modern Italy*, 11:2 (2006), 189–209; Andrea Mammone, 'A Daily Revision of the Past: Fascism, Antifascism, and Memory in Contemporary Italy', *Modern Italy*, 11:2 (2006), 211–26; Joshua Arthurs, 'Fascism as "Heritage" in Contemporary Italy', in Andrea Mammone and Giuseppe A. Veltri (eds.), *Italy Today: The Sick Man of Europe* (London: Routledge, 2010), 114–27.

19. Pamela Ballinger, 'Who Defines and Remembers Genocide after the Cold War? Contested Memories of Partisan Massacre in Venezia Giulia in 1943–1945', *Journal of Genocide Research*, 2:1 (2000), 11–30; Gaia Baracetti, 'Foibe: Nationalism, Revenge and Ideology in Venezia Giulia and Istria, 1943–5', *Journal of Contemporary History*, 44:4 (2009), 657–74; Martin Purvis and David Atkinson, 'Performing Wartime Memories: Ceremony as Contest at the Risiera di San Sabba Death Camp, Trieste', *Social and Cultural Geography*, 10:3 (2009), 337–56.

20. Ruth Ben-Ghiat, 'A Lesser Evil? Italian Fascism in/and the Totalitarian Equation', in Helmut Dubiel and Gabriel Motzkin (eds.), *The Lesser Evil: Moral Approaches to Genocide Practices* (London: Routledge, 2004), 147. Cf. James Walston, 'History and Memory of the Italian Concentration Camps', *Historical Journal*, 40:1 (1997), 169–83; Robert S. C. Gordon, 'The Holocaust in Italian Collective Memory: *Il giorno della memoria*, 27 January 2001', *Modern Italy*, 11:2 (2006), 167–88.

21. Uhl, 'Of Heroes and Victims', 186.

22. *Der Spiegel*, 25 January 1988, front cover, cited in Peter Utgaard, *Remembering and Forgetting Nazism: Education, National Identity and the Victim Myth in Postwar Austria* (New York: Berghahn Books, 2003), 161. The image is available online at: <http://www.spiegel.de/spiegel/print/d-13528122.html>. On the *Heldenplatz*, see Thomas Bernhard's play of that name.

23. Steven Beller, *A Concise History of Austria* (Cambridge: Cambridge University Press, 2006), 304–6.

24. Ido de Haan, 'Paths of Normalization after the Persecution of the Jews: The Netherlands, France, and West Germany', in Richard Bessel and Dirk Schumann (eds.), *Life after Death: Approaches to a Cultural and Social History of Europe during the 1940s and 1950s* (Cambridge: Cambridge University Press, 2003), 69.

25. Ido de Haan, 'Routines and Traditions: The Reactions of Non-Jews and Jews in the Netherlands to War and Persecution', in David Bankier and Israel Gutman (eds.), *Nazi Europe and the Final Solution* (Jerusalem: Yad Vashem, 2003), 437.

26. Vladimir Tismaneanu, 'Communism and the Human Condition: Reflections on *The Black Book of Communism*', *Human Rights Review*, 2:2 (2001), 125–34. In February 2005 the Law on French Colonialism imposed on school teachers the obligation to teach pupils about the 'positive side' of French colonialism; after much criticism, it was repealed by Chirac a year later.

27. 'François Hollande Sorry for Wartime Deportations of Jews', *Guardian* (22 July 2012), online at: <http://www.guardian.co.uk/world/2012/jul/22/francois-hollande-wartime-roundup-jews>. See also the film *The Round Up* [*La Rafle*] (dir. Rose Bosch, 2010).

28. Ludivine Broch, *Ordinary Workers, Vichy and the Holocaust: French Railwaymen and the Second World War* (Cambridge: Cambridge University Press, forthcoming).

29. Andrea Mammone, '*The Eternal Return?* Faux Populism and Contemporization of Neo-Fascism across Britain, France and Italy', *Journal of Contemporary European Studies*, 17:2 (2009), 171–92.

30. Graham, *The War and its Shadow*, 131–2.

31. Michael Richards, 'Between Memory and History: Social Relationships and Ways of Remembering the Spanish Civil War', *International Journal of Iberian Studies*, 19:1 (2006), 86; Francisco Ferrándiz, 'Cries and Whispers: Exhuming and Narrating Defeat in Spain Today', *Journal of Spanish Cultural Studies*, 9:2 (2008), 177–92.

32. I am grateful to Helen Graham for the wording of this sentence.

33. Carolyn P. Boyd, 'The Politics of History and Memory in Democratic Spain', *Annals of the American Academy of Political and Social Science*, 617 (2008), 142–3. See also Carsten Jacob Humlebæk, 'Political Uses of the Recent Past in the Spanish Post-Authoritarian Democracy', in Max Paul Friedman and Padraic Kenney (eds.), *Partisan Histories: The Past in Contemporary Global Politics* (New York: Palgrave Macmillan, 2005), 75–88; Paloma Aguilar and Carsten Humlebæk, 'Collective Memory and National Identity in the Spanish Democracy', *History & Memory*, 14:1–2 (2002), 121–64. For a moving example, see Ramón Sender Barayón, *A Death in Zamora* (Albuquerque, N. Mex.: University of New Mexico Press, 1989).

34. Allan Pred, *Even in Sweden: Racisms, Racialized Spaces, and the Popular Geographical Imagination* (Berkeley and Los Angeles: University of California Press, 2000).

35. For example: David Cesarani and Paul A. Levine (eds.), *'Bystanders' to the Holocaust: A Re-evaluation* (London: Vallentine Mitchell, 2002); Holmila, *Reporting the Holocaust*.

36. For example: Mette Bastholm Jensen and Steven L. B. Jensen (eds.), *Denmark and the Holocaust* (Copenhagen: Institute for International Studies, 2003); Gunnar S. Paulsson, 'The "Bridge over the Øresund": The Historiography on the

Expulsion of the Jews from Nazi-Occupied Denmark', *Journal of Contemporary History*, 30:3 (1995), 431–64.

37. Sørensen, 'Narrating the Second World War in Denmark since 1945'.

38. Peter Hervik, *The Annoying Difference: The Emergence of Danish Neonationalism, Neoracism and Populism in the Post-1989 World* (New York: Berghahn Books, 2011), xiii.

39. Regula Ludi, ' "Why Switzerland?" Remarks on a Neutral's Role in the Nazi Program of Robbery and Allied Postwar Restitution Policy', in Martin Dean, Constantin Goschler, and Philipp Ther (eds.), *Robbery and Restitution: The Conflict over Jewish Property in Europe* (New York: Berghahn Books, 2007), 183.

40. Ludi, ' "Why Switzerland?" ', 202; Michael R. Marrus, *Some Measure of Justice: The Holocaust Era Restitution Campaign of the 1990s* (Madison: University of Wisconsin Press, 2009), 17.

41. Damir Skenderovic, *The Radical Right in Switzerland: Continuity and Change, 1945–2000* (New York: Berghahn Books, 2009), 340.

42. Damir Skenderovic, 'Transformations and "Direct" Successes on the Right-Wing Fringe: Switzerland as a Model for Europe?', in Nora Langenbacher and Britta Schellenberg (eds.), *Is Europe on the 'Right' Path? Right-Wing Extremism and Right-Wing Populism in Europe* (Berlin: Friedrich-Ebert Stiftung, 2011), 159. This is literally true as well—the SVP produced some very striking posters for their anti-minarets campaign.

43. Teun Pauwels, 'Explaining the Success of Neo-liberal Populist Parties: The Case of Lijst Dedecker in Belgium', *Political Studies*, 58:5 (2010), 1009–29.

44. David Arter, 'The Breakthrough of Another West European Populist Radical Right Party? The Case of the True Finns', *Government and Opposition*, 45:4 (2010), 484–504.

45. Jens Rydgren, 'Is Extreme Right-Wing Populism Contagious? Explaining the Emergence of a New Party Family', *European Journal of Political Research*, 44 (2005), 413–37; Tim Bale et al., 'If You Can't Beat Them, Join Them? Explaining Social Democratic Responses to the Challenge from the Populist Radical Right in Western Europe', *Political Studies*, 58:3 (2010), 410–26; Cas Mudde, 'The Populist Zeitgeist', *Government and Opposition*, 39:4 (2004), 541–63; Tim Bale, 'Supplying the Insatiable Demand: Europe's Populist Radical Right', *Government and Opposition*, 47:2 (2012), 256–74.

46. Rév, *Retroactive Justice*, 282, 296. The Terror House also receives considerably more funding than Budapest's Holocaust Memorial Centre, which in November 2012 was in dire financial straits.

47. Martin Evans, 'Memorials, Monuments, Histories: The Re-Thinking of the Second World War since 1989', *National Identities*, 8:4 (2006), 319–21; James Mark, 'Containing Fascism: History in Post-Communist Baltic Occupation and Genocide Museums', in Oksana Sarkisova and Peter Apor (eds.), *Past for the Eyes: East European Representations of Communism in Cinema and Museums after 1989* (Budapest: Central European University Press, 2008), 352.

48. William Outhwaite and Larry Ray, *Social Theory and Postcommunism* (Oxford: Blackwell, 2005), 184–6.

49. Rév, *Retroactive Justice*, 238.

50. See <http://www.huffingtonpost.com/2012/11/27/marton-gyongyosi-jew-list_n_2196744.html>.

51. János M. Rainer, '1956: The Mid-Twentieth Century Seen from the Vantage Point of the Beginning of the Next Century', in Terry Cox (ed.), *Challenging Communism in Eastern Europe: 1956 and its Legacy* (London: Routledge, 2008), 6.

52. James Mark, 'Antifascism, the 1956 Revolution and the Politics of Communist Autobiographies in Hungary 1944–2000', in Cox (ed.), *Challenging Communism*, 25.

53. Mark, 'Antifascism, the 1956 Revolution', 26.

54. Mark, 'Antifascism, the 1956 Revolution', 47.

55. Mark, 'Antifascism, the 1956 Revolution', 48.

56. Dovilé Budryté, '"We Call it Genocide": Soviet Deportations and Repression in the Memory of Lithuanians', in Robert S. Frey (ed.), *The Genocidal Temptation: Auschwitz, Hiroshima, Rwanda, and Beyond* (Lanham, Md.: University Press of America, 2004), 79–95.

57. <http://defendinghistory.com/new/34584>.

58. Victor Neumann, *Essays on Romanian Intellectual History* (Timişoara: Editura Universităţii de Vest, 2008), 117.

59. Gabriela Cristea and Simina Radu-Bucurenci, 'Raising the Cross: Exorcising Romania's Communist Past in Museums, Memorials and Monuments', in Sarkisova and Apor (eds.), *Past for the Eyes*, 275–305.

60. Jan Tomasz Gross with Irena Grudzińska Gross, *Golden Harvest: Events at the Periphery of the Holocaust* (New York: Oxford University Press, 2012).

61. Sebastian Rejak and Elżbieta Frister (eds.), *Inferno of Choices: Poles and the Holocaust*, 2nd edn. (Warsaw: Oficyna Wydawnicza RYTM, 2012).

62. Stuart Elden and Luiza Bialasiewicz, 'The New Geopolitics of Division and the Problem of a Kantian Europe', *Review of International Studies*, 32:4 (2006), 627.

63. Maria Mälksoo, 'The Memory Politics of Becoming European: The East European Subalterns and the Collective Memory of Europe', *European Journal of International Relations*, 15:4 (2009), 653–80. See also Claus Leggewie, 'A Tour of the Battleground: The Seven Circles of Pan-European Memory', *Social Research*, 75:1 (2008), 217–34; Robert Bideleux, 'Rethinking the Eastward Extension of the EU Civil Order and the Nature of Europe's New East–West Divide', *Perspectives on European Politics and Society*, 10:1 (2009), 118–36; Ulf Brunnbauer, 'Remembering Communism during and after Communism', *Contemporary European History*, 21:3 (2012), 493–505.

64. Text of the Seventy Years Declaration online at: <http://defendinghistory.com/70-years-declaration/29230>.

65. Jörg Hackmann, 'From National Victims to Transnational Bystanders? The Changing Commemoration of World War II in Central and Eastern Europe', *Constellations*, 16:1 (2009), 176.

66. For a relatively optimistic stance, see Jeffrey Blutinger, 'An Inconvenient Past: Post-Communist Holocaust Memorialization', *Shofar: An Interdisciplinary Journal of Jewish Studies*, 29:1 (2010), 73–94.

67. Evans, 'Memorials, Monuments, Histories', 333. See also Maria Todorova and Zsuzsa Gille (eds.), *Post-Communist Nostalgia* (New York: Berghahn, 2010); Gregory Carleton, 'Victory in Death: Annihilation Narratives in Russia Today', *History & Memory*, 22:1 (2010), 135–68.

68. Alexandra Goujon, 'Memorial Narratives of WWII Partisans and Genocide in Belarus', *East European Politics and Societies*, 24:1 (2010), 6–25.

69. Nurit Schleifman, 'Moscow's Victory Park: A Monumental Change', *History & Memory*, 13:2 (2001), 5–34.

70. Lisa A. Kirschenbaum, 'Commemorations of the Siege of Leningrad: A Catastrophe in Memory and Myth', in Peter Gray and Kendrick Oliver (eds.), *The Memory of Catastrophe* (Manchester: Manchester University Press, 2004), 111.

71. Adamovich and Suvorov, cited in Nina Tumarkin, *The Living and the Dead: The Rise and Fall of the Cult of World War II in Russia* (New York: Basic Books, 1994), 207, 211–12.

72. Benjamin Forest, Juliet Johnson, and Karen Till, 'Post-totalitarian National Identity: Public Memory in Germany and Russia', *Social and Cultural Geography*, 5:3 (2004), 368.

73. Ilya Prizel, 'Nationalism in Postcommunist Russia: From Resignation to Anger', in Antohi and Tismaneanu (eds.), *Between Past and Future*, 337.

74. James V. Wertsch, 'Blank Spots in History and Deep Memory: Revising the Official Narrative of the Molotov–Ribbentrop Pact', in Kõresaar, Lauk, and Kuutma (eds.), *The Burden of Remembering*, 37–56.

75. Tony Wood, 'Russia Vanishes', *London Review of Books*, 34:23 (6 December 2012), 41.

76. Tatiana Zhurzhenko, 'The Geopolitics of Memory', *Eurozine* (10 May 2007), 9, online at: <http://www.eurozine.com/articles/2007-05-10-zhurzhenko-en.html>.

77. Zhurzhenko, 'The Geopolitics of Memory', 8–9.

78. Ann Douglas, 'War Envy and Amnesia: American Cold War Rewrites of Russia's War', in Isaac and Bell (eds.), *Uncertain Empire*, 122.

79. Judt, *Postwar*, 803. Jens Kroh, 'Erinnerungskultureller Akteur und geschichts politisches Netzwerk: Die "Task Force for International Cooperation on Holocaust Education, Remembrance and Research"', and Harald Schmid, 'Europäisierung des Auschwitzgedenkens? Zum Aufstieg des 27. Januar 1945 als "Holocaustgedenktag" in Europa', both in Jan Eckel and Claudia Moisel (eds.), *Universalisierung des Holocaust? Erinnerungskultur und Geschichtspolitik in internationaler Perspektive* (Göttingen: Wallstein, 2008), 156–73 and 174–202; Lothar

Probst, 'Founding Myths in Europe and the Role of the Holocaust', *New German Critique*, 90 (2003), 45–58.

80. Avi Beker (ed.), *The Plunder of Jewish Property during the Holocaust: Confronting European History* (New York: New York University Press, 2001); Dean, Goschler, and Ther (eds.), *Robbery and Restitution*; Martin Dean, *Robbing the Jews: The Confiscation of Jewish Property in the Holocaust, 1933–1945* (Cambridge: Cambridge University Press, 2008).

81. Juan J. Linz and Alfred Stepan, *Problems of Democratic Transition and Consolidation: Southern Europe, South America, and Post-Communist Europe* (Baltimore: Johns Hopkins University Press, 1996), 344–65.

82. Vladimir Tismaneanu, 'Democracy and Memory: Romania Confronts its Communist Past', *Annals of the American Academy of Political and Social Science*, 617 (2008), 166–80; Ruxandra Cesereanu, 'The Final Report on the Holocaust and the Final Report on the Communist Dictatorship in Romania', *East European Politics and Societies*, 22:2 (2008), 270–81.

83. Carolyn J. Dean, 'Recent French Discourses on Stalinism, Nazism and "Exorbitant" Jewish Memory', *History & Memory*, 18:1 (2006), 43–85.

84. Adam Hochschild, 'In the Heart of Darkness', *New York Review of Books* (6 October 2005), 39–42; Ludo de Witte, *The Assassination of Lumumba* (London: Verso, 2002); Martin Ewans, *European Atrocity, African Catastrophe: Leopold II, the Congo Free State and its Aftermath* (London: Routledge, 2002).

85. Caroline Elkins, *Britain's Gulag: The Brutal End of Empire in Kenya* (London: Jonathan Cape, 2004); David Anderson, *Histories of the Hanged: Britain's Dirty War in Kenya and the End of Empire* (London: Weidenfeld and Nicolson, 2004).

86. Kenneth O. Morgan, 'The Second World War and British Culture', in Brian Brivati and Harriet Jones (eds.), *From Reconstruction to Integration: Britain and Europe since 1945* (Leicester: Leicester University Press, 1993), 45 (national ego); David Reynolds, 'World War II and Modern Meanings', *Diplomatic History*, 25:3 (2001), 470 (German domination); cf. Wendy Webster, '"Europe against the Germans": The British Resistance Narrative, 1940–1950', *Journal of British Studies*, 48 (2009), 958–82.

87. Caroline Elkins, 'Race, Citizenship, and Governance: Settler Tyranny and the End of Empire', in Caroline Elkins and Susan Pedersen (eds.), *Settler Colonialism in the Twentieth Century: Projects, Practices, Legacies* (New York: Routledge, 2005), 203–22.

88. Matthew Connelly, 'Taking Off the Cold War Lens: Visions of North–South Conflict During the Algerian War for Independence', *American Historical Review*, 105:3 (2000), 739–69.

89. Edward T. Linenthal and Tom Engelhardt, *History Wars: The Enola Gay and Other Battles for the American Past* (New York: Henry Holt & Co, 1996); Phillips P. O'Brien, 'East versus West in the Defeat of Nazi Germany', *Strategic Studies*, 23:2 (2000), 89–113; Mark A. Stoler, 'The Second World War in US History and Memory', *Diplomatic History*, 25:3 (2001), 383–92.

90. John Torpey, '"Making Whole What Has Been Smashed": Reflections on Reparations', *Journal of Modern History*, 73:2 (2001), 333–58; Elazar Barkan, *The Guilt of Nations: Restitution and Negotiating Historical Injustices* (Baltimore: Johns Hopkins University Press, 2000).

91. Richard H. King, '"What Kind of People Are We?" The United States and the Truth and Reconciliation Idea', in Wilfred M. McClay (ed.), *Figures in the Carpet: Finding the Human Person in the American Past* (Grand Rapids, Mich.: Eerdmans, 2007), 496.

92. Christopher J. Le Mon, 'Rwanda's Troubled Gacaca Courts', *Human Rights Brief*, 14:2 (2007), 16–20.

93. Jeffrey C. Alexander, 'On the Social Construction of Moral Universals: The "Holocaust" from War Crime to Trauma Drama', *European Journal of Social Theory*, 5:1 (2002), 5–85; Daniel Levy and Natan Sznaider, 'Memories of Europe: Cosmopolitanism and its Others', in Chris Rumford (ed.), *Cosmopolitanism and Europe* (Liverpool: Liverpool University Press, 2007), 158–77; Gerard Delanty, 'The Idea of a Cosmopolitan Europe: On the Cultural Significance of Europeanization', *International Review of Sociology*, 15:3 (2005), 405–21.

94. Mark Mazower, 'The Strange Triumph of Human Rights, 1933–1950', *Historical Journal*, 47:2 (2004), 379–98.

95. Eric D. Weitz, 'From the Vienna to the Paris System: International Politics and the Entangled Histories of Human Rights, Forced Deportations, and Civilizing Missions', *American Historical Review*, 113:5 (2008), 1313–43.

96. Michael Rothberg, 'The Work of Testimony in the Age of Decolonization: Chronicle of a Summer, Cinema Verité, and the Emergence of the Holocaust Survivor', *PMLA*, 119:5 (2004), 1243.

97. Richard Ned Lebow, 'The Future of Memory', *Annals of the American Academy of Political and Social Science*, 617 (2008), 25–41.

98. Prizel, 'Nationalism in Postcommunist Russia', 334.

99. Georges-Henri Soutou, 'Was There a European Order in the Twentieth Century? From the Concert of Europe to the End of the Cold War', *Contemporary European History*, 9:3 (2000), 330. See, for examples: Jeffrey S. Kopstein, 'The Politics of National Reconciliation: Memory and Institutions in German–Czech Relations since 1989', *Nationalism and Ethnic Politics*, 3:2 (1997), 57–78; Jan C. Behrends, 'Jan Józef Lipskis europäischer Traum: Zur Geschichtskultur in Polen, Russland und Deutschland nach 1989', *Themenportal Europäische Geschichte* (2007), online at: <www.europa.clio-online.de/2007/Article=246>; and the forum 'Truth and Reconciliation in History', ed. Elazar Barkan, *American Historical Review*, 114:4 (2009).

100. Michnik, 'Letter from the Gdańsk Prison 1985', in *Letters from Prison*, 86. Or, as he put it later: 'We have plenty of historical examples of revolutions that began as a struggle for freedom and ended in despotism, from Cromwell to Napoleon, from Khomeini to other recent examples.' Michnik, 'The Strange Epoch of Post-Communism', 233.

CONCLUSION

1. Jan Karski in Chamberlin and Feldman (eds.), *The Liberation of the Nazi Concentration Camps 1945*, 181; *The Collected Writings of John Maynard Keynes*, ii: *The Economic Consequences of the Peace* (London: Macmillan for The Royal Economic Society, 1971 [1919]), 188.
2. Judt, *Postwar*, 537. See also Leonardo Paggi, 'Antifascism and the Reshaping of Democratic Consensus in Post-1945 Italy', *New German Critique*, 67 (1996), 101–10, esp. 108.
3. Mark Fisher, *Capitalist Realism: Is There No Alternative?* (London: O Books, 2009).
4. Aldous Huxley, *Brave New World* (New York: Perennial, 1969), xiii. Or, as Zuckerman's interlocutor, Klenek, so delicately puts it in Philip Roth's *The Prague Orgy*: 'Less liberty, better fucks.' Philip Roth, *Zuckerman Bound: A Trilogy and Epilogue* (New York: Farrar Straus Giroux, 1985), 723.

Picture Acknowledgements

1. Photo: Iain Masterton/Alamy
2. Photo: Ghetto Fighters' House Museum, Israel
3. Photo: akg-images/ullstein bild
4. © Gerhard Richter, 2013
5. Photo: AFP/Getty Images
6. Photo: © Marko Krojač
7. Photo: Robert Harding Picture Library Ltd/Alamy
8. © Peter Kennard. Photo: © Tate, London 2013.
9. Photo: © Hulton-Deutsch Collection/Corbis
10. Photo: epa european pressphoto agency b.v./Alamy

Maps: from Bernard Wasserstein, *Barbarism and Civilization: A History of Europe in our Time* (Oxford University Press, 2007)

Index